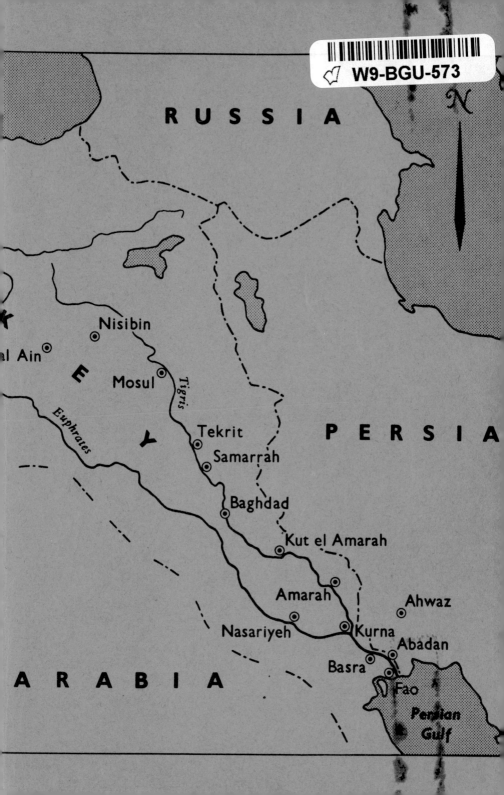

THE SIEGE

RUSSELL BRADDON
THE SIEGE

NEW YORK · THE VIKING PRESS

ILLUSTRATIONS

MAPS

ACKNOWLEDGMENTS

THE author would like to thank the following survivors of the Siege of Kut and others who helped him in his research.

Mr G. H. Allen; Abdul Majid Ali; Abdul Raman Al-Tikriti; Lt.-Col. L. A. P. Anderson; Mr A. Arris; Baroness Asquith of Yarnbury; Mr H. T. Barrett, D.C.M.; Lt.-Col. L. Bell Syer; Col. G. W. R. Bishop, O.B.E.; Mr G. H. Blower; Mr J. Boggis; Capt. G. H. G. Burroughs; Mr E. C. Burwood; Lt.-Col. J. W. Callaway, O.B.E.; Maj. A. S. Cane, D.S.O., O.B.E.; Maj. F. Castaldini; Col. R. O. Chamier, C.I.E.; Maj.-Gen. G. O. De R. Channer, C.B.E., M.C.; Mr G. H. Cheeseman; Lt.-Col. V. S. Clarke, M.C.; Mr H. J. Coombes; Brig. K. B. S. Crawford; Mr R. E. Croser; Mr H. S. Cullum; Mr G. E. Dowsett; Mr H. Eato; The Rt. Hon. Lord Elton; Mr W. S. Finch; Mr E. Firman; Mr R. Hague; Maj. J. H. Harris, M.C.; Hassan Al-Anbari; Mr A. Hayden; Maj. G. L. Heawood; Mr D. R. Holzmeyer; Mr A. G. Kingsmill; Khalis Azmi; Mr T. A. Lloyd; Mr E. J. Mant; Lt.-Col. J. McConville; Capt. H. S. D. MacNeal, M.C.; Maj.-Gen. J. S. Martin, C.I.E.; Col. R. V. Martin, I.M.S.; Maj. A. B. Matthews, D.S.O.; Brig. L. W. H. Mathias, D.S.O.; Sir John Mellor, Bart.; Maj. W. H. Miles; Mr P. R. Miller, D.C.M.; Mr J. T. Mills; Mr R. J. Murray; Sir Joseph Napier; Col. T. E. Osmond; Capt. F. W. Page-Roberts; Mr P. E. Palmer; Mr H. V. Plumb; Mr H. J. Porter; Mr F. N. Punchard; Lt.-Col. G. R. Rae; Lt.-Col. C. A. Raynor, D.S.O.; Maj.-Gen. H. H. Rich, C.B.; Mr A. E. Roach; Mr G. Roff; Col. E. W. C. Sandes; Mr W. J. Sherlock; Mr H. S. Soden; Col. W. S. Spackman, I.M.S.; Mr G. E. Sporle; Mr W. D. Swan; Mrs Margaret Taylor; Lt.-Col. H. G. Thomson, D.S.O.; Rt. Hon. R. H. Turton, P.C., M.C.; Mr A. Vanstone; Mr J. Wadham; Lt.-Col. H. G. Waldram, M.B.E., T.D.; Mr F. N. Webber-Willis; Maj. T. R. Wells, M.C.; Mr H. V. Wheeler; Mr A. J. Whitehand; Sqn.-Ldr. Winfield-Smith, S.C., D.S.O.

FOREWORD

THIS book began its life as a study of a siege. But then, because that siege made sense only in the context of the battles that led up to it, it began to grow backwards. And then, because those battles made sense only in the context of the personalities of the generals and politicians whose decisions prompted them, it began to grow sideways. And finally, because the battles and the generals seemed equally senseless in any context, it had to grow forwards, to examine the consequences of the siege – which were suffering and death in captivity.

Even so, such a book seemed an unnecessary exercise, since each of these aspects of it had already been most expertly covered in other and better books: except that each of them had been covered separately, and from one man's point of view only.

Eventually, therefore, this book became both a combination of those individual treatments and a mosaic of the experiences, recollections and remembered conversations of all those survivors of the Siege of Kut el Amarah prepared to be questioned at length by the writer.

Sir John Mellor, Major-General H. H. Rich and the late Lieutenant-Colonel G. R. Rae went to great trouble to provide lists of such survivors. I am deeply indebted to them for their help, as I am to all but three of those survivors who answered a questionnaire; to sixty-three of them who allowed me to question them in person; to the dozens of them who, from as far afield as Australia, wrote detailed descriptions of their experiences; and to the many who surrendered their treasured diaries and papers into my alien hands, to be used as I thought best.

In one respect I have broken faith with the majority of them. They knew General Sir Charles Townshend on the battlefield and in a siege, and believe him to have been a brilliant leader and a splendid man. I know him from the words of his apologia, *My Campaign in Mesopotamia*, and from the words of his orders, telegrams and communiqués, and believe him to have been a man who preferred expediency to truth, and self-advancement to the welfare of his command.

Even to say so thus baldly – far less to indict him in a long book – is brutal. The man is dead and cannot defend himself. Yet surely he defended himself as best he could in his apologia, which itself indicts

9

him? And, anyway, I am more concerned for the thousands who lost their youth and their lives in a frightful captivity directly attributable to him than I am concerned for him, whose captivity was luxurious and whose death, in 1924, was natural.

Generals have over their troops a power of life and death that is terrifying. Against that power there is no right of appeal. Except, perhaps in a book like this. Which, finally, was why I wrote it: and is why I dedicate it now to all those who suffered in Kut or captivity, because their fate was decided for them by idiots.

THE SIEGE

CHAPTER ONE

IT IS not only in this century that Britain has taken to abandoning old friends: she did it in the last. And it was not only in the last World War that she embarked on disastrous campaigns under disastrous generals: she did it in the First. Fortunately, she rarely indulges both vices simultaneously: but she did so in Mesopotamia in 1915 – and by 1916 had been given good cause to regret it.

Because it was then, at Kut el Amarah, after a futile siege of 147 days, that thirteen thousand British and Indian troops surrendered to the Turks and began a horrifying march into captivity. Kut el Amarah was the most humiliating disaster to have befallen a British Expeditionary Force since 1842 when, in a lunatic retreat from Kabul, sixteen thousand men died because of the decision of one half-witted general. It was to remain the most humiliating disaster until Singapore fell in 1942, because of the decisions of a series of half-witted military planners. In 1916, however, Kabul had been forgotten, Singapore was inconceivable and Kut seemed an unprecedented defeat at the hands of the despised Oriental.

As if this were not enough, no less than seven thousand of those thirteen thousand who surrendered at Kut died as prisoners of war: but only after a further twenty-three thousand casualties had been incurred in vain attempts to raise the siege that led to their captivity.

The immediate blame for the sufferings both of those who marched into captivity and of those who sought to relieve them must be attributed in equal parts to the general in command at Kut, his commander at Basra and his commander-in-chief in India: but it was not military ineptitude alone that precipitated the tragedy. Years of political ineptitude had also played their part.

They began with Gladstone's decision to discard a long-standing friendship with the Ottoman Empire the better to woo Tsarist Russia – and make pious noises about Turkish persecution of its Christian and Armenian minorities at the same time. They continued with such massive economies in successive Indian defence budgets that by 1914 there were barely enough troops, with barely adequate equipment, to contain the unsophisticated tribesmen of the North-West Frontier. They culminated in Britain's demands, upon the outbreak of the First World War, that India should equip and send overseas no less than four expeditionary forces – of which the last was the one dispatched to Mesopotamia.

Even in the nineteenth century this would have been a daunting enough operation for the Indian Army, but for the under-manned Indian Army of 1914–15 it was one which had to end in disaster unless Britain swiftly reinforced it: and in 1915 Britain was too preoccupied with disasters of her own in France and the Dardanelles even to notice, still less to avert, those of anyone else.

Germany, on the other hand, had worked tirelessly for more than fifty years to win the friendship of the Ottoman Empire. Loans were granted; railways were financed; Turkish soldiers were German-trained; Turkish Armies were German-equipped; German ships were assigned to the Turkish Navy; and German assistance against a hostile Russia was guaranteed.

It was not only at Turkey, however, that Berlin's diplomacy, from Gladstone's time onwards, was aimed. Her eyes fixed firmly on India, Germany intrigued to promote a Holy War – a Jehad – throughout the Middle East, even asserting that the Kaiser, as a direct descendant of Mohammed's sister, had embraced the Islamic faith and made himself its Defender. In this role, he would see to it that a giant airship, to which was attached an all-powerful magnet, would suck up into its bowels the King of England, the President of France and the Tsar of Russia, thus, at one swoop, depriving the infidel Powers of all their leaders.[1]

Great Britain was not, of course, unaware of Germany's Middle-Eastern aims and intrigues. Nor in 1914 (having recently converted a large portion of her Royal Navy from burning coal to oil, and thus made it dependent upon Middle-Eastern supplies of oil) could she afford to remain indifferent to them. When war with Germany was declared, she was therefore obliged to send a small naval force into the estuary of the Shatt al Arab to 'demonstrate'.

Two sloops, *Espiègle* and *Odin*, and an armed merchantman sailed forty-five miles up the shallow estuary, dropped anchor on the Persian side of the river, and waited to see how Turkey, who had not yet – to Germany's chagrin – declared war, would react.

Dilatory as ever, Turkey reacted not at all for a week; and then was

14

content merely to hand *Espiègle*'s commander a formal letter of complaint. 'Please you leave the Shatt before twenty four hours,' it concluded: to which *Espiègle*'s commander replied that, without Admiralty orders, he was unable to oblige. Like her sister vessels *Clio* and *Odin*, *Espiègle* was a new ship, built specially for service in the rivers of China, and her commander was not one to be bullied. Indifferent to threats, he left *Espiègle* where she was; an elegant, yacht-sized craft, gleaming white except for the ribbon of blue round her hull and the bright yellow of her funnel.[2] Two weeks later, the Turks having set up guns on their bank of the river, the British consul advised *Espiègle* to leave while she could.

In the meantime, having decided that she must act more positively to protect her oil supplies, Britain had ordered India Government to dispatch immediately to Abadan one brigade of the 6th (Poonah) Division, the rest of the division to follow as quickly as possible. If Turkey then declared war, the 6th Division – henceforth to be known as Expeditionary Force D – was to advance up the Shatt al Arab and occupy the riverside township of Basra.

Even before this order reached them, both the Viceroy, Lord Hardinge, and India's Commander-in-Chief, Sir Beauchamp Duff, had proved themselves reluctant allies. A request from the hard-pressed British Government for the loan of fifteen Indian officers had at first been refused, and was finally sanctioned only after the Viceroy had cabled, ' ... The Commander in Chief complains that he is absolutely crippled by this last measure ... '[3] A cable from Lord Kitchener in London, 'Can you manufacture any guns yourself?' had elicited from the Viceroy the prompt reply, 'Our manufacture of guns is negligible.'[3] A request from Whitehall, made at the suggestion of King George V, that troops from Nepal should be sent to Egypt, had provoked Sir Beauchamp Duff to demur that it was 'politically inadvisable at present to agree ... '[3]

Subsequently, invited to send Indian Army troops overseas to fight the common enemy, the Viceroy had cabled Whitehall that ' ... the Commander in Chief will never agree to any weakening of [his] frontier divisions'; whilst the Commander-in-Chief had cabled that the Viceroy could 'hardly sit quiet and see the whole control of Indian defence withdrawn from him altogether'.[3]

On their records, Hardinge and Beauchamp Duff must be regarded as failures in their respective wartime posts: but their recalcitrance is not wholly inexplicable. It was Queen Victoria herself who, as

Empress, had declared that India's wealth must be used to benefit the people of India,[4] and no Viceroy thereafter had risked alienating his Council by requests for any expenditure not instantly identifiable with the benefit of the monarch's native subjects. Hardinge was no exception: but Hardinge's error was that, without even consulting his Council, he arbitrarily refused every request for contributions to what was clearly a common cause, thereby creating the impression that India was reluctant to play a part in the First World War proportionate to that of Canada, Australia and New Zealand.

As to Beauchamp Duff, he had seen his Army reduced in strength and efficiency year by year, and now, in 1914, was required to defend a massive continent not only against tribesmen on the North-West Frontier, but against German subversion from Persia as well. To all requests for help outside India, therefore, his response was promptly and invariably uncooperative.

Since this was India Government's attitude towards mere requests, it is hardly surprising that Britain (anxious to protect oil supplies that lay within the zone of India's agreed responsibility) dispensed with requests and issued orders. It is still less surprising that, in almost all subsequent exchanges between India and Britain, there was something less than total rapport. By late 1914, in fact, as Lord Hardinge confessed to Lord Crewe, the Secretary of State for India, the relationship between Kitchener and Duff 'practically got to the bedrock'.[5] It was an unpromising start to a vital overseas campaign.

However, the 16th Brigade of the 6th Poonah Division was aware of none of this as its convoy sailed obediently from Bombay to the Persian Gulf. The brigade's one battalion of English troops – the 2nd Dorsets – were Regular soldiers accustomed to the whims of officialdom; its Indian troops had implicit faith in British leadership; its commanding officer, Major-General Delamain, was greatly respected; and the rest of the division, under General Sir Arthur Barrett, would soon join it, wherever it was going. As the convoy dropped anchor at Bahrain, to open its sealed orders and await – according to Sir Percy Cox, the political officer accompanying it – Turkey's declaration of war, the 16th Brigade was genuinely impatient for action.

Even more impatient were the Germans, to whom it seemed that an ungrateful Turkey would never declare war on Britain, nor an unresponsive Islam ever start its Jehad against the infidel: so Berlin decided to precipitate matters by ordering the battleships *Goeben* and *Breslau*, then stationed in the Sea of Marmara, to sail into the Black Sea and shell installations on the Russian coast. This they did, obliging Britain, Russia's ally, to declare war on Turkey, Germany's host.

As they sweated on their ships at Bahrain, Sir Percy Cox addressed the men of the 16th Brigade. Now that war between Britain and Turkey had been declared, it was their task, he told them, to protect British oil interests up the Shatt al Arab; otherwise the Royal Navy would have to depend for its oil on America.[6] Aware, then, both of the importance of their mission and of the undesirability of depending upon America for anything, Delamain's men sailed out of Bahrain and, next morning, crossed the bar of the Shatt al Arab and sailed up-river.

Almost at once, to port, they saw the Fort of Fao, and the sloop *Odin* shelling it; and, as they steamed past *Odin*, a Turkish flag was run up in front of the Customs House. It seemed there was to be a fight for their first foothold in this strange brown land. But when a party of Dorsets was put ashore, to make its way warily through groves of date palms, it met no opposition – and found Fao's fort deserted.

Espiègle having knocked out the Turkish guns opposite Abadan island, the 16th Brigade sailed up-river past the refinery with its seven chimneys, landed, and waited for the rest of the division to join it in this bleak desert land of shallow streams, date palms, filthy dogs, fearsome diseases and myriads of hostile insects.

Sit Arthur Barrett and his remaining brigade arrived shortly afterwards, and Barrett at once led his combined force against Basra. Brushing aside resistance that amounted to little more than skirmishes, he reached the outskirts of Ali Baba's fabled city and ordered an attack.

Yet already young men who had never before seen death had been horrified; death and killing are no less unpleasant because they are merely the result of a skirmish.

> We landed – God knows why. Dozens of men drowned before my eyes as we scrambled from boat to shore. No sooner on shore than we met terrible enfilading fire. Men dropped all around ... some with hands clasped around their middles. Gurkhas and Punjabis. Queer expressions on their dark faces ... It seemed an age, running head down towards a hail of lead. Could not see. Maybe I closed my eyes. It was awful. Screams of pain, rattle of fire, chatter of machine guns ... Dead lying in heaps. Stumbling over them. Felt a coward. Wanted to stop a bullet so I could get it over. Strange giddiness, then blindness. I fell.[7]

Advancing with the infantry were the regimental Medical Officers, each with an Indian assistant-surgeon, some stretcher-bearers and two drabis (mule drivers) – all insanely exposed. As the shells shrieked and crashed around them, mules and drabis stampeded, and young doctors had to round them up and start again looking for wounded. Everywhere men in pain. Everywhere men dying: a Dorset Captain, in agony, screwing his monocle into his eye – the monocle dropping out as he died. Maimed men crawling. Injections of morphia. [8]

To generals, a skirmish: to the fighting man, heaps of dead and stumbling over them. And Basra had still to be taken.

Advancing on the Turkish trenches and wire across open ground, the small lean Norfolks, precise as guardsmen, marched in extended order, their rifles at the high port. It was a movement magnificent in its arrogance – a movement designed to unnerve – and the defenders of Basra succumbed to it swiftly. Barrett's division stormed into the town and took possession of its motley bazaars and filthy canals, its silent groves of date and lime, pomegranate and lemon and orange, its sodden periphery of marshes, its mud-walled houses and its thousands of insanitary Arabs whom their conquerors instantly loathed.

Nor did the locals care much for their uninvited guests, whose horse-drawn guns seemed unable to turn a single corner in Basra's narrow streets without knocking down the wall of at least one house, and whose officers requisitioned even more homes for billets than had the Turks. In a state of mutual antipathy, each settled down to exploit the other. But at least – in a roadless land where every approach must be made by river – the back door to Abadan had been securely bolted and the Royal Navy's dread of becoming dependent upon American oil had been allayed.

Unless, of course, someone were to sneak through the back yard and break down the back door. Which might well be done, since the back yard extended north and west for more than fifty miles (the Tigris River flowing southwards through it all the way to the back door, and the Euphrates flowing eastwards all the way to the Tigris). Best, therefore, to seize as well the back gate to the back yard – where the blue Euphrates joined the yellow Tigris at Kurna, the original Garden of Eden.

And so, on December 9th, 1914, along with 1,200 prisoners and 9 guns, Kurna was taken; and taken so easily – Turkish resistance being so contemptibly feeble, though men were killed by it – that India Government quite recovered from its sulks and began to wonder whether Force D might not push 360 miles farther up the Tigris to Baghdad itself.[9]

But Lord Crewe cabled from Whitehall deprecating any advance beyond Kurna; Basra, as a port of disembarkation, lacked any kind of unloading facilities, not excluding wharves; and Barrett's division was short not only of mules and river vessels, but of artillery and hospitals as well; so India Government abandoned this pipe dream and settled temporarily for what it had.

General Barrett advised his men that there would be no more fighting unless they were attacked: in fact, that there *could* be no further offensive fighting until a light railway was built, more river transport provided and extra troops dispatched. His request for a railway having been already denied, and for extra shipping ignored, this did not, however, seem likely: so his men resigned themselves to garrison duties and a bitter Christmas either in filthy Basra or in the filthy Garden of Eden.

The British Regular detested Mesopotamia. Though tough and unsentimental, he was well versed in the Scriptures and had come to believe in the Garden of Adam and Eve. The evidence of his own eyes – a mud-hut village huddled round an open space from the centre of which grew the stump of an ancient tree; Temptation Square, the Arabs called it, and claimed that the stump was the original tree[10] – shocked him, as did the ludicrous Serpent Alley, Adam's Walk and Rib Road of Kurna.

Though a skilful scrounger (one battalion disembarking at Basra had offloaded not only its own equipment but also its transport's food supply for the next month, evoking from the captain of that vessel the comment: 'Forty-Third Light Infantry! The Forty bloody Thieves, more likely!') the British Regular hated the Arab who stole from, and even murdered, men wounded in battle.

Accustomed though he had been to the dirt and poverty of India, he hated the fleas that plagued him and the squalor that surrounded him in Basra, where he lived in tents on little islands of oily mud (each island linked to the next by a crude, plank bridge across the creek or canal or ditch that separated them) and suffered one sickness after another.

Waking up in their tents each morning they had seen in the face of one comrade after another the yellowish tinge of jaundice.

'Look at you!'

'Look at yourself!'

One after another, day after day, they reported sick.

'Carry on,' ordered their medical officer. 'You'll be all right.'[11]

And then there were the vicious mosquitoes. On sentry-duty each night men wore two suits of khaki drill and Balaclava helmets as protection from the mosquito; but when they came off duty their bodies were covered in lumps like acne, and their eyelids were grotesquely swollen.[12]

Only Crown and Anchor relieved their boredom: a game you couldn't win, but couldn't resist. 'Come along, me lucky lads,' the spieler shouted, congenial as a publican, altruistic as a shark, inviting them to drop their rupees on his grubby board, and lose them. 'Come along, me lucky lads. Drop it down, thick and heavy, where you like and where you fancy. My name's Tommy Fairplay. You come with a grey back shirt – and go with enough for a motor car.' And then, with the trickster's challenging grin, 'But not if I can bloody help it.'

Not if *he* could bloody help it. You *couldn't* win.

'Come on, bor – give us a start.'

'Me! I'm just going out on patrol.'

'Well, just give us a start. To get the others in. C'mon, put it on the diamond.'

'Ah!' Why'd one always give in? Irritably the rupee note was slapped on the diamond. And won. Delightedly the winnings were snatched up, and the winner went off on his patrol.

'Glad to see the last of you,' the boardman shouted. 'Now, come along, me lucky lads ... '[13]

Previously convinced that one needed only to march a bit, shoot a bit and play the odd game of football to be a soldier, the Regular found that marching and shooting and playing football were not enough in Basra and Kurna, so he began to adopt strange pets as well: and when one of them – a turkey, which slept every night under a different officer's bed, and attended meal parades, and ate everything upon which her beady eye alit – died of a surfeit of regimental buttons and gramophone needles, it seemed to him typical of the total ungodliness of Mesopotamia. In mordant doggerel he mocked the cradle of mankind:

> I've tried to solve a riddle.
> You wish to know it? Well ...
> If Kurna's the Garden of Eden,
> Then where the dickens is Hell?

But, unaware of these outpourings, Britain rested content with Force D's achievements at the end of 1914: and India accepted them with nothing less than complacency.

CHAPTER TWO

THIS complacency received a rude shock when Britain abruptly demanded a fourth brigade for Mesopotamia.

Having already cabled London that he was 'receiving complaints from the provinces that they are denuded of troops ... ', the Viceroy now rasped, 'We are strongly of the opinion that we have reached the limit of risk which can justifiably be imposed on the people of India, who pay for the Indian Army.'[1]

On February 25th, 1915, apparently as indifferent to Britain's perilous war-time situation as he seemed blind to the fact that India's imperial future would be brief indeed if Britain succumbed to Germany, he elaborated on this ungenerous theme. 'We feel that we have not been treated fairly', he advised; and, on March 3rd, dismissed London's pleas to the contrary with the flat assertion, 'I do not think that we ought to be asked to take further risks, and, in fact, we must refuse to do so.'[1]

To this Lord Crewe, abandoning diplomacy, responded from Whitehall by demanding a *fifth* brigade as well as a fourth. 'His Majesty's Government definitely order the strengthening of General Barrett's force at once,' he cabled – adding tartly that both the Viceroy and Sir Beauchamp Duff were entirely relieved of responsibility for the consequences of such a momentous Indian sacrifice.

The causes of this exchange were twofold. First, Whitehall had learned that the Turks were not only concentrating for a counter-attack on Kurna, but were also crossing into Persia to threaten the pipe-lines at Ahwaz on the River Karun, which led to Abadan and its refinery.

Second, Lord Kitchener's plan to land General Birdwood's Egypt-based army at the Gulf of Alexandretta (whence, against inferior opposition, it could swiftly have severed the Baghdad railway, and bled Mesopotamia to death) had been abandoned because Birdwood's force had just been earmarked for the proposed attack on Gallipoli.

So long as the Baghdad railway remained intact (and capable of transporting enemy troops from Turkey down to Mesopotamia), any rumoured threat to Ahwaz would inevitably agitate Whitehall; and Whitehall, by the beginning of March 1915, had become very agitated indeed. So agitated that when India declared itself reluctant to dispatch extra troops to protect Ahwaz, there seemed no alternative to ordering her to do so – even though Basra had neither wharves at which to disembark these troops, nor facilities wherewith to maintain them; and even though General Barrett had already sent back to India half of his sixteen hundred camels because there was no suitable grazing for them, and anyway no need for them in what he had understood to be a purely defensive operation. Hence Lord Crewe's final and peremptory cable: to which the Viceroy and his Commander-in-Chief responded with a gesture of almost childish petulance.

Provoked by what they regarded as Home Government arrogance, they decided to assert their independence by elevating Expeditionary Force D to the status of an Army Corps without Whitehall's approval. As well as the two fresh brigades Britain had demanded, they accordingly dispatched to Mesopotamia a new and aggressive commander, supported by a new and compliant staff, all of whom duly installed themselves in Basra on April 9th, 1915; from which moment, disaster became inevitable.

It was rendered inevitable by the interaction of the personalities of the Viceroy and his Commander-in-Chief with those of the new commander and his nominee (replacing General Barrett) to the command of the 6th Division: and by the nature of the army in India, from which Force D was drawn.

In 1914, the Indian Army consisted of only 76,000 British and 159,000 Indian troops, supported by too few guns, virtually no transport, virtually no munitions factories and a very poor hospital service.[2]

Against the sporadic and ill-organized attacks of unsophisticated Frontier tribesmen, however, this Army had been adequate. Even under the command of generals so old-fashioned that they bore nicknames like Old Bow and Arrows, it had been adequate. It had fought small skirmishes; extricated itself from the occasional ambush; defeated its opponents by superior discipline and rifle-fire in mountainous terrain that offered plenty of cover; and, when surrounded or outnumbered, had simply holed up until a relief force arrived to rescue it.

A small expedition sent in 1895 to Chitral, in Kashmir, had proved the efficacy of this simple tactic. Finding itself suddenly and greatly outnumbered, it had withdrawn into the fort at Chitral and there, doing little but refuse to surrender, had survived for forty-six days until Major Aylmer v.c. led a force from Peshawar to relieve it. A captain called Townshend, to whom the leader of the expedition, a medical officer, had assigned military command throughout the siege, had returned to England to be promoted, lionized, made a Companion of The Order of the Bath, granted an audience with the Prince of Wales and commanded to dine with Queen Victoria.

Sometimes, on the other hand, it had been the tribesmen who holed up in a fortress; whereupon it became the unenviable duty of some gallant officer under furious fire to blow up the massive gates behind which the enemy skulked. It was at Nilt, in 1891, that Aylmer had won his Victoria Cross – but not a dinner with Queen Victoria – for doing no less than that.

In short, the Indian Army of the nineteenth and early twentieth centuries had won its small battles against its uncivilized foes by gallantry, frontal attacks and superb discipline. It had won because its sepoys trusted the sahib implicitly, knowing neither how obsolete were his tactics nor how obsolete his weapons. It had won them because inadequate transport had been no great hindrance against an enemy who had no transport at all; and because its reactionary generals were opposed only by feudal chieftains leading disorganized rabbles.

But in Mesopotamia, sooner or later, a fragment of this same Indian Army would inevitably find itself confronted by a very different enemy, very differently led, in very different terrain; an unpalatable fact to which Sir Beauchamp Duff and the Viceroy had allowed themselves to be blinded by Force D's too-easy victories at Fao, Basra and Kurna.

Force D had won its early battles against an ill-led force of inferior Turks and unenthusiastic Arabs, who were anyway handicapped by an impossibly long line of communications; but, refusing to perceive these basic facts, India had decided that the enemy at Fao, Basra and Kurna – poor soldiers, reluctant to fight, lacking the leaders to make them fight – had been typical of the entire Turkish Army.

Unfortunately, the real Turkish soldier, the Anatolian Turk, was the most stubborn defensive fighter in the world – as those due to land at Gallipoli were soon to discover. Superbly skilled in the art of digging and concealing entrenchments; almost impossible to dislodge once he had dug in; capable of marching for days on end; and savagely disciplined by officers who would shoot him without compunction if he failed to hold his ground, he was a formidable enemy.

Even more significant was the fact that Field Marshal von der Goltz, one of Germany's greatest strategists,[3] was soon to assume command of these impressive troops in Mesopotamia; and that von der Goltz would eventually have to hand, in the person of General Khalil,* a man determined to make them fight.

Most significant, however, was the fact that no one in India believed either that this Anatolian Turk was a good soldier, soon to be imaginatively deployed and boldly led, or that he would shortly be marching south to Mesopotamia.

Though never as contemptible as India seemed to believe, the Turkish Army of 1915 was not, of course, invincible – its great deficiency being a shortage of river transport. Training, courage, equipment and von der Goltz notwithstanding, the Turk was as incapable of sustaining without adequate shallow-draught shipping an attack on Basra, five hundred miles down-river from Baghdad, as Force D, likewise ill-equipped, was to be incapable of sustaining an attack on Baghdad, five hundred miles up-river from Basra. But given lines of communication of equal length and difficulty – that is, at any point above Kut el Amarah – the Turkish forces available would always be able to hold their own and were quite capable of defeating their enemy.

And that capability became a certainty when India made Expeditionary Force D an Army Corps and instructed Sir John Nixon, its new commander, to make plans for a possible advance on Baghdad – an instruction it concealed from the British Government.

Nixon, a dashing cavalry officer, was a secretive, thrusting man with a thick moustache, a beaky nose and a strong but ungainly physique. The fact that his directive seemed designed less to protect Britain's oil supplies than to overrun the whole of the Basra vilayet – and then possibly to advance on Baghdad itself – was so entirely to his taste that, the better to put it into effect, he at once asked India for another cavalry brigade, a Pioneer battalion and a divisional commander as aggressive as himself.

As to his request for a cavalry brigade and a Pioneer battalion, India (grudging as ever) denied it – and Lord Crewe instructed that Gallipoli, not Mesopotamia, was the main theatre of war in Asia Minor. Even the protection of Suez ranked higher, Lord Crewe declared, than that of Mesopotamia, where 'a safe game must be played',[4] since it was important as a theatre of war only to protect Ahwaz and Abadan.

* A widely used phonetic spelling of Halil – the Turkish 'h' being guttural.

24

The Turks themselves now emphasized the wisdom of Lord Crewe's injunction by attacking from Nasariyeh (on the Euphrates) towards Kurna (at the junction of the Euphrates and the Tigris). With a force of thirty thousand – mainly Arabs and Kurds – they challenged at Shaiba: where, irresolutely led after an enterprising amphibious advance across marshes and floodland, the 6th Division simply stood in its trenches and, on two consecutive moonless nights, allowed itself to be thrown into such confusion that one unit even fired on another. But on the third day, General Melliss – a small, elderly man, brave to the point of recklessness – took command. 'Reconnaissance at full force at dawn', he ordered:[5] and at dawn his battalions advanced.

By now, however, his Mohammedan troops had come to accept the Turkish propaganda that to invade Mesopotamia was to desecrate sacred soil. Ordered to charge, they remained stubbornly flat on the ground, their trenching tools shielding their heads from enemy fire – until their British officers, wielding the flat of a sword on the soles of their feet, persuaded them that discretion was the better part of religion. Then, leaping upright, they followed the rest of the division into action.

'Men must be a bit crazy to bring off a charge like that. We yelled and jabbed ... It is amazing how one can adapt to slaughter ... Yet it proved very different from sticking stuffed sacks in training camp.'[6] 'Come on, you sons of Allah,' they screamed – then stuck bodies, not sacks, and retrieved bayonets from flesh with what their instructors in training camps had termed the 'jinking twist', and stuck another body. 'You got to get the other fellow before he gets you.'[6] Bayonets glistening with blood; suffocating clouds of grey dust.

'I was weary and sick. My stomach was gone. *"Stop blubbering, you."* I needed that to snap me out of it.'[6]

For a whole day, in which as many succumbed to heat-stroke as to enemy bullets, and rifle barrels were too hot to touch,[7] the outcome of the battle was so much in doubt that even Melliss considered a withdrawal. At least, he decided, he must withdraw his wounded, so he sent orders via a wounded subaltern to his distant Supply and Transport Corps that they should immediately rush up all available carts and mules. 'Have you got an indent?' the wounded officer was asked by a Supply Corps major.

'I hardly think this is the time for indents, sir.'

'What? Oh – I see.'[8]

Four abreast, then, and at the gallop, the carts careered towards the field of Shaiba, under the command of a very junior subaltern. The

Turks mistook them for reinforcing guns and troops and began to withdraw. Quite suddenly, as if they had lost interest in this particular patch of desert, apathetic rather than fearful, like a football crowd dispersing after a dull match, thousands began to drift away from the battlefield. Melliss's men charged; the Arabs fell on their Turkish allies; and victory went to the 6th Division, who found themselves in possession of a hundred square miles of corpse-littered, fly-swarming sand.

To his surprise the young officer whose careering carts had turned defeat into victory was not summoned to Basra to be congratulated by all the generals. He was not even congratulated by a captain: he, who had won the Battle of Shaiba. So, following the practice of students in Indian universities, he awarded himself the gallant order of 'Failed D.S.O.' and congratulated himself instead.

'Damned young puppy,' growled his seniors in the Mess when he told them. 'You could be shot for that sort of insolence at Quetta or Aldershot.'[9]

'A regular soldier's battle,' commented Melliss happily, unaware of its true victor's discontent. 'A real battle.'[10] A battle for which the Turks were to remember him as a general worthy even of the title Pasha. A battle, however, in which the British regiments of Force D learnt to mistrust some of their Indian comrades-in-arms.

Shaiba gave Force D a glimpse of wounds more shocking than any they had seen before, and of a hospital service that appalled them. Accustomed to injuries caused by tribesmen's bullets, they shrank from bodies blasted by Turkish shells. Expecting that the fearful mutilations would at once be expertly treated, they shuddered at the sight of rent flesh fastened together with safety pins, and of phenol pumped from a tin fly-spray into gaping, purple flesh that seethed with maggots; and they watched in disbelief as the delirious victims of heat-stroke were passed naked from one end to the other of a horse-trough full of tepid water.

Basra's hospitals were, in fact, a disgrace – and had been for months. In January, operations had been carried out on a table on a windswept veranda, an officer who had endured an appendisectomy lay on the floor with twenty-one other officers, tended by only one orderly, until he was discharged: and now, months later, it was no better – for the troops, worse; for Indian troops, much worse. In a climate notoriously hot, Basra's so-called hospitals – many of them just a collection of tents with almost no sanitation – boasted no ice, no electric fans and no nurses.[11] Nevertheless, quite a few of those who endured these conditions survived and were shipped back to India, whence they wrote letters home which were hardly paeans of praise. But Britain was far away, its public opinion slow to mobilize, and nothing was done.

As to Nixon's second request – that his nominee should replace General Barrett as commander of the 6th Division – India accepted it: and so the man who twenty years ago as a captain had won fame and a Queen's hospitality for surviving a siege at Chitral set sail from Karachi.

Now a fifty-four-year-old major-general, Charles Vere Ferrers Townshend, student of military history and implacable careerist, a tall, ugly man with an ovate skull – the original army egg-head – passed the slow days of his voyage up the Persian Gulf reflecting how Mesopotamia, granary of the ancient world, had in earlier times been destroyed by the Persians, recaptured by Belisarius, and allowed to erode into desolation by the Ottomans.[12] 'Where the Turk passes,' a proverb runs, 'the grass ceases to grow', and for centuries no grass had grown in Mesopotamia: but Townshend was not dismayed. Brashly self-confident, he envisaged himself a second Belisarius and wrote in his diary, 'Who knows that I shall not eventually become Governor of Mesopotamia?'[12]

For a descendant of that Lord George Townshend who, when Wolfe was killed, had succeeded to the command at Quebec, and later became a Field Marshal, such grandiose ambitions might not have been out of place: but for the son of a poor man whose expectation of inheriting a family title had early been extinguished, such ambitions, in the social and military climate of the late nineteenth century, should have been pure fantasy.

Charles, however, had been fortunate. His grandfather, the fifth marquis Townshend, conscious of the fact that only a bachelor heir stood between the title and his grandson, had provided him with a good education: and Charles had repaid his grandfather by working hard, though without distinction, until, as a Marine subaltern, with a taste for theatre and numerous theatrical friends, he was posted to Egypt in 1884 at the age of twenty-three.

Finding life there dull, and opportunity for advancement negligible, he applied for a transfer to the Indian Staff Corps.[13] Instead, he was sent south to Suakin, whence, bored by garrison duty, he wrote asking Lady Townshend, his grandmother, to pull strings and obtain for him a commission in the cavalry. He was assigned instead to the Egyptian

Camel Corps and, on Wolseley's expedition to relieve Khartoum, fought in some desperate desert battles until Gordon was murdered and the campaign abandoned.

His two-year-old application for a transfer to the Indian Army at last approved, he spent the next nine years in India, enjoying the moments of action, hating the months of garrison routine, and constantly seeking, through influential relatives, a transfer back to Egypt.

Unsuccessful in these attempts, he took part in that 1891 campaign against Hunza tribesmen in the course of which Captain Aylmer won his Victoria Cross; and, after it, remained in the Hunza district as Military Governor – an extraordinarily inflated title for a mere subaltern acting under the guidance of a political officer whose responsibilities included also the districts of Northern Kashmir and Chitral.

His negligible duties among the Hunza tribesmen concluded, Townshend resumed his attempts to procure a transfer to the Khedive's Army in Egypt.[13] But in 1893 fresh troubles broke out in Chitral: so he at once forgot his passion for Egypt (believing that promotion was to be gained only as a result of military action) and applied for a return to northern Kashmir. Two years later, he was to be besieged in Chitral's fort, along with a force of four hundred men led by his one-time political officer, Surgeon-Major Robertson.

Robertson assigned him military command of this siege, and he conducted it skilfully enough, but soon found himself contemptuous of the quality of most of his Indian troops. He also refused even to contemplate the idea of any sorties from the fort against the tribesmen investing him, insisting that the risk was too great and that he meant 'to sit tight until we are relieved ... '[13]

And so, for forty-six days, by killing his horses and salting away their flesh, halving rations and maintaining at any cost his access to the river, his water supply, a few yards outside the wall of the fort, he sat it out. He was relieved by Aylmer, and allowed to return on leave to England to be lionized – the Prince of Wales even offering to support any application he might care to make for a transfer to the Brigade of Guards.[14] However, General Kitchener offered him command of a battalion in Egypt, which – contriving to be released from the Indian Army – he accepted.

In 1898, at the Battle of Atbara against the Mahdists, he led his men in a brilliant charge and won Kitchener's congratulations – a piece of good fortune he was to exploit whenever possible over the next sixteen years. Later he took part in the Battle of Omdurman, married the daughter of a titled Frenchman, resigned his commission in the Egyptian Army and returned to England to renew both his string-pulling and his theatrical friendships. An amusing man, who by virtue of his grandfather's death was now heir presumptive to the bachelor sixth marquis, his company was as much appreciated by actors and actresses as theirs was by him.

He applied to the Commander-in-Chief for a transfer to a British line regiment but was snubbed,[15] and promptly sought a staff appointment back in India; and, failing there also, a post in South Africa where war seemed imminent. But no sooner had he been installed as Assistant Adjutant-General to the Military Governor of Bloemfontein than he found himself dissatisfied and, remembering the words of the Prince of Wales, began intriguing for a transfer to the Brigade of Guards.

He was offered instead a post as a major in the 2nd Battalion of the Royal Fusiliers, which he accepted. But when his new regiment returned to England, he found that he could not get on with his commanding officer and did not enjoy garrison duties at Dover: so he applied to the War Office first for a staff job, then for a regimental command back in South Africa, and finally for permission to reconnoitre privately the roads leading from the United States of America into Canada, in case those two countries should ever go to war! Doubtless glad to get rid of him, the War Office agreed.[15]

Returned from Canada, he was posted to the 1st Battalion Royal Fusiliers in India, where the Commander-in-Chief was now General Kitchener. At once he pestered Kitchener for promotion and a transfer out of the Fusiliers but was told curtly to stay with his regiment: and was obliged to do so until it returned to England.

In 1905 his bachelor cousin, the sixth marquis, married – thus threatening his hopes of succession to the title – but his social ambitions were somewhat placated by an appointment to Paris as Acting Military Attaché. Here he stayed until 1906, when he found himself back in India, a full colonel.

In 1908 he was transferred, as a brigadier-general, to the Orange River Colony – whence, almost at once, he returned on a deviously contrived leave to London, to let it be known that he would much prefer a major-general's command in Cairo!

He had to wait three years, and then was given a major-general's command in East Anglia: but, dissatisfied as ever, he volunteered for overseas service, and was posted back to India where, in 1913, because of his advanced ideas about training, he fell foul of one superior, a

General Sir Percy Lake, and earned the praises of two others, Generals Sir John Nixon and Sir Beachamp Duff, the latter his new Commander-in-Chief.

Now known to his brother officers as 'a bit of a ladies' man', he was also variously described as 'Frenchified', 'a thruster – you know, the sort of feller that *will* ride too far ahead and destroy the scent for the hounds and drive the Master mad', 'a man who'd sooner go to a theatre than a shooting party. *That* sort of man', and, 'the only real general in the entire Indian Army: but not exactly a gentleman!'[16]

When war broke out in Europe, Townshend the Thruster grew frantic at the thought of the opportunities he was missing for command, promotion and military glory in France. He pestered the War Office, Sir John French, Kitchener, his wife and everyone else he had ever known to procure him a transfer home, lamenting constantly that otherwise 'I look upon my career as finished':[17] but all of them except his wife had had a surfeit of his importunings, so he was left where he was.

But then Britain insisted that India send a second division to Mesopotamia, India Government decided to make Force D an Army Corps, and the newly appointed Corps Commander, General Sir John Nixon, remembering how much he had approved Townshend's methods in 1913, decided that this was the commander he wanted to take Barrett's place. Sir Beauchamp Duff, not averse to the appointment, wired Townshend, 'I have selected you for command of one of the divisions now in force. Orders will follow',[18] and Townshend – restless, ruthless, highly professional and loyal only to his own relentlessly driving ambitions – headed for Basra.

On April 23rd, 1915, he sailed up the Shatt al Arab between thick belts of date palms which reminded him of Luxor on the Nile.[18] The heat was more intense than he had ever known – perceptibly hotter even than the Persian Gulf he had just left – and the farther north he travelled, the hotter it became.

Landing at Basra – which those more romantic than observant were apt to describe as the Venice of Asia Minor, because of its canals and its deceptive beauty from afar at dawn and dusk – he went at once to the British Consulate, which now was General Nixon's headquarters, and reported to his new Commander.

Nixon wasted no time. Convinced that he had been sent to Mesopotamia to instil into Force D a spirit of aggression, he was only too willing to put into effect India Government's instruction to take over the whole of the Basra vilayet, and either forgetful of or indifferent to Lord Crewe's deprecation of 'any advance beyond Kurna'. Accordingly, he told Townshend that he was at once to prepare to evict the Turks from their positions outside Kurna and advance ninety miles up the Tigris to Amarah – the most important town on the Tigris south of Baghdad.

Very willing to obey, Townshend set off immediately to inspect his troops, finding the physique of many of his Indians less impressive than that of the British,[19] and accepting without surprise the advice that some Mohammedan troops (for whom he had had no time since Chitral) had fought poorly at Shaiba. Then he travelled up-river by launch to reconnoitre, from the top of a rickety wooden tower, what would be the starting-point for his first battle as a commander – the Garden of Eden.

He found it to be a small, squalid island surrounded by an apparently limitless muddy lake from whose surface protruded only the occasional sandhills, oases of palm trees and clusters of mud huts. The snows had thawed on mountains far to the north, and the Tigris had inundated every low-lying area between Baghdad and Basra. The Turks were entrenched on three island sandhills straddling the invisible channel up which Townshend's transports must sail from Kurna to seize Amarah. Standing on the top platform of the observation tower, his binoculars to his eyes, Townshend thought he might as well be expected to fight his way across Lake Michigan in America.[20] Three or four thousand yards away lay the sandhill redoubts he must capture first, and about ten thousand yards beyond them loomed a crescent of sandhills, from which the enemy could lay down fire to support these redoubts. Beyond that protruded two more positions, from which supporting fire could be laid.

Intelligence reports advised that the enemy positions were strongly fortified and manned altogether by 6 battalions of Turks, 600 Arab riflemen, 1,200 Marsh Arabs, 10 guns and a gunboat: and against this well entrenched force, across miles of water, through shell- and rifle-fire, marsh reeds and mines, his 6th Division would have to punt its way in hundreds of small native boats, supported by guns on makeshift barges and rafts.

'I had reason to think', he wrote, 'that Wolfe's job at Quebec was a fool to mine,' because, if *he* were in command of the Turks, he would rout any such attack as he was now obliged to make.[20]

Aware that most of his officers viewed the impending battle with something less than confidence, he might equally have reflected upon the promise he had made to Lady Nixon, just before he sailed from India to join her husband. 'I shall succeed,' he had assured her then, 'or never return.'[21] Certainly it looked unlikely that he would succeed.

Having observed the fall of a few artillery shots, he put away his binoculars, climbed down the ladder from the observation tower, boarded his launch and sailed back to Basra.[22] It was April 25th, and the first landings had just been made at Gallipoli.

CHAPTER THREE

BACK at Basra, he requested General Nixon to come and see for himself the difficulties inherent in the attack that was to be launched from Kurna. Nixon did so – thereby encouraging Townshend to suggest that the 12th Division, under General Gorringe, should co-operate in the advance by leading his men eastwards into Persia, heading north and then cutting back westwards across unflooded plainland to the Tigris, to take the enemy in the rear.

Nixon vetoed this suggestion. Though Persia, the source of British oil, was officially neutral, most of her tribesmen sympathized with the Turks (on grounds of a common religion and a common antipathy to the Russians), and the least violation of their neutrality could, Nixon feared, be sufficient to fling them into the Turkish camp – for which neither India nor Britain would ever forgive him.

Also Britain had insisted that Ahwaz be made secure and its oil-pumping renewed – and that, not any outflanking manœuvre up the Tigris, was Gorringe's task.

Having denied Townshend the co-operation of the 12th Division, Nixon further aggrieved his sensitive subordinate by depriving him of part of the 6th Division. A brigade must stay behind to cover Basra at the strongly entrenched fort of Dirhamiyeh, he ordered, and Townshend bitterly lamented that 'even Bonaparte could not have succeeded with methods like this'.[1]

He was in the habit of comparing his tactics and strategy with those of Bonaparte; and now, reflecting grimly that one battalion was more than adequate to hold a strong fort (which no one, since it was surrounded by water, intended attacking any way)[1] he felt as aggrieved as ever the Frenchman had at St Helena.

He was also in the habit of criticizing his superiors – had done so in the Sudan, in Chitral, in the Royal Fusiliers and lately in India – so it is perhaps not surprising to find him, within four days of meeting his new commander, indulging the habit again: but it did not bode well for the future.

Nixon, indeed, gave him ample grounds for criticism. Hundreds of tasks in Basra that should have been done by non-combatants were currently being done by men from the 6th Division. Everywhere Townshend looked he saw fighting troops employed as clerks, military policemen and batmen: but he asked for their return in vain, being promised that their numbers would be made up by reservists and territorials, who would arrive too late for the battle he must fight at Kurna.

'Truly a heart breaking state of affairs,' he commented, 'for one imbued with the principle of Economy of Force':[1] and he frankly confessed that he, like Bonaparte, von Moltke, Wellington and Clausewitz, was conspicuously imbued with that greatest of military virtues. Heartbreak and Bonaparte's inadequacy in the face of the battle he must fight notwithstanding, he proceeded energetically to prepare for it.

Bellums – a cross between a dugout and a rowing-boat – would be required in vast numbers. He ordered three hundred and twenty-eight for the brigade that must attack the first three redoubts.

But bellums provided no protection for men punting across flat water towards entrenched and hostile islands. For each battalion he ordered an advance guard of thirty-two boats armoured with machine-gun shields.

Nor are bellums easy to manœuvre. The Marsh Arab may glide like a shark in his, but not the infidel soldier. For each boat, then, he ordered that two men were to learn the art of punting – the second a reserve, in case the first should be shot.

Crews of one N.C.O. and nine men had to be assigned to every bellum; and picks, shovels, ropes, poles, paddles and caulking equipment (to plug bullet holes) as well. He ordered the crews to be assigned – care being taken that they were not all big men, or the bellum would sink – and the equipment collected.

Mines would wreak havoc against his advance by steamer and bellum from Kurna; he offered the local Arabs four hundred rupees for every mine they discovered.

Barges and rafts for each of his eighteen-pounder guns and howitzers, for his four- and five-inch guns and his battery of mountain artillery, would be required: he ordered their preparation.

A line of communication had to be organized – its personnel drawn from fighting troops: resentfully, he ordered that they be made available.

A naval flotilla of three armed sloops, four armed launches and a weird variety of even smaller craft – including horse boats with guns stuck on them – had to be improvised, and then so deployed that it could act both as escort and field artillery. Swiftly usurping overall command from the Senior Naval Officer, Townshend ordered that it be incorporated in his operational plan.

Undeterred by this plethora of unlikely military detail, he worked tirelessly (inevitably finding an historical precedent for the task confronting him in that which had confronted Abercrombie at Aboukir in 1801)[1] and returned each night to his billet in Basra, where his Greek host made him comfortable. His troops, meantime, sweltering and waterlogged all day, devoured by mosquitoes all night and maddened by sandflies each dawn, hated their life at Kurna.

Deciding that he needed a new orderly, Townshend asked if there were any Norfolks who would apply for the job. A slight, boyish-looking twenty-three-year-old called Boggis decided that being a general's orderly would be better than the mud and heat of more battles like the one he had just fought at Shaiba.

As he marched into Townshend's office, he was surprised that the man sitting at the table should be so short: but Townshend gave him no time for further appraisals.

'Ah,' he said, 'Boggis! I see you come from Raynham.'

'Yes sir. I worked at the Hall as a boy.'

'Just what I want,' said Townshend – the Hall being the family seat he hoped one day to inherit – and Boggis became an orderly.[2]

Training and preparation continued throughout May. The *Lusitania* was sunk on the 1st – but no one cared about that at Kurna. Gorringe and his 12th Division, after initial reverses, secured Ahwaz and restored the flow of oil to Abadan – but no one cared about that at Kurna. Lord Crewe – belatedly advised by India of Nixon's decision to advance to Amarah, and only slightly mollified by the news that Ahwaz was now safe – growled that, 'on the clear understanding that the General Officer commanding D force is satisfied that he can concentrate a sufficient force at Amarah to defy an attack during the Summer from Baghdad', the advance would be sanctioned:[3] but no one even knew, let alone cared about that at Kurna.

All that mattered at Kurna was training for the coming battle and doing promptly what the General asked. Because the General was everywhere: and the General could be harsh.

'Boggis,' Townshend instructed, 'come with me': and dutifully Boggis followed his master – who was quite tall when he stood up, his

35

legs being long, even if his trunk was short – to an artillery shell dump. Thousands of shells were stacked carefully out of reach of the ubiquitous flood waters – except in one corner.

'Boggis – get me the Colonel.' Boggis returned with the Colonel. 'Can't you see the water's lapping round these bloody shells?' Townshend snapped. 'Move the bloody things.' And Boggis began to wonder whether the mud and heat of more battles like Shaiba might not be preferable to service with such a martinet. But when Townshend returned to his billet and immediately absorbed himself – as was his daily practice – in the study of a volume of military history, he forgot his fears.[4]

Nixon meantime had become perturbed by a message about himself and his proposed advances on Amarah and Nasariyeh. Dispatched by Crewe to Hardinge, and relayed to him from India, it read, 'We can send him no more troops and he must clearly understand that his action must be guided by this fact.' That was bad enough, since it made him the scapegoat for any failure by Townshend: but what followed was worse. 'Arrangements for the move in question must have been made some days back, and I am of the opinion that General Nixon should have submitted his proposals before the last moment ... only the Cabinet should decide questions jointly affecting civil and military policy.'[5]

If previously Nixon had not known that India's intentions in Mesopotamia differed vastly from Britain's, now he was painfully conscious of the fact. His plans to attack northwards up the Tigris, with the 6th Division, as far as Amarah, and westwards along the Euphrates, with the 12th Division, as far as Nasariyeh, seemed suddenly less attractive once Lord Crewe had cast upon him all the responsibility for any failures in either campaign. So he cabled India for guidance; and India reassured him.

Three days later, Joseph Chamberlain succeeded Lord Crewe at the India Office, and cabled the Viceroy, endorsing Crewe's policy of caution. The Viceroy countered with a cable arguing that it would be unwise to issue Nixon with explicit orders which might not suit a situation only he could assess: but he did promise that India would refuse to 'authorize any advance *beyond Amarah* for which [Nixon's] force is not adequate'.[5]

Apparently convinced, apparently not even noticing those fateful words 'beyond Amarah', which his Government had never even contemplated – still less sanctioned – Chamberlain argued no further; and the month ended with British and Indian intentions as to the role of Force D in Mesopotamia more at odds than ever.

On the afternoon of May 30th, in heat so searing that bully beef melted and spurted as soon as the tin was punctured,[6] Townshend once again climbed Kurna's observation tower to survey the tawny sea surrounding him. Here and there were dotted the yellow islands that were enemy redoubts; and, in the distance, the masts of a dhow. That crescent of sandhills, ten thousand yards away, would be 'the tough nut'.[7] He envisaged heavy losses – his hundreds of bellums stuck in thick reeds and every man in them shot down by the malevolent Arabs who dwelt therein, his wounded drowning and his sloops mined. And, as he descended the ladder, he decided that 'surely no leader had been called upon to fight so extraordinary a battle' as was he.[7]

But, 'It's all right, sir,' his servant, Whitmore, comforted. 'You'll have the Townshend luck'[7] – and Whitmore (soon to die of illness) spoke for the entire division, the myth of 'Townshend's luck' being widely accepted. With his alert grey eyes and his big nose, his confident manner and his easy conversation, Townshend had nothing about him of the lofty disdain of other generals. None of the remoteness of Nixon, whom no one ever saw. None of the arrogance of Gorringe, who had ordered the whipping of two Arabs because one of them had dropped some matting and frightened his horse.[8] Townshend was different. A nice man, Charlie was. Even his officers, delighted by his theatrical gossip, liked him. And everyone, of every rank, was anxious to go into action with him, if only because life at Kurna was so vile.

The Ox and Bucks' Forty Thieves, for example, had been there since first it was taken: and had had to endure not only the extreme cold of winter (before spring and floods combined to plague them with intense humidity and clouds of mosquitoes) but also the frenzies of banner-waving Arab hordes – nicknamed the Salvation Army – screaming and sniping at them from a distance every evening. Admittedly a few rounds of shrapnel always sent them melting into the mist,[9] but a battle would be welcome if it meant a chance to eliminate them entirely and escape from Kurna for ever.

'When Allah made Hell, he did not find it bad enough,' the Arabs were apt to say, 'so he made Mesopotamia as well.'[10] And for once the 6th Division, to whom the quintessence of Mesopotamia was Kurna, and the quintessence of Kurna the Arab, agreed with them. Lying that night in the mud beside their fully laden bellums, they were almost eager for the attack they were to launch next day.

The first day of the battle was brilliantly successful. At dawn, hundreds of bellums, each carrying ten men, moved slowly across open water and through clumps of reeds towards their island objectives. Supporting them, the heavy guns at Kurna, those of the naval flotilla and those on the barges and horse boats, smothered the three small sandhills with a murderous fire: to which the Turks replied so feebly that Townshend, observing from the crow's-nest of elegant *Espiègle*, was astounded by the incompetence of his opposing commander,[11] Halim Bey.

To Townshend, observing with a general's eye, a feeble retaliation: to his men in their bellums – punting, poling, pushing, pulling through thick high reeds; suddenly fainting with heat and falling overboard to drown, or have their throats cut by the lurking Marsh Arab; sliced open with shrapnel and reduced to lifeless, huddled, drill-clad meat by bullets – it was violence incarnate.

As the bellums reached the first enemy redoubt, threading their way like rats through the reeds,[12] their occupants splashed ashore, drenched with water and perspiration, only their sun helmets dry, to storm the Turkish trenches – and found them full of dead and wounded.

The sandhill islands had afforded the Turks no defensive timber (and nowhere, between Baghdad and Basra, is there to be found even a stone, let alone a rock) so their trenches, entirely without cover or reinforcement, and shallow (because otherwise they would fill up with water) had collapsed under the 'volcano of fire'[13] that had erupted upon them. And Townshend's men – advancing with the bayonet, ready to gouge out a ferocious enemy – were instead appalled by the sight of ghastly wounds, of corpses blasted completely naked, and of enemy soldiers grovelling to kiss their feet and beg for mercy.

They found some of the Turkish gunners secured by chains to the field guns they captured; and the guns bore the trade mark of Krupp. It seemed all wrong, somehow.[14] In the water around them floated the debris of battle: shattered rafts, shattered boats, shattered bodies; water bottles, sun helmets, haversacks.

As it had been at this redoubt, so it was at the second and third, and Townshend's first line of objectives was secured. But six thousand yards ahead lay the next line, that dangerous crescent of sandhills strongly supported by two positions farther away still – the only access to them a channel through a minefield. Ordering his infantry to bivouac till dawn, he instructed his armoured tugs, *Shaitan* and *Lewis Pelly*, to clear the way.

The tugs were greatly assisted in this by an elderly Turkish officer who, captured red-fingered at a keyboard, had readily confessed that the mines obstructing their passage were electrically operated and that it had been his task both to lay and to fire them. Ordered aboard *Lewis Pelly*, and then placed in the bow, he had co-operated in the subsequent sweeping with conspicuous enthusiasm – while the men who had defeated the force of which he was part dug themselves hip-holes in the sand and fell asleep.

The following dawn, as every gun opened fire on the crescent of sandhills at Bahran, the myriad bellums advanced slowly up the Tigris: but from Bahran came no answering fire.

Astounded, the 6th Division approached its objective in silence; until one of their three reconnaissance aircraft roared overhead to drop a message in a canister, to which was attached streaming ribbons of red, white and blue. 'Bahran abandoned', the message revealed, the enemy being in full flight (if a frantic scuttle aboard anything that floated may be so described) northwards through the flood waters.

Townshend's innate aggression and ambition now asserted themselves. At Atbara, against the Mahdists, he had deliberately charged not one line of trenches but three,[15] thereby winning the congratulations of Kitchener, who was his operational commander:[16] at Kurna, then, why not do the same – and win the renewed congratulations of Kitchener, who was now Britain's Commander-in-Chief?

But Townshend was not merely an aggressive and ambitious soldier, he was also a student of military history and a general (for those days) of unusual flexibility, and history had taught him that an enemy in flight is an enemy to be kept on the run. History as well as instinct combined, therefore, to demand pursuit. Ordering some of his men to occupy Bahran, and others to hack away the mine cables that blocked his advance beyond it, he advised that he personally, on *Espiègle*, intended pursuing the Turks as far as Ezra's Tomb, twenty miles upstream. His troops, he said, were to follow him when boats became available.

Arriving at Bahran by river steamer – an ungainly vessel, flat-bottomed and paddle-wheeled, the ugly duckling of her breed – General Nixon approved this audacious plan and Townshend sailed off, accompanied by some staff officers and twenty-five soldiers, and escorted by the sloops *Odin* and *Clio*, the tugs *Shaitan* and *Lewis Pelly*, the launch *Sumana* and the paddle steamer *Comet*.

But the invisible channel so writhed through belts of flooded marshland, and the Navy's ignorance of the tortuous Tigris was so profound, that one or other of the flotilla was constantly aground, and Townshend began to fear that he would never close with the enemy's troop-laden shipping. *Espiègle* was steered by hand-wheel between decks, and he had to listen to a ceaseless flow of orders and acknowledgments, none of which indicated a hot pursuit.

'Two turns to starboard.'

'Two turns to starboard, sir.'

'One turn to port.'

'One turn to port, sir.'

'Hard to port.'

'Hard to port, sir.'[17]

All day it went on, the hundred-and-fifty-foot vessels awkwardly twisting and blindly probing for the narrow channel that snaked between inundated banks. Townshend, again perched on the crow's-nest, peering urgently ahead, seeing nothing but floodland and dense banks of bulrushes, fretted at the slowness of their progress.

By 5.30 that afternoon, however, they had closed to within eight thousand yards of the fleeing Turkish vessels *Mosul* and *Marmarice*; and, as *Espiègle*'s shells struck home on both, it seemed for a moment that they might be halted. But the hits were not mortal, and, as darkness fell, and Townshend's tiny flotilla approached the blue dome of Ezra's Tomb, both enemy ships vanished into the night.

Townshend, however, was not so easily thwarted. Leaving his staff at Ezra's Tomb to organize the advance by echelons of his division, he resumed the pursuit and by 4.20 a.m. had again sighted the gunboat *Marmarice*. *Espiègle* shelled her, and she went aground, listing and on fire.

Unfortunately *Espiègle* also went aground: so Captain Nunn, the Senior Naval Officer, and General Townshend pulled off in a boat to inspect their victim, finding her abandoned, two lighters full of ammunition alongside her. They took prisoner some wounded Turks – who told them that their Arab allies had murdered other Turkish casualties as they attempted to escape through the marshes – and returned to *Espiègle*.

Because *Espiègle* drew too much water to continue with any speed, Nunn and Townshend transferred to the armed steamer *Comet* and, escorted by *Shaitan*, *Lewis Pelly* and *Sumana*, continued their pursuit. Deep inside enemy territory, closing on a hostile force of thousands, surrounded by Arabs who, given the opportunity, would slaughter them without compunction, their total complement less than a hundred soldiers and sailors, they sailed boldly up the Tigris, driving the Turks before them.

Two miles on, they found the steamer *Mosul*, flying a white flag. On board her were a company of infantry and a group of officers waiting to surrender – it being their allies, the Arabs, of whom they were afraid.

At 11 a.m. the pursuit was resumed, *Comet* leading the flotilla, her paddles threshing the brown water, her broad hips butting the submerged flanks of her lifelong companion, the Tigris. At 2.15 in the afternoon, she and her escort escaped the flooded marshlands and found themselves sailing between green plains from which date palms stooped despondently over them, and raddled huts of reed and mud, and tents of crude cloth, stared at them blindly.

For hour after hour the same scene, as *Comet* made her bustling progress; but Townshend was now reflecting that an army might manœuvre 'with ease, on either side, as far as Amarah'[17] – and *he* had only two brigades. How many brigades could his enemy muster? And where were they? But he continued his pursuit.

Though still extremely hot, it had become so much less humid that he did not notice the heat; was so intent upon pursuit that he forgot even to eat; and those with him were so excited they forgot even to offer him food. They passed more villages; and noticed, with a mixture of elation and contempt, that they were bedecked with white flags, all their inhabitants (whose lack of loyalty to anyone was both notorious and justifiable) salaaming enthusiastically.

They reached Kilah Salih at 3.20 and, with one puny three-pounder, put to flight a patrol of Turkish cavalry. The local sheikh came hurriedly aboard to pay his respects to the new master. Townshend ordered him to collect food for fifteen thousand troops who were, he said, at his heels.[17]

His division, of course, had nothing like fifteen thousand troops, and those it did have could still – for all he knew – be stuck in the marshes on any one of a million bends or shoals in the impossible River Tigris; but he felt confident that the sheikh would lose no time sending on to the Turk, by camel, advice of his order; and the news that fifteen thousand British troops were imminently due at Kilah Salih would, he felt, encourage the enemy not at all. As darkness fell, he tied up for the night, satisfied with the day's achievements.

Next morning, at 5, *Comet*, *Shaitan*, *Lewis Pelly* and *Sumana* resumed their impudent advance, plunging on to Abu Sidrah, seventy-eight miles from Kurna: and there, at last, Townshend decided to halt. Amarah lay only twelve miles upstream, and surely the Turk would make a stand for Amarah? Surely less than a hundred men and four small boats could not storm a town with a garrison, a customs house and all the supplies necessary to re-equip the six Turkish battalions who had fled from Bahran? Better to wait for his leading brigade before he attacked.

Not so, argued Nunn. Having bluffed successfully so far, why not bluff all the way?

'No,' demurred Townshend, 'I won't do anything foolish. I must unite some troops before attacking; for there is sure to be a defence.'[17]

But then, an hour later, he decided to be foolish! Sending the tug *Shaitan* ahead as an advance guard, he took the final gamble.

As *Shaitan* approached Amarah, hundreds of Turkish soldiers were streaming across a boat-bridge to embark on a steamer; so the tug opened fire – and one round was enough not only to prevent any further embarkations, but also to cause the precipitate disembarkation of those already aboard.

Almost incredulously, *Shaitan*'s sailors watched hundreds of soldiers scuttling away through the narrow streets of the town: then, utterly incredulous, saw most of them falter, turn about and, hands held high, return to the front just as *Comet* threaded her way through dozens of maheilas to tie up by the Customs House.

At once Amarah's Governor, accompanied by the garrison commander and thirty officers, came on board and surrendered. Then a message arrived from the barracks that an entire battalion wished to surrender. A coxswain and a private[17] were sent ashore to oblige them, and they marched to the river and allowed themselves to be herded on to a large iron lighter. Amarah, with a population of twenty thousand, had fallen to a hundred men and General Townshend – who, grimly aware that both Turks and Arabs might at any moment come to their senses,[17] was already transmitting downstream a torrent of messages demanding the swiftest possible arrival of all his transports.

But it was Turks, not reinforcements, who first were sighted – a large force of them, approaching across the plain; the force Gorringe had defeated at Ahwaz, hundreds of miles to the south-east. Impudent as ever, *Shaitan* opened fire with her small gun, and the force fled precipitately north.

That evening, Townshend and Nunn entertained two of their captive officers to dinner, conversing with them in French – and with one another in English when they had anything confidential to say. Thus, as the two Turks regaled them with stories of the contempt in which Halim Bey was universally held, the Englishmen agreed that their thousand prisoners must that night be marooned in their lighters in the middle of the river where, under the noses of the flotilla's guns, they would be denied any chance of the revolt they should have started hours ago.

It was only then that Townshend discovered that one of his guests spoke perfect English; so he kept the man on *Comet* all night and most of the following morning,[17] and his thousand prisoners remained compliant.

The more opportunist Arabs, however, had by this time decided that Townshend's fifteen thousand, wherever else they might be, were certainly not at his heels. By dawn they had begun looting the buildings along Amarah's front so brazenly that *Comet*'s machine-gun had to open fire on them. Whereupon those surviving withdrew into the centre of the town, there to resume their looting. But then the first transports arrived, squads of Norfolks doubled ashore with their bayonets fixed, and, abandoning their loot, the Arabs fled. Townshend's victory was complete.

CHAPTER FOUR ·

GENERAL Nixon arrived by steamer and, receiving Townshend's report of a considerable victory achieved without 'a butcher's bill',[1] congratulated his divisional commander warmly.

His warmth was understandable.

Even for planning an advance from Kurna to Amarah, without prior consultation with the British Government, he had been sharply rebuked by Lord Crewe, and the anxiety this rebuke had caused him had not been assuaged by Townshend's simultaneous insistence that the 12th Division's support in the battle to come was essential. Convinced that the Turk had no stomach for fighting, and no leader capable of inducing him to fight, Nixon – accepting all responsibility for the coming action – had nevertheless decided not only that Townshend must attempt the advance, but that he must attempt it without Gorringe's division, without one of his own brigades, without a portion of his field artillery and without conventional supply troops.

And events had proved him right. Feebly led by Halim Bey, the enemy had fled and Amarah, the most modern and important town south of Baghdad, had fallen to him at a cost of almost no casualties at all.

Townshend's response to his commander's congratulations was, typically, neither wholly warm nor unequivocally dutiful. Convinced that his ninety-mile gamble – now dubbed 'Townshend's Regatta' – had been fraught with disaster; that it had succeeded less because of its audacity than because he, inspired, had thought to demand food for fifteen thousand; and that, had he been delayed only a few hours, the enemy – strengthened by the force from Ahwaz – would have stood at Amarah and routed him, he glumly reflected that no one but he and his men properly appreciated the enormous difficulties inherent in the operation.[1]

Perhaps it was reaction to the excitement of the last four days that induced this mood, or perhaps the illness which was to strike him down ninety-six hours later was already affecting him. Whatever the cause, over the next few days he found himself less and less in accord with his commander.

He requested the return of his brigade from Dirhamiyeh fort: but Nixon said first it must help Gorringe take Nasariyeh.

He declared it essential that the bulk of his division encamp on the bank opposite Amarah: but Nixon insisted on keeping it inside the town, so that Amarah's excellent arsenal and profusion of stores might be kept under direct military control.

He requested that at least six months' reserve of supplies be brought up-river: but Nixon refused, quoting India Headquarters' authorization of a six weeks' supply only.

He requested that he be allowed to concentrate his entire force at Amarah: but Nixon assigned all his field artillery and most of his miners, Pioneers and sappers to General Gorringe for the coming attack on Nasariyeh; and Townshend was furious. Not for a second did he consider that the 12th Division had no field artillery of its own: it was *his* artillery and *he* wanted it.

Nixon, in fact, acceded to only two of Townshend's requests at that time – that an airfield be constructed outside Amarah; and that each post on his ninety-mile line of communications be guarded against marauding Arabs by double companies only, the balance of his troops at once to rejoin him – thus terminating that 'dissemination of force' which to him, as it had been to Napoleon Bonaparte, was anathema.

Yet strangely – since the withdrawal of his field artillery was dissemination in its most crippling form – he never suggested that Nixon should apply to India for more artillery to support the 12th Division. Probably because he was not interested in the 12th Division – his one interest in life having always been the promotion and advancement of Townshend.

In fifty-five years, he had allowed no other interest to distract him, least of all loyalty to other people or causes. He had never allowed the needs of any branch of the service, or any regiment, or any command to inhibit his single-minded intent. Constantly intriguing for transfers to different branches of the service, or different regiments, or new commands, he had striven always for one thing only – promotion.

Ever since his grandfather's death, he had lived in the hope of becoming the seventh marquis Townshend: and ever since he had sailed for Mesopotamia, he had lived in the hope of becoming Governor of Baghdad. But whereas the family title would become his by virtue of the death of his childless cousin, the governorship of Baghdad would become his only by force of arms – *his* arms and *his* division – which must *not* be disseminated.

The victor is entitled to his trophies of war and Townshend, who had achieved a most notable victory, knew exactly the trophy he wanted. It was an enormous Persian carpet, at the moment gracing the floor of the Customs House. Twelve Arabs carried it out on to the quay and twelve Arabs industriously beat it clean; then it was carefully rolled and packaged and sent back to Raynham, where subsequently it graced the dining-room of Vere Lodge, Townshend's house on the estate he expected to inherit.[2]

But no one grudged him his spoils of war: everyone liked Charlie. Liked him, in fact, as much as they disliked Gorringe – nicknamed The Blood Orange – who had even had his men doing skeleton drill, until Melliss made him stop it. 'They won't fight any better for that,' Melliss had told Gorringe.[3] So the drilling had stopped: but not the endless block-house duties on the canals leading from Persia into the Tigris. There Gorringe's men – tired after their long march from Ahwaz – had to halt every Arab maheila while Sudanese policemen, black-skinned, red-fezzed, searched for contraband arms. In the day-time, it was a hot, thankless task; at night, as the jackals howled, the hyenas uttered their fearful laugh and murderous Arabs lurked in the gloom, it was a positive ordeal.[4] Unfairly, Gorringe was blamed for that, too: but his men refused to forget the thrashing he had ordered the two Arabs who had frightened his horse ('and him supposed to be a God-fearing man', they muttered),[5] and blamed him for everything.

Returning from a reconnaissance, Townshend succumbed to that vomiting and diarrhoea which had already incapacitated eleven hundred of his men. He was at once shipped down to Basra, where it was hoped there would by now be ice and electric fans and such other facilities as befit a sick major-general: but Basra's hospital had remained as primitive as ever, so Nixon put him on a ship to India.

Desperately ill, but promising to be back in a month, Townshend sailed for Bombay. And even though – as he himself modestly recorded – 'it was only my splendid constitution that pulled me through';[6] even though 'I had a narrow shave for my life that voyage',[6] by June

46

11th, when he reached Bombay, he was out of danger, and his return to Mesopotamia was assured.

Whilst Townshend languished and then grew strong in Bombay, his men languished and then fell ill in Amarah – which they detested.

Arriving as conquerors, they had been agreeably surprised by Amarah – although the legend that it lay on the site of the Garden of Tears (whence Adam and Eve had made their exit from the Garden of Eden) should perhaps have made them wary of first impressions. But they had not been wary, they had been impressionable: and, at first sight, Amarah had been impressive. Its river-front houses, two-storied and flat-roofed, had looked so elegant, their bay windows framed with intricately carved wood and elaborate cornices. The quayside, sprouting a forest of masts set into the decks of sturdy maheilas, had looked so exotic. The narrow streets, teeming with Jewish and Chaldean women in brilliant robes and strange head-dresses, had looked so inviting. The bazaar, glowing with a multitude of bulbous copper pots and ewers, with fresh fruit, golden dates and red meat, had looked so fascinating. Compared with Basra and Kurna, Amarah had seemed a metropolis. Compared with the filthy, hutted settlements that littered the banks of the Tigris, Amarah had looked like paradise. But Amarah the elegant, the exotic, the inviting, the fascinating was a short-lived illusion.

Amarah was heat so intense that men fainted. Amarah was glare so blinding that even the sepoys complained. The major in charge of the Bridge Train had indented India for sun-glasses, which, when they arrived, proved to be of the cheapest bazaar variety. His sepoys tried them once and threw them into the river.[7] Worse than any of this, though, Amarah was unhealthy: it was a thief-ridden incubator of dysentery, sunstroke, malaria and paratyphoid.[8] For all of which maladies the so-called hospital found itself utterly unprepared. Lacking beds, staff and drugs it could do little to cure; and its only prophylaxis was an order that all ranks remain in the shade from nine in the morning till six in the evening.

Cooped up in their billets, bored and bad-tempered, playing ruinous games of Crown and Anchor, the 6th Division succumbed more easily than ever to the sapping heat, the malarial mosquito and the many diseases bred of the Arab habit of defecating in the first convenient alley. Yet Nixon's headquarters had still not provided hospital ships to take them down to Basra; had still not insisted upon the purification of drinking water; still had no ambulances; still allowed men to live and succumb to heat-stroke under single-fly tents; and still had no intention of asking India to make good any of these deficiencies.[9]

Nor, after nine months of war, was Force D short only of medical supplies. It still had insufficient river craft even for a line extending only to Amarah; it still had artillery for only one of its two divisions; it still had no railway line from Basra to Nasariyeh; it still had no wharves at Basra; it still lacked replacements for its dead, wounded and sick; it still had only five aeroplanes; was still deficient in such necessities as wire-cutters, telephones, water carts, Very lights, rockets, mosquito nets, sun helmets, periscopes, telescopic sights, flares, bombs, hand-grenades, blankets and clothing;[9] and (except for shipping) Nixon had still failed to ask India for any of them.

In spite of which, on June 11th, 1915, Nixon signalled India that his next objective must be Nasariyeh: and India Government not only agreed but added, 'So far as we can see, all advantages, political and strategical, point to as early a move on Baghdad as possible' – although Baghdad lay three hundred and fifty tortuous miles upstream of Amarah!

CHAPTER FIVE

୧୨ୡୡ୶ଚ

T HE geography of Mesopotamia is confusing enough without the added confusion of military and political strategy: but place the right hand palm downwards, fingers extended, and there is a guide to the various operations of Force D in 1915.

The wrist is the Persian Gulf; the vein running up the back of the hand is the Shatt al Arab – running up past Abadan to Basra; the little finger is the Karun River – at its tip, Ahwaz and oil; the thumb is the Euphrates – at its tip, Nasariyeh; the junction of the thumb and first finger is Kurna; the first finger is the Tigris – at its first joint, Amarah; at its tip, Kut el Amarah; and running sluggishly down from the tip of that first finger to Nasariyeh at the tip of the thumb, is the shallow Shatt al Hai.

By June 1915 Nixon controlled the wrist and the back of the hand (Abadan and Basra), the little finger (Ahwaz, with its oil), the junction of first finger and thumb (Kurna) and the first finger as far as the first joint (Amarah). The Turks held the tip of the first finger (Kut el Amarah) and the tip of the thumb (Nasariyeh). And it was Nixon's contention that the Turks – denied access down the first finger to Kurna and Basra, because he held the first joint – would march and sail from Kut el Amarah, the first-finger tip, down the Shatt al Hai to Nasariyeh, the thumb tip, then along the thumb itself (the Euphrates) to Kurna – and so threaten the hand under which Force D held most of Basra province. To protect the hand, he argued, he must seize all of the thumb and all of the first finger – the second and third fingers being unimportant since they pointed only into desert and marshes, and not even the Arabs wanted them.

Thus he argued (conveniently ignoring the fact that the Shatt al Hai is quite unnavigable for a full seven months each year, and navigable only in the shallowest draught vessels with the utmost difficulty the other five) and thus India approved.[1] But Whitehall did not, and on June 14th Chamberlain cabled Hardinge saying so.[1] The Viceroy countered with a cable that, in India's opinion, the advance on Nasariyeh

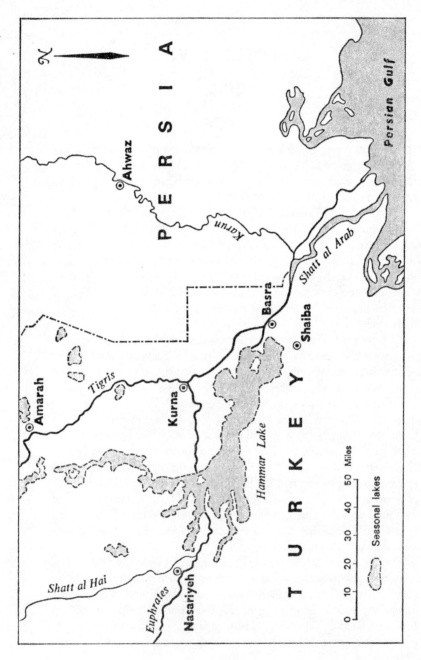

The setting for Townshend's Regatta

must be made: and when, by June 21st, no reply had been received from Chamberlain, he ordered Nixon to commence as soon as possible the operation Whitehall had vetoed once already.[1]

Nixon moved swiftly, ordering one of the 6th Division's brigades, under General Delamain, to move upstream to Ali Garbi, two of them to remain at Amarah, and the fourth to assist General Gorringe's division in its advance along the thumb to Nasariyeh.

It reads easily enough on paper: but to do it, in Mesopotamia, is a different thing.

In the first place, Gorringe's 12th Division had two months ago fought fairly severely to take the little-finger tip, Ahwaz, and had there and since then suffered about fifty per cent casualties.

In the second place, part of the division had pursued its defeated enemy north-westwards across desert and marshes for six long weeks in which drinking water became so scarce and brackish that for the last few days of the march they had been able to drink at all only because the men of the 6th Division – having taken Amarah before the Turks could reach it – had filled a number of pitch-lined bellums with fresh water and towed them along canals and through marshes to meet their tired and thirsty compatriots.[2]

In the third place, this weary, depleted force had almost at once had to reorganize at Amarah, then – advised by Gorringe, 'I've got a nice little job for you'[3] – unite with its other brigades at Basra and prepare to slog its way sixty-eight miles westwards along the Euphrates and through its marshes to Nasariyeh: sixty-eight miles against reputedly strong Turkish forces whose new commander, Nureddin,* was allegedly as tough as Halim Bey had been feeble.

Fortunately for Nixon, Gorringe was an ideal commander for a relentless slog. A big man, highly coloured, deeply tanned, officious and utterly without tact, he reminded those less insensitive than himself of an enormous he-goat, and allowed nothing – not Turks, Nureddin, counter-attacks, casualties, swamps, Marsh Arabs or deeply entrenched redoubts – to stop him.

He too was fortunate in his colleagues, one of whom, leading the 6th Division's 30th Brigade, was General Melliss of Shaiba fame, who had won a V.C. as a younger man, been mauled by a lion as a big-game hunter and was affectionately known as Old Blood and Thunder. He was given to roaring like a bull when enraged; and when in doubt he attacked.

* Contemporary British spelling for Nur-ud-Din.

The advance to Nasariyeh, however, was not to be a matter merely of marching resolutely and fighting stubbornly all along the Euphrates: it would also involve crossing a shallow lake and its attendant marshes, enduring the full heat of Mesopotamia's indescribably vicious summer, and holding at bay hordes of Arabs now as disenchanted by the British as they had been for centuries by the Turk.

A dispossessed race, whose once fertile land had been reduced to desolation by Ottoman incompetence, the Arabs had long since learnt that looting, not loyalty, was the quality that paid. They had learnt to hover on the fringe of civilization, marauding when they could, scavenging as opportunity offered, and slaughtering with utter impartiality anyone rash enough to stray alone. The Turks had taught them to loathe masters; and the British – who described them simply and collectively as 'bloody horse bastards and shit bags'[4] – had gone to no pains at all to convert them.

'While walking along the wharf I saw a soldier with a party of Arab prisoners. When he lined them up and counted them, he found one missing, so he grabbed another from the crowd to make up the number.'[5]

'One Arab came on to the bank to sell his goods. I selected what we wanted and began to haggle about the price. Then I shouted "Go!" Edwards and Shuter grabbed the goods ... and ran. A gentle push, and the Arab was down the bank.'[5]

'The General sent the Political Officer to the village to tell the people that, if they did not supply us with food, we would blow them up.'[5]

'I fired at 500 yards ... [The Arab] fell, but got up, holding his shoulder, and ran on. I asked the Sergeant for another go. "No, let him get away with it," he said. At 2 p.m. we took up positions two hundred yards back and had a bit more sport with Arabs when they tried to get back into their village. We did not try to hit them – just make the dust fly.'[5]

The Arab was to the British Regular what the hare is to the greyhound; but these hares (whose sight was phenomenal, whose accuracy with ancient rifles incredible, whose mobility through swamps snakelike) had learnt to hate: and when the time came, they took a brutal revenge.

But that time was not yet. For the moment the infidel still advanced and their masters still withdrew: and, as both sides plunged through Hammar Lake, wading and towing their Mississippi-type paddle-steamer behind them, the Arab murdered all who straggled or, wounded, were left behind.

> We were in a very bad position, [an officer wrote to his mother] as the night before one of the barges got stuck in the mud and had to be left. This, of course, drew the enemy's fire, and we happened to be in a direct line ... It really wasn't at all pleasant ...
>
> We can't dig trenches ... only mud walls, as water is just below the ground. Meanwhile the 24th had gone out in boats ... with some mountain guns to attack some sandhills. They had an awful time. Five out of thirteen officers killed and a hundred and thirty casualties ...
>
> Next day, stood to arms at 3.15 a.m. and then started absolute torture till 7.30 p.m. Couldn't move; not a breeze; and awful heat. Time goes very slowly and we had seven heat strokes. One died. We had to dig for drinking water, which was beastly ...
>
> Next day I came down here to hospital ... No attendance and no food arrangements: but we got double fly tents. Today it's been 110° in our tent ... [6]

By July 18th, after weeks of precarious battle, Gorringe's force had pushed its aquatic way through lakes and swamps, across creeks and palm groves, to the outskirts of Nasariyeh itself. And there Nureddin waited.

As did such an army of huge mosquitoes that British troops vowed they were carnivorous and the Gurkhas referred to the events of the following days as the Battle of Lam Kutta, the battle of Long Legs – of long mosquito legs.[7]

Those same Gurkhas dragged along to one of their English subalterns a filthy Arab, who was, they claimed, a spy.

'Channer,' the filthy Arab spy addressed the startled English subaltern, 'it's Arnold!' Whereupon Channer ordered the release of Captain Arnold Wilson, who had been absent for some time on yet another of his notorious reconnaissances and had now returned to report.

'Don't go that way,' Channer advised, as Wilson headed off, 'it's frightfully dangerous.'

'Absolute balls,' Wilson retorted, and carried on.

A law unto himself, he always did as he liked. 'You should have a bath,' his fellow officers complained each time, filthy, lank-haired and very malodorous, he came into the Mess. 'I can't,' he always replied. 'I'm an Arab!' And it seemed to them that he never had had a bath and never would have.[7]

If Channer had been disconcerted by Wilson, he was doubly disconcerted a little later by General Melliss, who ordered him to advance into a palm grove as yet unreconnoitred. Greatly daring, the young subaltern explained this fact to the General.

'Get on with it,' rasped Melliss, who had a fever that made him impatient of delay, so Channer and his men advanced into the palm grove and were at once pinned down by the fire of a Turkish picket. Dropping flat to the ground, they were fighting for their lives when Channer became aware that a newcomer had flung himself down beside him.

'Look here,' said General Melliss, 'I got you into this, it's my job to get you out of it. I'll go back for help.' But at that moment – perhaps recognizing the great victor of Shaiba – the Turks withdrew, and Melliss was spared his self-appointed mission.[7]

One Turkish position after another had to be stormed. As they waited for their turn to attack, the veteran Norfolks sat comfortably back in a nullah, opened up their haversacks, took out their old newspapers and read them thoughtfully – to the astonishment of the young Territorials who had just joined them as replacements and were feeling slightly nervous. Ordered to prepare to advance, the Norfolks folded their papers, replaced them in their haversacks, and rose to their feet: the Territorials were most impressed.

Minutes later, these same Norfolks were fighting with the confident precision of Caesar's legions. A badly wounded sergeant, supported by a bearded Sikh, staggered back to the rear. He had just destroyed a machine-gun nest: and severely wounded though he was, he carried back with him the machine-gun he had captured.[8]

The Turks resisted Gorringe's advance with everything available, including ancient muzzle-loading rifles and guns that fired an obsolete segmented shell, through whose exploding fragments the fever-ridden Melliss was seen indifferently striding across open ground. A staff officer, with an enormous water bottle in one hand and an umbrella in the other, marched beside him. The water bottle he tipped at regular intervals on to the sponge with which Melliss mopped his forehead. The umbrella he held over Melliss's head.[9] It was a very British battle: and it was too much for Nureddin's scratch force of inferior Turks and opportunist Arabs, who retired up the Shatt al Hai and headed for the safety of Kut el Amarah, abandoning Nasariyeh to Gorringe.

Entering the town's broad boulevards, some of Gorringe's junior officers were disconcerted by the corrupting, heady, brutish sense of power which is the conqueror's prerogative.[10] They found themselves kicking Arabs out of the way and ordering prisoners to be locked in cellars; and felt helplessly ashamed. It was twenty-four hours before their arrogance subsided[10] – as a result of a very British ceremony. Before a formal parade, the crescent flag was hauled down, the Union Jack was run up – to hang limp in the still, humid air – and a victory salute of twenty-one guns was fired. At which solemn moment the power-crazed conquerors could only think, 'Thank God! Now we can get some meat and vegetables and have a decent wash.'[11]

For others, there were less agreeable roles than that of flamboyant victor.

'A corporal was told to take the equipment off the dead, but after dealing with one he said he could not do any more because of the gases escaping from the mouth when the belt was taken off. The Sergeant looked at me. "All right, sir, I can do it." I tied my handkerchief over my mouth and took off all the remaining equipment.'[12]

Though corpses putrefy swiftly in a land where the thermometer climbs easily to a steamy 130° in the shade, the Marsh Arab had had no hesitation in digging them out of their graves to strip them even of the blankets which were both their coffins and their shrouds; and 12th Division had at last learned to remove everything from its dead before it buried them.

'We dug separate graves for the officers, and one long one for the men.' Social distinctions in those days were exquisitely maintained. 'We covered their faces with palm leaves and removed the identification discs.' A gesture of tenderness? Probably not. Probably they were ordered to. Else how explain the bleakness of, 'I was not allowed to keep Sergeant Colebrook's whistle. It was late when we finished.'[12]

Knowing none of this, those whom illness or injury had denied the chance to fight this last stage of the battle for Nasariyeh regretted missing it.

'I am very disappointed,' wrote the officer whom heat-stroke had briefly dispatched to what Basra light-heartedly called its hospital, 'as I did not take part in the charge that turned the Turks out of their trenches. Three of us [from hospital] joined the battalion the night before and were sent on a barge with the semi fit men as reserves – so missed the great show of this war! It was very annoying: but we weren't fit, and wouldn't have been much use for twenty four hours work.'[13] His understatement was typical of the class from which he came: so were his concluding words. 'Many thanks for the chocolate. It's rather melted: but when we get to ice, I'm sure it'll be all right!'

As celebrated for his administrative zeal as he is for his stiff upper lip, the English officer decided to teach the inhabitants of Nasariyeh the virtues of segregated sanitation. The Arab habit of retiring with a tin of water to a convenient corner and there defecating in full view of everyone was simply not good enough. So the West Kents were ordered to supervise the construction of rush-mat latrines – one for men, one for women – and to ensure that they were used. But the West Kents fought a hopeless battle. Against Turks armed with bayonets they were invincible: against Arabs armed with a tin of water they could do nothing but boot them away from one corner in the certain knowledge that they would promptly withdraw to squat in another.[14]

British battle casualties had been only five hundred, compared with a thousand Turkish dead, but sickness had struck down many more. Reinforcements had barely kept pace with the daily toll exacted by heat and the malarial mosquito; and those replacements who had arrived were neither at ease nor invariably made welcome.

'They would charge for the grub when it was dished up … This officer had told them that if they joined a *regular* regiment they would not get any grub unless they grabbed it.'[15] From Amarah to Basra, from Ahwaz to Nasariyeh, in the 6th Division and the 12th Division, similar incidents occurred: and the Regular soldier's genial philosophy of 'March a bit, shoot a bit and play a bit of football' became less genial in the face of such military solecisms.

'The sick, the lame and the lazy,' the West Kents called their replacements, and showed them no sympathy at all. Yet they were all either young volunteers just out from England via India, or older British railway-men who had spent many years in India; and, in a land where everything was unfamiliar, they needed sympathy.

The Territorials, for example, had been shipped to India in quite shocking conditions: but it had been useless to protest.

'I don't like meat with my porridge,' one had complained of the maggots floating therein.

'Nonsense,' the duty officer had told him. 'You've never been better fed in your life.'[16]

And when they arrived in India, Duff had treated them with arrogant contempt, reporting to London that they were quite unfit for Frontier work against Pathans, and that it was out of the question to think of using them against the Turks. As soon as replacements to fight the

Turks were required, however, he had changed his tune and bundled them onto the first available convoys to Mesopotamia, rather than forfeit troops from his own regiments.[17]

En route to Basra, one of them had refused his cholera inoculation – the effects of which were rumoured to be horrible. 'Look here,' his officer had gently explained, 'This is a battalion order.'

'Yes sir, but I don't hold with it. I've been a medical man all my life, and I don't hold with it.'

'A *medical* man? I thought you were a tailor?'

'Yes sir, but my brother's a dentist!'[18]

'You wasn't all the way with them,' a Regular explained. 'They was allotted to us, twenty at a time – and some of 'em was only bloody boys'[19] – which they were, some of their buglers being no more than sixteen years old. 'You should have brought your nannies with you,' muttered a colonel at Amarah.[20]

And it was not only those in the ranks who suffered: for many officers it had been no better. Just arrived at a Mess in Basra, the replacement subaltern who was subsequently to award himself a Failed D.S.O. had attempted polite conversation with a Regular major.

'*You* can't talk to *me*,' the major had snapped.

'Why the hell not?'

'You are a junior wart and you are *not* entitled to talk to a major in the Mess. Junior warts are the lowest form of military life.' There and then the junior wart – who had resigned a good job in India so that he could go to a war he was sure would kill him – had decided that he disliked Regular officers and would have as few dealings with them as possible in the future.[21] Not for him, nor for those brilliant students of Oxford and Cambridge who had quit the cloistered elegance of an academic life for the flies and dirt of Mesopotamia, the ludicrous ritual of saluting the major at their first meeting every morning, of springing to attention when the colonel entered the Mess, of bridge and silent conformity. They were sick of springing to attention. Sick of the aloof stares through outraged monocles that rebuked their slightest idiosyncrasy. Sick of muttered 'damned young puppies'.[22]

For so many of them the story had been the same. Anxious to serve their country, they had abandoned their vocations or sought permission from their master, India Government, to volunteer. Almost invariably India Government had refused. So they had resigned from their good, safe, comfortable jobs and volunteered anyway. Then, along with other volunteers or reservists of lesser ranks, in drafts of forty or fifty, they had crossed India to be shipped to Basra: gunners and infantrymen, Anglo-Indians and Englishmen.

When one such draft had stopped at Nagpur railway station, they had rushed into the refreshment room. The train had hooted and begun to pull out even as they drank their much-needed tea, so, dropping their cups, they had careered back to their carriage and leaped on board – pursued by an infuriated babu, who ran alongside their compartments loudly demanding the name of the officer in charge.

'Mellor,' the officer shouted.

'I hold you personally responsible,' the babu had screamed, panting and running, 'for the payment of thirty cups of tea. Under section 256 of Government of India Act Number ... ' but Mellor never heard which Act it was made him personally responsible, to the Nagpur railway refreshment room, for the payment of thirty cups of tea: he only knew that no one liked Territorials.[23]

Not, of course, that all such replacement officers longed for the affection of their elders and betters. Fastidious, cultured and highly articulate, some of them even despised them.

'I don't think I like him. He hasn't got any manners.'

'I know, but he *can* give an order! I must say I admire the way he says "Go and inspect that kit." I always find it so damned hard not to say "You might go and inspect it," or "Go and inspect it, would you." '

'Yes, that's splendid. But I still don't think I like him. He still hasn't any manners.'[24]

Lack of manners was not the only failing of those whose alma mater had been Aldershot rather than Balliol: they didn't read books, either. And they positively despised poetry, unless it was written by Kipling. And they were much more at home with Urdu than they were with the language of Shakespeare or Homer.

Volunteers with minds of their own, youngsters from England's green and pleasant land, students and teachers, tradesmen and craftsmen, scholars and aesthetes, first shunted round India, then cast into the steam bath of Mesopotamia, now abandoned among Regulars popularly believed to eat their young, these Territorial replacements felt very far from home. Only the Norfolks – perhaps because they had been away from England for so long – received them with warmth.[25]

The reservists called up from India's railways were no more at home. Years ago they had completed their term of service as Regulars, taken their discharge in India and accepted civil employment. Now, middle-aged and unfit, they were required to fight, march, wade and live rough in the most exhausting and worst-supplied of all the theatres of the First World War. 'Always keep one for yourself,' they were advised by the Regulars, who knew it all. 'Don't let yourself get taken alive by the Turk' – and, within twelve months, though not by their own hands, most of them were dead.

By his advances northwards to Amarah and westwards to Nasariyeh, Nixon had already vastly exceeded the original and explicit objectives laid down for Force D by the British Government, and he now abandoned any pretence of playing that 'safe game' upon which both Crewe and Chamberlain had insisted. Now, he claimed, to protect Nasariyeh from an assault down the Shatt al Hai, and Amarah from an attack down the Tigris, he must take Kut el Amarah at the junction of both.

Inevitably, India supported his claim. Either ignoring or ignorant of the fact that without river transport Kut was the point of no return for either a British or a Turkish force, the Viceroy cabled Chamberlain, 'Now that Nasariyeh has been occupied, the occupation of Kut el Amarah is considered by us to be a strategic necessity.'[26]

In fact it is more likely that expediency rather than strategy motivated the Viceroy's lunatic demand. Let Force D capture Baghdad, and not only Mesopotamia's two and a half million Arabs but every tribesman from Persia into Afghanistan would acknowledge Britain's supremacy in the Middle East and the inviolability of India's North-West Frontier. At one stroke, the nightmare that had haunted generations of Viceroys and Indian commanders-in-chief would be exorcized.

Convinced that the Dardenelles campaign would so preoccupy the Turks as to make their reinforcement of Mesopotamia unthinkable, Beauchamp Duff and Hardinge argued vehemently for permission to seize Kut, one hundred and fifty river miles upstream of Amarah – and, once it had been seized, intended pressing equally hard for an immediate and further advance of two hundred river miles to Baghdad. All of this, in spite of the fact that Duff, the Commander-in-Chief, had never visited, and never would visit, the theatre of war about which he so confidently advised, and had still made no attempt to equip his Mesopotamian Corps with the vital supplies it so conspicuously lacked.

Thus: Supply ships from India still anchored in mid-river at Basra and lay in lines waiting weeks to be off-loaded by maheilas.

The hospital service, now flooded with sick and wounded from the Nasariyeh advance, had become, if possible, worse.

There were no more reservists or Territorials in India to send as replacements to a force about to be committed to a series of bloody battles, in which victory would require it to hold both what it had taken *and* an enormously extended line of communications – in a land swarming with armed, mounted and hostile Arabs.

Britain, needing every man she had for the Western Front, was as incapable as India of sending reinforcements.

There was insufficient artillery to prepare an advance across bare desert against the most stubborn defensive fighter in the world, who would be waiting in trenches so cunningly concealed as to be difficult to detect anywhere, and impossible to detect in the heat haze of Mesopotamia.

India neither had nor could manufacture the guns necessary to make good this deficiency.

Britain's entire manufacturing capacity being absorbed by the demands of the war in Europe, Home Government could not make it good either.

Yet for what had once been regarded as so minor a theatre of war that its needs must rank second even to those of Egypt, there had now been conceived a strategy which presupposed the logistics of a major campaign.

An apathetic Whitehall, raped by an importunate Simla, had simply decided, it seemed, to lie back and enjoy it. But when the strategy thus unhappily conceived was born, and became delinquent, neither parent proved willing to support it, or was even capable of doing so. Instead, they flung their bastard offspring into the arms of General Townshend and ordered him to foster it.

Convalescing in India, Townshend stayed at Simla with Lord Hardinge and, though so weak that he was hardly able to walk upstairs,[27] contrived frequent conversations with the Viceroy and the Commander-in-Chief – 'both of whom were very flattering over the Kurna–Amarah operation'[27] – and made a point of talking with as many officials as possible in an attempt to discover whether or not India Government intended him to march against Kut el Amarah.

Some said yes; some no; the Foreign Department deprecated any such idea;[27] and on August 8th, 1915, Townshend wrote a letter to General Sir James Wolf Murray, in England, which made absolutely clear his own reactions to all that he had heard.

I believe I am to advance from Amarah to Kut el Amarah directly I get back to my division ... The question is, where are we to stop in Mesopotamia? ... We have certainly not got good enough troops to make certain of taking Baghdad ...

We can take no risks of defeat in the East. Imagine a retreat from Baghdad and the consequent instant rising of the Arabs of the whole country behind us, to say nothing of the certain rise, in that case, of the Persians, and probably the Afghans, in consequence ...

Of our two divisions, mine, the 6th, is complete: the 12th (Gorringe) has no guns! Or divisional troops! And Nixon takes them from me and lends them to Gorringe when he has to go anywhere.

I consider we ought to hold what we have got and not advance any more as long as we are held up, as we are, in the Dardanelles. All these offensive operations in secondary theatres are dreadful errors in strategy: the Dardanelles, Egypt, Mesopotamia, East Africa – I wonder and wonder at such expeditions being permitted in violation of all the great fundamental principles of war, especially that of Economy of Force. Such violation is always punished in history.

I am afraid we are out in the cold out here. The Mesopotamian operations are little noticed, though we are fighting the same enemy as you have in the Dardanelles, plus an appalling heat ... The hardships in France are nothing to that.

I have received great praise ... and have established a record in the way of pursuits ... [27]

The letter was completely in character. It revealed a gift for strategic appreciation amounting almost to prescience. It revealed Townshend's chronic tendency to criticize his superiors, and his obsession with his own affairs to the exclusion of all others. It revealed his habitual lack of generosity to colleagues – whom he praised only if they were of inferior rank to himself – his tendency to whine and his almost embarrassing immodesty.

He was, however, neither the first general nor the last to criticize his superiors, to be obsessed with himself, to lack generosity and to whine and boast, and these unprepossessing qualities were of no significance as he wrote to Murray. What was significant was his military judgment, which history would prove to have been flawless.

Two days later, Townshend lunched with his Commander-in-Chief: and after lunch had a long conversation in Duff's study, in the course of which Duff told him that probably he would have to advance to Kut as soon as he got back to Amarah. Duff said that Nixon had strongly advocated this advance – but that sanction had not yet arrived from England.[27]

Strangely, Townshend did *not* then repeat to his Commander-in-Chief the point he had so vehemently stressed in his letter to General Murray – written only forty-eight hours earlier – that Force D should be content to hold what it had and advance no further than Amarah: instead he promised to throw Nureddin out of Kut and into the river Tigris![27]

But, having thus ingratiated himself, he went on to hope he would not be asked to proceed against Baghdad with his *present* force. For that, he suggested, he should have a fully armed corps.[27]

A creature of habit in all his intrigues, he was again attempting the gambit he had played when asked whether he was happy with his brigadier-general's posting to the Orange River Colony, and had replied that he would prefer a command in Cairo – which would have ensured his promotion to major-general! A fully armed corps under his command, when he advanced (as Duff clearly wished him to advance) to Baghdad, would ensure his promotion to lieutenant-general.

'It is not for me,' he reports himself as saying to the Commander-in-Chief,[27] 'to point out the grave risks of continuing the strategic offensive with inadequate forces and with no troops on the two or three hundred mile line of communication behind me' – thereby doing so nevertheless.

'Not one inch,' Duff then allegedly replied, 'shall you go beyond Kut el Amarah, unless I make you up to adequate strength.'[27]

Only Duff could substantiate this dialogue; but Duff is dead. He may well have said what Townshend reports him as saying – and thereby implied that Townshend deserved to be made up to lieutenant-general – but Townshend's apologia for Townshend's war is not always governed by an impeccable regard for accuracy. In this same conversation with his Commander-in-Chief, for example, he describes his line of communications as being two or three hundred miles long! An imprecise definition, to say the least; but one typical of almost every figure quoted by him in his autobiography written after the war, *and* in his reports to Headquarters written during it.

Townshend, in short, was inclined to cheat, with both numbers and words. At least two-thirds of his division were subsequently to pay for this defect with their lives.

For the moment, though, declared fit to return to Mesopotamia, he reported again to his Commander-in-Chief, who complained that everyone was asking him for more troops, and that he had not a single man to give. On the other hand, the news from every theatre of war was bad. In France, defeat followed defeat. In Persia and Afghanistan, Germany was regarded as the likely victor of the war. At Gallipoli, that very day, an unknown Turkish colonel, Mustafa Kemal, had launched a devastating counter-attack. And to India it seemed that Russia might now win the race to occupy Baghdad. In Duff's opinion, it was time Force D notched up another victory.

Townshend travelled by train across the plains to Karachi, which he found exhausting in his 'weakened state';[27] sailed on the *Dumra*, a fast mail-boat, into a monsoonal gale, 'which further distressed' him;[27] arrived at Basra on August 21st, and reported to Nixon, who told him that Nureddin's force was entrenched astride the Tigris at Essinn, a few miles downstream of Kut el Amarah.

Nureddin was reported by Intelligence to have 11,000 men at Essinn, a further 12 battalions due to arrive there by raft in four days' time, 5 battalions, earmarked as reserves, at Khanikan, and the dubious support of numerous conscripted Baghdadis and Arab tribesmen. As well as assembling this not inconsiderable force, Intelligence reported, Nureddin had constructed a number of bridges across the Tigris to facilitate the swift movement of his artillery, and had prepared strong positions well upstream of Kut, in case he should be obliged to withdraw from Essinn and defend Baghdad elsewhere.

Nixon's only reaction to these reports of formidable Turkish opposition was one of impatience at Britain's delay in sanctioning his advance against it. Finally, on August 23rd, he instructed Townshend to 'disperse and destroy' the enemy, and to occupy Kut el Amarah.

For this purpose, Townshend would have at his disposal the 6th Division, those troops and guns taken from him to support Gorringe's attack on Nasariyeh, the 7th Lancers, some extra howitzers, heavy artillery, field guns and 4.7s, the armed steamer *Comet* and the launch *Sumana*, two aeroplanes and two pack wirelesses.

No mention was made of extra shipping, Nixon being apparently convinced that the nine paddle-steamers, two tugs and thirty-three lighters which had been barely adequate to sustain a 140-mile line of communication from Basra to Amarah would now suffice for a 290-mile line of communication to Kut. And no mention was made of hospital ships. With good reason. There *were* no extra river craft, and

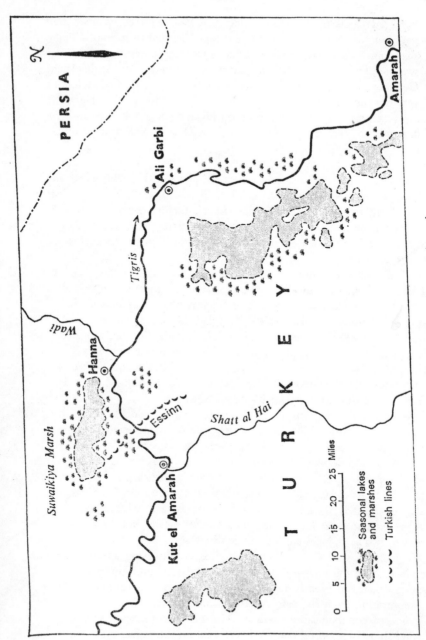

The Tigris from Amarah to Kut el Amarah

Surgeon-General Hathaway's timid request for *one* hospital ship, made a fortnight earlier, had been ignored by India.

No mention was made of reserves or reinforcements, because neither were available; nor of Very lights, telescopic sights, wire-cutters or any of the rest of the material of a modern war, because Nixon had still not thought to ask for them. No ambulances were requested for the wounded because the ordinary unsprung transport cart was considered satisfactory for this purpose.

Townshend protested at none of these deficiencies and did not even suggest that they might, at some time in the future, be made good. Instead, promising to send his plan of operations from Amarah, and to telegraph as soon as he was ready to take the first step in his advance to Kut, he remarked that, should he rout Nureddin at Essinn, outside Kut, and then at Ctesiphon, outside Baghdad, he might also pursue him into Baghdad.[27]

He was, he said, willing to 'take that responsibility' because, to 'destroy' a 'dispersed' enemy, one *must* pursue. So, leaving the bulk of his force at Ctesiphon, and using his flotilla, he would dash into Baghdad with only one battalion, rescue the European women imprisoned there, take some prisoners, and dash out again – thereby achieving a spectacular coup, but avoiding an apparently enforced withdrawal.[27]

Thus, within seventeen days of writing a brilliantly prescient letter about the folly of advancing anywhere beyond Amarah, Townshend not only agreed with enthusiasm to Nixon's order that he advance ninety miles to Kut el Amarah, but also, unprompted by Nixon, suggested that he would almost certainly pursue the enemy another hundred and ninety river miles to Ctesiphon, and perhaps the entire two hundred river miles to Baghdad.

As to why he did so, there is no evidence at all – except his character.

Indisputably, he was a man ambitious to the point of egomania: a man whom the lure of promotion had goaded throughout his career to such incessant intriguing and importunate letter-writing that he had incurred constant snubbing and rebuke, yet had persisted. To such a man, the smallest hint of condonation seems enthusiastic approval. And had not Nixon ordered him to disperse and destroy? And had not Beauchamp Duff promised him, 'Not one inch shall you go beyond Kut el Amarah unless I make you up to adequate strength'?

To a man of Townshend's temperament, these two dicta may well have combined to suggest that he need only offer Nixon a second Regatta up the Tigris from Kut to be rewarded by Duff with a corps, which would enable him to seize Baghdad and, as a lieutenant-general, become its governor.

It would, to him, have been no more than a huge, but logical, extension of his elevation, as a subaltern, to the governorship of Hunza. It would have been a glorious, but logical, projection of his charge through three enemy lines at Atbara. It would all have made sense to Townshend. But only within the context of Beauchamp Duff's promise and of Nixon's fatal instruction, 'disperse and destroy the enemy's forces'.

If, however, it was not his Commander-in-Chief's rash promise that led Townshend to tempt Nixon with visions of a dash into Baghdad, he might still have suggested it because he was the victim of a curious form of moral cowardice. Townshend could be brutally logical and explicit on paper, and neither bullets nor danger alarmed him on the battlefield; but, confronted by any superior officer whose views differed from his own, he usually told him what he wanted to hear.

Confronted by a Commander-in-Chief who favoured an advance beyond Amarah, Townshend had indicated his firm intention of seizing Kut. Confronted by a Corps Commander who aimed even higher, he had lightly suggested dashing in and out of Baghdad itself. And to neither Duff nor Nixon had he at any time mentioned that such violations of fundamental strategic principles would be punished by history.

Whatever Townshend's motives for thus compromising with his convictions, compromise he did; and Nixon's reaction was both consistent and predictable in a man who still believed that the Turk disliked fighting, was badly led and fled when attacked with determination. To Nixon, Fao had proved it, as had Basra, Ahwaz, Kurna, Amarah and Nasariyeh. Kut, Ctesiphon and Baghdad would merely prove it again.

So confident of this was he that he finally told Townshend, 'If you intend entering Baghdad, send me a wire so that I can enter with you!'[27] – and Townshend's last opportunity to talk sense was lost. Had he then, nevertheless, contemplated a few belated words of warning, an interjection by Sir Percy Cox, Nixon's Political Officer, effectively stifled them. 'If you *were* to go into Baghdad,' remarked Sir Percy, 'it would have almost the same political significance as if you were to enter Constantinople:'[27] and to Townshend such a prospect was irresistible. Ten weeks later his original convictions were to reassert themselves: but by then it was too late.

In the company of a thousand Territorials and reservists, Townshend sailed that afternoon for Amarah. The bow of *Julnar* had been divided by a piece of rope into two sections: Townshend, with his A.D.C., sat in one section, four reinforcement officers sat in the other – watching fascinated as the hero of the Regatta immersed himself in a volume of military history.

The sun blazed down on the awning that sheltered them; date palms slid slowly by; an occasional flight of teal flashed overhead; the occasional camel, sour-lipped, loped past – Townshend, absorbed in his study of past campaigns, than which he believed there to be no better guide to the strategy of future campaigns, was oblivious to them all.[28]

Though committed to lead into battle a division already weakened by a thousand casualties of one kind or another (and brought up to strength only by an influx of 'the sick, the lame and the lazy') he exuded confidence. Though no better-equipped now than he had been against the feeble Halim Bey (except for two pack wirelesses, which would, if they worked, take the place of two primitive heliographs, which had rarely worked) he seemed untroubled by his promise to fling Nureddin into the Tigris. Like Montgomery in a later war, Townshend knew how to impress those he commanded.[29]

To the delight of his troops, he arrived at Amarah the following morning. For one thing, he was their Charlie: for another, the general commanding in his absence had been deaf and bad tempered, and they had liked him not at all; for a third, there were clouds in the sky for the first time in five months – which, in searing Mesopotamia, could be an omen only for good; and finally, now that Charlie was here, they would escape the Garden of Tears.

Observing the enthusiasm with which he was received, his officers remarked wryly that 'a dog takes to the master who shows him sport',[30] and were careful themselves to refer to Townshend as Alfonse, because he looked Frenchified, rather than emulate their troops' eulogies. A fine man, Townshend was, the rankers told one another. A *good* man. Not the sort of man that shakes hands with you, mind; but a lovely man.[31] One could never, the officers agreed, call Townshend, who was unusually ugly, a lovely man: but, for all their reticence, they liked the man who had become a frequent visitor to their Messes. His vast repertoire of bawdy stories and theatrical anecdotes provided a stimulating change from the grumpiness of his deaf and liverish predecessor, who had required them to practise close order drill and play hockey – 'for all the world as if we were still at Quetta'[32] – and he was vastly preferable to Nixon, whose unconcealed ambition had earned him the nickname the Baron of Baghdad.[33] In short, Townshend's division was loyal to him and had every confidence in him; and Boggis was glad to rejoin him as his orderly.

Townshend promptly justified his division's confidence in him by scrapping the plans drawn up by Staff at Basra during his absence in India. Their idea had been that he should prepare to attack Kut el Amarah by concentrating two of his four brigades almost a hundred miles upstream at Sheikh Saad: but Townshend, who considered Sheikh Saad too close to Essinn to permit the slow business of a concentration to be conducted in safety, chose Ali Garbi, seventy-five miles upstream, instead. And, outraged by the suggestion that he should disseminate his forces, he planned to concentrate there not just two brigades but his entire command.

He would concentrate his entire command, that is, when the rest of it had been returned to him! At the moment, he was still without the brigade given to Gorringe a month ago to assist in the capture of Nasariyeh. Irritably, as he drew up a plan of operations which was a copy of Napoleon's favourite offensive manœuvre (because, as he often told his Staff, 'the great principles of strategy never alter'),[34] he made a note that he must harry Basra for its return.

Staff at Basra forestalled him by sending a telegram asking how, once he had evicted Nureddin first from Essinn and then from Ctesiphon, he proposed executing his pursuit into Baghdad? By Naval Flotilla, he replied, his division following by route march:[34] and, having disposed of Basra, returned to planning a blow against Nureddin's weakest point at Essinn with the greatest number of his own men.

Von Moltke had declared that a general-in-chief must contain 'the front of an enemy with part of his force, whilst he uses his principal effort against the enemy's flank' – and Townshend would have liked nothing better than to follow von Moltke's precept.[34] Unfortunately, such a precept demanded superiority of numbers, copious reinforcements and rapidity of movement, none of which was available to him. Morosely he thought of Hannibal and Charles XII of Sweden and Napoleon Bonaparte in 1812 – who had all met disaster because of deficiencies such as his – and inevitably he decided to write a private letter to Nixon. In this, he first delivered his commander a thinly veiled lecture on the virtue of Economy of Force and the vice of Dissemination, then requested the prompt return of his missing brigade, and finally advised that he would be ready to advance as soon as his promised shipping reached him.[34]

On the same day, he formally demanded 750 mules and 150 carts over and above the 740 and 330 of each respectively he already had.

The following day, after the first of his ships had arrived, he began to move his division up to Ali Garbi and, in a flurry of activity, scouring his convalescent depot, found no less than 350 men he considered fit to rejoin their units. Ordering the balance to do garrison duty, he instructed his medical staff to prepare for six per cent casualties in the coming action at Essinn and returned to his Headquarters.

On September 2nd, Basra wired brusquely that he could not have his extra mules and carts; and complained that, by making this demand, he had delayed operations by a fortnight. At once Townshend dashed off another letter to Nixon.

> I feel very hurt ... You have given me a most serious and important operation to carry out – the most important and serious one that I know of in the last thirty years ... Who can tell what manœuvre I may not have to make? There is a possibility of my entering Baghdad, and perhaps not by river ... As for MGGS saying I have delayed operations a fortnight by my demands for transport, I must suppose he was not serious ...[34]

But Major-General, General Staff, *was* serious. Having rejected Staff's ready-made plan for his advance, and alienated himself by his condescending lectures on strategy, Townshend had failed to prepare his own plans in time to advance when Nixon wanted him to advance, which he had promised Nixon he would do on his return from Simla. Basra was angry with him.

But, in his anger, Nixon had failed entirely to perceive with what cunning Townshend had begun to play with words in his most recent telegram – failed to perceive it, perhaps, because no one in those days seems to have been capable of drafting a telegram in anything that resembles disciplined English. Even so, Basra Staff should by then have become wary of Townshend's words.

On August 25th, he had suggested a pursuit into Baghdad with a naval flotilla and one battalion. On August 29th, he had stipulated that his pursuit would be by naval flotilla only. But now, on September 2nd, in his fury at being denied extra mules and carts, he asserted, 'There is a possibility of my entering Baghdad, *and perhaps not by river.*'[35] And no one at Basra even noticed that here was not only coercion but a significant change of plans as well. Given an inch,

Townshend would always demand two hundred miles; given a pen, he usually cheated; and had he, as a result of his latest ploy, been given his other mules and carts, he would instantly have claimed that 'perhaps not by river' had meant 'by an advance across the desert' and demanded from Duff an Army Corps as promised to him at Simla.

Four days later he played with words again. 'It seems to me', he wrote to Nixon, 'that Nureddin has been reinforced.'[36] He did not state categorically that Nureddin *had* been reinforced: he merely said it seemed so to him – and even his original estimate of the force available to Nureddin had been a characteristically imprecise 'seven to eight thousand'.

He cheated on this occasion not to procure more mules, but to enhance in Nixon's eyes the victory he felt certain would be his. For two months General Delamain's brigade had sat alone, on Nixon's orders, at Ali Garbi. Nureddin, Townshend believed, could easily, and should promptly, have wiped it out. Because he had not, Townshend believed him 'ignorant of the art of war'[36] and was now confident of defeating him.

'You will never find me making tactical errors like that,' he wrote to Nixon – who must have been as outraged by his subordinate's immodesty as by the implication that his sending Delamain to Garbi had been an even worse tactical error than Nureddin's failure to exploit it. 'I am afraid my advance will seem slow to you, but it cannot be avoided when I have to battledore and shuttlecock my transport to fetch up troops and stores in homeopathic doses ... When I do get within punching distance of Nureddin, you can rely on my taking him by the collar.'[36]

By September 10th, having shipped 11,080 men and 30 guns seventy-five miles upstream to a city of tents at Ali Garbi, and being ready to give battle, Townshend joined his division. Between him and Essinn lay only Sheikh Saad, held by a Turkish detachment. Two days later, the 6th Division began its long march.

They set off at first light – about 4 a.m. – and marched till 8.30 that morning; by which time the temperature was 100° and heat rose from the desert in a haze so shimmering that a camel in the distance was mistaken for a column of infantry and Townshend himself was deluded into thinking he saw the enemy advancing in strength.[36]

Hour after hour the march continued, following the Basra–Baghdad telephone line – eleven thousand men pacing steadily, sweating through their tunics; webbing chafing their shoulders; rifle, bayonet, trenching tool, haversack and water bottle getting steadily heavier; 740 horses and mules, attached to 350 carts and thirty guns and limbers, dutifully plodding; team after team of indomitable oxen pulling heavy guns, sixteen to a gun, ungreased wooden axles squealing, iron wheels grinding; cavalry prancing; thousands of Indian non-combatants anxiously following, unmilitary but invaluable; and, chugging alongside, the flotilla and the shipping, the barges and lighters, the pontoons and danacks, towed in a long line, for bridging the Tigris whenever necessary. British troops in sun helmets; Indians in turbans. Officers, elegantly uniformed, riding chargers; men, drab in sensible khaki, pacing rhythmically in dusty boots and puttees. The desert in front of them endless; the distant Persian mountains, to the right, uninterested and aloof.

Bivouacking by the river, they pitched their tents, refilled their water bottles, collected camel thorn for fires, brewed tea, cooked a stew and settled to rest as well as they could. All the scurry, champing of bits, heat and apparent chaos of a division coming to a halt in echelons of brigades: in fact, a drill superbly performed – the familiar drill of India.

While orderlies set up their Messes, officers shot sand-grouse; and, after their meal, Townshend joined them. For them, even on a march, life retained much of its formal comfort. But for their troops, sweltering in single-fly tents, heads aching, feet burning, life was a bugger. Mesopotamia, they grumbled, was nothing but millions of miles of sweet F.A. with a couple of rivers like snakes in pain twisting through its middle.[37] Might as well go to the tent at the end of the line whence came the enticing call, 'Come along, me lucky lads. Drop it down, thick and heavy ... ' What the hell? What could you buy in the desert.[38]

Awakened at two the next morning, 6th Division ate, shrugged on its webbing and kit, re-formed and started marching again – the heavy-laden carts jolting springless on their iron-clad wheels across uneven stubble; guns being manhandled across dry ditches; wheels creaking; harnesses clinking; cavalry scouting; Arabs, from a safe distance, sniping; and, as the sun rose, dust rising in a cloud.

Certain that this was no mirage, the Turkish detachment at Sheikh Saad sensibly fled: and Townshend marched on, three more nights, to Hanna, Sannaiyat and Abu Rammanah, whence he sent all his ships back to Amarah, to bring up the last of his guns and supplies. It was to be ten days more before he considered himself ready to attack: ten days during which the enemy worked tirelessly to strengthen their defences outside Kut, at Essinn.

The Turkish positions straddled the Tigris, running a considerable distance outwards from the river on either side of it.

Their left flank was both longer and stronger than their right, and was split in two by two thousand yards of impenetrable, brackish marsh which lay, peanut-shaped, across their line, extending four thousand yards in front of it, and two thousand yards behind it. Beyond this their line continued almost to the edge of a second marsh, equally impenetrable and brackish.

Their right flank, on the same side of the river as Townshend's bivouac, was strongly entrenched in front of a ridge of hills, and could easily be reinforced across a boat bridge flung up by Nureddin for that purpose.

If he made a feint against this right and weaker flank, Townshend was convinced that Nureddin would be deceived into believing it his main attack. And if, at night, he could then cross all his troops unseen to the other side of the river, he could launch a surprise attack at dawn against and around the enemy's left flank. But to cross his troops he would need a bridge. He ordered the construction of a boat-bridge eight thousand yards downsteam, out of sight of the enemy.

Having decided to feint against the weak right flank and deliver his main attack on the strong left, he had still to find a means of turning this left flank and destroying it from the rear.

But the enemy's line (including the first marsh) extended ten thousand yards, almost to the edge of the second marsh.

He could therefore turn the enemy's left flank at only two points: between the end of their line and the edge of the second marsh – or round the back of the second marsh. Deciding to turn it at both, he submitted his plans to Nixon – who approved them and indicated his desire to be present at the battle.

Whilst Nixon travelled upstream, Townshend took the rare step of issuing a communiqué to his troops. First he gave them a formal message: 'The Secretary of State has telegraphed to Sir John Nixon wishing 6th Division a speedy and complete success to crown all their previous triumphs; and to assure them that their services are not forgotten.'[39]

Then he spoke to them as a uniquely popular general offering more sport: 'Major General Townshend wishes to say that 6th Division has fought five engagements in the last eleven months and has gained in the Empire a reputation second to none ... There is no need for him to remind the troops of what their King and Country expect of them, and he hopes that a good blow struck now may well end their Mesopotamian labours.'[39]

Three days later, Nixon arrived – bearing a telegram from Sir Beauchamp Duff, instructing that there was to be no advance beyond Kut – and the deaf General Fry rode out with his brigade staff to reconnoitre. Rode too close to the Turkish trenches, from behind which an ancient gun fired off a warning shot. A black missile bounced across the desert towards his party.

'Mind that cannon-ball, General,' a major shouted.

'Cannon-ball?' Fry muttered irritably, as it skipped past them. 'What cannon-ball?'[40]

On the night of September 26th, a portion of Townshend's force under General Fry took up positions a thousand yards from that part of the Turkish left flank which lay between the river and the first marsh. At dawn, it would be their task to attack and pin down this half of the stronger enemy flank, whilst Townshend feinted across the river.

Next morning, Townshend and Nixon climbed an observation tower, built the night before, to watch the first stage of the battle – the desert was flat, but not smooth: scarred, pock-marked, pimpled. To their right they saw Fry advance against furious shell- and rifle-fire until he was pinned down eight hundred yards from the Turkish trenches. To their left, they saw the delivery of their feint – thousands of men marching towards the Turks and ostentatiously digging in – and learnt that Nureddin, deceived by it, had begun to rush his reserve across his bridge to oppose it.

That night Townshend stood at the head of his boat-bridge and watched his Main Force (who, as part of his feint, had already marched eight miles that day) return to cross it and head a further six miles into the desert – so that, when dawn came, one-half of them could fall on the enemy's extreme flank, by the second marsh, and the other half march right round the marsh and cut in behind the Turkish line.

Only one thing gave him cause for anxiety. Some Punjabis from his rearguard had deserted. Would they tell Nureddin that the main dawn attack was to be launched against his *left* flank, and not, as he had deduced from Townshend's feint, against his right? Townshend worried with good cause. The Punjabi deserters did reveal his plan to the enemy commander, but Nureddin, busy with his Staff, deciding that it was a trick, ignored them.[41]

At dawn, Fry again attacked violently, and Townshend ordered every available transport cart to be rushed up from the rear towards him. In the grey half-light the Turks might mistake them for batteries of artillery and suspect an attack at divisional strength.

Whether or not they mistook Fry's brigade for a division, the Turks stood fast in their trenches and beat down their assailants with rifle- and machine-gun and artillery-fire that was witheringly accurate. Neither camel thorn nor flat ground offered cover to those who attacked: but still the machine-gunners, in teams of four, raced ahead, each Number One with his tripod, which he slammed down on to the gritty soil, each Number Two with the gun, which he slapped on to the tripod, each Number Three with his bullet-laced belts, each Number Four with his complement of spare parts.

Flat on the ground, shells bursting and bullets spurting all around them, Number One fixed the gun to its tripod by inserting a cotter pin, threw up his sights and passed the crank handle to Number Two, who, inserting the belt's brass tag, cranked in the first round. Then Number One started firing. Fired until his ammunition was gone – when Number Three sprinted back to the mule that carried more, and brought it up to him, if he lived so long. Fired until overheating or a broken case or a cross feed or a defective firing pin caused a stoppage – when Number Four, reading Number One's hand signals, brought up the proper tool, or the proper replacement, if he lived so long. The Turks disliked machine-gunners, and their mortality rate was high.

Flotilla fire supported Fry's attack – in itself a second feint. If Nureddin *did* suspect that the main attack would now fall on this side of the river, at least he must be led to believe that it would fall between the river and the first marsh. His attention must be distracted until the Main Force could fork round either side of the second marsh and turn his flank. From the top of their hastily erected tower, Townshend and Nixon looked anxiously six miles to the north-east, awaiting the flashes of gun-fire that would indicate their turning attack.

At last General Delamain reported by telephone that he was attacking between the second marsh and the end of the Turkish line. Peering through their binoculars, the two Generals saw smoke, and heard gun-fire – but could perceive no movement. Sandhills obscured their view.

And where, Townshend demanded, was General Hoghton? Why

was he not attacking from the other side of the marsh? Why did he not telephone? Nixon, saying nothing, watched and listened.[41]

Hoghton was not attacking because his column – which included cavalry and machine-guns mounted on carts – had lost itself on a long cold march across a dark desert devoid of landmarks; and he could not telephone because he had run out of cable; and he could not radio because he had no pack wireless; and his helio messages were invisible because of heat haze.

Unsupported by Hoghton, and with grossly inadequate artillery preparation, Delamain's men carried the trenches before them; but had to fight so desperately to hold them that by 11 a.m. it seemed likely that they would be driven back and that the whole attack would fail.

But then, frighteningly late, Hoghton fell on the enemy's rear.

'We marched miles and miles through that grim and silent night' – the order being that no man should speak or make any sound that would alert the enemy.[42]

Those who marched knew nothing of marshes, nothing of enveloping manœuvres: only that they marched, interminably and silently, away from the battle.

They were told that they must march eight miles. When dawn came, and they had marched what they believed to have been at least twenty, they could see nothing anywhere but empty desert.

'Blimey,' said a Cockney, 'we're lost!' And was threatened with every punishment in the book if he so much as breathed again.[42] Then the sun came over the horizon, red and irritable – and on their left hand. They were marching south. After five nights of marching north, now they were marching south. They were indeed lost. But still they plodded on.

An hour later, they saw strange contours ahead; and some minutes after that recognized them as the earth-works and supply dumps of a military force. And such dumps lie always to the rear of such forces. Then they knew why they had marched so far for so long.

'Prepare for action!' Deliberately they went through the familiar motions.

'Double!' As if they had just risen from a good night's sleep, they broke into the familiar, jogging trot. All around them the heat haze was shimmering, but they felt no heat, no tiredness. They were coming in on Johnny Turk, from behind.

Out of the haze their cavalry appeared and, deploying, they doubled behind it, bayonets fixed, towards an enemy facing the other way, oblivious of their approach.

They poured into Nureddin's communication trenches and ran swiftly, unseen (impossible now that they could be seen) towards the firing line, killing the small groups of cooks and servants and stretcher-bearers they met on their way.

They reached the rear dugouts – and took their occupants prisoner: then swarmed into the Turkish firing line. Johnny Turk stood on his firing-step, peering the wrong way. Johnny Turk was bayoneted in the back and pitchforked to the ground. Stick and jink: stick and jink. Jump the bodies. Stick and jink. Cries of pain; screams of 'Allah' – drowned by the din of the battle outside. Johnny Turk looking round, too late, consternation on his face as the bayonet impaled him. 'One after another we came upon them, all registering that rather silly look of amazement.' Clear one trench; rush into the next. Stick and jink: pitchfork; jump and run on.[42] Until they heard the sound of their own men charging towards them. Hoghton's brigade and Delamain's had joined hands.

At once the Turks between the two marshes retreated – at which moment Delamain's men were supposed to press home their advantage and cause a rout: but Delamain's Indians, after fifteen miles of marching and three hours of fierce fighting, were exhausted; and Hoghton's men were already asleep in the blood-stinking trenches they had taken from the rear; and neither brigade recovered until late afternoon – when, observing the approach of the Turkish reserve, they charged with the bayonet and put it to flight, for the cavalry to chop to pieces as it fled up-river.

Now only that part of the Turkish left flank which lay between the river and the first marsh stood firm: but it stood firm with that resolution for which the Turk is famed, and General Fry, who was supposed at this moment to sweep through it and join Delamain and Hoghton in what would become the destruction of Nureddin's force, found his brigade silhouetted by the late afternoon sun,[43] a perfect target if it moved so much as an inch.

For his hundreds of men there was then only one thing to do: dig in. Cautiously unhitching their trenching tools, not daring to raise a head or an arm or a buttock, they lay and breast-stroked desperate little mounds of gritty sand in front of their heads – then scraped desperate little indentations for each shoulder – then for each thigh – until finally, if they had not yet been killed, they had burrowed below

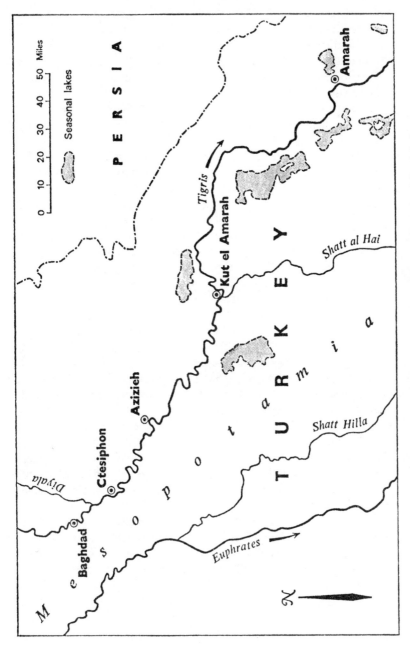

The riverline of the disastrous advance from Kut el Amarah to Baghdad

ground-level. Here, unable either to advance or withdraw, they were obliged to remain. There would be no bursting through the Turkish line for them.[44] Nureddin, it seemed, was to escape after all.

Frantically, therefore, Townshend asked his flotilla to proceed eight miles upstream to Kut and seize the enemy's ships – as *he* had seized *Mosul* and *Marmarice* en route to Amarah. Without ships to transport them, most of Nureddin's men and all his material would be cut off by Melliss's encircling cavalry: but the flotilla's way was blocked by an iron lighter secured with heavy chains.

Under furious fire, a lieutenant-commander went alongside the lighter in a dinghy and attempted to hack through the chains securing it to each bank; but he was shot dead, and his flotilla obliged to withdraw. Nureddin's shipping was safe, even though Nureddin himself, deceived and out-manœuvred, had been decisively beaten. As darkness fell, Townshend ordered Fry's guns to cease fire lest they hit Delamain's men in the rear of the Turkish lines, and, turning to Nixon, told him that the battle was won.

'They'll go in the night,' he assured his commander[45] – and, when daylight came, they had gone.

Only their wounded and thirteen guns[46] had been left behind. Upon the wounded, the Arabs had descended with their customary, murderous rapacity. Upon the guns, the victors gazed with wry amusement. They included ancient muzzle-loaders, beside which were stacked small heaps of cannon-balls – one of which, an English officer confessed, had even hit him. 'But only,' he explained, 'on the arse. And only on the long hop!'[47]

Seven hundred Turks had been killed or wounded; 1,289 had been captured; the rest, with most of their guns, had escaped. Townshend had been denied the full fruits of a brilliantly planned manœuvre against an enemy of almost equal numbers, fighting tenaciously from the strongest of defensive positions: but he had achieved a remarkable victory nevertheless.

And all was not yet lost. Surely he could do again from Kut what previously he had done from Kurna? Ordering Delamain to occupy Kut, and Hoghton to collect the dead and wounded (of whom he had lost 1,229), he joined his flotilla and set off in pursuit of Nureddin.

CHAPTER SIX

Townshend's plan to destroy Nureddin's force had failed for a variety of reasons, all of them beyond his control.

He could not have prevented Hoghton's late arrival on the scene of battle. He could not have foreseen that, when Hoghton did arrive, Melliss's poorly mounted cavalry would perform rather indifferently because it had not carried with it special cooking pots for its Sikhs and Hindus, who then had refused to pursue the retreating Turk and live on food from *Arab* cooking pots as they did so. He could not have foreseen that Delamain's Indian troops, unlike his Dorsets, would become so exhausted that they would be unable to press home their last morning attack. And he could not have foreseen that, quite untypically by their previous standards, when half their line collapsed the Turks in front of Fry would continue to resist instead of joining their compatriots in retreat.

What he should have foreseen was that, against entrenched positions like those at Essinn, held by fighters as tenacious as the Turks, whose numbers equalled his own, his losses were bound to be higher than the six per cent he had estimated.

In fact, they were almost twelve per cent, of whom the wounded suffered frightfully. Untended, they lay freezing all night – some to be stripped and murdered by Arabs – and, when daylight came, were placed on supply carts, unsprung, iron-slatted, and drawn across a cruelly uneven surface to the river bank. There, in fierce sun, they languished until they could be crammed on to the decks of iron barges and towed very slowly downstream to Amarah. What little water they were given was impure. What little treatment they could be given was ineffective. Their wounds went gangrenous, their broken arms and legs were splinted with wood from Johnny Walker whisky crates, and they lay in a morass of their own blood and excreta, assailed by millions of flies. Quite unnecessarily, many of them died.

Sir John Nixon, Sir Beauchamp Duff and Lord Hardinge had more important things with which to concern themselves than the plight of men wounded in an action it would have been wiser never to have fought. Their obsession was Baghdad.

Nevertheless, they made some appropriate noises. Duff sent 'Townshend, and Delamain, and all concerned, his heartiest congratulations on the very successful operations at Kut el Amarah', saying he was 'deeply aggrieved to hear of your unavoidable losses', and trusting that 'the wounded are doing well'[1] – although he knew that in the whole of Mesopotamia there was not a single ambulance, hospital ship or even hospital worth the name.

Nixon was no less hypocritical. Replying to King George V's congratulations and solicitude for the wounded, he assured His Majesty that the sick and wounded were well; that it was hoped many of them would be back in the ranks shortly; and that the spirit of the troops was splendid.[1] In reply to a similar message from the Viceroy, he assured His Excellency that he and the 6th Division had been inspired by His Excellency's congratulations to the victors and solicitude for the wounded; and hastened to reassure His Excellency that the wounded *were* doing well, it even being expected that a certain number would 'recover here and rejoin ranks'.[1]

Having thus disposed of the formal and the trivial, Basra, Simla and Whitehall turned their attentions to more important things – such as whether or not to compound their atrocious indifference to Force D's physical well-being with an atrociously reckless decision that it should march on Baghdad. First, though, they decided to give Townshend an opportunity to repeat his Regatta – which would absolve them from the responsibility of making any decision at all.

Whilst Delamain's men marched towards Kut – westwards, now, because of the need to follow the river, and the feckless way it constantly changed its course – Townshend and his flotilla ploughed upstream. Nureddin's troops marched somewhere ahead; but even Turks must rest occasionally, whereas ships need not, and Townshend was entitled to hope that, when he caught up with them, they would surrender to him as Halim Bey's battalion had done at Amarah.

But beyond Kut the Tigris gets steadily shallower and narrower, and its sandbanks more frequent. Five days later, after innumerable groundings, the flotilla had travelled only sixty miles when it drew into Azizieh – by which time the Turks, who had marched in large, well organized groups, their ships and supplies sailing ahead of them, were reported by aerial reconnaissance to be installing themselves upstream at Ctesiphon. The destruction of Nureddin's force at last seemed to Townshend an objective too risky to pursue.

Not so to Nixon, who (believing Nureddin's troops to be demoralized and routed) had already cabled Chamberlain in Whitehall, 'I consider I am strong enough to open road to Baghdad and, with this intention, I propose to concentrate at Azizieh':[2] and had also cabled Simla, asking whether he might not be reinforced by a division from France, so that, having taken Baghdad, he could hold it against inevitable counter-attacks.

Advised that Nureddin's troops, far from being demoralized and routed, were installing themselves in strong, previously prepared positions at Ctesiphon, he saw no reason to change his plans. In fact, now more than ever, he considered their implementation essential. Now, he said, Ctesiphon constituted a threat to the whole of Force D in Mesopotamia.[2]

It was the argument he had used to procure sanction for all his advances: for, like Townshend, he conformed always to a pattern. Kurna had had to be taken because it had constituted a threat down the Tigris to Basra; then Amarah, because it had constituted a threat down the Tigris to Kurna; then Nasariyeh, because it had constituted a threat down the Euphrates to Kurna; then Kut, because it had constituted a threat down both the Tigris and the Shatt al Hai to Nasariyeh, Amarah, Kurna, Basra and even Abadan. Now Ctesiphon was the domino whose fall would topple every other domino in his hand.

Always he wanted more: and always he seemed oblivious to his one true function in Mesopotamia, which was to protect Britain's oil supply, between Ahwaz and Abadan, and 'play a safe game'. Now, on the contrary, he considered it desirable to 'smash'[2] Nureddin.

Properly agitated, Chamberlain cabled Lord Hardinge, 'Will you kindly inform me what General Nixon's present intentions are as ... on account of navigation problems, there is no probability of the retreating enemy being caught up and smashed.'[2]

That same day, unfortunately, apparently unaware of the Secretary of State's cable, the British Cabinet cabled Hardinge that if, without reinforcements, Nixon could take Baghdad and hold it, there were political reasons in favour of his doing so.[2]

Nixon, swift to exploit such divided opposition, cabled that he had solved the navigation problems to which Chamberlain had referred: he would *march* all his men; and his ships, thereby lightened, would reach Azizieh without grounding! He did not point out that he had too few ships to sustain – from Basra, almost four hundred miles downstream – any advance beyond Azizieh: nor did he point out that these ships could not possibly sustain a permanent occupation of Baghdad. He merely said, 'We have overcome the difficulties of navigation,' and that was enough to mislead Whitehall into thinking both that he had devised a means of getting his ships upstream of Kut *and* that he had enough of them to support the advance he so ardently advocated.

Lord Hardinge abetted his advocacy by cabling that Nixon could, without much difficulty, with the forces at his disposal, take Baghdad and capture and destroy all enemy shipping there. To hold Baghdad, on the other hand, he would need another division – which India, naturally, could not supply.

Between them, Nixon and Hardinge thus placed Whitehall in a distressing dilemma. Embattled Britain desperately needed a victory somewhere, but there was no prospect of one in France; in Gallipoli there was every prospect of defeat; and in Central Europe Germany was thrusting steadily towards Constantinople. Nowhere, in any of the Allied theatres of war, was there a glimmer of hope: except, perhaps, at Baghdad.

On October 8th, in his customary execrable English, Chamberlain cabled Nixon, 'To both occupy and hold Baghdad, what addition to your present force are you confident will be necessary?'[2]

Nixon replied, 'No additions are necessary to my force to beat Nureddin and occupy Baghdad; of this I am confident.' But to hold Baghdad he would, he said, need another division, and a cavalry regiment.[2]

He had doubtless been forced to this qualification by a recent series of messages from Townshend who, forthright as ever at a distance, had advised an immediate withdrawal from Azizieh to Kut, unless political considerations, and the Dardanelles campaign, demanded otherwise. In this case he would require either an Army Corps, or an extra division and a cavalry regiment[3] – either of which, of course, would have ensured his promotion to lieutenant-general.

Such advice was far from acceptable to Nixon: particularly since it came from a subordinate who had once suggested the pursuit of Nureddin into Baghdad by river, had subsequently suggested a pursuit by land, and had never suggested that for either type of pursuit he would need more than the enlarged division under his command.

Nixon's Chief of Staff therefore wired Townshend and rebuked him for not accepting his commander's appreciation that enemy strength at Ctesiphon was only four thousand bayonets, five hundred sabres and twenty guns. 'It is the Army Commander's intention', the message continued, 'to open the way to Baghdad, as he understands another division will be sent from France.' Accordingly, Townshend was to send his commander a plan of operations – not criticisms of his strategy.[4]

At this stage, even at a distance, Townshend's forthrightness deserted him. Though he doubted the assertion that another division would be despatched to Basra from France; though he knew that even if it were it could never be shipped to him in time to support him in battle – and even if, miraculously, it arrived in time, it could not conceivably be supplied by vessels too few and too slow to supply even his own division; nevertheless, he wired that Nixon's expectation of a division from France had made 'all the difference in my appreciation'.[4]

Actually, his appreciation had become gloomier than ever. If he advanced to Baghdad, he would have a line of communications five hundred river miles long – with only Gorringe's incomplete division to guard both it *and* the keypoints Ahwaz, Kurna, Amarah, Kut, Nasariyeh and Basra. Napoleon, with an army of 213,000, had failed to capture Moscow and guard 570 miles of communications: how could Force D, with only 25,000, take Baghdad and guard 512 miles of communications?[5]

Against this realistic but gloomy assessment (confided to his diary, and reproduced in his post-war apologia) there can, of course, be levelled his suggestion at Basra, repeated from Amarah, that a pursuit to Baghdad was both likely and feasible; a divergence in his views which he has never explained. But it can be understood if one remembers that at Basra he had merely said what Nixon wanted to hear: and that at Amarah he had repeated it because he had become convinced that Nureddin (having failed to destroy Delamain's exposed brigade at Ali Garbi) was unskilled in the art of war. He had become equally convinced that he would destroy Nureddin's force at the coming battle of Essinn; and that nothing would then stand between him and Baghdad.

In the event, however, Hoghton's brigade had attacked the Turkish rear so late that Delamain's Indians – exposed to vicious shell-fire as they attacked an entrenched enemy (a type of warfare quite alien to them) – had been too dispirited to make their final thrust; Fry's last thrust had been parried by a section of the line that should have crumbled, but did not; his flotilla had been prevented from advancing by a skilfully placed block ship; and Nureddin's entire force had retreated in good order because cavalry that should have cut and harassed it into a disorganized rabble had been nobbled by a lack of cooking pots.

The Battle of Essinn, though convincingly won, had left between Townshend and Baghdad a large, well organized enemy force: and once the shallows of the Tigris had denied his flotilla a successful pursuit of that force, the conditions upon which he had predicated an advance to Baghdad had ceased to prevail. He had pursued Nureddin for sixty miles without catching him: now it was time to come home.

He may well have rationalized thus. He certainly opposed Nixon's suggestion that he should now attempt to smash Nureddin at Ctesiphon: but his opposition was brief, and his subsequent compliance equivocal.

'It is not discipline to protest,' he commented of this compliance in his autobiography. 'My long experience of the army, and, in particular, my acquaintance with military history, told me that ... my duty was to warn my commander.' Having once warned Nixon, it became his duty, he considered, to obey him. Wellington had had to obey at Cintra: he must obey at Azizieh.[5] But, disbelieving Nixon's argument that a division from France would be available to support him, it was certainly *not* his duty to assert that 'that makes all the difference in my appreciation'.

He had cried wolf to Nixon too often already. He had depicted the action confronting him at Kurna as one that would have daunted even Bonaparte: and had won it with ease – as Nixon had expected. He had depicted the action confronting him at Essinn as the 'most important and serious in the past thirty years': and had won it convincingly – as Nixon had expected. And now, when Nixon expected him to destroy Nureddin at Ctesiphon – when, for once, to cry wolf would have been justified – he declared that his wolf had become a sheep: which, not surprisingly, Nixon interpreted as an unwonted vote of confidence in himself and his plans.

Townshend's past exaggerations therefore contributed as much to the ensuing tragedy as Hardinge's failure to pass on to Chamberlain the advice (now in his possession) that Force D had too little river transport to sustain the advance he advised, and as did Duff's total inability, as a Commander-in-Chief, to cope with anything more sophisticated than Frontier warfare against tribal Pathans.

In London, the Cabinet, believing Force D's river transport to be adequate, discussed the possibility of further reinforcing Nixon.

From Simla, the Viceroy and Sir Beauchamp Duff expressed themselves glad to hear it, but stressed again that all such requirements must come either from Britain or the Western Front: they themselves could provide none.

In Mesopotamia, Headquarters Staff began to interfere so blatantly in the planning of the battle to be fought at Ctesiphon that Townshend wired asking who was commanding the operation.[5] Nixon hurriedly replied that of course Townshend was to command: but Townshend – involved with plans that catered as much for the withdrawal he considered inevitable as for the victory his commander considered a foregone conclusion – was not mollified.

Peevishly, and imprecisely as always, he reported that his planes had observed 'at least three or four thousand' Turks entrenched at Ctesiphon. Almost insolently he reminded Nixon's Staff, 'I shall want all land transport you can get me, *as asked for previous to Kut*. I trust that, as *you* have decided on forward move, you are taking all steps to hire camels, donkeys, maheilas, etc.'[5] Anxiously, he noted that Germany's successes in Serbia must bring Bulgaria into the war on her side – so strengthening Turkey's stranglehold on Gallipoli that troops from there might soon be released to fight in Mesopotamia. Even more anxiously, he accepted Delamain's report that the Indians in the 16th Brigade, having suffered forty-five per cent casualties at Essinn, lacked the will for further assault. Grimly cautious, and convinced that Nureddin's force would be equal in numbers to his own, he worked at his plans.

On October 14th, ignoring the fact that England had ordered Townshend to remain where he was until a decision had been made about reinforcements, Nixon's Chief of Staff wired asking him when he was prepared to resume the offensive, because his delay in doing so had induced certain Arab chieftains to treat with the Turks. Townshend's retort was a demand for barbed wire and searchlights with which to strengthen his already formidable position at Azizieh.

'What on earth are your engineers doing?' Nixon furiously telegraphed – pointing out that Azizieh was already surrounded with more than thirty miles of wire. Such defensive ideas, he stormed, were like 'fungus destroying the offensive spirit.'[5]

Nixon's relationship with Townshend was deteriorating almost as rapidly as the health of Townshend's troops who – deprived of vegetables – were succumbing in large numbers to beriberi. Their morale, on the other hand, except for some of Delamain's Indians, was high. As convinced as Nixon that the Turk could easily be beaten (particularly by Charlie, the Man of Mesopotamia) they positively favoured a march on Baghdad.[6]

Townshend's British troops, full of confidence, ignored such unpleasantnesses as beriberi, heat and flies, and, according to their rank, went fishing or sand-grouse shooting. India may not have been able to ship to Mesopotamia a single Very pistol or telescopic sight, but it had had no difficulty in finding cargo space for hundreds of sporting guns. Basra may not have been able to transport upstream a single splint or water purifier, but it had had no difficulty in delivering promptly, to the officers at Azizieh, guns ordered specifically for the destruction of small birds. First things, with Simla and Basra, came first.

Not that anyone so thought of it at the time: no one questioned, then, the validity of the social hierarchy. Indian troops did not doubt the social superiority of British troops; British troops did not doubt the social superiority of their officers; and superiority was marked by privilege. So troops who had no canteens, cigarettes, beer or comforts of any kind, never doubted that their officers were entitled to servants, cigarettes, whisky and sporting guns. Nor did the officers, who knew that privileges impose responsibilities. In return they must be prepared to 'show themselves' at all times, regardless of danger. In less than a month, most of them were to be killed doing it. Meantime, their brother officers at Nasariyeh – ordered to play polo,[7] though they had neither ponies, kit nor sticks – envied them the chance to fight as officers should, to be the first to enter Baghdad:[7] and those in Kut – ordered to 'stand by for Baghdad' – prayed that they would be summoned to Azizieh in time to participate in the final triumph.[8]

At Azizieh, therefore, there were no doubts, except in the mind of General Townshend: but his doubts had come to be shared by Whitehall – which had begun to wonder whether one division of reinforcements would be sufficient to hold Baghdad. Would even two divisions, Whitehall had begun to wonder, be sufficient? General Staff must consider the matter, Whitehall cabled Simla, asking whether this delay would affect the outcome of Nixon's proposed advance.[9] The Viceroy replied that such a delay would in no way alter the outcome of Nixon's advance on Baghdad; it would merely make it more costly.[9]

Whitehall, advising that it was prepared to send two divisions of reinforcements at some unspecified time in the future, suggested that India might like to avoid this costly delay by temporarily providing *one* division with which to support the immediate occupation of Baghdad.

To the surprise of no one in Whitehall, the Viceroy replied, 'After consultation with the Commander-in-Chief, we agree that in no case could I undertake to supply from India, even temporarily, a further force of the strength of one division.'[9]

London began to have more doubts, believing that in three months' time Turkey would be able to muster sixty thousand troops against Nixon's proposed occupation of Baghdad. Perhaps the advance should be abandoned? On the other hand, perhaps it shouldn't, because Allied prospects in Gallipoli were so uncertain, and Arabs everywhere were showing such pronounced signs of joining the Turkish cause that the capture of Baghdad would be of incalculable political value.

All the more reason, the Viceroy argued – urged on by Nixon and Duff – to risk the occupation of Baghdad with the least possible delay. So long as Britain would send two divisions to Mesopotamia as quickly as possible (and unless Britain immediately advised him to the contrary) he proposed ordering Nixon to march on Baghdad at once.

'If Nixon is satisfied', Chamberlain replied, 'that the force he has available is sufficient for the operation, he may march on Baghdad. Two divisions will be sent to him as soon as possible, but ... will take time to dispatch.'[9] Simla had won.

With arguments based on a wilful ignorance, or disregard, of all the facts, Simla had persuaded its hesitant British masters to sanction an advance deplored by their military experts. Confident that the eventual arrival at Basra of two divisions of reinforcements from France would deter sixty thousand Turks from retaking an occupied Baghdad, Simla never even considered that, with the river transport then available to Force D, those two divisions might just as profitably be sent to Botany Bay for all the good they could do five hundred miles up the River Tigris. Chamberlain's last cable was dispatched from London on October 23rd, 1915. From that moment the reputations of Hardinge, Duff, Nixon and Townshend were doomed; the fate of thirteen thousand of Townshend's troops was sealed; and the deaths of thousands more in the Relief Force became inevitable.

CHAPTER SEVEN

C OMMITTED to an operation which he believed to be misconceived, Townshend took no pains to conceal his discontent. Of his Indian replacements he wrote, 'I have never seen such a wretched class of recruits in the whole of my Indian experience.'[1] Of Indian reliability in general he was so doubtful that he summarily dispatched back to Basra an entire Trans-border battalion. About the tardiness of his maheila convoys from Kut he complained vehemently in his diary; and about his division as a whole he wrote glumly and privately to the Viceroy, 'These troops of mine are tired, and their tails are not up but slightly down.'[1]

Although all the evidence indicates this statement (except for a small minority of Indians) to be blatantly untrue, it is as an indication of Townshend's frame of mind, rather than as a lie, that it is interesting. His acquaintance with military history may have inhibited him from protesting against his commander's orders more than once, but his acquaintance with Lord Hardinge apparently entitled him to denigrate his commander's wisdom without compunction.

Elaborating his theme, he wrote that his Mohammedan soldiers were 'not pleased at approaching the sacred precincts of Suliman Pak – or Ctesiphon' – where lay the body of the Prophet's barber! His troops were not 'confident and have had enough. The British soldier and the Sepoy, as the Roman soldier did under Belisarius, look over their shoulders and are fearful of the distance from the sea; and go down, in consequence, with every imaginable disease.'[1] Almost every word of which was untrue.

His Mohammedan troops had been shielded from the knowledge that they would one day fight upon the holy soil of Suliman Pak by Townshend's own long-standing policy of referring to it always as Ctesiphon, which meant so little to those under his command that most of them were unable even to pronounce it. Sestiphon, they called it; or Setiphon; or Pissedupon – but never Ctesiphon. To allege that his

Mohammedans were not pleased at approaching the sacred precincts of a barber's tomb was therefore to confess that his security precautions had failed. Which they had not: and which, if they had, he would never have admitted to anyone as influential as a viceroy.

To mention the few as if their dubious fears were shared by all his Indian troops was to libel the majority, who were still 'nimak hilal' – true to their salt. In the earliest days of the Indian Army the sepoy had been paid in salt, and had insisted that he must be worth it. Nimak hilal had been his creed then, and it was his creed now: and to prove that he was worth his salt he would follow his English officer anywhere, not excluding Sestiphon, Pissedupon or even Suliman Pak. All he needed was his officer.[2]

Townshend's statement that his troops were not confident, and had had enough, is bluntly contradicted by every survivor of those days and belittles their subsequent conduct in battle. Much as they detested Mesopotamia, much as they detested Azizieh, sick as they were of marching and fighting, living in shorts and tunics, eating bully beef and biscuits, they would go anywhere, do anything for Townshend: and Townshend's statement that, like Belisarius' Romans, his troops were so constantly fearful that they went down with every conceivable disease is refuted by the medical return of November 10th – on which date only fifty-four Indians and seventy-five British of his entire division were sick.

Townshend lied to his Viceroy perhaps because it was *his* tail that was down; or because he wished, as usual, to exaggerate the difficulties confronting him; or because he hoped that the Viceroy would relay his remarks to the Commander-in-Chief, thereby reminding him of his promise 'not one inch beyond Kut unless I make you up in strength'; or because he wished, good and early, to exonerate himself from any shred of responsibility for what he foresaw as impending disaster; or, which is most likely, for all these reasons together.

In the meantime, however, he did everything required of a divisional commander about to take the offensive. He probed upstream to El Kutunie and, having forced the Turks to abandon it, burnt their camp and blew up their fortified positions. He pestered G.H.Q. for the return from non-combatant duties of his hundreds of British troops. He sent a gunboat downstream to protect his maheila convoys from the unwelcome attention of marauding Arabs, and raged to his diary, 'Damn this convoy, which is delaying all my steamers, and has been made to sail from Kut to Azizieh against my wishes.'[3] (He was entitled to rage. Maheilas sail slowly on any waters; against the fast-flowing Tigris, when the wind blew from the wrong quarter, they had even been known to sail backwards. Yet it was in maheilas that Nixon's Staff insisted his supplies be transported to him. He required 208 tons of supplies a day, and received 150.)[4]

He dispatched a brigade to El Kutunie, whence it was to reconnoitre the road ahead to Zeur, and finally – having ordered his officers and men to shed every superfluous ounce of kit, having filled in all his redoubts and reduced Azizieh to a small fortified post – he declared himself ready to begin the march whose objective was Baghdad.

His staff were full of optimism;[5] he himself exuded confidence, telling his men, 'Nureddin is within punching distance. I'll put him out for the count,'[6] and advising a startled subaltern, 'I may be very ugly, but I'm a great man.'[7] Nixon, with an entourage of Staff officers and censors, had already joined him, to the dismay of his junior officers, who believed Nixon wanted only to claim the honours of *their* entry into Baghdad and become a baron immediately.[8]

By bringing with him so large an entourage, Nixon demonstrated his conviction that Baghdad would be captured. His estimate of the enemy's strength at Ctesiphon was 13,000 troops and 38 guns; and he remained unimpressed by Townshend's exaggerated counter-estimate of 20,000 troops and '40 or 50' guns. At a special church parade he even appeared on his horse and, riding up to the Dorsets' immaculate ranks, shouted, 'One more go, Dorsets! You'd be sorry to miss this one.'[9] And so, on November 15th, the march began.

But it had to be halted when three of the division's steamers (which carried all its supplies) dropped so far behind that they could not even be seen, and a fourth (which carried the division's entire supply of fuel) had to go back to look for them. Ordering the construction of a bridge across the river so that he could advance a small column along the opposite bank, Townshend delayed his advance on Zeur.

Inevitably, the major in charge of the Bridging Train had too few pontoons and was obliged to improvise with native boats. Strolling down to inspect the finished product, Nixon asked if the boats were satisfactory.

'No, sir.'

'Why don't you use pontoons?'

'Only eighteen pontoons are authorized, sir.'

'Wire India for more,' Nixon ordered one of his staff officers. 'How many do you want?'

Reflecting that a pontoon cost more than a hundred pounds, the major wondered whether he dared ask for twenty. India Government was notoriously mean. Before he could speak, Nixon suggested, 'A hundred?'

The major was dumbstruck.

'Two hundred?' Nixon persisted.

'Fifty, sir,' said the major; and Nixon instructed his staff officer to wire for them at once.[10] But he might as well have wired for a million: there were none available in India.

On board the *Méjidieh*, Boggis made sure that Townshend was comfortable. Each day he drew a bucketful of water from the Tigris and, having strained it through a lime-stone filter, took it by launch to one of the gunboats, where it was converted to soda water and bottled: all of this so that he could place a whisky and soda by the General's side as he read his books or wrote up his diary. At meal-times he made sure that the General had Vichy water to drink; and between meals, plum cake to eat. Townshend was partial to plum cake. At night he slept on deck, close to the General's cabin – and shivered under his single blanket.[11]

Townshend's missing ships reached him on November 18th, as did news of a Turkish advance – 'five or six thousand'[12] strong – upon Zeur. The next day, advancing his entire force in two columns, five thousand yards apart, Townshend forced the Turks to withdraw, and bivouacked at Zeur, fourteen miles from Azizieh.

At Ctesiphon, on the right-hand side of the river as Townshend faced them, the Turks, thirteen thousand strong, were waiting for him in two strongly fortified lines, each anchored to the Tigris at its right flank, each more than two miles long. On the opposite side of the river, they were waiting for him in two much shorter lines: but the approach was impossible – nothing but rough ground, dry water-courses and old canals, which would impede his guns and cripple his cavalry. He must attack the longer and stronger lines.

About five miles behind these lines, the Diyala river flowed parallel until it joined the Tigris; between the lines, and closer to the Tigris, towered the colossal ruins of Chosroe's ruined Arch, once a part of his palace banqueting hall; in front of it, an ancient mound, marked on the maps as a high wall, ran out for a short distance from the river.

Townshend's troops proceeded next day to Llaj, with its groves of tamarind and casuarina[13] – from which Ctesiphon lay only a short march away – and there he made his final preparations.

One of his pilots, Yeates Brown, certain that Nureddin would be discomfited if the telegraph wires behind his lines were cut – thus denying him the benefit of any advice from Baghdad – volunteered to fly across the Turkish entrenchments, land on the desert behind them, blow up several poles, return to his plane, take off and fly back to Llaj. Townshend agreed and the primitive biplane (grossly overladen with an observer, spares, oil, extra petrol and explosives) duly wafted into the air, crossed the Turkish position at Ctesiphon and made a perfect landing between the enemy's second line and the Diyala River – but refused to come to a halt until it had collided with a telegraph pole, which knocked off one of its wings. At once a horde of Arab horsemen appeared, and pilot and observer were borne off in triumph to Baghdad, where they were put on display and spat upon.

In the Dorset Mess that night – a picnic tea in the open air – an officer with a taste for the macabre sketched a group portrait of all his companions. Inviting each man present to close his eyes and jab with a pencil, he passed his sketch around, announcing happily that anyone jabbed with the pencil could expect to be more painfully jabbed in thirty-six hours' time! Four hits were registered: one on Colonel Wheatman's spine, one on Major Clemson's shoulder, one on Captain Miles's groin, and one on the leg of a subaltern who had been three times wounded already. 'The blighters are going to get me again,' the subaltern groaned – and everybody laughed.[14]

Elsewhere there were more serious conversations.

'Are you confident of winning?' Nixon asked Townshend.

'Yes,' Townshend replied. 'I shall win all right.'[13]

According to the gospel of Bonaparte and von Moltke, he would preoccupy (though he preferred the word 'paralyse') the Turkish first line with an attack by his Minimum Force under Hoghton – who would have to advance across flat ground that offered no cover – then outflank the first line and attack the second with his Main Force of two columns under Hamilton and Delamain, concealed during the night behind some low sandhills and a canal embankment. Having thus surprised Nureddin, he expected both Turkish lines to retreat from their prepared positions either to the Tigris on their right or to the Diyala at their rear. Whichever it was, they would be trapped: and his artillery, flotilla guns and Melliss's flying column of cavalry would be able to decimate them. Then Hoghton, Hamilton and Delamain could press home a last annihilating attack, and the short road to Baghdad would lie open.

That night, on deck, attempting to sleep, Boggis shivered more than usual: and Townshend's dog was so cold that he crept up to Boggis and snuggled against him. Each warming the other, they fell asleep.

Boggis awoke to a fearful yelping and found Townshend thrashing his dog. Struggling upright, he demanded, 'What are you doing that for, sir?'

'He was sleeping with you!' Townshend snarled, still thrashing. 'He's *my* dog and he's got to learn.'

'He's a harsh bastard,' Boggis decided. But he was puzzled nevertheless. Townshend was devoted to Spot, as he was to his horse.[16]

Hoghton's column – accompanied by every available cook, batman and clerk – set off ostentatiously from the scented woods of Llaj at 2 p.m. on November 22nd. It was their task to preoccupy, or paralyse, the Turks: and, making as much noise as possible, they did everything they could to convince the enemy that it was the whole of the 6th Division that now was advancing upon them.

At 8 p.m. they halted, a few miles from Ctesiphon, to water and spend an anxious night. If the Turks attacked, they would be wiped out. Denied even the solace of a cigarette, because Townshend had forbidden smoking on pain of court martial, they sat and waited, as did the enemy in his trenches at Ctesiphon, both of them listening to the lapping of the Tigris and the rustle of wind through camel thorn and desert grass,[17] each straining to catch the faintest sound of the other. Looking up at the stars, Hoghton's troops thought, 'They can see them at home' – and suddenly home seemed more remote than ever.[18]

Meantime, under cover of darkness, Hamilton, Delamain and Melliss – having advanced their columns with wheels and harnesses bound with sacking and straw[19] to ensure absolute silence – had taken up their assigned positions across the desert, behind the sandhills and the canal embankment. They would attack and penetrate and outflank the Turkish lines just as soon as Hoghton had joined battle in the morning.

Thus far everything had gone smoothly and only the arrival of a cable advising that thirty thousand Turkish troops were en route to Baghdad, under a general called Khalil, and that the German Field-Marshal, von der Goltz, had finally assumed command of all operations in Mesopotamia, gave cause for anxiety.[20] If this report of thirty thousand enemy reinforcements were true, Townshend's force must expect a mauling: but Nixon decided that it was not true – and the operation proceeded.

At first light, Hoghton's column moved forward, expecting a hail of fire with every step it took through the short desert grass.

Nothing happened.

A silent desert: and nothing to be seen on it except a towering ruined arch and a high, blind, mound-like wall. On the scarred, pocked, acned face of the desert, not a trace of a trench: not a sign of a Turk: not a whisper of a shell.

Yet all the time the certain, eerie knowledge that thirteen thousand eyes were peering along thirteen thousand sights – at them: and that thirty (or forty) guns awaited only a brief command to send over a barrage of shells – at them. Warily they plodded forward, Indians and British alike. Puzzled, they crossed patches of burnt grass. But still nothing happened: still the battle did not start.

Time passed and the darkness lightened: and all the time Hamilton, Delamain and Melliss had to wait, passively. They must not attack until Nureddin, believing Hoghton's column to be Townshend's Main Force, joined it in battle and was so paralysed by it as to be unable to resist their own violent thrusts on his left flank and to the rear of his first line.

Yet all the time the light grew brighter – and their chances of surprise slighter.

7 a.m. – and still Hoghton's column had not engaged.

7.30 a.m. Not so much as a rifle shot: all hope of surprise lost: so Hamilton asked could he start his attack without waiting for Hoghton.

Townshend agreed, and, riding up to his British battalion, Delamain announced, 'There you are Dorsets – it's all yours;'[21] and almost at once Townshend heard a roar of musketry.[13]

This finally provoked the Turks in front of Hoghton to open fire, with their artillery to support them, with fearful accuracy. At last those circles of burnt grass made sense. They had been carefully sited. Days ago, Nureddin's guns had fired registration shots on them and now, as Hoghton's men pushed forward, they laid a deadly bombardment. But Townshend's ruse had worked. Nureddin's first line was paralysed.

And soon, as planned, the whole of the 6th Division was attacking confidently. The outflanking movement succeeded brilliantly – so brilliantly that the Turks were obliged to face about in their first line trench and try to clamber out to repel those who came running in at them from the rear. Hundred of them fell backwards, bayoneted through the neck or chest, their heads stove in with rifle butts: the rest fled to their second line.

Sensing victory, Hamilton's men and Delamain's charged the

second line, confident that it would be too demoralized to stand: but were wrong. Packed together, so that they fought shoulder to shoulder, the Turks showed no sign of demoralization. Their rifle-fire was cool and accurate, their bayonet and bludgeon work fanatically dour. Hours passed before enough of them were killed for some of their line to be occupied. And then, for hours, they counter-attacked.

Nor, contrary to plans, had that part of the first line confronting Hoghton conceded defeat – and Nureddin was not routed.

Though the Dorsets stormed redoubt after redoubt, and the Norfolks clubbed and bayoneted their way into the second line, and the Forty Thieves savaged everything in front of them, and Townshend rode boldly along the line, showing himself to his men, the enemy was not routed.

Though officer after officer was killed, and messengers had horse after horse shot from under them, and Townshend could reach Delamain only by dismounting from his horse and walking along a trench carpeted with Turkish, Gurkha and Punjabi dead, Nureddin continued to resist.

Unperturbed either by the eleven Gurkhas lying dead around him or by their Turkish victims – each with his head split open, or cut off, by Gurkha kukris – Townshend watched the course of the battle. Binoculars to his eyes, he missed nothing: nor was he afraid to peer over the top of the trench to gain a panoramic view.[22] He was cool, quiet and completely in control.

'Boggis!'

'Sir?'

'A change of clothing.'

'*Now*, sir?'

'I always change at this time.'

Frantically scurrying, Boggis made his way a mile to the river through the shot and shell of a violent battle: then made his way even more frantically back.

'Your clothes, sir.'

'Thank you, Boggis.'[23]

Deliberately Townshend stripped and stood naked among his dead troops and his living officers: then slipped on a silk vest, silk underpants, a khaki shirt, his breeches, boots and sun-helmet, and, picking up his binoculars, eating a piece of plum cake passed to him by a junior staff officer,[24] resumed his inspection of the battle.[25]

With two out of every three of their officers killed, the Indians began to lose their cohesion and confidence. Townshend summoned his Pioneers to march from the Arch to the middle of the first line, to strengthen what he called the Water Point. Advancing parallel to the line of battle, the Pioneers reached their destination with only two of their ten officers surviving.[26] 'Not far off,' wrote one of them, 'and within a few yards of the Turkish wire, a feeble cry attracted me to poor little Venis, shot through the body, paralysed and dying. When I got to him all he did, in spite of his own agony, was point to a figure lying face downwards and just ahead of him, and cry in a broken voice: "Oh, Spackie, they've killed Riddell!" And there was Riddell, shot through the head and body, his fair hair clotted with blood and sand. I gave the poor boy a strong shot of morphia and he died in a few minutes with his head on my knee.'[27]

And then, reinforced by the advance guard of those thirty-thousand of whom Nixon had been warned only the day before, Nureddin counter-attacked all along the line.

Counter-attacked with such ferocity that, at the end of the day, Townshend was obliged to pull back to the first line of trenches, a stream of wounded preceding him, a stream of leaderless British and Indian troops following them.

For an hour or more, in the second Turkish line, these men had found themselves without officers and with no idea what was expected of them. Units had ceased to exist. A few West Kents fought beside a few Gurkhas: a handful of Norfolks with a handful of Punjabis. Ammunition ran out. Volunteers ran back across the open plain to the mules who carried the boxes of bullets, and returned to the trench, opening the boxes and handing out the five-round clips. 'Pass 'em along, me lucky lads. Who'll say no to a bunch of fives?'[28] Slapping in the clips, they started to fire again. Fired and fired. All of them exhausted and thirsty and hungry – and Johnny Turk coming at them endlessly, bombing them from one stretch of trench to the other.

Until at last a few Indians had simply climbed out of the trench and begun to run backwards.

'Cowards,' screamed the British.[29]

The Indian withdrawal became a rout. Useless for their Indian N.C.O.'s to bellow at them: they followed only their British officers, who were dead. Hundreds of them streamed away from the battle. Then British troops began to follow them.

'Cowards,' screamed their more determined compatriots: but they no longer cared.

Observing this flight, Townshend ordered his staff and generals to advance and halt it. Pistols in hands, showing themselves, shouting, manhandling and bullying, they stemmed the tide, giving the rabble they opposed time to collect its wits, time to remember what Arabs did to those who fled into the desert. All the way from Essinn to Llaj they had seen Turkish stragglers whom the Arabs had murdered. Their throats cut; their guts stuffed with rubble; flies blackening their bloated corpses. And those upon whom the women had fallen, shockingly mutilated. Better to be killed by the Turk than fall into the hands of the Arab or his woman.[29]

Fighting for their lives, Townshend's exposed men found their rifles jamming with dust, and were obliged to kick back the bolt after each shot – thereby exposing their heads to the sniper's bullet.

Separated from their battalions, men formed scratch units and fought till they had no more ammunition. Then they lay low: and fell instantly asleep. Until attacked with the bayonet, when they withdrew according to the textbook. Run back a few yards; kneel; aim, fire – without bullets. *Click click click* their empty rifles went: but what Turk, amidst the colossal explosions of all those howitzer shells, could tell that? Run back a few yards more; kneel; aim; *click click click*. In perfect formation to fresh cover. Lie down again. And sleep.[30]

As he reorganized his mutilated force, Townshend hoped that Nureddin would disengage. The Turk was notoriously averse to attacks across open ground, and his losses that day had been more appalling even than those of 6th Division: surely, under cover of darkness, he would withdraw now beyond the Diyala?

Though the Nureddin of Essinn may well have done so, the Nureddin of Ctesiphon did not dare to. Along with the reinforcements that had reached him that day had come Khalil Pasha; and Khalil had left a sick-bed in Mosul simply to be present at this battle, and to ensure that it ended in a Turkish victory.[31]

Uncharacteristically, therefore, and to Townshend's surprise, Nureddin returned to the attack. Time after time, the Turks stormed their way into Townshend's trenches. Time after time, with grenades, rifle butts and bayonets, they were driven out again. No detail escaped Townshend's eye. Where his Indians seemed hard pressed, he ordered up his British Regulars, a company here, a company there. Where the enemy appeared, he ordered artillery fire. In danger of being overrun, he stood his ground and drew his revolver. Advised by Hoghton that the situation on his left flank was desperate, he retorted that it was desperate everywhere, and insisted that his luckless subordinate stand fast. In what had become a killing match, he remained confident that the Turk would tire first. Nixon, complete with entourage, may have departed for the safer climate of Kut, but Townshend had no intention of following him until the enemy had disengaged. And that night, at last, Khalil agreed to a withdrawal beyond the Diyala.

For the moment, then, the victory was Townshend's. But only by default. And, if this was victory, defeat could hardly have been worse.

Across the plain of Ctesiphon there sprouted a forest of reversed rifles, bayonets in the sand: each marking the resting place of a man killed or wounded.[32] Of his 8,500 bayonets, he had lost 4,000.

From all sides came the moans of his wounded – whose agonies had only begun.

His guns were short of shells; no more would reach him; and eight miles away, across the Diyala, his enemy was re-grouping, preparing to resume the attack.

Baghdad – only yesterday a glittering prize – had become another of Mesopotamia's treacherous mirages: the brutal reality was that he must extricate what remained of his division and, constantly harassed by the enemy's pursuit, retreat. Where? From Ctesiphon to Llaj, from Llaj to Zeur, from Zeur to El Kutunie, from El Kutunie to Azizieh, from Azizieh to Kut? It would depend how far and how fast Nureddin chased him.

Having destroyed his stronghold at Azizieh a week ago, the earliest point at which he could hope to stand was Kut: yet even that, he had months ago insisted, was too far upstream of Basra to be safe. By his own definition, only Amarah was safe: and Amarah lay 250 miles downstream; say 130 if he marched in a straight line. But marching in a straight line, ignoring the course of the river, his force would die of thirst, and the Arabs would ambush all his unescorted ships.

He had foreseen it all, yet had protested least to those whose decisions had affected him most. A flexible commander, whose temperament demanded nothing less than a carefully planned victory, he must improvise a withdrawal – which everywhere would be interpreted as defeat – and surrender the initiative to his enemy. Townshend's luck had at last run out.

One of the reconnaissance planes flew back to Kut, where its pilot was at once assailed with questions. 'I don't really know,' he muttered, 'but I think it's all over. We've had a heavy knock.'[33]

At Amarah, on the other hand, a battery of Anglo-Indian gunners –
'Bombay Fizzers' to the patronizing Regulars – was commanded to
fire a salute in honour of a victory at Ctesiphon! Obediently they
loaded their field guns with blanks, stood by them and fired. *Phut*, went
the guns: and the Arabs for whose benefit the salute had been ordered
were not impressed. At once live shells were slammed into smoking
breaches and the salute was fired again: this time so impressively that
the Arabs cheered and one of the Fizzers fainted.[34] There could have
been no apter commentary on the battle Nixon had demanded, the
results of which its survivors now surveyed.

Trenches were full and spewing over with dead. Piles of Turkish
corpses, dyed yellow with lyddite,[35] lay everywhere. In every irrigation
ditch the water ran red as those who were slightly wounded attempted
to keep those who were helpless or unconscious from drowning. Every
dried-up water-course was littered with wounded who, frozen overnight, groaned with thirst now that the sun was high. A crazy convoy of ammunition and commissariat carts jolted load after load of
bleeding men to the river's edge – passing an endless line of men who
preferred to crawl.

The carts had no springs, and only straw or corpses to cushion their
iron-slatted floors. In each there were three lying, three sitting. For
some, a journey of ten miles to the hospital vessels provided by
Surgeon-General Hathaway and India Government – steel barges and
lighters, which would be towed by paddle-wheel steamer first to Kut,
then all the way to Basra. No beds; a few straw mattresses for the lucky;
bare, hot iron for the rest.

All that day the wounded were collected – among them Colonel
Wheatman, with a spine wound, Major Clemson, with a shoulder
wound, and a subaltern, thrice wounded previously, now shot in the
leg.[36] Captain Miles had been spared: but only for the moment.

A handful of doctors and orderlies slaved to ease the suffering of
men whose agony was exceeded only by their bewilderment, but there
was little they could do.

As more than 3,500 wounded waited to be transported to Kut on two
small steamers and the barges which, like unwholesome parasites, clung
to them, Townshend united his force in the shelter of the High Wall,
replenished them with food, water and ammunition and told Nixon's
sole representative left at Ctesiphon that he would not allow his
men to be annihilated for political reasons only.[37] If they were, he
asserted, all of Mesopotamia would fall. It was November 24th: he

would withdraw on the morning of the 25th: and now he would eat.

'Boggis!'

'Sir?'

'Set up my table by the Arch. And for God's sake' – as a shell fell near them – 'don't get all my plates broken.'

Boggis collected the cart on which Townshend's Mess gear was stored and led it towards the shade of the Arch, threading his way among the wounded, the mules behind him plodding mulishly.

A shot breathed past him and he whirled around – to see a wounded Turk loading his rifle.

'Johnny!' a Gurkha shouted, pointing at the Turk. 'Me finish!'

Leaving the Gurkha to his happy business, Boggis set up the General's folding table, placed on it the General's unbroken china, opened one of the General's tins of meat, and a bottle of the General's Vichy water, adjusted the General's folding canvas chair, and awaited the General's pleasure.[38]

Delamain, meantime, tall and calm, concerned as always for his men, walked along the top of High Wall until he saw the C.O. of the Dorsets standing below him with about two hundred men. 'Where's your regiment, Colonel Herbert?' he called.

'Here, sir,' replied Herbert of a battalion that had attacked Ctesiphon almost a thousand strong. Shaking his head, Delamain walked on.[39]

Next day Townshend issued two communiqués. In the first, which was addressed to his Indians only, he said.

> It must be fully understood that … I am moving back to Llaj because of the food question. There is a road from Baghdad, which comes in between us here and Llaj, where the enemy could with guns stop my ships. I do not want my troops to be starved nor to make them live in constant want of water. In short, it is *akal ki bat* which takes us back to Llaj. Many troops, who are coming from France and will reach Basra in a week or ten days'-time, will join this force to take Baghdad.[40]

To all his troops, he said:

> … I cannot express my admiration and gratitude for the heroism displayed by all ranks. To show with what stern valour you fought, you drove four divisions out of a very strong position and

forced them to retire beyond the Diyala River. But our numbers were too few to put them to rout. We have had 4,000 men killed and wounded, the Turks losing many more than this figure. You have added a brilliant page to the glorious battle roll of the Army in India, and you will be proud to tell them at home that you fought at Ctesiphon.[40]

Meantime, Nurredin had also been uniting and regrouping, only his cavalry remaining south of the Diyala. Eventually he ordered them back too: but the order failed to arrive and they continued their reconnaissance, thus observing Townshend's withdrawal to the High Wall. Advised of this, Nureddin realized that Townshend intended to retreat and ordered his troops to reoccupy Ctesiphon's second line that afternoon.[41] Watching this move, Townshend ordered that his withdrawal should begin that night: and at 8.30, in perfect order, every man, gun, horse and cart marched off.

Not a shot was fired; each column moved with precision and in silence; all the shipping – gunboats, steamers, tugs, lighters and barges – swam stealthily alongside; and Townshend, head on chest, rode with the rearguard. Those who watched him were reminded irresistibly of Napoleon on his retreat from Moscow.[42] As doubtless he intended they should be.

CHAPTER EIGHT

HALTING hourly, marching with disciplined precision, the 6th Division reached Llaj, whence Townshend telegraphed Nixon at Kut that ' ... with 4,500 casualties ... and brigades reduced to less than a full strength British battalion, it would have been madness to have remained at Ctesiphon.'[1] Adding that Nureddin had been seen advancing in four colums (one of which had obviously intended to cut him off from Llaj) he commented, 'Had I been pinned down by one column and ... cut off by the other, you must know what the result would have been. I know well. Here I remain: and demonstrate up bank immediately?'

Townshend seemed almost himself again. His 4,000 casualties had become 4,500; the implication that his commander did not understand basic military tactics was only thinly veiled; and he was forthright to the point of bluntness.

To Nixon's staff, he wired even more assertively. He did not need food; he would stay at Llaj till he 'had eaten up his supplies'; he would then march to Azizieh; and he would there concentrate for his advance on Baghdad! He supposed his second division *would* be sent to him at Azizieh? He desired to know when it would arrive.[2]

Confronted by this message, one could uncharitably assume that Townshend was playing some obscure game of blind general's bluff, its aim being to make Nixon's foolish decision to advance on Baghdad look doubly foolish.

He himself had declared that the enemy was four divisions strong: how then could he expect to hold him off at Azizieh with the remnants of four brigades each reduced to 'less than a full strength British battalion'?

He himself had reduced the defences of Azizieh from those of a stronghold to those of an outpost: how then, with the enemy on his tail, could he hope not only to stand there but from there, to advance again on Baghdad?

He himself had damned the slowness of Force D's maheila convoys: how then did he expect them adequately to supply not only his own force but a new division as well?

And just what did he imagine his enemy was going to do while he sat contentedly at Llaj – only a night's march from Ctesiphon – 'eating up his supplies'?

It is easy, and logical, thus to challenge the integrity of Townshend's telegram from Llaj – but uncharitable. Vain and ambitious he had always been, but never idiotic. The fact is – must be – that the Townshend who wired to Nixon's staff from Llaj was no longer the Townshend who had written to General Murray from Simla.

There were good medical reasons why this should be so. In July, after a long chase from Kurna to Amarah, during which he had eaten too little and stood in the sun too long, he had fallen suddenly ill – so ill that he believed himself lucky to have survived. In August, still complaining of weakness and exhaustion, he had found himself back in Amarah, in temperatures as high as 125°, required immediately to plan and lead an operation he believed to be fraught with disaster. He had won his first battle at Essinn: but Nureddin had escaped. More than ever, then, he had dreaded a battle for Baghdad: but Nixon had insisted.

So, after three sapping months of planning, fear and frustration, he had fought at Ctesiphon and spent two gruelling days in the sun and two nerve-racked nights in the cold. It was the sun, Townshend thought, that had struck him down at Amarah in July. The sun at Ctesiphon – in addition to too short a convalescence in India and too much work, anxiety and disappointment since that time – could well have done it again.

From the age of twenty-three to fifty-four, Townshend's diaries, letters and cables had revealed a man of ruthless consistency. But from the moment his convalescence had begun in India, consistency had vanished.

His head ringing with the gossip that Duff favoured an advance on Baghdad, he had abandoned his own convictions, and offered to take Kut. Then he had offered Nixon a raid on Baghdad. By river, he had suggested – or perhaps by land! He had fortified Azizieh with over thirty miles of wire – and then de-fortified it.

By the time of Ctesiphon, as he thrashed his dog and risked his orderly's life for the sake of some clean underwear, he was showing signs of strain. After Ctesiphon, in his telegrams, communiqués, diaries and autobiography, he reveals himself as a man whose mind was governed almost entirely by wishful thinking.

'I shall stay at Llaj,' he telegraphed, 'until I have eaten up my supplies.' Yet none of those who survive remember any supplies at Llaj. 'Here I remain,' he blustered, 'and demonstrate up bank immediately' – as if Ctesiphon had never happened. 'I suppose my second division will be sent to me at Azizieh?' Yet no one knew better than he how long it would take to ship a division from Basra to Azizieh.

But whatever his delusions at Llaj, at least they were short-lived. No sooner had he dispatched his telegrams than his aerial reconnaissance reported that an advance guard of 12,000 enemy infantry and 400 cavalry were advancing upon him from Ctesiphon. With a large enemy force only three and a half miles away, he ceased to delude himself.

Not so Nixon, whose Chief of Staff now wired that Townshend's grandiloquent plans had been approved – and that a third of his new division would reach him at Azizieh by December 15th. But Townshend no longer intended to advance from Azizieh. He did not even, any longer, intend standing at Azizieh. Once more, he had changed his mind. 'I shall again refuse battle,' he wired, 'and fall back to Kut el Amarah in all probability, as Kut is a strategical point we are bound to hold ... Should [the enemy] follow to Kut, so much the better. We ought to destroy him in that case ... The further we get him from Baghdad, the more chance, in our next battle, of knocking him out altogether.'[2]

Having shed one delusion, he seemed determined at once to shroud his mind in another. Kut, which he had described to Murray as a position undesirably remote from Basra, now became 'a strategical point we are bound to hold'. Although he knew it to be without defences, except for the old Turkish lines at Essinn which faced the wrong way, now it became a battle-ground so unfavourable to the enemy that 'we ought to destroy him'. His four weak brigades now became a force strong enough to defeat a Turkish army. Why did he say any of it? Perhaps to prevent Nixon from ordering him to make any stand up-river of Kut. Perhaps to remind Duff that he had not yet been brought up to his promised 'adequate strength'. Perhaps – and most likely – because he had begun to remember Chitral.

There, hard pressed as he was now, he had withdrawn into a fort, slammed its gates and sat out a forty-six-day siege – from which he had emerged a hero, the darling of Britain, the guest of his Queen. Kut was surrounded on three sides by a loop in the River Tigris: and a wide river on three sides was as good as three high walls. Kut's fourth and open side could easily be entrenched. Let the Turk then attack it and he would find it more dangerous than any gate. Behind his three river walls and his line of fortified redoubts, he could sit out another siege; and, when he was relieved, a hero again, he could take command of an adequate force, seize Baghdad, become its governor ... and who knew what else? First, though, he must get to Kut. Which meant that he must forestall any notions Nixon had of ordering him to stand and fight anywhere else, and march as far from Llaj as possible.

Instructing his men to rip their tents with their bayonets, but to leave them standing – in the hope that Nureddin would thereby be deceived at least until dawn – he ordered an immediate departure for Azizieh.[3]

He marched his men twenty-two miles that night. Time after time, one or other of his ships ran aground: but he marched on, relying upon them to catch up. The armed tug *Shaitan* was beached with leaking plates: ordering it to be scuttled, he abandoned it. Like flies round a corpse, Arab horsemen lurked at the rear of his plodding column: ignoring them, he marched on. Irrigation canals and nullahs blocked the progress of his wheeled guns and transport: ordering his sappers to dig ramps in and out of them, he drove his force on. And finally stood at the gates of Azizieh and watched his men march in.[2]

Even there, however, he did not let them rest. All the wounded were to be put aboard the *Méjidieh* and her two attendant barges. All Azizieh's stores, including the kit his troops had shed on their march to Ctesiphon, were to be destroyed.[3] All the barbed wire round Azizieh was to be uprooted and thrown into the Tigris. The supply column must be loaded and a boat-bridge dismantled. It was a chaotic afternoon.

Each regiment was allowed two hours to scavenge through its abandoned kit. Any man who found his own bag could take away anything he was prepared to carry another fifty miles.

Thousands of bags in a huge dump, thousands of men, each searching for his own. Some were lucky, and left with vests and socks, tins of tobacco and boots: the unlucky did not, realizing bitterly that their socks and vests and boots and tobacco were in the hands of Arabs who, risking the few sentries left to guard the compound, had pilfered every night for the past eleven days.

Officers also looked hopefully for the kit they had left behind them, the fortunate ones debating anxiously which of their treasures (from shooting guns to silver flasks) to take with them, and finally abandoning such accoutrements of war as plumed helmets, full-dress uniforms and ceremonial swords: which was too much for the Forty Thieves. 'Hey,' protested a corporal, 'we can't leave all *this* to the Turks!' and a party of twelve added some very exotic equipment to their normally prosaic kit[4] – including half a side of bacon. Officers were no less enterprising. One who found his box selected from it a sleeping valise and a pair of silk pyjamas: and took them with him when the march continued.[5]

Another found a stack of mail – and in it a magnificent parcel addressed to himself, Lieutenant J. Mellor. Excitedly he opened it, expecting Christmas fare, but found a file of papers, stamped with the marks of officialdom all the way from Nagpur to Rangoon, dealing with the claim of a railway refreshment room babu for the payment of thirty cups of tea – and ordering him to forward forthwith, to Nagpur, the sum of fourteen rupees. Carefully re-wrapping his magnificent parcel, he carried it away and threw it into the Tigris.[6] He must be forgiven his failure to perceive that first things still came first: he was a very young man.

Next morning, a trickle of replacements reached Azizieh, including some Hussars and half a battalion of the West Kents, who had spent the previous night marching twenty-one miles, only to end up where they began, which had not pleased them.[7]

They were even less pleased when, swinging into Azizieh, and being greeted with shouts of, 'How many are you?' – to which they had replied, 'Half the West Kents,' – Townshend's troops had grumbled, 'That's no bloody good. We need half the British Army!'

'Where do you reckon you're going then?' a Dorset shouted to a Hussar.

'Up-river, with you.'

'Then you're coming *down*-river with us,' the Dorset rasped.[8]

After a meal of bully and biscuits, the newly arrived West Kents were ordered to load sick and wounded on to the *Méjidieh*. 'I could hardly believe my eyes,' one reported of the sprawling, unwashed, ill-fed men he handled. 'I'll never forget that sight.'[9]

Other replacements were on their way, including the salute-firing Anglo-Indian gunners from Amarah. Full of zeal, they had shrugged aside the less agreeable aspects of Mesopotamia, determined to prove themselves the equal of those whose blood was pure, determined to live down that pejorative 'Bombay Fizzers', and had been disappointed when they were halted at Kut because all Nixon's ships were at Azizieh, full of wounded, and because Nixon had become anxious about his line of communications, which was suddenly threatened by large forces of Arab horsemen.

What troops, Nixon's Staff wired Townshend, could be spared to disperse this disagreeable threat? Generously, Townshend ordered Melliss to rush the 30th Brigade downstream: the rest of his force, men and ships would leave Azizieh the following morning, the enemy by now being less than six miles behind them.

That night, 6th Division prepared itself for a further march: prepared itself as soldiers do. The officers of an artillery Mess bought a hen, to be eaten when finally they halted. Captain Miles slept luxuriously in his valise and silk pyjamas. Those assigned to the rearguard bemoaned their fate. Horses and mules, heads down, waited patiently in their lines. And sleeping troops shivered. It was November 29th, and winter had begun.

Next morning they marched south, heading for Umm al Tubul, the Mother of Tombs, leaving behind them a deserted camp, a blazing store-house and an exploding bargeful of aviation bombs. Nureddin – alerted by smoke belching black in the distance against the desert's bleached sky, reading it correctly as a signal that Townshend had once more declined an invitation to battle – set off in pursuit.

After only four miles, Townshend was compelled to order a ten-minute rest: already men were abandoning kit they had picked up at Azizieh – including the side of bacon: already there were stragglers, and Arabs waiting to kill and strip them the instant it was safe to do so. From the resting column, men trudged back across the desert, looking for their friends.

'He was lying on the ground, and when I told him to get up he said he was finished. I took his rifle, grabbed him by the collar, pulled him to his feet and kicked him. "Now come," I said. He hung on to me and, as luck would have it, we caught up. "Any more tricks and you get your throat cut," I said, giving him half a biscuit and a piece of bully.'[10]

They reached Umm al Tubul at noon, their shipping with them. But Melliss and his brigade marched on, determined to reach Kut in time to strengthen the line below it, to make safe Nixon's departure for Basra from it: and in Kut itself a sentry standing at the head of the track that leads past the minaret into the town saw a dishevelled figure riding towards him on a donkey.

'Where's Headquarters?' the rider demanded, as he reached the sentry. An officer, the sentry observed. Dead tired. An officer on a *donkey*? Something had gone wrong.

'Down there, sir,' pointing.

Nodding, the officer rode away, down the track, towards Headquarters, slumped and dejected, leaving the sentry to stare anxiously into the desert. There'd been rumours, of course. Ever since that plane came back, there'd been rumours. Could it really be as bad as that, though? An officer on a donkey?[11]

Once again Townshend changed his mind – because of a misunderstanding with his Senior Naval Officer. Nunn, believing Townshend's men incapable of marching farther, had said that his ships would proceed no farther: Townshend, believing that Nunn had said his ships *could* proceed no farther, had halted his troops to protect them. And so, having twice declared that he would refuse battle with Nureddin,[12] he resolved to stay at Umm al Tubul until the following morning, and, if Nureddin closed on him, to attack.

This decision taken, he decided to recall Melliss – asking for volunteers to ride after him through a desert swarming with Arab horsemen. Two Lancer officers obliged him, and promising to recommend them for the Victoria Cross he sent them off on their mission, escorted by six Indians to whom he promised nothing.

For those who remained at Umm al Tubul, the night passed in silence – the silence of those who are exhausted, apprehensive and cold.

'Boggis!'

Boggis, shivering under his banket outside Townshend's tent, was startled into wakefulness. 'Sir?'

'Can you hear wheels?'

Boggis listened intently. 'No, sir.'

'Well, I can. Go and get Colonel Evans and we'll see if he can hear anything.'

Boggis brought back a rumpled Colonel Evans, a short, sturdy, red-faced man with a bristling moustache, whose language was reputedly worse than anyone's east of Suez.[13]

'Evans – can you hear wheels?'

'No, sir.'

'I can. There are Turks on the move out there. Why haven't the outposts reported it? See to it.'[14]

Evans returned to his own tent and woke all the officers sleeping near it. 'I want you to listen and tell me if you can hear anything,' he ordered.

They all listened, and heard nothing but the clinking of harnesses in their own horse lines. No one spoke and Evans glared at them ferociously, as if criticizing their silence.

'I think it's only the mules, sir,' one of them finally volunteered.

'I know *that*'s only the mules, you pissbegotten bugger: but what else can you hear?'

'Nothing, sir.'

'Well, the General can!'[15]

So orders were sent out for every man to stand to. Wearily the infantry deployed, and the gunners erected their monkey poles and climbed up on top of them to observe, and the Hussars prepared to fight their first battle in Mesopotamia.

A few miles to the rear, on a line of low sand dunes, fires began to flicker: and from those dunes a few shells whined overhead.

'Arabs,' said a brigadier. 'And a couple of camel guns. We'll attack 'em at dawn.'

But when dawn came they saw rows of tents on the crest of the dunes, and a mass of Turkish soldiery wandering round them. For a moment each side incredulously surveyed the other: then, as the British gunners reacted, and sent shell after shell to burst among tents and troops, blasting them aside, twelve thousand Turks advanced across open ground. Not hesitating a second, Townshend ordered Hamilton to attack them head on, Delamain to envelop and his cavalry to charge. But numbed by an immediate torrent of English shells the Turks' advance had already ground to an uneasy halt. It thus became the cavalry's prerogative to ride out and cut them to pieces.

The Hussars – mounted on tough Australian horses – charged in the classic manner, sabres murderously outstretched, galloping in line into the enemy, through the enemy, round and into the enemy again. 'Grand,' shouted the infantry. 'Grand'.[16]

Gun teams also galloped forward – foam-flecked tongues hanging out 'long as your arm' – to keep the shattered Turks in range. A horse had its leg blown off. No time to shoot it. Cut it out of the team and gallop on.[17] Clouds of dust, halt, unlimber, slam shell into breach, slam breach shut and fire over open sights into a greenish, frenzied, turbaned rabble, which broke and fled.

Townshend's infantry deployed on the sand dunes, revelling in the prospect of a fight on open ground.

A Norfolk with both legs broken ignored his injuries. Spreading his ammunition carefully round him, he continued his deliberate fire, round after round.[18]

Comet and *Firefly* raced upstream, to add their fire to Nureddin's discomfiture: and still the enemy fled. Whereupon Townshend disengaged, ordering his brigades to fall back in echelon.

The dead and wounded were retrieved in the inevitable carts. Guns were re-limbered and galloped back to their lines – where the horse with the shattered leg waited to rejoin its team: where again there was no time to shoot it, because the march must be resumed at once. Now, for the first time, a few officers doubted a decision of Townshend's sufficiently to ask themselves the question that was to haunt them for the next two and a half years. 'Had we pressed home our attack against the fleeing Turk,' they asked themselves, 'would there be any need to continue this retreat?'[19] Because Townshend had not called off the attack so that his exhausted troops might rest: on the contrary, his orders were that they were to start at once on a twelve-hour march of thirty-six miles.

He may, of course, they realized, have suspected a trap. Or he may have feared for the safety of his shipping, *Comet* having already gone aground, and *Firefly* – a new monitor, pride of the flotilla – having been disabled, a shell through her boiler. Or he may have decided to lead his force back into Kut and do no more until such reinforcements reached him as would make an advance on Baghdad an undoubted success. But, whatever his reason, at 7.30 a.m. he had disengaged, and Melliss, returning post haste, found that he had missed the battle and was required to do no more than head off any pursuit that might threaten the division's continued retreat.

Once again infantry and cavalry, field artillery and howitzers, supply carts and followers, steamers and barges, launches and pontoons, prepared to move, and the horse with the shattered leg fought viciously to evict its replacement from the team of four to which it had always belonged, until finally someone shot it.[20]

Giving his orders for the march, Delamain pointed to three Dorset privates. 'You go with the 66th Punjabis. Don't let them run.' Quite unselfconsciously three white privates took up their positions in the Punjabi ranks, ready to march beside Indian officers, and to order them not to break into a run.[21]

The column set off, a long line of men, animals, carts and guns, led by the Indians, who were obviously nervous. With an enormous march ahead of them and in spite of the Dorset privates, they were almost trotting: and the line behind them began at once to lengthen and straggle. From his rearguard post, Townshend glared ahead.

'What's *happening* up there?' he snarled. 'Has everyone gone mad?'

'Seems so, sir,' Boggis replied. Grunting, Townshend kicked his horse to a gallop, charged to the head of the column and brought the Indians to heel. He didn't really like them: he never had.[22]

He marched his men without pity all that day, and at sunset gave no sign of calling a halt. A worried Delamain suggested that at least they might stop long enough to fill their water bottles and have a drink.

'Once these men get down to the river bank,' Townshend retorted, 'we shan't collect them for hours. They'll lie by the water, drink and fall asleep like logs.'[23] Still Delamain protested.[24] 'Look,' Townshend grated, 'how do I know that the Turks aren't only a mile or so behind?' – and kept his column marching.

It reached Shadie, thirty-six miles from Umm al Tubul, at 9 that night. The launches towing his pontoons had been so often ambushed by Arabs swarming on the river bank that their native skippers had panicked, one after the other, and, cutting their tow-ropes, abandoned all his vital bridging materials.[26] Of his troops, those who had fallen behind had had their throats slit by Arabs; and for the rest there was no food, no camp and nothing to comfort them. Lying exactly where they halted, they slept in columns, in the cold night air, on the cold desert sand, as he had said they would, like logs.[27]

Townshend waited only to see his rearguard safely arrived before boarding *Méjidieh* to inspect his casualties. Ever since Chitral he had hated such inspections,[28] but he forced himself to do it: and was appalled to learn that one of his hospital barges had grounded upstream and been captured by the Turks. He would have been even more appalled had he realized how the Turks had cared for those who thus became their prisoners – not because they were cruel, simply because their medical supplies were even less adequate than those of Force D. The fate of the Dorset lieutenant who received his fourth wound at Ctesiphon was typical. Too late, the Turks amputated his leg, and he died of gangrene.[29]

It was not, however, Townshend's duty to comfort his wounded; they, God help them, had become Surgeon-General Hathaway's responsibility. Townshend's duty was to lead his force to safety, and safety, to him, now meant Kut – one day's march away.

His division had carried out a perfectly executed six-and-a-half-day retreat, and he did not doubt that it would hold Kut as securely as Surgeon-Major Robertson's tiny force had held Chitral twenty years ago.

CHAPTER NINE

AWAITING the 6th Division's arrival at Kut there was little but filth, thousands of sacks of ginger, a high degree of military chaos and a population of six thousand utterly unreliable Arabs.

No one had ever anticipated that this drab town (suspended in a loop of the Tigris which itself resembles a uvula at the throat of the Shatt al Hai), with a back yard of desert that extended to Baghdad itself, would ever be anything more than a supply dump and a base hospital.

The town of Kut (a bazaar, a clutter of mud houses, a maze of narrow alleys and a mosque) clung to the tip of the uvula like an ulcer, the bazaar being closest to the river: and beyond the town, looking up-river from the bazaar, there were groves of date palms and lime trees to the left and right, some brick kilns and a filth-littered wasteland 3,000 yards long and 2,700 yards wide from one side of the looping Tigris to the other. Opposite the bazaar, across the Tigris, lay a small village and a liquorice factory.

Uninviting though it was, Kut was one of the few posts held by Force D upon which any kind of planning had been brought to bear – largely because its senior medical officer had been treated so rudely by Basra when he attempted to suggest overall improvements for Mesopotamia's Medical Service that he had subsequently concentrated all his energies elsewhere. Intended as a supply dump and a minor base hospital for nine hundred casualties, it had been well stocked with everything needed for both, the hospital accommodation consisting of a number of huts and ꞌ nts in one of the palm groves. But, as barge-load after barge-load of neglected and filthy casualties came alongside, it seemed that even this careful planning must soon break down.

Those already in the hospital were shipped downstream to Amarah and Indian stretcher-bearers began plodding from the river to the hospital (which soon became full again, and then overflowed) back to the river with an empty stretcher, back to the hospital with a casualty, back to the river, interminably.

Doctors and orderlies could do little more than clean each wound, label each casualty and send him back to the river to be shipped either to Amarah or to Basra.

An R.F.C. officer watching this dismal procession, calculating that it would take a month to clear all the wounded, suggested that he and his mechanics might help. They had a lorry: why not use it to carry five stretcher-loads at a time from the river to the hospital, and a full complement of stretcher-bearers back to the river again?[1] Gratefully, the doctors accepted his suggestion; and so, as the flow of casualties to and fro grew faster, the R.F.C. made the first of its many contributions to the welfare of Kut.

Young Territorials made their contribution more arduously, digging shallow trenches from the mud fort at the right rear of Kut, on the river, straight across to the river on the far side. Some of them were twenty, some eighteen, several were sixteen. Country boys most of them, Mesopotamia staggered them, as had everything since they had left England: the vastness of the ship on which they had sailed and the vastness of the Tigris; the limitless brown flatness of the desert; the exotic blueness of the exotic dome on Ezra's exotic tomb; the hugeness of the fish the Arabs scooped out of the river in their frail circular nets; the stink of Kut; the way the sand fell back into their trenches as fast as they dug it out. But soon, as they reached the firmer subsoil, they settled down: and their defences began to deepen.[2]

Townshend's grotesque column of sleeping men awoke so stiff that they could barely move. Calves and thighs seemed to have locked; backs and shoulders ached too intolerably even to contemplate the burden of packs and rifles; and they were hungry. Groaning, they hauled themselves to their feet as N.C.O.s barked orders and officers peered bleakly down from the comfortable backs of chargers. It was definitely a shit pot war.[3]

At least, though, they were spared the tedium of 'getting fell in'. They already were fell in. They had slept fell in.

Excruciatingly, the last leg of their march began. Ahead lay Kut, and endless cups of tea, and comfortable billets, and beautiful nurses, and lovely tins of bully beef. Dazed and aching, they plodded on.

A signals officer decided to cut the telegraph lines that ran along their route. No sense letting Nureddin use them to send messages back to Baghdad. Exhausted signallers dragged themselves up poles that seemed a hundred feet high and, clinging with one arm and both legs, attempted to cut the lines with pliers held in one hand. But the line was too tough; or the pliers too weak; or one hand not enough. Panting, they slid down to the ground – and severed the lines with rifle-fire.[4]

By midday, men were falling out of the column in scores. Townshend ordered his supply carts to the rear. No straggler must be sacrificed to the Arab now.

An hour later he halted, accepting the fact that his troops must rest. But not for long; Kut was their objective. Nevertheless, at 6 in the evening, only five miles from Kut, he allowed them to bivouac for the night. Once again, each man slept where he halted.

For Townshend, there was no rest. Brigadier-General Rimington, Kut's G.O.C., had ridden out to meet him, and now there were decisions to be made. Rimington's news was that Nixon, having already steamed out of Kut heading for somewhere safer, had wired, 'Please tell Townshend that Army Commander must leave situation to him as to how far he falls back. But Army Commander's intentions is to concentrate reinforcements as far forward as possible.'[5]

Rimington gave it as his personal opinion that it would be difficult so to entrench Kut's vast backyard as to prevent an enemy turning manœuvre; that it would require only a small enemy force to invest Kut; that the bulk of Nureddin's troops would consequently be free to reoccupy their old stronghold at Essinn – from which any British force sent to relieve Kut might subsequently find it difficult to evict them; that 6th Division's alternatives to accepting a siege were either to occupy the old Turkish trenches at Essinn or to evacuate its wounded and stores by maheila and march on.

Townshend's answer was swift – and probably premeditated. Difficult as Rimington had made it sound to prepare Kut against a siege, he was going there. His men were too exhausted to march 'even an inch' beyond it.[5]

Rimington might well have retorted, 'Then how will they almost immediately manage to dig about six miles of trenches and fight off the Turks?' but he did not do so. Probably no brigadier-general would have done so to a major-general – least of all to one as distinguished as Major-General Charles Townshend.

And even if he had, Townshend would doubtless have countered that not only did Essinn's old lines face the wrong way, but they could easily be turned by a force as numerically superior to his own as Nureddin's army; or, worse, be ignored and left to starve as Nureddin drove down-river to Amarah. And if he were not to stand at Essinn, how much farther must he march his exhausted men? To Garbi? That was 70 river-miles. To Amarah? That was 150 miles. No – they were exhausted. Not another inch could they go.

Or was it Townshend who was exhausted; who could march not another inch? Because his decision to accept a siege – though instinctive to the hero of Chitral – was entirely alien to a military historian.

'To make war,' Frederick the Great had always insisted – and Townshend was apt to quote him – 'is to attack': to withdraw into Kut was simply thereafter to *be* attacked.

'Movement is the law of strategy,' Foch maintained – and Townshend was apt to quote him too: to withdraw into Kut was to accept a role of total immobility.

Military history bristled with sieges, and Townshend could quote them all: yet now chose only to remember Plevna, where Osman Pasha had once delayed an entire Russian army. What Osman had done, he could do: and the following morning, December 3rd, 1915, he watched his division stumble into Kut.

CHAPTER TEN

c√§§§√

As 6th Division struggled into the sanctuary of a river-looped wasteland, the precision of a once-superb fighting machine vanished. In unecheloned disorder, guns jostled men on foot, men on foot clung to the stirrups of isolated cavalrymen, and supply carts rattled blindly through them all. Kut's doctors, orderlies and Territorials rushed out to help, taking tea and ten thousand chapattis with them,[1] doing what they could to comfort and console.

'Would you like a hot bath?'

'My dear chap, you save my life. Haven't had my clothes off for ten days.'[2]

The gunner officers arrived, too tired even to eat the hen they had brought with them all the way from Azizieh.[3]

Melliss arrived, his breeches slashed from thigh to calf by an enemy sabre.[4]

Thousands of troops arrived, sun-helmeted men in boots too heavy to lift, in shorts and tunics black with sweat and dirt, and were ordered to halt by the shallow trench that ran from one river bank to the other.[5] Thousands more followed them in, and were deployed in the groves and the town.[6]

Some of them, as they arrived, were sprawled on lurching gun-carriages, sound asleep. Dorsets plodded beside Gurkhas, and Norfolks beside Punjabis. A trumpeter bent down from his saddle suggesting that a Regular, whose boots dripped blood, should get up behind him.

'I never fell out of a march in twelve years,' the man muttered. 'And I shan't start now.'[7] Thousands of men who wanted only mug after mug of tea and an eternity of sleep. Gulping down the one from dixies brought out by Kut's tiny garrison, they stumbled off to indulge in the other.

'Thus,' wrote Townshend, 'was the retreat successfully concluded'[8] – and neither then nor later considered how much his own orders must have contributed to his troops' exhaustion.

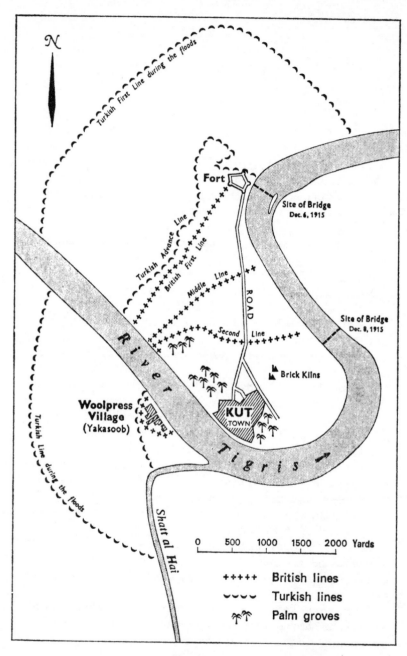

N

Turkish First Line during the floods

Fort

Site of Bridge
Dec. 6, 1915

Turkish Advance Line

British First Line

Middle Line

ROAD

Second Line

Site of Bridge
Dec. 8, 1915

Brick Kilns

River

Woolpress Village
(Yakasoob)

KUT
TOWN

Tigris

Turkish Line during the floods

Shatt al Hai

| 0 | 500 | 1000 | 1500 | 2000 | Yards |

+ + + + +   British lines

⌣⌣⌣⌣   Turkish lines

🌴🌴🌴   Palm groves

Kut besieged

On the first night, he had marched them only a few hours and then halted until the enemy arrived and forced him into a second leg of twenty-two miles. Arrived at Azizieh, he had gone unhurriedly about the business of removing or destroying its stores and had then marched only part of the day to Umm al Tubul – where he had deliberately invited battle. An hour and a half after he had had his battle, he had flogged his force thirty-six miles in twelve hours to Shadie: but after Shadie, he had ordained two short legs to Kut.

From Ctesiphon to Kut, therefore, he had ordered three marches that were unreasonably short and two that were excessively long. Nothing is better calculated to exhaust a large column of men. Unlike generals on horseback, troops require a rhythm to their march. Given that, they will cover phenomenal distances, regardless of thirst and hunger. Denied it, they will stumble into exhaustion; and Townshend had denied his division all sense of rhythm simply to 'eat up' his supplies at Llaj, uproot some barbed wire at Azizieh and fight precisely the battle he had previously insisted he must avoid at Umm al Tubul. In consequence, his force had staggered into Kut and collapsed into sleep. Properly led, it could have arrived there in the same or less time, and in reasonable condition.

It might then even have marched on to Garbi, and thence to Amarah, and so avoided the fate that befell it: but Townshend never even considered that. Instead, as soon as they awakened, he set them to digging the trenches that would lock them inside the looping maw of the Tigris. Three lines of trenches, dozens of saps, dozens of dugouts and dozens of gun-pits all had to be dug. Cables, along which his messages could be tapped out in morse, had to be laid from his Headquarters in the town to each of his four brigade headquarters.[9] Telephone lines had to be connected, and barbed wire strung in seven-tiered fences with eleven-tiered aprons[10] in front of the first line and round every vulnerable point. Shells and ammunition had to be carried to gun-pits and trenches.

Mole-like, ten thousand of his men must burrow underground: and they must do it in twenty-four hours. They did it, these men who had been too exhausted to march another inch, and, having done it, had a further twenty-four hours to wait before the Turk, no less weary than they, eventually caught up with them.

Thus committed to a siege, Townshend rationalized its necessity. As Osman had paralysed a Russian advance and saved Turkey, so would he paralyse a Turkish advance and save Mesopotamia. He would fling a bridge across the Tigris and attack the enemy either straight up the desert from his own back yard, should they decide to invest him, or across the river, should they try to march past him – thereby maintaining a posture as offensive as it was passive. He would dominate the junction of the Tigris and the Hai, gateway to both Amarah and Nasariyeh. With his guns he would blow out of the river the ships with which the Turks would otherwise supply an offensive against Basra. He would save southern Mesopotamia from the Ottoman hordes.[11]

Theoretically it was splendid – heroic even – but it took no account of the fact that the Turks were as short of shipping as Force D, and as incapable, therefore, of sustaining an offensive against Amarah or Nasariyeh as Force D had been of sustaining one at Ctesiphon. Nor did it take account of the fact that Force D, with its chaotic Marine administration at Basra and its own shortage of ships, would be incapable of mounting an offensive strong enough to smash the force about to besiege him, unless he was prepared to hold on as long as Osman had done at Plevna – which he was not! On the contrary, though he himself had required nearly nine weeks to concentrate his force and capture Kut, he was about to demand that a relief force be concentrated and capture Kut in less than a month.

Meantime, in yet another communiqué, he advised his weary troops:

I intend to defend Kut el Amara and not to retire any further. The honour of our Mother Country and the Empire demands that we all work heart and soul in the defence of this place. We must dig in deep and dig in quickly, and then the enemy's shells will do little damage. We have ample food and ammunition, but N.C.O.'s must husband ammunition and not throw it away uselessly. The way you have managed to retire some 80 or 90 miles under the very noses of the Turks is nothing short of splendid and speaks eloquently for the courage and discipline of this force ... [11]

As his men dug deep and quickly and his engineers strung up mile after mile of barbed wire, he telegraphed Nixon that he intended standing at Kut and that he had a month's rations for his British troops, two months' for his Indians, and ample ammunition to deal with the three enemy divisions he must expect to face.[11] He hoped he would be relieved 'by a month'.[12]

Nixon, now a sick man, replied: 'The Army Commander is glad to hear of your decision and is convinced that your troops will continue to show the same spirit in defence as they have shown throughout your operations.'[13]

The British public did not share the Army Commander's enthusiasm. Led by the press at first to expect a victory at Ctesiphon, and then told only that Townshend had 'withdrawn his force to a position lower down the river',[13] they had been shocked finally to learn of a full retreat. Perturbed by their outcry, the Cabinet had even debated whether Townshend should stay at Kut or not, but had failed to reach a decision.[14] Had it known that Townshend was about to agree that the exhaustion of his twenty-five Indian bridge-builders, and the need to improvise, made the construction of his much-vaunted offensive bridge an impossibility, the British Cabinet might have debated more incisively: but the Cabinet did not know it.

'This will have a serious bearing on the result of the operation,'[15] Townshend admitted to Colonel Evans, his Chief Staff Officer: but he did not admit it to Nixon. No bridge meant no offensive posture – no attack and no movement. Frederick the Great and Marshal Foch would have disapproved most vehemently. Even Nixon might disapprove. So the following day Townshend merely wired Nixon, 'As it is reported that von der Goltz is at Baghdad now, in command of the Turkish Army of *six* divisions, I shall expect him to turn this place, leaving a force at Kut to contain me. The relieving force will probably have to fight a second battle of Essinn. It is only violation of Economy of Force if you send up reinforcements in packets.'[16]

Having thus told his commander not only how to suck eggs but which particular egg to suck, it is not surprising that his answer came only from Nixon's Chief of Staff, who declared that it was hoped to relieve him within two months – meantime relief forces were being concentrated north of Amarah, at Ali Garbi.[16]

Relief in two months, Townshend immediately retorted, would mean the loss of the 6th Division, which would be a disastrous blow to British prestige both in Mesopotamia and India. Perhaps, he suggested, he should after all retire to Ali Garbi?[17]

Perhaps aware that Nixon was sufficiently rash to attempt in a month what had taken him nine weeks, Townshend had at last considered the one step that might have saved his force – a further withdrawal to Ali Garbi: but it was too late.

Nixon replied with two telegrams. The first conveyed Sir Beauchamp Duff's congratulations on the Pyrrhic victory of Ctesiphon, claiming that 'All England and Paris are talking of your wonderful success and brilliant achievements – and so they ought.'[18] The second advised that relief in two months meant relief 'within' two months, and that to withdraw to Ali Garbi was not a military necessity, whereas to control the mouth of the Shatt al Hai was. 'You speak of six enemy divisions facing you,' Nixon went on. 'On December 5 … you spoke of only three' – and quite clearly he chose to believe in the smaller of his subordinate's constantly attendant wolves: therefore – 'retirement from Kut should not be contemplated' and, even if it were, 'Essinn position seems indicated, not Ali Garbi … It may be possible, enemy wishes only to contain you while concentrating on Nasariyeh. Have you considered this?'[19]

Poor Townshend: his twelve days of semantic manœuvring had so confused Nixon that on the one hand he had ordered Kut to be held to deny the Turks access to Nasariyeh, and on the other had suggested that the Turks might propose advancing on Nasariyeh whether Kut was held or not.

Far from denying Nixon the initiative, by keeping him constantly off-balance, Townshend had compelled him to issue an order that made no sense, but must be obeyed. Because of this he now admitted that he had *two* months' rations for *all* his troops.[19]

If the Turks were to attack Nasariyeh, his stand at Kut would become strategically pointless: but if he were now to decide to avoid a siege because of that, his orders were to stand at Essinn where his ten thousand combatants, in nine thousand yards of entrenchments, would swiftly be turned. Compelled to choose between a pointless siege and a pointless withdrawal, he opted for the siege and, adverting momentarily to the dangers inherent therein, decided to reduce the number of mouths to be fed in Kut, and to press meantime for a speedy relief.

Why, though, did it have to be speedy? Why his decision to put his troops on full rations, thereby compelling relief attempts within the month? Why did he make no attempt to search Kut and unearth the supplies of food which Arabs notoriously hoard – especially in a town that was a centre of the grain trade? The answer to these questions can only be hypothetical: but it ought, at least, to be debated.

Townshend's career had been marked by a relentless pursuit of promotion, and his next promotion would be to lieutenant-general – in command of a corps. Unless, however, he was relieved within two months, command of the second corps which by then would have been concentrated in Mesopotamia would almost certainly go to his junior, Major-General Gorringe, who then would become a lieutenant-general and deny Townshend not only his promotion but also the command of that force which eventually would take Baghdad. And Townshend knew enough of military history to be sure that that would be the end of his career. As a retired major-general, he would be lucky even to be knighted. Seen in this light, his lavish allocation of rations, his failure to unearth hidden grain and his demand for an impossibly early relief all make sense.

Townshend, in fact, made only one concesssion to the normal demands of siege rationing: he despatched down-river as many of his useless mouths as possible. When his engineers had flung a bridge of derelict boats – gissaras and danacks – across the river from the fort, he ordered his immobilized cavalry brigade and all his superfluous transport to proceed at once to Ali Garbi.[20]

Those who had to stay behind watched the cavalry's departure with something between envy and suspicion. A mounted radio operator, leading five other horses, was halted on the bridge.

'Where do you think you're going?'

'Taking these animals to join the rest that are leaving, sir.'

'Get back to the fort. They'll need you there.'[21]

The sand at the far end of the bridge had become so churned that it had begun to react like quicksand, and the only way to defeat it was to hit it at the gallop. Across an undulating, swaying, improvised roadway, therefore, the remainder of the horses, mules and even camels, positively thundered. It did the seams and the timbers of the supporting native boats no good at all.[22]

Aeroplanes eat nothing, but are useless unless they fly, so Townshend ordered them away too. Unfortunately, two of his aircraft were grounded, waiting for repairs: their pilots and a team of mechanics stayed in Kut, working on the planes.[23]

Men in hospital eat food: Townshend ordered all his shipping, except the tiny *Sumana*, to evacuate as many as possible of them downstream.[24]

Arabs eat food, and Kut contained six thousand of them. Townshend sought permission to evict the lot: but Basra, on the advice of Sir Percy Cox, refused.[25] The Turks would massacre them, Cox maintained, and British prestige would suffer throughout the Islamic world.[26]

But non-combatants also eat food, and of them Townshend had nearly 3,500: yet made no attempt to evacuate them. Those were days when officers required several servants; when British troops could not be seen carrying water or cleaning latrines – tasks fit only for natives; when Mohammedan troops could not be seen burying corpses or sweeping manure, which were tasks fit only for lesser castes. Without bhistis, Townshend's troops would have gone thirsty. Without sweepers, Kut would have been submerged in excreta. Without drabis, horses and mules would have starved. Without bearers, sick and wounded would have died untended. So Townshend retained his numerous camp-followers and Kut's rations lasted a month the less because of them.

Observing the departure of Townshend's cavalry, supply line, shipping and planes, the German staff officers accompanying the Turkish 6th Army ordered an immediate investment. Ignoring Kut's furious gunfire, the Turks began to dig in on the sandhills more than a thousand yards from Townshend's front line, and then, with that skill and zeal for which they are notorious, to sap forward, yard by yard, hour by hour, always closer.

The British Cabinet surveyed the situation prevailing between the Balkans, the Dardanelles, Mesopotamia and Egypt and at last reached a decision: Townshend should withdraw to Ali Garbi! But whatever the Cabinet might have proposed, it was Turkey who now disposed: so the 6th Division remained in Kut.

By this time Townshend's troops were all properly deployed and industriously digging. The fort – a crown-shaped edifice of mud and wood – was the point on the right flank, on the river's edge, from which the first line ran a mile and a half straight to the river on the other side.

Young Territorials now found themselves side by side with Regulars and excited by the prospect of battle. Though the Regulars told them war was bloody horrible, they were still excited. They wanted it to start. They wanted a go at the Turks. Then a shell exploded near them – and some of their friends fell down and didn't get up again. They were bloody, and still, and their faces had a funny look on them: and, confronted by death for the first time, the youngsters were no longer excited – just shocked, and vengeful.[27]

Some hundreds of yards behind the first line ran the middle line: and behind that what Headquarters, with impeccable British logic, called the second line.

As the Turks dug closer, 6th Division burrowed more frenziedly than ever. And the enemy began to snipe: from the sandhills in front;

from the desert across the river from the fort; from the desert across the river by the town. It gave the men in the lines the disagreeable sensation of being vulnerable from all sides.[27] Only deep down would they be safe – at least eight feet down, with a parapet in front, and a step to stand on when one had to fire, through as small a loophole as possible, or warily round a sandbag. Dig six, seven, eight feet down. Build more saps, and stronger dugouts and longer, deeper – much deeper – communication trenches, because the Turks were constantly sniping and constantly sapping closer.

Already each man in the trenches had accepted that henceforth this was his life, his home. They just dug and ate, dug and slept, their officers living with them, sleeping in dugouts, messing in dugouts, making do with a quart of water a day, just like them, busy, like them. The gunner officers had not even had time to eat their hen, which now they had christened Mrs Milligan.

Because they were not yet deep enough, those near the fort used anything and everything to strengthen their parapets. Haversacks, kerosene tins and oil drums packed with earth took the place of sandbags: as did tins of potato meal, tins of jam and eighty-pound baskets of luscious golden dates; and window-sills from Arab houses were better than nothing for timber.

Turkish guns began to arrive and to shell everything in sight, adding the mournful whine of shrapnel to the vicious snap of musketry, and the hospital huts and tents in the palm groves at once proved vulnerable. So the bazaar – a roadway flanked by tiny stalls set in cubicles, each with its wooden shutters to enclose its stock at night, the whole covered with a roof of thatching – was commandeered, its stall-holders evicted, its wooden shutters torn down, its cubicles turned into diminutive wards, its filthy roads swept clean, and beds and patients, orderlies and doctors, supplies and medicines moved in – on hand-carts. Meantime, timber from huts and canvas from tents was filched by everyone to revet dugouts.

General Melliss, accompanied always by two dogs, was everywhere. 'Where the hell is that bugger Delamain?'[28] he would shout, to the delight of his troops, if not of Delamain, whose language was more fastidious.

To discourage the locals from treachery or spying, twenty were taken hostage. Roofs were strengthened to protect those lucky enough to be billeted in houses. To provide a bridge-head at the confluence of the Tigris and the Hai, the small settlement across the river, whose liquorice presses had been mistaken for wool presses, was occupied, and dubbed Woolpress Village. To provide access to pickets and gun-pits and trenches to the west and east of the town, lanes wide enough to accommodate transport carts were knocked through dozens of houses – to the fury of their occupants, who demanded compensation, and to the especial fury of one who found grinning sepoys bursting through the walls of his harem, apparently intending to drive a corridor across his Persian carpets, beneath his glittering chandelier and through the ranks of his nubile if smelly maidens. Which, disregarding his unamiable expletives, was exactly what they did.[29]

To ensure constant communication with the outside world, two wirelesses were installed, along with the small motors that constantly re-charged their batteries, beside a woolpress near the bazaar, each precious instrument protected from the blast of Turkish shells by bales of angora wool. From his Headquarters – a two-storied house in the middle of the town – Townshend kept Boggis and his radio operators busy with a torrent of messages to Nixon, and to his friends in London – actors and Gaiety Girls.[30]

Tapping them out, to be received at and relayed from Ali Garbi, the signallers grinned, and told one another that Charlie was a bit of a ladies' man. Then their wool bales were taken from them – to protect Charlie's Headquarters – and they were less pleased,[30] even though they did not doubt that Townshend was as fearless as ever. He protected his roof with bales of wool, and built up the low wall surrounding it with steel plates not because he was afraid, but because it was his duty to survive and because most of his time had now to be passed either in his house or on its roof.

Already his daily routine had become instinctive. Leaving his truckle bed at 6 each morning, he climbed to the flat roof to survey the surrounding desert and the build-up of the force investing him. After breakfast at 8, he drafted orders for his force and messages for Basra; the latter, rolled up and tied securely, Boggis delivered to the wireless station. Until lunch-time at 1, he studied military history and wrote in his diary. Then more observation, more orders, visits and inspections. Dinner at 7; and bed when he considered it safe to retire.[31]

The bridge across which the cavalry had departed was too close to the enemy's lines, and he ordered it to be pulled back from the fort, and anchored instead to the end of his second line, and guarded on the far bank by a double company. It still looked vulnerable, but he would not order it to be dismantled. So long as he had access to the opposite bank, he could maintain the illusion that his force could rush out and wreak havoc among the enemy whenever he chose – even though his sappers had warned him that guns could cross it only if they were man-handled. Drawn by horses, his guns would shake the whole thing to pieces.[32]

He never referred to the fact that the building of such a bridge on December 6th had been dismissed as an impossibility on December 3rd, and he never discussed his reasons for moving it to a new position where the Turks could easily attack it. He just left it there, and mean-time, everywhere else, so deployed his men and guns that each avenue of enemy approach was held by a Minimum Force, his Main Force being poised to strengthen any point at which an attack might be launched against him.

At last Kut felt like a fortress besieged, and, because of it, generated its own confidence.[33] The British enjoy the challenge of chaos: like to bring order into chaos even if it seems order only to them. Charlie had organized everything with complete authority. He *looked* so authorita-tive[34] as he walked with his dog, Spot, ignoring enemy shells, furious when Spot fled at the first explosion, which he invariably did. But Townshend's men didn't mind that.[35] Things were ship-shape. Their trenches were almost deep enough. Their firing-steps high enough. Their sandbags and loop-holes gave a wide enough field of fire. Their rations – bully beef and biscuits – arrived regularly by hand cart and were boiled into bully stews on fires in the saps where the latrine bucket was.[36] The latrine to which the Dorsets always referred as 'Yer tis' – which, to the vast amusement of the Norfolks, was how they said 'Here it is.'[37] The bucket that the sweeper emptied into an incinerator – whose contents he somehow persuaded to burn.

The bhisti brought them their daily quart of water, even though the Turk sniped him as he drew it from the Tigris. The guns by the brick kilns blasted off at the Turk as often as he blasted off at Kut. Kut was safe. Well … safe enough, so long as you could rely on the Punjabis. Unfairly, Townshend had made everyone suspicious of the Punjabis. The Gurkhas were all right, but one couldn't be sure of the Punjabis.[38]

The newly arrived Territorials couldn't tell one Indian from another. Except the Gurkhas: the little ones, like boys, always laughing. 'They don't laugh when they got their bloody kukris out,' the Regulars advised.[39] The Regulars knew everything. Even how to sleep on the fire-step. And it was cold sleeping on the fire-step, with only one blanket to keep you warm.[40] Galvanized iron over the saps would help.

127

Difficult to get though. And rifle grenades would help:[41] only there weren't any.

The pilots who had hoped to fly out of Kut now found that they couldn't. The engine in one plane wouldn't go, and someone had scrounged a wing off the second to revet his dugout! Determined to be useful, the two pilots decided to help the sappers make rifle-grenades, for which purpose chopped-up telephone wire, nails and guncotton were sealed into jam tins, bully tins, any kind of tins, and fixed to a rod, to which was attached a detonator. Insert the rod down a rifle barrel, light the fuse on the jam tin, fire the rifle, explode the detonator and away grenade. Simple! Except attaching the detonators was dangerous.

'You're the most careful bloke on the flight,' Wells was told by Winfield Smith. 'You'd better do it.'[41]

Thus Kut got its rifle-grenades, while the Turks got thirty-two field guns, five howitzers and an eighteenth-century mortar: and the siege began in earnest.

At Basra the chaos was complete and there was nowhere Kut's agreeable sense of achievement to compensate for it. Ships lay in line, midstream, waiting days to be unloaded by maheila. Dockside control was non-existent. Reinforcements were arriving, but there was no means of getting them upstream to Amarah; and most of their equipment lay in the holds of other vessels still on the high seas. But it was the final breakdown of Force D's hospital arrangements that most demoralized those who waited, or were garrisoned, at Basra.

Six months previously Chamberlain had cabled from London suggesting that Force D, about to advance from Amarah under Townshend, might need more doctors, nurses, medicines and hospital comforts. He wanted Sir Beauchamp Duff to give some thought to the matter of extra doctors and nurses; English charities were anxious to make good any deficiencies of comforts.[42] But, loftily declining English charity, Lord Hardinge had sought to deter Chamberlain from further enquiries about India's duty to provide an adequate medical service. 'My Government [has] arranged for doctors and medicines,' he had lied, because Force D was then seventeen medical officers and fifty sub-assistant surgeons short of its establishment.[42]

But letters from the worst casualties of Essinn, who had been shipped to India to convalesce, had begun to filter through to their families in England, and complaints from them to filter through to the Government. Chamberlain had written a letter to the Viceroy advising that he

(*Left*) Lord Hardinge, Viceroy of India

(*Right*) Sir Joseph Chamberlain

(*Left*) Lieutenant-General Sir Percy Lake

(*Right*) Major-General Charles Townshend

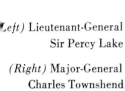

(*Left*) Major-General Melliss

(*Right*) Major-General Gorringe

(*Left*) Nureddin

(*Right*) Khalil Pasha

Kut town, before the siege: six thousand inhabitants,
mud bricks and very dirty

had heard that India Government had perhaps *not* made proper arrangements for doctors and medicines. And then had written again, because a Member of Parliament had passed on to him an officer's letter which described the assertion that Force D's medical arrangements were adequate as 'eyewash'. Therefore he urged that no expense 'be allowed to stand in the way of the best provision that science can suggest'.[42]

Parsimonious as ever, India Government had ignored him: until Chamberlain had become so perturbed that he had cabled the Viceroy, 'I do beg you to urge Duff to go thoroughly into this matter.'[42]

He had also cabled Nixon, 'On arrival wounded Basra, please telegraph urgently particulars and progress:'[42] and Nixon – having just witnessed the return of nearly four thousand casualties from Ctesiphon – had been in a proper position both to do so and to ensure that something be done about it.

Certainly something had needed to be done.

Force D, at the time of Ctesiphon, had only two small hospital ships: not well equipped – but designated hospital ships. Between them they could accommodate five hundred casualties. At Ctesiphon there had been nearly four thousand, who were crammed on to steel lighters and anything else that would float, and towed very slowly, through hot days and freezing windswept nights, five hundred miles down the Tigris.

The *Méjidieh*, with six hundred casualties on board and two crammed lighters in tow, had reached Basra festooned with stalactites of excreta, and exuding a stench that was offensive from a distance of a hundred yards. She had laboured downstream for thirteen days and nights. On her decks, and on the exposed decks of her lighters, men lay huddled in pools of blood, urine and faeces, their bodies slimed with excrement, their wounds crawling with maggots, their shattered bones splinted in wood from whisky crates and the handles of trenching tools, and their thighs, backs and buttocks leprous with sores.[42]

Replying to Chamberlain's urgent cable, Nixon had therefore reported: 'Wounded satisfactorily disposed of. Many likely to recover … Medical arrangements, under circumstances of considerable difficulty, worked splendidly.'[42] And in all of Basra, apparently, there had been only one man courageous enough to nail him with his lie.

Major Carter, Medical Officer in charge of the hospital ship *Varela*, having watched the arrival of the *Méjidieh* with horror and examined some of her unfortunate passengers with a mixture of outrage, compassion and revulsion, had demanded an interview with Nixon: who, ill and testy, had found his remarks so objectionable[42] that he had ordered Surgeon-General Hathaway to deal with him. Surgeon-General Hathaway had accordingly threatened to put him under arrest, said he would have his ship taken away from him and called him 'a meddlesome, interfering faddist'.[42]

In India, Sir Beauchamp Duff had behaved no less shamefully. To the Viceroy he had observed that Chamberlain's anxieties were based only on complaints from individuals; that such complaints were usually frivolous, and that unless Chamberlain was prepared to name names, *his* complaint must also be regarded as frivolous.[42] And this in spite of the fact that his own Chief of Staff, Sir Percy Lake, had acquainted him with the contents of a letter from Surgeon-General MacNeece which had declared of the treatment of Ctesiphon's wounded that 'the whole position was bad'.[42]

As if this were not enough, when a fellow general had dared to bring to his notice what by now was common talk all over Delhi – that many of Force D's hospitals were no better than filthy, tented hovels – Sir Beauchamp Duff had threatened to dismiss him unless he stopped interfering.

The one concesssion he and Nixon had been prepared to make at this grievously late state of their war had been to order suitable river steamers from England. It would be a year before they sailed up the Tigris: meantime, Force D, about to suffer appalling casualties as it attempted to beat Townshend's successive and impossible demands for almost immediate relief, would have to make do with supply and medical services which were as scandalous as they were inhuman.

CHAPTER ELEVEN

OUTSIDE Kut, Nureddin had assembled an imposing army and a formidable array of guns, realizing that he must reduce its garrison before he could dispatch his shipping round the long, looping stretch of river in which it lay suspended. First, though, attempting a bluff, he sent Townshend a letter, inviting him to surrender.

Townshend's troops, Nurreddin wrote in elegant French, had done all that could be expected of them and now, enfeebled as they were, should lay down their arms: and even if enfeeblement were not sufficient reason for surrender, it would be unchivalrous of Townshend, by his continued occupation of Kut, to expose its peaceful citizens to the horrors of bombardment, against all the laws of civilized warfare.[1]

Townshend, well aware that each of his British troops was consuming daily a pound of meat, a pound of bread, three ounces of bacon, four ounces of onion, six ounces of potatoes, three ounces of jam, one ounce of tea, and two and a half ounces of sugar, plus salt, butter and cheese, and that his Indians ate equally well, was disinclined to regard any of them as enfeebled. So he thanked Nureddin for the courtesy of summoning a capitulation before delivering a bombardment, reminded him that his friends the Germans not only had no compunction in occupying towns, but did so in a manner peculiar to themselves, regardless of the laws of civilized warfare,[1] and declined to surrender. Convinced that all Germans were Huns, all Turks Asiatics, and all Arabs 'merciless and cowardly scoundrels',[1] he had not hesitated to patronize the German-staffed, Arab-supported Nureddin: who retorted by bombarding Kut.

As thirty-two guns, five howitzers and an ancient mortar poured their converging fire into an area of four square miles, the 6th Division experienced a type of warfare stranger and more violent than anything it had known before. From every side, from every angle, shells screamed in. Date palms were decapitated; Arab houses collapsed in clouds of dust and splintered lathes; mules and horses were disembowelled; and

Kut's own guns – all forty-three of them, including the four 4.7s mounted on barges and manned by a handful of sailors – retaliated briskly.

Kut's Arabs reacted strangely. Convinced that Turkish bombardments killed infidels only, they echoed the shrill whine of approaching shells with their own shrill whistling, and jeered at the infidels' fear: until an Arab house, with all its occupants, was obliterated – whereafter their whistles and jeering ceased.[2]

The British, on the other hand, began to take pride in being able to distinguish one type of shell from another, and positively enjoyed the infrequent roar of the medieval mortar, nicknamed Flatulent Flossie, which hurled at them a missile the size of a football that landed with a thud and exploded at its leisure. But their complacency was shaken when the Turks decided to tighten the noose by attacking the double Punjabi company which, on the far side of the river, guarded Townshend's bridge. The Punjabis counter-attacked: but when their British officer, wounded for the third time, fell to the ground, they retreated across the bridge into Kut.

At once Melliss galloped up and ordered them back, and then crossed the bridge himself and helped them fight off a fresh attack. In spite of this, the enemy installed himself so close to the bridge that it seemed possible he would seize it and his compatriots be able to storm across it into the heart of Kut. Melliss galloped from the river to Headquarters and, rushing in to Townshend, asked what should be done about the bridge.

'Don't bother me,' snapped Townshend, who was in one of his more Napoleonic moods, 'I'm thinking.'[3] But some time later, deciding that the bridge must be blown, he called for volunteers.

Two came forward, Lieutenants Sweet and Matthews, and it was agreed that late that night they would take a small party to the river bank, crawl on to the bridge, lay their gun-cotton, cut the cables anchoring each supporting boat, and explode their charges. In theory then (if they had not long since been killed: and no one believed that they could possibly survive) every boat would be destroyed or sunk, and nothing of value would be left for the Turk. That Kut would also be completely without bridging material, and therefore without any means of either escape or assault across the river, seems not to have occurred to Townshend. Within three days of justifying his defensive posture by insisting that his bridge made it an offensive–defensive posture, he was deliberately destroying his one means of taking the offensive. His bridge gone, there would be no way out of Kut except by swimming the river or storming the series of impregnable Turkish lines lying across the northern neck of the peninsula.

After a long day, in which they must have contemplated their imminent deaths a thousand times, Sweet and Matthews gravely shook hands with the other officers in their respective Messes[4] and made their way through the darkness along the second line trench to the bank of the river. As soon as they left the trench they would be at the mercy of a thousand Turkish rifles. Infinitely cautious, they crawled to the river bank.

Not a shot.

Carrying eight pounds of gun-cotton each, and escorted by a handful of Gurkhas, they crept barefooted on to the bridge and laid their charges.

Not a shot.

Withdrawing with equal stealth, the Gurkhas slashed the cables anchoring each of the supporting boats, Sweet and Matthews lit their fuses, and the entire detachment fled.

Still not a shot.

And then, with a roar, the bridge blew: and the Turkish detachment near by, eating their evening meal, were too stunned even to move.

Townshend immediately wired Basra recommending both officers for the Victoria Cross: but, when morning came, much of the bridge was found to be stuck midstream. Some of its boats had been waterlogged, and a hidden sandbank had stranded others.[5] Realizing that the first thunderstorm would sweep what remained of his bridge into enemy hands, Townshend ordered his field guns to blow it up: and, as one shell after another blasted asunder his precious danacks and gissaras, leaving the tiny *Sumana* and some wayward maheilas his only means of crossing the river, he must have known that his role had become that of a wholly passive defender.

The pattern of siege life began to develop: long bright days, and even longer nights, lit only by kerosene lamps and flickering candles.

Across the river, in Woolpress Village, two hundred tons of barley were discovered, but Townshend did not bother to order *Sumana* to bring it back for storage in Kut.

From the first line to the middle and second lines of his defences, the communication trenches ran so shallowly that men had to crawl through them – and still were shot dead if they attempted it in daylight.

Above ground, no one was safe – except Mrs Milligan, who pecked with impunity, swooping on bullets as they spurted into the dust, convinced that they were worms.

In their dugouts, officers whiled away the time playing bridge, and risked the sniper's bullets to dash across to friends for yet another rubber. Disdainful of such Aldershot behaviour, the more intellectual of their puppies played patience, or sat on the fire-step, bulky in greatcoats but shivering nevertheless, and wondered how it would be to be dead, and remembered more tranquil days at school, and read the classics of more civilized times.[6]

At Townshend's Headquarters a sapper major arrived with an urgent mission, 'Good morning, sir. I've come to build you a dugout.'

'I won't have one.'

'Those are my orders, sir.'

'Thank you, but I don't want one.'[7]

In their dank, communal courtyards the Arab locals also began to dig dugouts. From their exposed lines in the palm groves all the horses and mules were pulled back into the alleyways of the town itself. Needing fuel for their cooking fires, Townshend's men began to strip Kut's houses of their woodwork – to the fury of their occupants. In their makeshift wireless room, operators took it in turn to sit with headphones to their ears, receiving telegrams from down-river; and, late at night, they adjusted their crystal sets in the hope of picking up faint messages tapped in the Navy's peculiar three-letter code between one warship and another in the distant Mediterranean.

From Basra came a message from Lieutenant-General Sir Fenton Aylmer, v.c., to Major-General Charles Townshend: 'Have just assumed command Tigris Line. Have utmost confidence in defender of Chitral and his gallant troops to keep flag flying till we can relieve them. Heartiest congratulations on brilliant deeds of yourself and your command.'[8]

Townshend's reaction to the arrival of another lieutenant-general in Mesopotamia was not, as one might expect, grudging. He had by no means abandoned his hopes of achieving that status himself, but it was Gorringe's promotion, once Aylmer had superseded the ailing Nixon, that he dreaded. To Aylmer, his old colleague-in-arms, the man who had relieved him twenty years ago at Chitral – surely an omen now? – he therefore telegraphed most cordially, 'Thanks from 6th Division for your inspiring message. Your confidence shall not be misplaced. Grateful thanks from myself. Am proud to serve under you.'[8]

Aylmer may have had the utmost confidence in Townshend, but what he saw on his arrival at Basra can have left him with no confidence at all in his commander, Sir John Nixon – whose policy it now was to send each new batch of reinforcements on a fourteen-day march upstream, dispatching their equipment after them, the first-line transport after their equipment, and their second-line transport (which included their blankets and medical supplies) after that. Sleeping cold in a Mesopotamian winter for fourteen successive nights, many of the troops who should have strengthened Aylmer's Relief Force were soon in hospital instead.

Equally alarming to a sapper general expected to lead a most difficult military expedition were the facts that he was short of bridging materials and signalling equipment; that his reinforcements had never trained together as a division; that they lacked experience;[9] and that Nixon, relentlessly pressed by Townshend, was insisting that this raw, ill-equipped, ill-supplied, incohesive force should advance at once to the relief of Kut.[10] As he left Basra for Amarah, Aylmer cannot possibly have felt cheerful.

Nor, it seemed, did England feel cheerful. Chamberlain anxiously cabled Townshend asking if the Turks had heavier guns than he; how many barges, containing what, had he lost during and since the retreat from Ctesiphon; what was his view of the present situation; how long did he anticipate he could hold out; and what was the physical condition of his troops?[10]

For Townshend these queries came as a heaven-sent opportunity to increase his pressure on Nixon, and his reply was a characteristic admixture of opportunism, fact, disloyalty and deceit.

'My strategic offensive', he cabled – having dealt with the trivia of Turkish guns and his own losses of barges and shipping – 'has received the usual check common enough in history when the offensive has not got sufficient troops nor a constant flow of reinforcements.' Explaining that Hannibal, Charles XII and Napoleon had all failed for the same reason, he managed to imply that, in his case, the fault had been Nixon's, and even hinted at worse shortcomings by detailing the manner in which Nixon should now be making amends. 'The situation can be quickly remedied by rapid concentration of forces, and relief for my beleaguered force, uniting all forces at Kut for the final advance on Baghdad. Example: Wellington's resumption of the offensive after his retreat from Burgos to the Portuguese frontier.'[11]

No suggestion could have been less scrupulous – or less considerate of the lives of those who would be thus quickly concentrated for his relief – because no one had better cause than Townshend to know that Force D, with its tiny fleet of river steamers, was incapable of transporting from Basra that sufficiency of troops, and of maintaining from Basra that constant flow of reinforcements without which he, Hannibal, Charles XII and Napoleon alike had failed.

Regardless of cost, Townshend wanted a swift relief and the concentration thereafter of all available troops at Kut – whence, naturally, following his immediate promotion, the command would become his for the final advance on Baghdad. Chamberlain had offered Townshend a last chance to retrieve glory out of self-inflicted ruin: and he leapt at it.

'The fighting value of my troops,' he explained, 'has naturally much decreased since Ctesiphon (though discipline maintains) and I am very anxious as to the result if enemy makes a determined onslaught with very superior numbers' – which frightening possibility he might well have considered *before* he marched his division into Kut rather than a week after he had done so. 'We are constantly shelled all day and I am very anxious to be relieved in say ten to fifteen days.'[11]

These exchanges, between Aylmer and Townshend, and Townshend and London, took place on December 10th, 1915. 'I am very anxious', he had warned, 'as to the result if enemy makes a determined onslaught ... ' Yet that same day, from dawn till night, the Turks had attacked his first line with great determination – and had been repelled. They had shown no greater a desire than hitherto to die in the open, and Townshend had not been surprised by their failure.[11] Let the Turks dig in only three hundred yards from his own first line – he would hold them. Let them sap forward – he would still hold them. He knew his Turks; he knew his division; and, in spite of his warning to Chamberlain, he was as confident as any of his very confident troops that he would never succumb to an onslaught.

To starvation, yes. Bazain, he knew well, had fatally locked up the best army in France at Metz – and starved. And Mach had starved at Ulm; and Cornwallis at Yorktown.[11] But *he* did not intend to starve at Kut. He would first compel a relief: if possible, and he had done his best to ensure it, within ten to fifteen days.

The following day, Kut was bombarded more heavily than ever: there were 202 casualties, and the Arab locals began to suspect that the garrison might fall. As they sold chapattis and tobacco to those troops lucky enough to be billeted in the town rather than the trenches, they therefore charged a commission of one rupee for each ten-rupee note they changed. They no longer trusted paper currency: an infallible warning of impending crisis in any Asian country.

As if to crystallize these Arab doubts, the Turks resumed their bombardment at dusk. As if to demonstrate to the Turks the Arab hope that this was a Holy War, the muezzin climbed his minaret and pierced the roar of shells with a clear ululating call to the faithful. Whereupon his ungrateful co-religionist shelled the minaret, lest the British should be using it as an observation post.[12]

As darkness fell, and the bombardment ceased, whilst the Turks prayed and ate, curious British troops stole cautiously from the palm groves to the place where Flatulent Flossie's latest bomb had so thunderously exploded: and, in an age of steel, found fragments of manganese bronze. The Turks – whose rifles had the latest telescopic sights, whose 10.5 centimetre guns were superior to anything in the armoury of Kut, whose equipment was in almost every respect more modern than that of Force D – still thought it sensible to supplement the devastating power of twentieth-century guns with the futile bombs of a museum mortar. Fascinated, the British collected hundreds of shards of ancient bronze, and converted them into souvenirs of Kut.[13]

Their meal over, the Turks began lobbing bombs at the barbed wire in front of the first-line trenches, and fired thousands of bullets flat across the ground. They aimed at nothing: just fired and fired – all night. For them, it was safe: for their enemy, noisy, dangerous and the pattern of many nights to come.

Aylmer arrived at Amarah on December 12th to prepare for the relief of Kut. In Mesopotamia there were now (as well as Townshend's division in Kut, and Gorringe's at Ahwaz, Kurna and Nasariyeh) two new divisions and some cavalry, all of which Aylmer wished to concentrate at Garbi so that he could attack in force on January 31st, 1916. But Nixon demanded an attack by January 3rd – when only one division would have assembled at Garbi. Within three weeks, therefore, Aylmer must collect a staff, train his troops, make his plans, advance forty-five miles and, with his one ill-equipped division, defeat either three or six enemy divisions, according to which, if either, of Townshend's disparate assessments he was most disposed to believe.

Townshend made his task no easier by harassing him constantly with telegrams full of ominous news. The Turk had fired five thousand shells into Kut in two days. He had been attacked two days running. The enemy's trenches were only fifty yards away and their snipers were tireless and enterprising. It had been a mistake not to evict the six thousand locals. Admittedly the women and children would have died of thirst in the desert and the men been killed by the Turks; but alive, in Kut, they spied on everything and then, floating on inflated goat skins, swam the river at night to tell Nureddin all they knew. And that was not all – Hoghton, whose men manned the fort, distrusted one of his Indian battalions and wanted it replaced with Norfolks, which was impossible because the Norfolks were needed as a reserve. Casualties were mounting daily; including Ctesiphon, they totalled five thousand. He was, he insisted, very fearful of a determined Turkish assault.[14]

In short, Townshend did not intend that Aylmer, who had relieved him in 1895, should enjoy a second's relaxation until he had repeated the performance – and that by the beginning of the New Year at the very latest.

Generals see things one way, troops see them another: and Townshend's troops shared none of the apprehensions he conveyed to Aylmer. They trusted him completely. They were more phlegmatic than he. They had grown accustomed to the nightly uproar of grenades on their wire and rifle-shots whistling across their heads, and slept through it all. Not comfortably, because it was cold: but slept. And survived, they thought, because they shivered. One of their number had stolen an officer's sleeping valise, and been found in it, in the morning, frozen to death.

They had just as quickly learnt to cope with snipers. At first they had been disinclined to believe that a man more than six hundred yards distant could hit them. Kut, after all, was not Bisley. But when an officer was shot dead by a sniper who lay in the sandhills a thousand yards away, and a sergeant was shot dead by a sniper across the river seven hundred yards away, and Captain Miles – whose fate had been prophesied by a pencil jab on a rough sketch on the eve of Ctesiphon – was at last shot through the groin, they changed their minds, and retaliated.

A hand waved across a loop-hole or to the side of one's protective sandbag was enough to bring a shot. Enough hands waved often enough across enough loop-holes and to the side of enough sandbags could pin-point the position of a sniper. Then wave a hand, let him shoot – and fire back while he reloaded.[15] At least it was something to do. Something positive to do in a life that otherwise consisted only of standing-to before dawn, eating ample but monotonous rations, sitting in the same few feet of the same trench between the same men, being visited daily by the same officers and ordered about by the same N.C.O.s, eating again, sleeping on the fire-step, washing in the morning and beginning it all again.

Not a heroic life: just dangerous and monotonous. It was the bhistis who were heroic. Little brown men in grubby turbans and loin-cloths who took their goatskin bags down to the river every day, defying the sniper, and trotted back to the trenches on their spindly legs to give every man a quart of water. A quart in which to wash and shave, from which to drink all day. But every drop of it drawn from the river, and carried from the river, by these hundreds of Gunga Dins.

And the sappers were heroic – out in the open, in front of the trenches every night, repairing the wire the Turks had cut to ribbons with their bombs and shells. Or, more dangerous still, burrowing a tunnel forward under no-man's land, right up to the nearest Turkish saps, to lay mines that could be blown if ever the Turks tried another attack.

For those men fortunate enough to be stationed back in the town, life was less monotonous because there were Arabs with whom they could trade, and the Crown and Anchor boys to whom they could still lose their money: but *they* couldn't snipe back at snipers, and even their life was an austere one. Only the officers contrived a degree of sophistication. They slept in separate, individual dugouts, with little niches cut into the hard-packed sandy walls to hold their books of verse and hair-brushes and private tins of jam; and shaved every day; and managed to buy delicacies for their dugout Messes; and visited one another when they were off duty. And only the Flying Corps men – for whom, in a siege, there was no prescribed role – had the satisfaction of inventing jobs for themselves. In which they were greatly assisted by the volatile mind of Winfield Smith.

Why not, suggested Winfield Smith, go back to Roman times and make a ballista? Rifle-grenades were proving somewhat unsuccessful: so why not *catapult* bombs into the near-by Turkish trenches?[16]

When that failed to prove successful either, he suggested that they modify their stock of aerial bombs for use in a mortar.[17] In what mortar? the sappers asked. They had already improvised a wooden mortar, its wooden barrel bound with stout wire, and it had blown itself to pieces.[18] In what mortar, therefore? In the mortar they would make out of a cylinder from the engine of one of their marooned aircraft, said

Winfield Smith, whose boyish if mad enthusiasm was almost irresistible. Industriously, therefore, they set about converting cylinders and bombs, confident that one day they would produce a weapon of war.

Front-line dugouts still needed timber: the R.F.C. decided one dark night to take a load on their lorry as far as the second line – whence it could be manhandled along the communication trench to the first line.

'I know the way,' volunteered Winfield Smith. 'I'll walk ahead and guide you.'

In pitch darkness they set out, the lorry grinding gently forward, Winfield Smith guiding them confidently onwards. And onwards. Until a hail of bullets told them that somewhere in the night they had erred and strayed. Cutting their motor, they dropped to the ground.

'Where are we?' they whispered to the troops entrenched in front of them.

'The front line!'

To start their motor again would be to advise the Turk – only a hundred yards away – that they were attempting a withdrawal: and then, even though he could see nothing, he would open up and annihilate them. But to remain where they were was also, eventually, to be annihilated by the Turks' maddening random fire. There was only one thing to do. In complete silence, they must push their lorry back whence they had come.

Theirs was a slow and anxious progress, which eventually they found blocked completely by the men of the second line who, taking advantage of the darkness, had thoughtlessly lengthened their trench. So they had to dig a long ramp into it, and a long ramp out of it, and then push their clumsy vehicle down and up, and by that time they had decided that transport was not their métier. For the future they would concentrate on things more creative.

To Winfield Smith the provision of a water supply seemed the R.F.C.'s next and most logical contribution. Admittedly the bhistis allowed nothing to stop them drawing water from the exposed banks of the Tigris, but too many of them were being killed, as were Arab women and children, sent out by husbands and fathers too sensible to risk it themselves. A water supply would prevent this slaughter: but a water supply from the low-lying Tigris would involve pumping, and Kut had no pumps.[19]

So the R.F.C. mechanics made the pumps; Winfield Smith found an engine; the engine was connected to the pumps, whose pipes were pushed each night into the river – not too deep, or they would choke with mud: not too shallow, or they would float – and the mortality rate among Indian bhistis and Arab ladies declined appreciably.[19]

Little else broke the monotonous cycle of cold nights, noisy days, life underground, cold nights, noisy days. Except that a camel got itself shot between the opposing lines and lay there, very dead, exuding the most powerful stink whenever a bullet hit it, which was frequently.[20] And the walls of the fort had proved so feeble that shells tore gaping holes in them, through which the Turks could view everything within. The bastion – a small section of the fort that jutted out from the rest, the jewel on its crown – was particularly vulnerable. So a trench had been dug inside its breached wall, and a breastwork of galvanized iron had been erected behind it, one sheet of iron a foot or so behind another, the gap between them packed with earth, to screen the movements of those within. It was neither bullet- nor sound-proof, but it looked imposing.

Rafters protrude raggedly from the walls of Arab houses, Arab carpenters being a lazy and unaesthetic tribe, so British soldiers, desperate for fire-wood, took to prowling Kut's dark and narrow lanes and pruning the ragged rafters hard back against their mud walls. The Arabs were not pleased, but for the moment could find no suitable retort to the statement, 'Well it's doing nobody any good sticking out like that, is it?', and by the time they had found one had lost all their projecting rafters.

Thus Kut began to settle down, to create a way of life out of the siege; to accept two weeks in the first line, then relief and two weeks in the second, then back to the first again, the little Gurkhas carrying sandbags on which to stand so that they could see over the parapet.

The siege produced its eccentrics and its characters. Mullins, the padré who kept saying, 'I wish I could take a bottle of whisky up to the front line'; Spooner, another padré, never at a loss for an apt text; Melliss, swearing and encouraging, always accompanied by his dogs, who hated cats and pursued them incessantly; Delamain, whom fortnightly he relieved, precise, intelligent, much admired; Evans, the G.S.O.I., calling those who displeased him 'pissbegotten buggers'; the Crown and Anchor boys, who now owned most of the garrison's money; the Fat Boy, a local Arab of enormous girth; Jones, made up to officer after the departure of the cavalry, but insisting to his ex-civil-service colleagues from Rangoon, the Eurasian gunners, 'I'm still one of you', and scrounging the wing of an aeroplane to prove it; Wells, attaching temperamental detonators to makeshift rifle-grenades;

Winfield Smith, a combination of Heath Robinson and Walter Mitty; Sweet and Matthews, the heroes; Woolpress Village's solitary donkey, growing happily fat on the tons of barley in which Townshend had displayed no interest whatsoever; and Townshend himself, who would get them out of it.

'We'll be out by Christmas,' they said, and, Christmas being only twelve days away, were prepared to wait in patience.

The Turks seemed equally prepared to wait, not moving from their trenches, and Townshend began to suspect that they were mining towards his fort. The tribesmen at Chitral had tried the same thing, and he had only prevented them from breaching one of his walls by sending out a raiding party which had killed almost all of them.[21] Not daring to risk any massive breaching of his fort, he sent out two raiding parties to clear the Turkish trench nearest it. They killed thirty and brought back eleven prisoners and were elated by their success: but he refused to order further sorties.[22]

Sorties out, he argued, inevitably involve a withdrawal in: and too many withdrawals sap morale![22] It was a strange argument. Had it any validity, athletes would become demoralized by consistent high jumps of eight feet, because eight exhilarating feet up meant only eight depressing feet down; no one would ever sail round the world, because to do so is only to end up where one started; and no one would strive for success because in the end one will only die. But it was an illuminating argument, because it threw into sharp relief the man's incorrigible distaste for anything less than signal success. Failing that, he preferred to do nothing. In fact, it is probable that he refused to contemplate further sorties because he disliked everything that was not essential to his continued safety. 'The risk is too great,' he had said when sorties were proposed at Chitral. 'I mean to sit tight until we are relieved ... We might sally out, of course when we [see] the relieving column.'[23] But he had not done so: and at Kut was less inclined to do so than ever.

At Chitral the latrines had been in the stable picket and the stench had been appalling: but he had regularly visited his troops in the stable.[23] At Kut, though he disliked illness and suffering, he regularly visited his men in the bazaar hospital. And, as he told them that Aylmer would soon have them out, that Aylmer knew what he was doing; as he told them bawdy stories and moved from man to man, his grey eyes bright, saying, 'After this I'm looking forward to a spot of leave. After this you won't see my bum for dust',[24] everyone agreed that he was a lovely man. Except his officers, who said simply that his visits were as bright as sunshine! Certainly, they agreed, he was vain: but he wasn't boastful. And one *had* to admit, didn't one, that after the Regatta, not to mention the *perfect* battle he had fought at Essinn, he might well have become boastful.[24]

To the officers closest to him, however, he was obviously sick, the victim of nervous exhaustion,[25] and to Aylmer and Nixon he offered nothing but gloom. Twelve thousand Turks were investing him; one of his senior officers was ill and another had been wounded in the head; and how crazy it was that only seven British officers were allotted to each Indian regiment. At Ctesiphon, as those seven had been whittled down to two or three, his Indians had panicked.[26] Hoghton still didn't trust them at the fort, and all indications were that the big enemy thrust would be against the fort. They shelled it constantly, and it was constantly crumbling. He could have advised that this was all for the best because the breached walls were at once so strengthened by his tireless sappers with sandbags and entrenchments that they became quite formidable: but he chose not to. He preferred his messages sombre.

The enemy, he was prepared to admit, was quiet, but he was still suffering 'forty or fifty' casualties a day. His defences, he had to admit, were now 'quite respectable':[26] but the old fort was more a handicap than a help, and if 'those the Gods love die young', then he hoped they had adored the officer responsible for its visually impressive but structurally puny design![26]

Admittedly, the Russians were attacking von der Goltz's troops in Persia, but he hoped Britain would ask Russia to menace Baghdad as well, and so take 'the strain off me'.[26]

In theory a sortie could help Aylmer's relief attempt, he conceded, but he felt obliged to advise Aylmer that it would take twenty hours – using the *Sumana* to tow fifty maheilas to and fro – to transport his seven thousand fighting men across the river to meet and assist any advancing relief force: and to bring across their guns and stores (without which they would, of course, make no significant impact) would take another eleven days, 'if my men work day and night'.[26] Good and early, Townshend was indicating that his true intention was to sit gloomily tight until someone else relieved him.

CHAPTER TWELVE

THOUGH Christmas was only two days away, the Turks showed no goodwill. Their compatriots had just driven the Allies out of Suvla and Anzac Bays, and, with this example from Gallipoli to encourage them, they shelled Kut more violently than ever.

Even the hospital was hit, its thatched roof set on fire and many of its wounded received fresh wounds. Townshend visited the Indian section of the hospital, but the medical officers were too busy giving anti-tetanus injections to talk to him, and he, as usual, felt disinclined to talk with sepoys. Then a shell crashed through the roof and Spot fled, so he left too,[1] and complained to his headquarters that there were too many British troops stationed in the town rather than the trenches.[2] He wanted as many of them as possible as close as possible to the enemy, whose major onslaught he expected by the minute.

Even so, much of his line must be held by native regiments griev-ously short of British officers. Deciding to make good this deficiency, he offered commissions to any of his 2,700 British troops who would volunteer to join an Indian regiment.[3]

The offer was only briefly debated by his troops – even by his favourite Norfolks.

'It isn't awfully attractive,' one confessed to his friend. 'The Turk gives rather special attention to the white officer of a native regiment.'

'Won't you apply then?'

'Not me.'

'Well, I'm going to. It'll be better than mucking about like this.' He was commissioned that day and, one star on his shoulder, joined an Indian regiment in the front line.[3] His name was Ormiston.

Every day, Reuter's news was telegraphed to Townshend from Basra and the news of the partial evacuation of Gallipoli had come as a shock to him: but all he could do was await Nureddin's pleasure, and, as a seasonal gesture, allow his officers to send messages home for Christmas.

To his wireless operators the gesture was far from welcome: not because they themselves failed to qualify for this privilege, but because they were hard pressed already. There were Townshend's messages to transmit, Aylmer's and Nixon's to receive, and a monitoring service to be maintained. There were also two officers, one in Kut and one downstream, playing an interminable and maddening game of chess, radioing in and out their every frivolous move.[4] There was already too much to do, but still the privileged messages came rolling in: and so rigid was the system of the day that the rank and file took no exception at all.

All that night, the Turks poured rifle-fire into the fort and blasted its barbed wire with grenades. At 5 in the morning – December 24th – they began shelling Woolpress Village: and continued to do so for three hours.

Obviously an attack was coming: but where? At the fort on the north-east corner of the perimeter? Or at Woolpress Village across the river, on the south-west corner? For four hours Kut waited; and then, at noon, after a bombardment which breached the fort's wall and cut every telephone line between the fort and Headquarters, the enemy, to the accompaniment of bugle calls and hoarse screams, advanced in close formation.

Ignoring the withering fire of four maxims, artillery and thousands of rifles, they swarmed forward, evicted the Indians from their trench, poured up to the walls of the fort and into the breached wall of the bastion, and killed Second Lieutenant Ormiston.[5]

The Eurasian gunners were given bayonets and ordered to man the breastwork of galvanized iron and dirt that lay only a yard behind and above the bastion trench now held by the Turks. Grenades burst among them, spouting metal and black powder. 'Fall back,' an officer screamed.

'No!' countermanded their major. 'Stand fast!'[6]

So thirty-three gunners of mixed blood stood their ground, blocking the way into the fort, into Kut. Eleven were killed and eight wounded: but fourteen continued to stand their ground. Until the Forty Thieves, two hundred strong, came bludgeoning in with butt and bayonet and blasting with jam-tin bombs, and behind them the Pioneers.

'Sahib,' begged a very young sepoy at the breastwork, 'how do I load this rifle?' He had been trained on Lee Metfords and the workings of a Lee Enfield were beyond him. In the uproar of point-blank battle, his officer loaded his rifle for him. Five times he fired and each time shouted, 'Laga! ... A hit.' Then his officer re-loaded the Lee Enfield and the cycle began again.[7] It continued for hours.

Dorsets and Pioneers, Norfolks and Rangoon Volunteers, Indians and Turks, Englishmen and Turks, all round the fort and inside the bastion, bursting bombs, exploding shells, rifle-fire and machine-gun fire. Very lights soaring into the cold black sky, bullets whanging against galvanized iron, orders shouted in babbling voices, wounded moaning and being dragged to safety, a Turkish officer, sword in hand, hanging across the barbed wire, gaseous stench from the riddled camel ... Christmas Eve in Kut.

Against infuriated Turkish assaults, the Ox and Bucks retaliated with equal fury. The enemy continued to force his way into the bastion: at a range of ten yards, Turks and Britons lit their fuses and hurled their grenades, leaped forward and gouged with bayonets.

Watched by von der Goltz, Turkish support troops walked into a volcano of howitzer fire – enormous black and yellow eruptions of metal and lyddite – and, faltering, soon retired. But around the fort and in the fort, their brothers fought viciously in a din so prodigious that grenades exploded unheard and gunners were deaf to the detonations of even their own artillery.

At last the Turkish attack lost its momentum, and began to ebb. Fighting their way backwards, jabbing and lunging, they slowly withdrew, offering a perfect target as they climbed out of the trenches they had captured and over the deep piles of their own dead. One after another, brutally and efficiently, as they clawed their way above ground over their comrades' bodies, they were shot dead.[8]

Von der Goltz departed for Baghdad; the battle subsided; and only the dead, the wounded and a lone distracted Turkish dog were visible beyond the parapets of Kut's first line. Two thousand Turks had been either killed or wounded: and Townshend had lost 382 – which brought his casualties since December 3rd to a total of 1,625.

As the entire garrison talked of the heroism of the Rangoon gunners and the Forty Thieves, the wounded of the 6th Division were carried back to the hospital, and the Turkish wounded lay groaning beneath the parapets they had failed to storm, or across the wire that had snared them.

Against an enemy who had fought so well there could be no rancour, and for men wounded as these were wounded there could be nothing but compassion: so Townshend's tired troops crawled on to their parapets to help them in – but were promptly sniped. The Turks must be left where they lay until they died. On Christmas Eve, it somehow seemed all wrong.

On Christmas Day it seemed even worse. At least they should be given something to drink. But how to get it to them without being shot? If only they could drag themselves up on to the parapet, one could pull them in then. But the parapet was too high. A lot of energy had been expended to ensure that it was. Just as well. Bound to be another attack soon. And look at that poor bloody dog. 'Hey, doggie. Hey, Fido. Come on, boy! Come on.' But Fido wouldn't come. Just darted from corpse to corpse. Poor Fido. Otherwise, everything quiet. Too quiet. Apprehensively they sat deep in their trenches and prepared to eat a Christmas dinner of bully beef and biscuits, and a tin of pineapple and condensed milk[9] shared between six. At which moment a sandstorm snarled its way across the desert. Shrouding themselves in blankets, they ate their gritty Yuletide food.[10] And, when darkness fell, they filled dixies with food and water, hung them from the end of their bayonets, poked them through their loopholes and called softly to the Turkish wounded, 'Hey, Johnny!' That same night their officers had eaten a five-course meal which had included asparagus, plum pudding, whisky with water from the Tigris[11] – and sand.

In the hospital, some fifteen hundred men lying on bug-ridden charpoys cared little what day it was. Haggard medical officers and orderlies moved swiftly from one wound to the next, pouring iodine. Those who needed bedpans rarely got them. Those fortunate enough to have a mug of tea could place it, between sips, only on the earthen floor – where immediately it swarmed with ants.

'Aren't you going to do *any*thing for me, you callous bastards?'
'They're not callous.'
'Then what *are* they?'
'Scarce!'[12]

Too many casualties; too few orderlies and doctors; too little room in the cubicles that had been stalls, on the swept earth that had been a roadway; too little protection from sun and shells under the thatched roof; operations performed on a wooden table by the light of kerosene lamps; the roar of shells day and night; a great willingness to be discharged to bell tents in the palm groves rejoicing in the title 'Convalescent Depot' – that was hospital life for rankers in Kut. And all the time the knowledge that the Turks (across the river on three sides, in a series of trenches on the fourth) were tightening their grip.

On Boxing Day, Townshend was elated to observe that Nureddin was sending away column after column of infantry.[13] Obviously his osses on Christmas Eve had been more than he could stomach. Townshend telegraphed Nixon and Aylmer that the enemy was raising his siege.[14] But twenty-four hours later he found himself still securely invested, and realized that Nureddin had merely divided his force, and sent the larger part of it to Essinn to oppose Aylmer's coming attempt at relief.[15]

Unaware of such distant manœuvres, which anyway were invisible to men living eight feet below ground-level, Kut set about restoring its battered defences. Even though two Indians deserted, and another enemy division was reported to be marching towards Essinn, Kut remained confident, its only real anxiety being the Turkish wounded, who still lay under the parapets of the front line, and Fido, who remained alone and distracted.

Under a white flag, a mounted Turk appeared, escorted by an orderly, and a young Dorset officer was ordered to go out and meet him, to learn the purpose of his visit. Feeling utterly vulnerable, he marched across no-man's-land, his own orderly beside him, cursing the fact that his tender years had convinced his C.O. that he would remember his schoolboy French better than any other Dorset officer.

Face to face with the Turkish officer – or rather face to knee, because the Turk remained mounted – he inquired in his ill-remembered French what the other wanted. To deliver a letter to His Excellency General Townshend, the Turk replied, and to obtain from him immediate permission for a truce to bury the dead.

The Dorset officer declined to allow the Turk to ride into Kut, examining all its defences as he did so, but sent his own orderly to Townshend with the letter; and, while he and the Turks waited for Townshend's reply, had an agreeable conversation about the Germans, whom neither of them liked, and about the Bosporus villa that belonged to the Turkish officer's uncle. 'You must let me entertain you there after the war,' said the Turk. At which moment Townshend's reply was delivered by the British orderly and the Turk, handing the Dorset officer a box of fifty cigarettes, saluted and returned to his own lines.[16]

Suspecting an Asiatic trick, and insisting upon the rules of military protocol, Townshend had replied that he would agree to a request for a truce only when it came from Nureddin himself. Meantime, dead and wounded must lie where they were.

Worried by his prisoners' reports of the imminent arrival of fresh Turkish divisions, Townshend wired Basra that he hoped Aylmer

148

would start his advance from Ali Garbi by January 3rd, and so reach Kut well before January 10th. And what news, he asked, of reinforcements, and the Russians?[17]

Aylmer replied that his relieving force now consisted of approximately two divisions and a brigade of cavalry[17] – which, against the five enemy divisions already opposing him at or below Kut and the three more allegedly on their way from Baghdad, might have seemed inadequate to anyone. Not, however, to Townshend, who continued to urge an early attack. Nor to Nixon, who still was insanely optimistic, and impatient, apparently, of Townshend's nagging. Somewhat curtly he informed Townshend that there was *no* news of the Russians.[18]

The Turk meantime, denied success by direct attack, had resorted to the more disagreeable weapons of siege warfare. His snipers began to use dum-dum bullets, paying particular attention to Arab women and children drawing water at the river's edge, and pamphlets appeared urging Indians to murder their British officers. This being too dangerous, a few Indians shot themselves instead – blowing off toes and fingers, in the hope of being sent to hospital; but they failed in their purpose because powder scorches betrayed their wounds as self-inflicted. Thereafter, those sufficiently determined shot themselves through a fold of cloth.

As the year ended, the nights grew colder. So cold that wooden crosses began to disappear from the cemetery, to be used as fire-wood, and a billion lice, appearing from nowhere, snuggled into the seams of any garment covering warm flesh. One night there were none of them: the next, Kut was infested, and remained infested until the spring, when, just as abruptly, every louse vanished – to be replaced, in sequence, by fleas, mosquitoes, sandflies, scorpions and centipedes.

The second line (in fact, the third) had by this time become a veritable warren of trenches and dugouts, the latter roofed with galvanized iron and covered with dirt. It was unwholesome and disagreeable. The middle line, since it collected all the shells that missed the first line, was worse; and the first line was hell. The camel outside it stank most horribly; the Turkish dead were putrefying; monotony was relieved only when someone was sniped; and there was nothing to do, nothing to see, no one to talk to, and only bully to eat.

In the town it was better. There one could at least go up on to a flat roof and look for miles in every direction; see the enemy lines growing longer by the day; see the masts of his shipping up-river and his huge camp beyond the far bend, his wounded trudging back to some unknown destination, and Arab camel trains setting out across the desert, carrying whatever it is that camels carry. Up on the roof one could look east at the snow-capped Persian mountains, which were neutral, or south-east where men were free. Just a few miles downriver. A man could walk it in a couple of hours. Just a few miles, a couple of hours, to freedom. It was a strange feeling.

Strange, too, for officers billeted in town to realize that while they slept in beds, read in front of coal fires and enjoyed occasional hot baths,[19] their brother officers slept in valises in holes in the ground, shivered like their men and washed in a dish of cold water. *C'est la guerre*, however. And even they had their casualties. Wells, for example, as he dutifully attached detonators to rifle-grenades, had observed some dust inside one of the detonator tubes. He had endeavoured to clean it out with a stick and blown most of the fingers off his right hand, because the dust was fulminate of mercury.[20]

Since its makeshift detonators were obviously dangerous, Kut wired downstream for more to be dropped by aeroplane. Gracefully the plane flew overhead, carefully the detonators were dropped in a package which landed miles away in the desert, and gracefully the plane sailed off again.

'Did you receive detonators?' Basra enquired.

'I'll give you two guesses,' replied Townshend.[21]

Thus, manning their three lines of trenches, watching from their roofs, lying in their hospital beds under their red blankets, sitting in their gun-pits by the brick kilns, making grenades and periscopic sights in their workshop, sending their messages down to Basra, picking lice out of their clothing, and mounting a picket to preserve the cemetery's crosses from further desecration, Townshend's men saw in the New Year.

CHAPTER THIRTEEN

THE first day of 1916 was not without its excitements. A sepoy on sentry-duty in the middle line suddenly raised his rifle, fired at one of his Indian officers, missed, leapt the parapet and fled towards the first line, obviously hoping to hurdle it and desert to the Turks: but he was seized, sent back for immediate court martial,[1] and sentenced to death by shooting at sunset.[2]

The first enemy aeroplane flew overhead and the R.F.C. decided to manufacture an anti-aircraft gun.[3]

Aylmer, replying to Townshend's suggestion that he should push his force up to Kut by January 10th, objected to this premature advance unless conditions in Kut absolutely demanded it. If he had to, he would ship one division as far upstream as possible and then march it against the Turks at Kut by January 4th. He preferred, however, to concentrate his entire force at Sheikh Saad and advance with that on January 9th.[4]

Townshend cannot have liked this message. Not only did it deny him the immediate advance he desired, it denied him it for a reason he less than anyone could refute: that such an advance would involve the dissemination of the maximum force available. Hoist with his own petard, he remained silent until the sun had set, the court-martialled sepoy been shot and the Turks begun their nightly bombardment.[5] Then, as Turkish shells burst through his roof, killing two of his signallers, he sent his reluctant reply. Quoting the inviolable laws of Economy of Force, he agreed that the Relief Force should advance united on January 9th.[6]

Two Turkish divisions, ignoring Kut completely, marched down-river to reinforce those already dug in at Sheikh Saad and Essinn – to the great surprise of many of Townshend's officers, who had believed him when he had said that, by accepting a siege, he would effectively block any enemy advance beyond Kut.[7] Then two thousand more troops and six guns contemptuously by-passed them, and only the arrival of a Turkish officer under a flag of truce distracted Townshend from the realization that he himself was doing nothing.

The Turk bore a letter from Nureddin which suggested a truce to bury the dead. Playing the game the Turkish way, refusing to come to the point, Townshend mockingly suggested that the Turks in Persia should invade Afghanistan. And perhaps India after that? And here was a box of cigarettes for Nureddin. And he would give Nureddin his answer 'tomorrow'.

On receiving the cigarettes, Nureddin ordered a tremendous bombardment of both Kut and Woolpress Village, which Townshend considered ungrateful of him,[8] and which Woolpress interpreted as the prelude to a serious onslaught against itself. Determined to help the Villagers, *Sumana* opened up for the first time with her twelve-pounder and blazed away for hours. Next day her commanding officer was himself bombarded – with furious memos from Head-quarters demanding instant explanations in triplicate as to why he had dared fire his gun without orders.[9] That same day a brief truce was agreed and the Turkish dead were buried in the Turkish manner, very shallowly in no-man's-land,[10] each corpse lying with its buttocks towards the enemy. *Sumana*'s commanding officer considered that the Turks had perfectly made his point.[11]

Aylmer asked Townshend to confirm Basra's advice that he was opposed, between Sheikh Saad and Kut, by 30,000 combatants and 83 guns. More like 20,000 and 32 guns, Townshend retorted, of whom, anyway, '4,000 or 5,000' had been lost since the siege began![12]

The figures 20,000 and 32 guns were, for him, quite unusually precise. That they were also false no one knew better than he, who had, from the earliest days of the siege, noted the arrival of every Turkish reinforcement. Basra's estimate, based on aerial reconnaissances and Townshend's own telegrams, was accurate.

Why then did Townshend counter Basra's estimate with a contempt-uously reduced and uncharacteristically precise appreciation of his own? Why else than that he was determined Aylmer should attack immediately?

Townshend's exaggerations and imprecisions were invariably employed to his own advantage; but where lay the advantage to him in compelling Aylmer, with two inadequate divisions, to attack a Turkish force of great superiority? Or in misleading him as to the number of men and guns opposing him? The truth is that such an advantage could have existed only in the mind of a man no longer completely stable: and the tragedy was that such a man had for five months been the dominant brain in Mesopotamia.

Aylmer decided to launch his attack on Kut from Sannaiyat, fifteen miles downsteam of Essinn. First, though, he must clear the Turks out of Sheikh Saad. Accordingly he dispatched part of his force to Sheikh Saad with orders to take it, advance to Sannaiyat and wait there for the rest of the corps. But Sheikh Saad – expected to fall easily and quickly – refused to fall at all. Aylmer had to bring his entire corps into action against a Turkish rearguard that fought stubbornly and skilfully. Far from concentrating for a decisive blow against Essinn, he was unable even to reach the point from which that blow was to be delivered.

Unaware of this, Townshend sent Aylmer, his superior, a personal telegram in which he alluded to the tactics he had himself employed at Essinn. He hoped, thereby, he subsequently maintained,[12] to discourage Aylmer from the brutish and futile frontal attacks to which he thought him prone: and he apparently considered Nureddin so stupid that he would twice fall for the same outflanking manœuvre on the same field of battle. But, in the event, it mattered neither way: Aylmer never reached Essinn.

Basra suffered equally from Townshend's compulsion to dispatch unwanted (even when valid) advice. In deference to his suggestion that a feint from Nasariyeh might mislead Nureddin into fearing a relief attempt up the Shatt al Hai, Basra ordered Gorringe to demonstrate that day.[13] Dutifully abandoning its compulsory polo matches, the 12th Division therefore feinted: and was completely ignored by an enemy who, from superbly concealed trenches, in overwhelming numbers, was waiting for Aylmer's next attack at Sheikh Saad.

Aylmer's force flung themselves forward – and were slaughtered. His fresh British troops, convinced that no mere Asian would dare withstand them, were stunned by the Turks' ferocity; his Indians, knowing neither where they were, nor why they fought, despaired at the suffering of their wounded fellow sepoys; and his wounded, for nights and days on end, lay freezing and bleeding, untended and apparently abandoned.

'Sahib,' the wounded begged, 'sahib, water. Sahib, help.'[14]

But no water could be brought to them, and no help was available.

At best, they were wheeled off to the river bank on jolting carts, and there again abandoned: at worst, they lay and died of exposure, or neglect, or further wounds. Yet London had cabled on December 28th, 'Can British Red Cross help in any way with hospital supplies for your force?' and Lord Hardinge had replied, 'Nothing required at present. If anything needed in future, will not hesitate to ask you.'[15] After all, Force D had plenty of those curious Japanese fly-traps: what more did its hospitals require?

Expecting a counter-attack, conscious of the fact that he was making no ground at all and desperately in need of any move that might distract the enemy, Aylmer wired Townshend, 'Will you consider the advisability of making a sortie?'[15]

No suggestion could have been less welcome to Townshend, but it was difficult to refute. He knew that Aylmer's attack was failing – 'He won't get through,' he told one of his staff[16] – and he was a tireless advocate of the distant feint that removed immediate pressures. He had himself asked for a Russian feint on Baghdad to alleviate the pressure on Kut. He had himself asked for Gorringe to feint to alleviate the pressure on Aylmer. But now, when Aylmer asked *him* to feint to alleviate the pressure on Sheikh Saad, he was disinclined to do so. He therefore contrived a dialogue at the conclusion of which he was *ordered* to remain at Kut.

'Will you consider the advisability of making a sortie?' Aylmer had asked: a simple, direct, concise question. To which Townshend's reply was devious, irrelevant and cunning.

He could not, he complained, tell how many Turks still contained him, because he could not see into their trenches. He had not, he complained, been provided with the daily aerial reconnaissances of those trenches that had been promised him. Even so, he *had* contemplated a sortie. But might it not, if Aylmer were repulsed, be worth abandoning his guns and wounded, and cutting his way out of the encircling enemy?[17] He thus implied that he had decided against a sortie only because others had denied him vital information, and at the same time suggested instead something he knew Nixon would instantly veto.

Had he ever been prepared to cut his way out of Kut, he would have done it before the Turks so securely invested him, but fighting his way out had never been what Townshend had in mind. His intention was so to confuse the real issue with a hypothetical issue that Basra would quash them both. And in this he was wholly successful.

'Army Commander directs you not to resort to expedient of cutting your way out except in desperate extremity,' Basra telegraphed promptly. 'We have plenty of reinforcements here, which are being sent up as empty shipping is returned from up-river ...'[18]

His immediate objective achieved, Townshend at once endeavoured to nullify any future accusation that he had wilfully misconstrued Aylmer's message. 'I had misunderstood Aylmer,' he claimed, 'and thought he was sounding me out as to whether I could cut my way out.'[19] But Townshend the military historian could never have confused making a sortie with cutting his way out. Indeed he had himself banned sorties from Kut because they inevitably involved a withdrawal back whence they had started. Nor could the Townshend, whose French was perfect, possibly have confused 'sortie' with 'breakout'. Such confusion as there had been, therefore, was of his own deliberate creation, and all that Aylmer could do was to wire wearily back:

'In asking you to consider advisability of making a sortie, of course I only meant by way of creating a diversion and thus relieving pressure here. There is absolutely no idea yet of your having to cut your way out. I do, however, contemplate some delay in relieving you, as I am opposed by very considerable numbers.'[19]

A less insensitive man than Townshend would have been appalled by those words 'of course' and 'very considerable numbers'. A less courteous man than Aylmer would more bluntly have accused him of playing with words and deceiving with figures. But Townshend remained insensitive, and Aylmer courteous, and others paid the price.

Later that day, Aylmer wired again. 'Owing to the fatigue of troops ... I have been unable to make any progress.'[20]

Nixon also wired – with personal news. He was to be invalided home, would hand over to Aylmer in a few weeks, and would recommend to Simla that Townshend should succeed to the command of the Tigris Corps.

Townshend's pleasure at this advice – which would ensure his promotion and give him a second bite at the tempting apple that was Baghdad – must have been considerably dampened by the knowledge that it was meaningless so long as Kut remained invested and he locked up inside it. As to Nixon's loss of the command of Force D, however, he can hardly have regretted it. It was, in his opinion, Nixon who had forced him to the battle of Ctesiphon; and it was Ctesiphon which had precipitated his retreat into Kut.

Whether or not this thought occurred to Townshend at this time, it had some time ago occurred to the British press, which was now – disregarding its earlier description of the Mesopotamian War as a 'picnic' – angrily criticizing the decision ever to advance on Baghdad.

It had also occurred to the House of Lords, where Lord Crewe (doubtless under orders from the Government, because no one had more sternly advocated caution than he) defended the advance, and Lord Sydenham assailed it, but where all finally agreed that at least it had been a glorious failure, which, to the British, is sometimes even more gratifying than a moderate success.

On the other hand, both press and Lords demanded a scapegoat, and quite clearly Nixon was the man they had cast for that role. Posterity, they had decided, must blame Nixon for everything: for a viceroy's weakness and a commander-in-chief's ignorance; for India Government's failure to understand that, in a country devoid of roads and railways, river shipping is essential to a successful offensive; and for Home Government's failure to perceive that, in a campaign of its own devising, Hardinge, Duff, Nixon and Townshend had been, between them, almost certain to run amok.

As Aylmer's long day ended, he again wired Townshend giving his exact dispositions – against which fifteen thousand obstinate Turks stood in unassailable trenches. Mindful of Townshend's tactless allusions to the manœuvre whereby a frontal attack had previously been avoided at Essinn, he confessed that he did not think he would be able to outflank the Turk at Sheikh Saad, and warned that, until reinforcements arrived, his progress would be slow.[20]

For Townshend this was sombre news. As if to underline it, his staff reported that there had been a theft from his vital food stores of a thousand bags of flour.[21]

The following morning, apparently galvanized by bad news, Townshend seemed suddenly to have recaptured his confidence and flair.

Forced to accept the fact that Aylmer had been pinned down, and that his food stores had become vulnerable, he wired asking for an aerial reconnaissance, 'so that I can get a rough estimation of the Turks containing me here. There is no doubt that if I attacked their main camp and took it, and drove away steamers etc., it would bring the Turk's main force back here very quickly. But I must have no doubt about winning. My troops are very different to what they were two or three months ago.'[21]

It was a bold suggestion, as audacious as the Regatta itself, but already the crisis that had prompted it had passed. The Turks at Sheikh Saad, after three days without food, had withdrawn upstream overnight, and Townshend's newfound zest expired with their departure. As Melliss and Delamain conducted his defence for him, he began to devote his entire energy to the writing of telegrams and the study of happier campaigns in the nineteenth century.[22]

'I am pursuing', Aylmer wired: but, 'heavy rain makes movement most difficult.'

Pursuing was hardly the word for a ten-mile trudge through mud so glutinous that troops sank in it up to their knees and horses up to their bellies. Aylmer could only push on: but with a force whose casualties numbered four thousand, whose Indians had become dispirited, and whose untired opponents had had four extra days in which to entrench and reinforce.

Peering upstream from his roof, Townshend noticed that every Turkish vessel was dressed with bunting, and heard from every Turkish trench the sound of excited cheering. The Turks had just learnt that the Allies had fled from Gallipoli. Apparently still in high spirits, Townshend wired downstream that this jubilation was doubtless inspired by one of three events. Either it was the anniversary of Turkish pay-day. Or Enver Pasha had been assassinated. Or von der Pilsener – as he had dubbed von der Goltz – had arrived for an inspection.[23]

But with this message went the last of his exuberance. No longer able to delude himself that relief would come swiftly, Townshend was further depressed by the knowledge that Aylmer insisted upon deploying his force on both sides of the river. Townshend feared that Aylmer would find himself unable to concentrate quickly a strong enough Main Force on either bank to outmanœuvre an enemy ordered by von der Goltz to stand at every point between Sheikh Saad and Essinn.

As the day wore on, Townshend observed groups of lightly wounded Turkish soldiers from Sheikh Saad walking across the desert towards their upsteam camp. Two hundred at a time, five batches passed only a few miles from where he stood. But Aylmer had suffered nearly 4,000 wounded – which must mean about 650 dead – and the weather downstream was appalling. For Townshend, standing in brilliant sunlight, the outlook was gloomy.

No less so for Nixon. Harassed by the news of his unpopularity in England, he was pressed by Whitehall to extricate Townshend as quickly as possible. Townshend's food situation obliged him to attack anyway before the middle of January. Aware, however, that another premature attack would be as fatal to Aylmer's force as an attack made too late would be to Townshend's, he had to make an immediate decision. It was a heavy responsibility for any commander. For a man as sick as Nixon, it must have been agonizing. He decided that Aylmer must resume his attack.

The agonies of generals are rarely communicated to their troops – and are of no interest to them when they are – so Kut knew nothing of this. Kut knew only that the initial exhilaration of standing alone, of inviting the enemy to do his damnedest, had been supplanted by a spirit of wary optimism. 'What was an adventure has become a bed and breakfast kind of war.'[24] A bed and breakfast kind of war wherein the landlord provided no mattress, no heating, and very inadequate food. A war in which the commanding general was never seen by ninety per cent of his troops; in which Melliss and Delamain, however, had become part of the family in their respective brigades. Melliss, 'a lovely little man', prematurely aged but extrovert, fearless and admirably un-intellectual. Delamain, fearless, thoughtful and considerate. On his daily rounds, he had ordered, no compliments were to be paid. Men sitting were to remain seated. Men on duty were to ignore him.

'Who's that singing?' he had once demanded.

'Me, sir,' confessed a Cockney private.

'The liveliest man I've heard today,' Delamain congratulated. 'When we get home I'll buy you a barrel of beer.' (And, in 1919, did so.)[25]

All very admirable; all very domesticated and cosy – but boring. And dirty.

' "Instructions for cleaning clothing," ' a private read aloud from his *Soldier's Small Book*, which was full of helpful hints about how to salute, clean your rifle and survive life in the Army. ' "Stains from perspiration and sweat," ' he read, his voice singsong. ' "A solution of salts of sorrel – one quarter of a ounce to one pint of boiling bloody water – should be applied all over the garment with a clean hard brush. Finish by sponging well with cold water." Want to hear any more?'[26]

'No. Put a sock in it.'

It was fires Kut missed most. Not so much for warmth as for cooking. Long since, every bench from every Arab coffee house had been stolen and burnt – to the dismay of the male population, whose habit it had been to sit all day in a coffee house while the wives worked.

Doors had vanished from doorways and sills from windows. Finally liquorice root, hacked out of the earth, had become the only fuel. And there was not much of that.

Cigarettes were another worry. Men can survive without women, without food, comfort and medicine, but not without a smoke. Fortunately almost anything that burns will smoke, so the men of Kut began to smoke tea-leaves and ginger root – though some maintained that lime-tree leaves, which they called Brick Kiln Virginia,[27] were better – and, coughing like consumptives, resigned themselves to a life of tedium.

Not that life was entirely unexciting. The R.F.C.'s mortar – at last perfected – provided all who manned her with high excitement. Known as the Kut Baby, she was a stocky child, ungainly in looks and unpredictable in her moods. Her barrel – a Gnome cylinder corseted with wire to prevent her busting her gut – was mounted at a scientifically calculated angle on a wooden base, and into her barrel was inserted a bag of black powder whose fuse protruded through what had once been a spark-plug aperture. The powder rammed home, a bomb was inserted, with a short, slow-burning fuse through its base. Then the barrel was pointed in the general direction of Baghdad and everyone departed into the nearest traverse except the fuse lighter. Who, heroically alone, applied his match – and fled.

A long and anxious silence would ensue; sometimes very long, sometimes interminable, because nothing had happened. At other times Baby would merely burp, and propel her bomb just over the parapet. Or just inside the parapet, which was less amusing. And sometimes she blew herself up and became a smoking ruin, her wire-corseted barrel a wicked flower with black jagged petals, which was not at all amusing. Normally, though, she let out a full-throated roar and her bomb hurtled into no-man's-land where it exploded quite harmlessly. But there had been one occasion – at Woolpress Village – when a bomb stuffed with nails and chopped wire had sailed gloriously all the way to the Turkish trenches before it exploded, and the men of Woolpress had claimed a direct hit.[28] But no one in Kut had believed them; and the feat was never repeated, because Baby ran out of food. There were simply not enough twenty-pound bombs, or empty jam tins, to satisfy her unpredictable appetite.[29]

Down-river, however, Aylmer at last had plenty of bombs, and his opponents for once seemed to be entrenched in positions that were slightly less than impregnable. Given an element of surprise, he might just be able to turn their first line and destroy them before they could withdraw to their next position, three and a half miles farther upstream, in a defile at Hanna.

Advised of Aylmer's optimism, Townshend visited his troops in hospital to tell them that relief was on its way.

'You'll get us out, General,' they assured him. 'After getting us out of Umm al Tubul, you can get us out of anything.'

'Surely', he reflected, returning to his diary, 'no commander ever had a more devoted division than my Sixth.'[39] And, nauseating though his sentiment sounds, it happens to have been the truth.

Turkish infantry and cavalry

Gunboats on the Tigris. Though shallow in draught,
they constantly ran aground

Relief Force unloading facilities were not sophisticated

Troops advance in an attempt to relieve Kut

Employed as auxiliary supply vessels to Townshend
at Ctesiphon, craft like these were always slow
and sometimes even sailed backwards

CHAPTER FOURTEEN

F ROM his roof-top lookout Townshend, binoculars to eyes,
peered through slits in the steel plates that protected him from
snipers. Everywhere he looked there were Turkish trenches, thirty
miles of them at least,[1] double lines and treble lines, a noose around his
neck.

A distant Turkish soldier, kneeling by the river, filled a can of water,
placed it on his head and plodded towards his redoubt.

'Boggis.'

'Sir?'

'Rifles! See that fellow there?' – pointing – 'We'll have a go at him.'

Carefully both men aimed: but it was Townshend who fired first.
The can of water fell one way, the Turk the other.

'Mine,' said Townshend: and Boggis was unable to contradict him.
Not only was the General a good shot, the General was a general: who
now was singing happily to himself as he descended to his room, to
study his books and write his diary, 'When I was single, my pockets
would jingle, I long to be single again.'[2]

The following morning, Aylmer launched the attack he hoped
would rout at least one of the several forces standing between him and
Kut. Theoretically, his chances were good. On his maps, the Turkish
position was vulnerable. But his maps were not only inadequate, they
were inaccurate as well, and when his troops advanced, with only
maps to guide them, they found their progress blocked by flooded
ditches and canals that had no right to be there.

His artillery, particularly, was delayed, and much of his plans depended upon its punctual bombardment; and the Turks, as always, resisted stubbornly; and, as the minutes lost became hours, Khalil Bey
read Aylmer's intentions and moved his troops accordingly.

Monitoring Aylmer's messages to Headquarters in Basra, Kut's
wireless operators kept Townshend in touch with the battle that ensued.

The Turks were driven out of their first line and kept under pressure by Kemball, whereupon Younghusband was supposed to throw in his 35th Brigade to turn their flank and cut off their retreat to Hanna: instead, he sent a message saying that to do so would be a 'most precarious undertaking'.[3]

Taking the decision out of Aylmer's hands, Nixon, contemptuous as ever of the Turks, replied, 'Am confident that you and the fine troops under your command will achieve your objective.'[3] So Younghusband and the fine troops under his command rushed forward.

It was then that time lost put the Relief Force at Khalil's mercy: and it is not a general's duty to be merciful to an enemy who charges into the cross-fire of his carefully-sighted machine-guns. Younghusband's charge disintegrated, and only the cavalry could have retrieved the situation: but the cavalry at first dallied and then, attacking alone and late, were also savaged by Khalil's machine-guns. As night fell, Aylmer seemed to have no hope left of preventing his enemy from falling back intact and in good order to Hanna: and indeed, the Turks did withdraw, as was their custom, in the darkness. At noon the following day, Aylmer acknowledged that, for the second time, he had failed to destroy an enemy force roughly equal in numbers to his own.

This advice filled Townshend with such dismay that his messages over the next few days became markedly hysterical. He declared that his force was becoming seriously demoralized. He referred constantly to promises (in fact never made) to relieve him within a month: and he pestered Aylmer with advice as to how the next battle should be fought.[4]

To his own officers he behaved no less strangely. Field Marshal von der Goltz was known by all to be the man he really feared, and a constant watch was kept for any sign of his arrival outside Kut.[5] The day after Aylmer's second defeat, an officer on an observation platform in the foliage of a date palm was asked what he was looking for through his telescope.

'Von der Goltz,' he replied. 'When I see him, I'm to press this button.' And when he saw him, he did.[6]

At once three batteries of artillery opened fire on this most legitimate of targets:[7] but Townshend promptly and angrily ordered them to cease fire. Von der Goltz, he maintained, was the leading strategist in Europe: and just as British officers at Torres Vedras had refused to fire on Massena, so he refused to fire on the commander of the 6th Turkish Army.[8]

It is only from a message to Nixon, twenty-four hours later, that his true motive for so apparently an archaic act of chivalry can be deduced. Deliberately to spare the life of an elderly enemy Field Marshal was one thing: deliberately to spare the life of one whom he had himself described as the leading strategist in Europe, whose task it was to destroy a force commanded by Nixon, one of the worst strategists in the world, was another entirely. And the fact that it was *not* von der Goltz after all, but Khalil, who had refused to allow so elderly a gentleman to carry out such an ardous inspection and had taken his place,[9] is neither here nor there. But, as the morrow would prove, Townshend had an ulterior motive for ordering an almost inexplicable cease-fire.

Three days had passed since the Turks had foiled Aylmer's latest efforts, three days in which they had given every indication of a premeditated withdrawal to prepared positions from which they would willingly give battle. Meantime the weather had become atrocious and Aylmer had had an opportunity to reassess the problems confronting him. In less than a week he had lost six thousand men and, even with replacements, his force now numbered no more than nine thousand. Accordingly, he wired Nixon and Townshend:

> The position of affairs must be frankly faced. The enemy is blocking the entrance of the Hannah defile with very strong works ... designed to resist a heavy bombardment. I shall have opposed to me his whole 52 Division and two regiments of the 35th and 38th Divisions ... Emplacements for 19 guns have been seen, eleven of which are designed to fire across the river ... Behind ... is the Essinn position. It is impossible, in my opinion, to take the first position from this side [of the river] alone without losing half the force ... The best plan seems to me for Townshend to cross the river during the night, with such able-bodied men as he has ... and march well round [that flank of the] Essinn [lines which are] on the right bank [as he faces them]. I would cross about one division and one cavalry brigade at same time and march to join him and bring him back here. The opportunity is now favourable and may cease ... [He] would have to leave sick and destroy most of his guns and material. If Townshend thinks that this is possible, I shall issue orders for him to do so.[10]

There was, of course, not the least chance of Townshend agreeing to Aylmer's suggestion, but it was Nixon – from his sick-bed, on the last day of his command – who brushed it aside.

> I do not in any way agree with your appreciation of the situation [he said] or that same calls for Townshend to take the extreme step you propose. Only circumstances that could in my opinion justify this course would be a demoralization of your force, which I have no reason to suspect.
> You have been opposed from Sheik Saad by ... rather over 15,000 with, at outside, 41 guns, and you have twice defeated them. Townshend has reported a strong column of one division and 12 guns retiring to main camp west of Kut. Enemy have suffered losses estimated by you at 4,500 at Sheik Saad and 2,000 at Wadi. You therefore should have between you and Kut not more than 5,000 and possibly 27 guns ... The course you originally proposed ... should ... afford you opportunity of inflicting severe blow on enemy and effecting speedy relief of Townshend ... The course you now propose ... would be disastrous from every point of view.[10]

Thus Nixon's last decision as an Army Commander compounded all his previous idiocies. Aylmer's two bloody failures he described as victories, simply because the enemy had chosen, as planned, to withdraw after each of them. He rashly elected to believe Townshend's erroneous claim that half the Turkish force opposing Aylmer had already retired beyond Kut. He continued to believe that the plan he had imposed upon Aylmer would succeed. And he now added a grievous insult to an already mortal injury by describing that plan to Aylmer as '*your* original plan'.

To Townshend, as Nixon's dispatch was monitored and brought to him, it must all have been most gratifying: but not so gratifying that he could subdue his eternal compulsion to dash off some messages of his own.

He wired Aylmer 'supposing' he would now advance his Main Force upstream, leaving a Minimum Force to guard his shipping, and relying on Kut to block any enemy shipping movements downstream. He also reminded Aylmer that he could not get his own men out of Kut and across the river at more than 350 an hour.[11]

Aylmer's reply to Nixon was reluctant and resigned. 'I understand,' he telegraphed, 'that you desire me to get to Kut in such a way as to hold that place, together with Townshend, at least until his force can be removed entirely. The only way to relieve Townshend without ... his breaking out, is for me to force the defile [at Dujeilah] ... This I shall attempt to do.'[12]

Aylmer's was a sad decision. Sad because it had been imposed upon him; sad because it doomed his force to yet another and even bloodier failure; and saddest of all because it at last made explicit the hitherto unspoken truth that Kut, far from being a strategic point to be held at all costs, was simply a trap from which thirteen thousand men must somehow be extricated. If ever he managed to fight his way through to Kut – which he clearly considered improbable – Aylmer now accepted the fact, which Basra did not dispute, that it would be for the sole purpose of removing from it a force that had held it for more than six weeks.

Perhaps detecting the pessimism that had inspired Aylmer to open his reply with the words, 'I understand that you desire me ...', Townshend felt himself compelled to strike an heroic attitude. Wiring both Nixon and Aylmer, he advised that, if all attempts at relief finally failed, he would fight in Kut from trench to trench, and house to house, until no ammunition remained to him, whereupon – all hope past – the traditions of war would justify him in making terms with the enemy, as Junot had done in Portugal in 1808,[13] Junot having been then permitted by his respectful foes not only to return to France with all his men, arms and baggage, but even to sail thereto in an enemy vessel.

And now at last Townshend's extraordinary rage at the gunners who had dared to fire on von der Goltz was explained. He quoted Junot to Nixon on January 17th. Doubtless he had decided that he might one day have to emulate Junot's example, and hope for Junot's treatment, during his study period on January 16th – and it was on that day that his gunners had attempted to kill the man they and he had thought to be Field Marshal von der Goltz. To shell the enemy commander is hardly the way subsequently to extract from him the chivalrous treatment that Junot had received: and Townshend dreaded the thought of anything less than his chivalrous repatriation, whatever the fate of Kut might be. Major-generals do not become lieutenant-generals by languishing in captivity.

As usual when proposing something that might be ill received, however, Townshend had also contrived to confuse all the real issues by adding others he knew would be rejected in spite of their irreproachable sentiments: and Nixon obligingly replied to his 'trench by trench, house by house till no ammunition remains' bravado with an immediate veto on the break-out attempt he had no intention of making. 'By February,' Nixon promised, 'all columns now marching should have reached Sheik Saad ... Force will then total four full divisions, except for two brigades of artillery, and we should be able to resume the offensive ...'[13]

To this Townshend, incorrigibly self-righteous, replied that he personally had never wished 'to abandon Kut', indeed had only contemplated it at Aylmer's suggestion; and considered it his duty, on the contrary, to stay there and dam up enemy forces. On the other hand, even though he was delighted that Kut was not to be abandoned, he *had* been given to understand, when first he entered it, that he would be relieved within a month: the resumption of an offensive in February would mean a siege of two months at least.[13]

As he drafted his message, it obviously never occurred to him that it could scarcely endear him to Aylmer, whose grim task it was to attempt to relieve him, nor that it must create in the mind of the man who would take over from Nixon in less than twenty-four hours an impression of himself as a chronic mischief-maker. Even Townshend, knowing as he did that his new commander would be that same Sir Percy Lake who had so strongly disapproved his methods in 1913, would have wired with more discretion had he been in a normal state of mind.

On January 19th, 1916, Lieutenant-General Sir Percy Lake – a man with shaggy eyebrows, high cheek-bones and the sort of moustache through which soup would have to be sucked – assumed command in Mesopotamia. For more than a year he had been Duff's Chief of Staff at Simla and he therefore expected to encounter little at Basra with which reports from Nixon's staff would not have made him familiar. What he saw, in fact, shocked him profoundly and made clear to him at last the degree to which Nixon's secretiveness had distorted India's view of its war in Mesopotamia.[14]

Even so, he should not have been so shocked as he was. He knew that India had sent Sir George Buchanan, a harbour expert, to take over the administration of Basra port only a few weeks ago, and that Sir George was already returning to India, having been completely frustrated by Nixon. 'Director General of Port Administration and River Conservancy' was the resounding title India Government had bestowed on Sir George, but they had left it to Nixon to define his precise duties. Resentful of the intrusion, Nixon had argued so bitterly with Sir George, and defined for him so few duties, that he had returned in disgust to India – there to report that Basra's dockside arrangements were 'of the most primitive order', situated in 'a huge quagmire', and looking as if Force D had arrived 'only last week rather than a year ago'.[14]

After a single glance at Basra – whose ships now waited three weeks to be unloaded – Lake ordered the immediate construction of wharves, landing stages, roads and camps. After a brief glance at the telegrams exhanged between Nixon, Townshend and Aylmer, he must have known that something somewhere was seriously wrong. But he can hardly have been expected to discern that Aylmer's past two attacks had failed primarily because they had been foisted upon him by a Nixon who was stupid and ill and a Townshend who was brilliant but unbalanced – so unbalanced that, by the dispatch of one lie in particular, he had caused Nixon to insist that Aylmer should risk a premature attack.

As yet that lie lay comfortably embedded in the hundreds of other lies that had been told about conditions at Basra: but it had only a week to live, and its eventual exposure was an appalling start to the relationship between Townshend and his new Army Commander.

For the moment, though, Lake was less concerned with Townshend's problems than with Aylmer's – whose only boat-bridge had just been smashed by one of his steamers, which had broken away in a storm, whose next battle was to be fought at Hanna in forty-eight hours' time, and to whom it would be quite impossible to send the ten thousand infantry and twelve guns encamped at Basra because there was no spare shipping.[14] Yet Aylmer badly needed more troops, and his need for extra guns was little less than desperate.

The Turkish position at Hanna had always been a formidable one, but the recent heavy rains had made it almost invulnerable. It lay across a defile that stretched from the Tigris to a marsh so vast that it was impossible to march around it and attack from the rear; and it consisted of two lines, each a mile long. These lines Aylmer had to attack head on.

It was not an operation that any general could happily have contemplated – and the fact that Townshend claimed to have seen no less than two thousand Turks withdrawing past Kut, obviously from Hanna, made Aylmer no happier because he simply did not believe them to have withdrawn from Hanna: as, in fact, they had not. The troops Townshend saw passing Kut were reserves:[15] of which fact he was probably well aware, and should have been if he was not.

That night, Aylmer's troops marched to their starting-points. 'We waited from 11 p.m. till 4.30 a.m. with no blankets and bitterly cold ... There was a very heavy dew and it froze, so it was pretty beastly.'[16]

It remained pretty beastly whilst brigades deployed and guns took up their carefully assigned positions. They were to lay down a barrage of twelve thousand shells at dawn – after which, the Turk and his wire presumably flattened, the infantry would attack.

Unfortunately, the bombardment began not at dawn but at 7.30, and by then the Turks could see clearly every move to be made against them. Anticipating the barrage on their first line, they withdrew to their second: and when the shells crept towards their second, they returned to the first.[17]

In Kut it also rained; but the roar of Aylmer's futile bombardment could be clearly heard. Two young subalterns sat in a traverse, listening to the distant thudding, water lapping round their ankles, the downpour drenching them.

' "Say not the struggle nought availeth," ' one of them quoted.

'What?'

' "Say not the struggle nought availeth,
The labour and the wounds are vain ..." '

'Apt!'

' "The enemy fainteth not, nor faileth.
And, as things have been, they remain." '

'You are *not* cheering me up.'

' "If hopes were dupes, fears may be liars:
It may be, in yon smoke concealed,
Your comrades pursue e'en now the fliers,
And, but for you, possess the field." '[18]

Upon the field itself, assuming that their futile bombardment would offer them an umbrella under which to advance, the Black Watch began a long charge across open ground. But the open ground was a morass, the umbrella was full of holes, and their charge was reduced to a lurching, heaving plod through cloying mud. The Black Watch was slaughtered by an enemy unaffected by shells that had fallen where he was not.

Though a few of the Scots reached the Turkish trenches and stabbed their way into them, they were soon driven out by bombs, and then, lacking any kind of cover or support, had to recross that same murderous stretch of mud over which they had so recently advanced to regain their own line. Only two officers and fifteen men returned to the starting-point.

And on the other flank, out of two Indian battalions, only twenty-five men reached the Turkish trenches. Piecemeal attacks were destroyed wholesale all along the line.

In Kut, it still rained: and in their sap one subaltern still quoted Clough's apposite verse to the other.

'For while the tired waves vainly breaking
Seem here no painful inch to gain,
Far back, through creeks and inlets making,
Comes silent, flooding in, the main.'

His companion snorted, but he continued, quietly, with the final and more hopeful verse:

'And not by eastern windows only,
When daylight comes, comes in the light.
In front the sun climbs slow, how slowly!
But westward, look, the land is bright.'

But on the battlefield, no sun climbed slowly, and nowhere looked even faintly bright. On the contrary, the rain sheeted down, the enemy held fast and failure seemed imminent.[18]

Bombers were ordered to clear the Turks from their line. Each man carried an open haversack on his stomach, each haversack full of grenades: but when they reached the Turkish trench they found it full of corpses, Turkish and British, the rain washing the blood of the one over the limbs of the other. Unable either to wade through this pulp of human flesh or to jump it, they too were driven back to their own line.[19]

Every battalion attacked: every attack was repulsed. Only the dead held their positions in the Turkish lines: and only the wounded lay between one force and the other.

'All the officers except myself were hit, and about ninety per cent of the men,' wrote a captain of the Hampshires. 'A good many are missing, as we got into their trenches – but couldn't stay there.'[19] The attack had failed.

Aylmer telegraphed Townshend that a further assault in the afternoon would be impossible: his men were exhausted, drenched and frozen. To add to their despair, an icy wind was blowing, the rain was falling harder than ever, and the Tigris had begun to flood.

Some of the wounded drowned; some died of cold; many were picked off by the watchful Turk; all suffered agonies. One of them, shot through the leg, lay all day in no-man's-land. As bullets began to splash around him, once the battle had stopped, he scooped a wall of mud round his head, and then round his shoulders, and then round his legs, until he lay in a sort of mud coffin, lacking only a lid, the water inside it getting deeper with the rain and redder with his blood all afternoon.

Most of that night he lay there too. He was found by two stretcher-bearers, who carried him for more than three hours – dropping him twice as they fell into holes – to the ambulance point. Here he was given rum and lay for another three hours in the rain. Then on to a cart, to be wheeled to the river, where, sardine-like, he was packed on to the open deck of a boat – which reached Basra six days later.

'All my friends in the regiment are gone,' he wrote home. 'I don't know what will become of us.'[19]

Five days later he was put aboard a hospital ship. 'We are now on our way to Bombay – thank goodness. I think, after eleven months of Mesopotamia, one needs a bit of a change.'[19]

In Kut it was raining too. When the last scrap of wood had been sawn or torn off the last Arab house, when the last gnarled ginger root had been dug out of the sandy soil, when fires were no longer possible, there was a deluge: and the Tigris – suddenly a raging torrent – over-flowed its banks, flooding all the first-line trenches on the left flank. In spite of all the nights of dangerous work the Pioneers had put into the building of bunds, sudden shouts of 'Pani ātā ... pani ātā' from the Indians had preceded walls of water several feet deep bursting through parapets and sweeping straight down the trenches.[20]

That night, men stood knee-deep in water, sodden blankets over their heads and shoulders, and slept. When they awoke, their blankets had frozen hard to the side of the trench and their feet were frost-bitten.

'I can't send you to the hospital,' the assistant surgeon apologized. 'All I can do is bandage your feet.' There being no bandages, he used their filthy puttees, and sent them back to the line.[21] Chlorodine for dysentery, quinine for fever, puttees for bandages: it was all he could do.[22]

In the horse lines, animals sank to their withers in mud: in the town, one much-used stretch of road lay under a foot of water, so the engineers built it up with thousands of sacks of ginger;[23] in the gun-pits, guns sank to the axles of their iron-rimmed wheels; in no-man's-land, hundreds of Turkish corpses were washed out of their shallow graves; in the first line, a smiling sixteen-year-old appeared with an armful of great-coats. 'Thanks,' said his Hampshire and West Kent seniors. 'Now get out of here.' The front line was not for sixteen-year-olds. On the left flank, men fought desperately to dam the running water and – losing the battle, wet to the waist, their legs slimy with mud, their puttees sodden and their boots squelching – had to with-draw under fire. Fortunately the Turkish trenches were also inund-ated, and they too were evacuated. Enemies who had only hours ago stood 150 yards apart at the most, now faced one another across a thousand yards of watery mud.

Inevitably it was Melliss, conspicuous in his red-banded general's cap, who made an inspection of the flooded trenches. Wading knee-deep along the new line, he spoke to almost everyone.[24] 'Good morn-ing, sentry ... All right, my man? ... What a bloody business, eh?'

And to men in the first line, almost submerged and groping in the deep brown water: 'What're you doing there?'

'Looking for rifles, sir. Got lost when we were helping one another out.'

'Keep it up.'[25]

To others, standing waist-deep in their new positions: 'Pull down some sandbags. Stand on them.'[26]

A bullet splashed into the mud by his head. 'Take that cap off, sir,' his men implored. 'The snipers'll get you.'[26]

'Balls!' And waded off to talk with the sepoys. Only General Melliss and the Gurkhas – who had passed the night of the floods telling one another stories[27] – and Mrs Milligan seemed happy that day in Kut.

Flooded and fuel-less, its hopes of relief dashed once again, and with only fourteen days' rations remaining, Kut accepted that January 21st had been its worst day yet. Soberly, Townshend put everyone on half rations and, six weeks late, ordered a house-to-house search for hidden hoards of grain.

That evening, Aylmer sent a second telegram.

We have made two assaults on enemy's entrenched position here without success. I shall renew attack tomorrow but acknowledge ... it appears rather a forlorn hope. My losses have been very heavy.

The only way you can help is to make a sortie on a large scale and endeavour to defeat what is in front of you, returning into Kut again. Success would mean that the enemy now opposing me would probably retire from this defile ... If you can do this, please do it soon.[28]

Townshend's response was predictably unhelpful. Conditions at Kut, he said, were just as bad as they were at Hanna; all his 6,450 combatant troops were fully occupied coping with inundations; perhaps Aylmer should await more reinforcements before attacking the defile for a third time; and finally – anticipating Aylmer's argument that he must help if he was to be relieved before his food ran out – he *now* had rations for another twenty-seven days!

Having thus parried every argument that Aylmer might deploy against him, he then went on to the offensive. 'I cannot understand why all these troops are returning from opposing you,' he jeered.[29]

Aylmer, ignoring Townshend and his jibe, sent off a wire to Lake advising that captured Turks had told him he was opposed by at least nine thousand infantry and twenty-six guns. 'I am quite certain,' he remarked, with crushing irony, 'that Townshend has observed most carefully: but, if all troops marching westward during past fortnight be deducted from enemy in front of me, I should only have had to fight about 5,000 yesterday.'[30] Townshend's lies were coming home to roost: but the biggest of them all was still flying high.

Aylmer's desire to relieve a man who refused to co-operate from Kut on the one hand, and deliberately minimized the opposition to be over-come at Hanna on the other, cannot – at the personal level – have remained overwhelming. Over a period of three weeks, the only sensible words he had had from Townshend were those that had sug-gested he delay his third attack till reinforcements arrived. Learning now that his troops, without his permission, had withdrawn some thirteen hundred yards from the Turkish lines, he decided to accept this advice – doubtless well aware that nothing could be less pleasing to Townshend than the delay in his relief thereby incurred – and telegraphed Lake that his troops, after severe losses in the severest conditions, were in no state to achieve the impossible.[30] Without demur, Lake agreed, instructing him merely to regroup and meanwhile to send his ships back empty to Amarah, where Gorringe would be organizing reinforcements as they arrived from Basra.[30]

To Townshend this order apparently implied so intolerable a delay in Aylmer's next relief attempt that, ignoring everything he had previously said, he at once asserted that only three courses of action now lay open to him. He could either attempt a break-out (not a sortie); or maintain his stand to the last cartridge and the last ounce of food; or negotiate with the enemy, offering them Kut in exchange for the free passage of his troops and guns, as Junot had done in 1808 at Lisbon. And of the three, he said, he considered the break-out – Plan A – the best.

If he was bluffing, Lake's reply must have appalled him: because Lake agreed that a break-out in co-operation with an attack by Aylmer might indeed be the best course. Before making his final decision, however, Lake said he proposed visiting Aylmer's Headquarters to review the situation for himself.

Immediately Townshend set about confusing the break-out issue he had himself initiated. He remained, he wired, perfectly prepared to break out, but the success of such an attempt would, of course, depend purely on luck – and General Melliss disapproved the idea entirely because it must fail if the Turks, as they could scarcely fail to do, dis- covered his troops trying to sneak across the river at night.

That the success of a break-out attempt would depend largely upon luck, and that it would fail if the Turks unluckily discovered what was being attempted, can hardly have been news either to Lake or to Aylmer, as Townshend was doubtless aware. He therefore proceeded to debate the subject in an entirely fresh context. On December 3rd he had roundly declared that he had rations for only a month; and then on December 6th, being advised that relief could only come 'within two months', discovered that he had rations for sixty days; on the morning of January 21st, he had wailed that he had rations for only ten more days; and then, on the afternoon of January 21st, to circumvent the desirability of a sortie, he decided that he had rations for another twenty-seven days. Now, on January 24th – to nullify the validity of a break-out – he insisted that, by killing his horses and mules, he could provide his troops with rations for another *fifty-six* days.

In case this was not enough to justify his 'sitting tight', he next, in a wire to Aylmer, resorted to bravado and sentimentality. It was only the raging Tigris he feared, not the enemy (to which Aylmer would have been entitled to ask why then had he not crossed the river during any one of the forty-nine nights before January 21st when it was shallow), and anyway, 'it is a terrible thing for me to leave behind the wounded and sick … who have all trusted me … I am going to abandon them like a thief in the night'. (To which again Aylmer might well have asked why then had he twice, on January 8th and again today, suggested it?) 'I know my first duty is to try to save all my able bodied men, and to the Government, and I was the first to tell you and Sir John that I would attempt to cut my way out if you were repulsed.' (To which Aylmer might well have retorted: 'But only to confuse Nixon when all I wanted was a sortie: and only because you were confident that Nixon would veto your first offer as now you hope Lake will veto your second.')

But then, at last, Townshend came to the point.

> I do not see why we should not hold on here for another two months ... in which case Army Commander could call troops from India – or even Australians from Melbourne ... The Turk is a mediocre fighter in the open, but formidable behind a wall or trench. The divisions in front of you are the same as fled when we closed with them at Essinn last September, and the same as at Ctesiphon, but [that] was of course because their flank was turned and [because] we attacked in columns on fronts not more than six or seven hundred yards a brigade. I hope you will weigh the matter well with Army Commander. Remember, my being able to cross the river at night without detection is, I may say, a case of spinning a coin.[31]

Townshend's vision of Sir Percy Lake having merely to say the word to inspire Australia's youth – all of which apparently lived in Melbourne – to rush to the aid of Townshend was almost as ludicrous as his claim that the Essinn and Ctesiphon positions outflanked by him in the dry days of summer had presented no more difficulties than Hanna's marsh-moated quagmire in the deluges of winter now presented to Aylmer.

Townshend's assertion that Aylmer faced the same enemy at Hanna as he had himself faced at Essinn and Ctesiphon was as specious as his assertion that those who *had* faced him had instantly fled. Aylmer faced many more Anatolian Turks than Townshend had done. Aylmer faced a Nureddin whose resolve had been stiffened by the advent of von der Goltz and General Khalil – upon whose arrival at Ctesiphon it had been Townshend who had been obliged to flee, not the Turk. And those who had fled from him at Essinn, and in the first part of the battle at Ctesiphon, had done so *not*, as he claimed, when he closed with them, but only after he had turned their flank. At Hanna,

174

there was no flank for Aylmer to turn: there was the Tigris on the left and a vast expanse of marsh to the right.

With whatever indignation, or contempt, Aylmer may have viewed this last effusion, he declined to continue the dialogue that night: which probably explains yet another telegram from Townshend the following morning. Having thought the matter over, Townshend confessed, he had now decided that he and Lake and Aylmer were wrong: it was Melliss who was right. An attempted break-out *would* fail. Or, if it did not, it would involve the abandonment of '4,000 or 5,000' combatants, as well as all the sick and wounded[31] (whose numbers he chose not to provide, presumably because Basra already had them and they therefore allowed of no advantageous imprecision).

Nor was this the sole result of his nocturnal cogitations. Overnight his food position had changed dramatically for the fourth time in four days: he now had 'sufficient' rations not for fifty-six days, but 'ample' rations for eighty-four.[31]

Kut therefore must be held, he asserted resoundingly, and the Turks denied any opportunity of advancing down the Tigris. Should he abandon Kut, Amarah and Nasariyeh would fall and all the territory won in 1915 be ingloriously lost. Indeed, it had been for these reasons alone that, on his own decision, he had halted and dug in at Kut, and would, if necessary, remain there for eighty-four days more. Reinforcements to Aylmer's corps, he advised, should be good white troops, not Indians, whose morale he found inferior. The Turks would not dare attempt again to overrun him. The coming floods would favour Aylmer, who had more gunboats than Nureddin. And he himself could best help as Osman Pasha had helped when, besieged at Plevna in 1897, he had delayed the Russians for almost five months and so saved Constantinople.[31]

Aylmer's reply to this spate of hypocrisy and condescension was superbly succinct and damning. 'It must be acknowledged,' he wired Lake, 'Townshend's [latest telegram] throws a completely new light on the situation ... Had it been communicated to me before, [it] would certainly have modified much that I have unsuccessfully attempted to do and [much that] I have proposed. I no longer desire to adopt Plan A.'[32]

As always, Townshend had to have the last word. Worried by Aylmer's caustic reference to his suppression, for more than seven weeks, of his true ration potential, he blandly asserted that there had been no need to look for extra food 'until the question arose as to whether I could be relieved or not ... The Arab population of Kut is 6,000, distinctly hostile ... a positive danger ... I did not want to search for food until obliged ... I knew there was much food in town, but not so much as we discovered.'[33]

Thus he had his last word: but he would have done better to bite it back. Kut's Arabs were unarmed and a danger to its garrison only because they had to be fed. Townshend had abstained from searching their houses for food not for fear of provoking them but for the same reason as he had abstained from collecting Woolpress Village's early-discovered two hundred tons of barley: he simply had not been interested, at that stage, in building up his supplies of food. His sole interest had been to compel a relief within, at the most, a month.

'I knew there was much food in the town,' his telegram admitted. No superhuman intellect was required to know it. *All* Arabs in *all* towns hoard and hide food. Yet he had never looked for it; had issued false deadlines on four occasions, each one implying that he *had* looked for it; and had finally done what he should have done seven weeks earlier only because he would otherwise have been obliged to attempt a break-out.

'Sit tight until we are relieved' had always been his motto, and it remained his motto: for the moment, though, he must explain to his troops how it had come about that they had had to sit tight for so long – and might have to sit tight for eighty-four days longer. So the following morning he issued the first of his famous Kut communiqués – the opening sentence and final paragraph of which were extraordinary for their malicious disloyalty to his superiors; the balance of which was proved by events to be nonsense.

The Relief Force under General Aylmer has been unsuccessful in its efforts to dislodge the Turks entrenched on the left bank of the river, some fourteen miles below the position at Essinn, where we defeated the Turks in September last, when their strength was greater than it is now. Our relieving force suffered severe loss and had very bad weather to contend with. They are entrenched close to the Turkish position. More reinforcements are on their way up river and I confidently expect to be relieved some day during the first half of the month of February.

I desire all ranks to know why I decided to make a stand at Kut during our retirement from Ctesiphon. It was because so long as we hold Kut the Turks cannot get their ships, barges, stores and ammunitions past this place, and so cannot move down to attack Amarah. Thus we are holding up the whole of the Turkish advance. It also gives time for our reinforcements to come up river from Basra and so restore success to our arms; it gives time to our allies, the Russians, who are now overrunning Persia, to move towards Baghdad. I had a personal message from General Baratoff, commanding the Russian Expeditionary Force in Persia, the other day, telling me of his admiration of what you men of the 6th Division and troops attached have done in the past few months, and telling me of his own progress on the road from Kirmanshah, towards Baghdad.

By standing at Kut, I maintain the territory we have won in the past year at the expense of much blood, commencing with your glorious victory at Shaiba, and thus we maintain the campaign as a glorious one instead of letting disaster pursue its course down to Amarah and perhaps beyond.

I have ample food for 84 days, and that is not counting the 3,000 animals which can be eaten. When I defended Chitral some twenty years ago, we lived well on attar and horse flesh, but, I repeat, I expect confidently to be relieved in the first half of the month of February.

Our duty stands out plain and simple. It is our duty to our Empire, to our beloved King and Country, to stand here and hold up the Turkish advance as we are doing now: and with the help of all, heart and soul with me together, we will make this a defence to be remembered in history as a glorious one. All in England and India are watching us now and are proud of the splendid courage and devotion you have shown. Let all remember the glorious defence of Plevna, for that is what is in my mind.

I am absolutely calm and confident as to the result. The Turk, though good behind a trench, is of little value in the attack. They have tried it once, and their losses in one night in their attempt on the Fort were 2,000 alone. They have also had very heavy losses from General Aylmer's musketry and guns, and I have no doubt they have had enough.

I want to tell you now that, when I was ordered to advance on Ctesiphon, I officially demanded an Army corps, or at least two divisions, to perform the task successfully. Having pointed out the grave danger of attempting to do this with one division only, I had done my duty. You know the result, and whether I was right or not; and your name will go down to history as the heroes of Ctesiphon, for heroes you proved yourselves in that battle. Perhaps by right I should not have told you of the above, but I feel I owe it to all of you to speak straightly and openly and to take you into my confidence. God knows, I felt our heavy losses, and the sufferings of my poor brave wounded, and I shall remember it as long as I live. I may truly say that no General I know of has been more loyally obeyed and served than I have been in command of the Sixth Division. These words are long, I am afraid, but I speak straight from the heart, and you see I have thrown all officialdom overboard. We will succeed; mark my words. *Save your ammunition as if it were gold.*[33]

CHAPTER FIFTEEN

B OGGIS had naturally been one of the first to learn of Townshend's belated order to search for hidden food, and whilst the Hampshires and Norfolks and West Kents went purposefully from house to house, he had conducted his own investigation.

'Subedah,' he said to an Indian major standing with him in the courtyard, 'does that wall strike you as funny?'

'No, sahib.'

'But look! It's so thick. There's nothing behind it but a street: why's it so thick?'

'I don't know, sahib.'

A sepoy was ordered to knock a hole in the wall with a pick-axe, and dozens of sacks of barley were found stacked neatly between a false front and the real wall behind.[1]

In almost every house and courtyard the story was the same. In sacks, in earthenware jars, in the walls, under the floor, in the rafters, cache after cache of grain was uncovered. Where two sacks were discovered, one was confiscated: the Arab had to be left with something for himself. Where a larger hoard was discovered, most of it was carried into the courtyard until a cart could be sent by Supply to collect it, and the sentry posted to guard it be relieved.

Such sentry-duty was not popular: the Arabs objected to their treasure being stolen. Each courtyard served all the houses surrounding it, and one felt lonely and vulnerable standing guard over a pile of confiscated grain, watched by all the resentful householders. But Arab hospitality frequently prevailed, and often the anxious sentry, waiting for Supply to relieve him, was offered some kebab or a chapatti. Invariably he would refuse, for fear of its being poisoned; then the Arab would insist, and the sentry would indicate 'after you', and, smiling, the Arab would eat first.[2]

Naturally, Headquarters sent Woolpress Village a message asking where was the barley it had reported in December to be there by the hundreds of tons? Woolpress replied that it had all been affected by rain, and much of it eaten by their solitary mule. Bitterly, then, Headquarters allowed it to be known that it suspected the garrison, not the mule, of eating much of the barley, although a single inspection of the fattest mule in the world would have dispelled such dark suspicions forever: but no one from Headquarters ever visited Woolpress Village. Exposed, isolated and even more susceptible to flooding than Kut, it was thought to be dangerous.[3]

Eventually, all the confiscated grain was collected from all the resentful courtyards and handed over to Supply, who carefully weighed each sack of it, added up all the weights and then sat down to a pretty calculation. X pounds of grain being available, out of which Y men must eat A pounds per day, and Z animals eat B pounds per day, how long would the grain last?

They arrived at this answer easily enough: but ... for British troops there was to be a meat ration, provided by killing so many oxen or horses or mules each day. Therefore, less grain would be needed each day for animals, and more would become available each day for men. How now to calculate how long the grain would last? And how to ensure that the last ounce of grain and the last ounce of meat were consumed on the same day? Daunted by such complicated mathematics, Supply decided to enlist the aid of that ingenious R.F.C. officer who had already sacrificed his fingers to the cause of rifle-grenades and who now thought he remembered that, as a schoolboy, he had learnt a formula for the solution of just such problems.[4]

Having racked his brains for some hours, however, the R.F.C. officer was compelled to admit that, if ever there had been such a formula, he had forgotten it: so he produced an answer by applying what he called 'first principles' instead. Of which Headquarters were so suspicious that they insisted Supply provide its own answer: but when the two answers tallied, the order was given for the distribution of grain and the slaughter of animals to begin at the rate calculated by the R.F.C., and Townshend notified Lake that Kut could eat for a further eighty-four days.

But an issue of grain is not much use to troops who have no fuel for cooking: what they needed was wheat and barley ground into flour and attar. A further search was ordered for millstones; many were found; but all worn so smooth as to be useless. Therefore, men familiar with stone-cutting were required. Stone-cutting Dorsets were withdrawn from the firing line to rehabilitate Kut's old, smooth millstones.[5]

But how could two donkeys plodding interminably round two mills grind enough grain a day to feed thirteen thousand men and a diminishing three thousand animals? The R.F.C. solved that problem also. With the Tigris in flood, there was no need for pumping: so the pumping machine was transferred to the axis of a millstone and the donkeys' pedestrian output was supplemented by a mechanized flow of twelve eighty-pound sacks a day.

Now only one problem remained. How, without wood for fires, to bake the flour into bread: how to cook the attar and the meat? Use that bargeful of crude oil that's tied up near the town, someone suggested. So ovens were fired with oil; and British troops cooked their meat, and Indians, whose religion forbade them horse-meat, their extra ration of attar, over a narrow, shallow trench containing an inch or two of thick oil ignited with kerosene.

The oil generated a fierce heat and a dense cloud of smoke which blackened everything it touched: but there was plenty of it, and Kut's feeding problems for the next three months were solved. Horse-meat was pleasant enough; mule-meat was sinewy; ox-meat was jaw-breaking;[6] and Woolpress Village's fat, corn-fed mule was delicious.[7] So were the pies baked for those officers who regularly shot starlings in Kut and sparrows in Woolpress Village[7] – to which starlings, like colonels and generals, never came. Townshend's troops ate adequately, if not well, and seemed happy enough: except for General Hoghton, who loved all animals so passionately that the mere thought of eating horse-flesh horrified and sickened him.[8]

In the hospital, on the other hand, as the rain thrashed at their matting roof and bugs assailed them by the million, men with malaria and bullet-wounds became the victims of strange appetites; and their friends, visiting them at night, were distressed at being unable to satisfy them. 'My mate was shot. He had a craving for an orange. Or a mango. But there weren't any. He died two days later.'[9]

'Tom?' a patient called as a gunner passed him. The gunner turned and recognized a boyhood friend, now a Dorset private, ginger-bearded, his head bandaged. The gunner sat on his charpoy.

'What happened to you?' he asked, scratching at his leg, which already the bugs were biting.

'Sniper.'

'How you getting on?'

'Ah! We're not getting much here.'

The gunner left him, returned to his dugout by the brick kilns, collected eight rupees from his companions, walked into the town, haggled with an Arab, bought a tin of condensed milk and took it happily to the hospital.

'Sorry,' said an orderly, 'you're too late.'[10]

Hospital was not a good place to be, however generous one's friends, however devoted the medical staff. No one allowed himself to be sent to hospital if he could avoid it: and if he was sent there, he begged constantly to be returned to the firing line. However cold the nights, in shorts and shirt and tunic, lying on the mud under a single blanket, living like a mole in a crudely roofed dugout, it was better than being in hospital. One knew what to expect in the trenches. So many hours on the firing-step, peering at nothing but the backsides of decomposing Turkish corpses through the key-hole slot in the shielded loop-hole; so many hours off – furiously bailing water; so much daily meat to be cooked over the black smoking oil-fire; one's daily loaf of bread; one's daily quart of water; one's friends. Nothing to do, of course. Nothing to read. No money – nothing to buy anyway, not in the trenches. No letters. Just the firing-step, the oil-fire, the dense black smoke, the cold nights, the talk of past meals and past pleasures. Like the football match in 1913 between Bristol Rovers and Crystal Palace.

'Found a sovereign in the mud, my mate did. So we paid an extra threepence each and sat in the grandstand. A marvellous day, that was.'

'Who won?'

'Crystal Palace.'[10] Nothing to do but talk. About 'away' matches his home team had lost.

'What's the first thing you want when you get home?'

'A hot bath!'[11]

Officers could get hot baths from their friends billeted in town. Officers' Messes still got an issue of firewood.[12] Still, who'd be an officer? Look what happened to Ormiston.

Nothing to talk about; nothing to do.

Cards would have helped. But there weren't any. No oranges, no mangoes, no cards. Roll on the middle of February. Roll on General Aylmer.

Lake arrived at Aylmer's Headquarters on January 27th, searching for a solution to a problem that was insoluble, his task made none the easier because his friend Aylmer had not only lost control at Hanna (when his troops had broken contact with the enemy) but was also clearly reluctant to resume the offensive.

Worse even than this, though, was the knowledge that the Tigris Corps – disillusioned by the futility of the battles Townshend had imposed upon it, resentful of those who censored out of every letter every smallest reference to military or medical bungling – having added yet another verse to its alphabetical catalogue of Force D's multifarious ineptitudes, was wont to recite:

> W stands for the Wonder, and pain,
> with which we regard our infirm and insane
> old aged generals who run this campaign
> we're waging in Mesopotamia.[13]

In fact, the generals then running the campaign were not so much infirm and insane as the victims of Duff, Nixon and Townshend who, between them, had manœuvred Force D into a position whence it could do little but destroy itself. Townshend would not (probably no longer could) attempt a break-out: but could not be abandoned. Between Townshend and Aylmer lay 35,000 well entrenched Turkish troops: but against those 35,000 (and a further 36,000 were en route from the Dardanelles) Lake could deploy only 40,000:[14] and to supply even those 40,000, his shipping and wharfage services were totally inadequate. The rain floods of January had proved a tougher enemy even than the Turks: but the floods of January would be as nothing to those that would come when the snows at the head of the Tigris thawed in March. Lake must, therefore, relieve Townshend in February: but Aylmer was reluctant. Nevertheless, he now gave Aylmer his orders to this effect.

Unaware of the pessimism with which the Tigris Corps contemplated its coming task, Kut went about its duties as cheerfully as ever. The Crown and Anchor boys still operated in a room in the barracks down by the serai, their 'Come along, me lucky boys' as enticing as ever. Not that the majority had any money to play with any longer. Like everything else, money was running out. Even the officers' Messes had at last run out of sugar (and almost out of butter). There was no salt for anyone and saltless horse-meat left a taste in the mouth that was curiously metallic.[15] The nights were so cold that ice formed on the water.[16] But the Tigris had dropped four inches[17] and that – to a community who had spent a week bailing as frantically as sailors adrift in a leaking lifeboat – was what mattered most.

Once again Kut's inventors went to work. Remembering the Turks' dazzling display of flares and Very lights on Christmas Eve, they produced for their own troops what they modestly described as an Illuminated Rifle-Grenade – which their less imaginative compatriots described as a tin on the end of a long metal rod.

The inhabitants of Woolpress Village, offered the use of this rare missile, examined it with suspicion and demanded to know how it worked. Somewhat impatiently their sappers explained that the tin contained materials that would burst into brilliant light, and a small parachute that would allow the light to float slowly down over the enemy's lines, so exposing any Turk who moved above them to the devastating fire of the Village's snipers.

Almost convinced – because the Villagers had never quite trusted its sappers since the Baby had so devastatingly become a black lily of smoking metal – they inserted the rod of an illuminated grenade into the barrel of a rifle, pushed the rifle through a loop-hole, lined it up with great precision, lashed it securely into place, tied a long piece of string on its trigger, retired into a traverse – and pulled the end of the string.

Whereupon, to the joy of all – especially the sappers – the grenade soared off on its appointed course, the parachute fluffed open and the flare burst into magnificent light, evoking from friend and foe alike a great roar of approval. But the parachute then drifted back over the Village, casting a pitiless glare over its every position, while the Turks remained shrouded in impenetrable darkness: so the C.O. of Woolpress Village declined to use any more Illuminated Rifle-Grenades,[18] and the sappers returned to less lethal pastimes – like making bricks out of mud and straw, against the day of the coming floods, or knitting socks with wool from unravelled scarves.[19]

Every day the Tigris dropped a few inches and the trenches dried out a little more until, by the middle of the first week of February, conditions had reverted almost to normal. Except that there was now a thousand yards of no-man's land between the opposing forces: and the Turk would never attack across an open thousand yards. For the first time in two months, therefore, Kut's garrison was able to relax. Only the morning and evening bombardments, and the constant risk of being sniped, now endangered them: and to those they had long since become inured.

Sniping, in fact, had even become a sort of game. British sharpshooters, for example, regularly attempted to shoot holes in the blades of Turkish shovels each time they appeared above the ground, casting their spoil out of ever deepening trenches, because shovels with holes in them don't dig so well and anyway shooting at them was something to do. Goodnaturedly, one of the Turks entered into the spirit of the game by exposing his shovel blade, then snatching it out of sight again, time after time. Every twenty seconds, the blade appeared, and British rifles crackled all along the line, trying to hit it before it vanished from sight. Up ... fire ... down. Up ... fire ... down. Time after time. Every twenty seconds. Then abruptly it would stop. Twenty seconds: no shovel. Thirty seconds: forty seconds: a minute – and still no shovel. Ah! There it was again. One shovel blade, with a bandage on it![20]

Townshend – urged to visit some other part of the trenches than those by the fort – decided to inspect an exposed redoubt; of which fact the officer in charge of the redoubt was warned by his brigade major, who said the General would arrive the following morning.

The officer concerned, dirty and dishevelled to a degree that no general would tolerate, at once told his orderly to bring him some water and, stripping off, began his toilet. At which moment Townshend, accompanied by his red-tabbed staff, appeared round the corner, demanding, 'Is there an officer here?'[21]

Dumbly the orderly pointed. 'Splendid,' said Townshend. 'Come along – I want to see everything. NO' – as the naked man attempted to drag recalcitrant shorts over wet legs – 'As you are! Your men'll enjoy seeing you like that.' And spent an hour inspecting everything.[22]

Next morning the brigade major telegraphed the redoubt. 'The General's regrets, he'll be unable to visit you today,' he said. 'Pressure of work.'

'He was here yesterday, sir,' his subaltern corrected – to the extreme displeasure of the brigade major, who, along with the entire Brigade Staff, had naturally wanted to participate in so splendid a ceremony as a G.O.C.'s inspection.[22]

Not all senior officers were so pompous, however. The colonel commanding the 66th Punjabis, for example, made it his nightly practice to go to the listening point nearest the Turkish lines and from it to shout at the enemy curses and insults of the most lurid kind.[23] To which the Turks retorted by shouting to his men, 'Indian soldier – why you stay there and no eat? Come to us and eat very much.'[24] But to no avail. The Punjabis had just had a large meal of camel stew – which their religion allowed them to eat, though it forbade the consumption of horse and mule – and were perfectly happy to stay with their colonel, whose insults they greatly admired.

Refusing to be outdone by their ingenious colleagues inside Kut, the R.F.C. outside it took off from their crude desert air-strips to deliver some gifts to the beleaguered garrison. Wobbling overhead in frail biplanes, they cast sack after sack into space and (these being pre-parachute times) watched them hurtle into the palm groves.

From below, thousands of eager British eyes watched the five-thousand-foot descent of the plummeting sacks. Mail at last: and that night their mail was brought up to them, along the communication trenches. Pull-throughs for rifles!

Then came another plane. This time it must be mail. This time it was newspapers for Townshend. And a millstone for the bloody grain.[25] As if they hadn't enough millstones. As if that bloody engine didn't chug chug chug all day and night anyway.[26] Why couldn't some-one bring some letters?[27] They never did, of course. Letters could wait till after the relief. What mattered was pull-throughs; and millstones; and newspapers for the General.

The only word they did receive was a message to the General from the Viceroy, who declared, 'The bravery and endurance with which you and the troops under your command have resisted the attacks of the enemy have excited the admiration of all and I am confident resistance will be maintained until help reaches you in near future. India thinks of you and your troops all the time.'[28] Which was the kind of message that made one suspect not only that nobody in India thought of anyone ever, but that something must be seriously wrong with the Relief Force – or why would the Viceroy be laying it on so thick?[29]

And what did he know about it anyway? What did he know about lice? Had he ever had to strip off and kill thousands of the little sods between *his* thumb-nails? Had he ever been driven so mad by their insatiable thirst for human blood he'd smeared himself with crude oil and nearly burnt his balls off?[30] Had he ever tried making bricks out of mud and bhoosa? Or eaten horse-meat without salt? Or been bitten by one of those sandflies that had suddenly decided to join the war on Turkey's side? Or visited a hospital that would have had Florence Nightingale banging him over the head with her lamp?[31] Or tried to get mules to pull a ration cart while the Turks were indulging in their regular evening strafe?

Now *there* was a thing! Almost the worst thing at the moment: try-ing to bring up the rations. A fatigue party would collect the raw meat from the slaughter lines, and the potato-meal that was supposed to thicken the stew when you cooked the meat, and the precious loaves of bread, and load it all on to a cart and set off through narrow alleys ankle-deep in mud and filth: and then the strafe would start, and the bloody mules would go berserk, and you'd have to manhandle them and the cart all the way to the communication trench. Let the Viceroy try that. Or at least let him give a medal to the quartermaster sergeants who did it night after night.[31] And another medal to the Indian sweepers, who collected all the night-soil from every trench, and cleaned up every street and alleyway in the wake of six thousand feckless Arabs, and never complained at all. Maybe they *were* used to it: but, without them, everyone would have died of disease long ago.[31] 'India thinks of you and your troops all the time' indeed! Why didn't India do something?

The Viceroy and Sir Beauchamp Duff, however, were not the men to do things – except dispatch the occasional cable to those whose sufferings or suspicions they felt might easily be allayed. After fourteen months of war, India Government had raised its income tax by not a single rupee, had refrained from imposing any taxes on war profits, had allowed only one in every hundred of its legion of British officials to leave their posts and enlist, and was still insisting that every penny of expenditure incurred by all four of its Expeditionary Forces be paid by Great Britain.[32] As a result, and not unnaturally, Britain had just decided to assume political control at least of the war for which she was paying; and in a few months' time was to go even further and assume military control as well. But that would be too late to save the garrison at Kut.

For them this first week of February 1916 was proving strangely irritating, now that the likelihood of another Turkish attack had vanished. For the troops, because of the lice and the saltless horse stews and the lack of mail. For the officers, because of the lice and the fact that puddings in their Messes had become a rarity. For Melliss and Delamain, because they interpreted the needs of the first line differently, so that saps built by Delamain, when his brigade was in the line, were filled in by Melliss a fortnight later, and they were clashing constantly.[33] For Townshend, because the news he had read in one of *The Times* newspapers dropped by plane had filled him with foreboding.

It had said that the 13th British Division had suffered four thousand casualties in one action alone at Gallipoli: and it was the 13th Division that was coming to Basra to reinforce the Tigris Corps. All along he had hoped for 'good British troops' to come to his relief: and now that they did, they came mutilated and probably downcast from the débâcle of Gallipoli.[34] And to add to his woes, his senior medical officer had just advised him that scurvy had broken out among the ranks of his non-meat-eating Indians.[35] Their gums exuded pus, their teeth had loosened in their sockets and their breath was foul. Every morning more of them appeared on sick parade. How long would Tigris Corps take to relieve him? How long could a force already afflicted with scurvy and its attendant anaemia survive?

CHAPTER SIXTEEN

⟨⟨⟨⟨

Having at last received the ten thousand troops and twelve guns that had perforce sat idle at Basra while he fought his unsuccessful battle on January 21st, Aylmer wired Townshend the plan for his next attempt. He would force the Hanna defile and attack Essinn with twelve thousand troops some time in the middle of February; but he would need every possible assistance from Townshend because his transport problem remained so crippling that at any one time he had supplies for only twenty-four hours.[1]

The exchange of telegrams that ensued became progressively less realistic. The possibility of floating a bridge across the river from Kut was mooted: yet the only material available for the manufacture of such a bridge was a heap of doors commandeered just in time to prevent them from being consumed as firewood.[2] A bridge of old Arab doors would naturally be a spectacular innovation, but no one believed that it would work, and many considered that those who attempted to cross it would inevitably drown.

His engineers had also told him they could run a cable to the far bank of the Tigris, loop it over a pulley, bring it back to the Kut bank and attach it to the bow of a maheila, the Kut end of the cable being attached to the stern. The action of the river's current on the maheila would then start the cable moving, and drag the maheila to and fro. A flying bridge, they called it.[3] Townshend could not deny its feasibility, but he liked the idea so little that when a break-out was again suggested by Aylmer, he made sure that his statistics should sound no more encouraging on their fourth airing than they had on their first.[4]

The possibility of feeding and supplying Aylmer's troops from Kut on the last day of their attack was debated: but it was no easier to get food and ammunition across the river than it was to transport troops. And how, anyway, would Aylmer's troops react to saltless horse-flesh?[5]

The only telegram that had about it the smallest ring of truth was one from Townshend; inevitably, but for once with an almost touching humility, he offered some tactical advice.

12,000 rifles [he observed] seems a very small Main Force out of 20,000 ... If you have any doubt of the result, would it not be wiser to unite all your forces before advancing, particularly with regard to 13 British Division? If this effort fails, it will be a grave affair ... Please do not mind my offering suggestions ... You can imagine how anxious I am. I have had continual strain on me since I advanced from Amarah in September last. The whole of the operations have been on my shoulders, and you know how ill I was when I left Simla to conduct the advance on Kut el Amarah ... [6]

At last it was out. ' ... and you know how ill I was when I left Simla to conduct the advance on Kut el Amarah': the clue to a series of strangely irrational decisions in a man normally capable of sustained and brilliant initiative. Yet no one had noticed that he was unwell at Amarah: and those closest to him, like Boggis, had always thought him immensely strong and resilient. Townshend had calculatedly impressed his replacement officers as he read military history on the river voyage from Basra to Amarah: he had impressed his command all the way to Ctesiphon and back to Kut with an appearance of mental and physical vigour. Only now, and only to Aylmer, did he admit the truth.

However tempted Aylmer may have been to accept Townshend's advice that he delay his next attack, Lake could not permit it. The 13th Division would not reach Aylmer until March 15th at the earliest – and long before then, one fresh Turkish division would be well on its way to Essinn and a second would be following.[7]

Townshend's response to this altered situation was in keeping with his character. Ignoring the imminent arrival of two fresh enemy divisions, he adverted strictly to the arrival of the 13th British Division – which, when added to the three new brigades said to be en route from India, would constitute a second corps on the Tigris: and a second corps on the Tigris predicated a second lieutenant-general. So he wired Lake asking for his name to be put forward to Duff as the commander of this new corps. Even in the middle of a siege, his mind could be distracted by the lure of promotion. Of his thirteen thousand invested troops he had recently proclaimed that 'no general ever had a more loyal or devoted command': but, mentally at least, he had already abandoned them in his pursuit of a larger command.

Having dealt with the matter of his own promotion, he turned his mind to lesser things, suggesting that Simla should seek from the Moulvi of Delhi and the spiritual leaders of the Sikhs, Dogras and Rajputs permission for his stubborn sepoys to eat the horse-flesh without which they would all succumb to scurvy.[8] Though prone to criticize Indian troops, he appreciated that their terror of transgressing this particular ban was real. The names of those who ate horse-flesh would be betrayed to their villages by those who had not weakened. No girl would marry such a man. No family would welcome back such a son. No father would give his daughter in marriage to the son of such a man. No daughter of such a man would be acceptable in marriage to the son of any other. He must spare them that, must obtain for them a dispensation that would keep them honourably alive and well. Of his nine and a half thousand combatant troops, seven thousand were sepoys. He needed them all: and they needed meat.

As against this, however, two other arguments prevailed: and had he not been so averse to Indian troops he would either have been aware of them already, or would at least have allowed those who *were* aware to acquaint him with them. For the fact is that even to cross the 'kala pani' – the black water, as the orthodox sepoy calls the sea – was a breach of his faith.[9] Having crossed it, he could easily be persuaded to accept the customs of the faithless, provided he was ordered to do so. In such cases, Sikhs were known to be not particularly fussy about what they ate; Gurkhas were known to be not fussy at all; and only the Moslem was truly anxious. But all of them would respond to an order,[9] which Townshend could and should have given on January 21st. Instead, he had waited until scurvy forced his hand and then had merely sought the permission of his sepoys' spiritual leaders for the consumption of forbidden meat.

Just as his Indians needed meat, so Kut needed dykes and bunds against the coming floods. Whether Aylmer reached Townshend by mid-February or not, nothing could stop the floods reaching him some time in March: and he must be prepared for them. He issued orders accordingly, and his sappers began laying their bricks of bhoosa and mud.[10]

As if provoked by these preparations – or perhaps by the way Aylmer's artillery so constantly bombarded their compatriots at Hanna – the Turks retaliated with a new weapon. Taking off from the desert beyond their camp at Shamran Bend, a German plane flew over Kut and bombed the guns by the brick kilns.

After a respite of over two weeks from such personal attacks – the daily strafes being impersonal and routine – this aerial onslaught seemed positively vindictive. The fact that none of the bombs hit anyone was neither here nor there: what mattered was that the enemy had regained the initiative, and that no amount of rifle-fire seemed to affect his German pilot; and, adding insult to injury, that fragments of the bombs he dropped, which had screamed most disagreeably as they fell and exploded even more disagreeably upon impact, revealed them to be British bombs, doubtless retrieved from one of the barges lost during the retreat from Ctesiphon.[11] Hurriedly, the R.F.C. set about improvising an anti-aircraft gun.

Two days later, from the roof of their billet, they were able to send a stream of bullets skywards from two machine-guns so mounted on a vertical axis as to enable them to revolve around it and be raised or depressed according to the angle between themselves and the enemy plane. Theoretically, a splendid weapon, but, in practice, ineffectual. Drift and elevation were a matter of guess-work and a machine-gun is designed to ingest its beltful of bullets from a horizontal posture. When vertical, two men must stand beside it and feed it devotedly: but Kut's Indian and West Kent machine-gunners invariably became so excited during air raids that they watched the plane, not the belt – and within seconds their gun jammed.[12] And the thirteen-pounder mounted on a turntable improvised from one of its own wheels, though splendidly explosive, was equally impotent. Disregarding the evidence of their own eyes, however, Townshend's troops assured one another that Fritz had had so warm a reception he'd think twice before coming again. And when he did come again, they forgot that they had ever said anything so silly and installed a number of empty shell cases (which could be loudly banged) as air-raid alarms instead. In a siege, as in captivity, the reality of today must never be used in evidence against the optimist of yesterday.

On the other hand, one must remain practical: and the Failed D.S.O. in charge of one of the donkey-operated mills was confronted, after one air raid, with a very practical problem. From the middle of the path that his donkey must tread there protruded the tail of an unexploded bomb, and he had no idea how to defuse it. Nor did he intend finding out, having learnt, since those far-off days of Shaiba, to do only what he had been told to do. And he had never been told to defuse bombs. But he *had* been told to grind grain. What he now had to decide was whether he should allow the donkey to resume its circular perambula-

The Relief Force were driven mad by flies

Townshend in Kut impatiently awaits a
Relief Force that will never arrive

Starving Kut needed a daily air drop of five thousand
pounds of food. A handful of planes like this, sacks
of food tied to the under-carriage, could not provide it

Indian troops sail upstream

A Tigris hospital ship

The Turks allowed some of Kut's sick and wounded
to be exchanged for Turkish prisoners held by the British

Kut surrenders and thirteen thousand men go into captivity

British prisoners of war never ceased to be astounded
by Turkish inefficiency. Major N.V.L. Rybot caricatures
a local but typical fire brigade

tion, and risk it killing them both, or keep the donkey idle, and risk his superior's wrath.

He resolved his dilemma by telephoning Colonel Evans – less formally known as 'Mushy' – who duly arrived and demanded irritably, 'Why the hell haven't you got that bloody mill working?'

'Because there's a bloody bomb there,' retorted the Failed D.S.O., 'and I don't understand bombs and I don't want to blow myself up.'

Mushy cast a contemptuous glance first at the bomb and then at his subordinate.

'What are you worrying about? Bloody thing won't go off unless you kick the pissbegotten thing,' he pronounced. 'Start grinding!' And strode back to his Headquarters, watched all the way by a disgusted and anxious wart. *He* had understood the Colonel's warning: but had, he wondered, the donkey?[13]

Chief of Staff India cabled Basra advising, 'Please inform Townshend that he can quote the Immam Jumma Musjid Delhi as saying there is no objection to Muselmans eating horse-flesh in stress of war, providing it is [properly killed by throat-cutting]. Leading Pandit Delhi says there is no objection to Hindus eating horse-flesh. We will get you similar authority from the leading Granthis as soon as possible.'[14]

Townshend duly and hopefully quoted the Immam and the leading Pandit: but still his sepoys refused to eat horse-flesh. It was not damnation they feared – it was being unable to marry off their daughters because they had transgressed without coercion. Every day, therefore, more and more of them reported sick with scurvy.

Every day also, at dusk, the German pilot flew overhead and dropped his bombs, contemptuous of the furious fire his leisurely runs provoked – although occasionally he would humour those below him by cutting his engine and allowing his plane to spin slowly downwards, as if it were mortally stricken. But then, just as everyone began cheering, he would restart his engine and roar back to Shamran Bend, waving amiably to his disappointed foes. Once he even looped the loop.[15] There was nothing Kut could do about him, except watch for his take-off, bang its empty shell cases, take cover in its favourite hidey-holes, listen to his exploding bombs, watch him depart, track down the banshee wailing of Arab women whose homes had been demolished and look for survivors.

Nor was there anything Kut could do about the shelling it endured every morning and every night. Nothing but cower, and dig out the wounded, and watch old Flatulent Flossie's great ball of bronze come soaring overhead to land with a thud and explode when it felt like it. In her time, Flatulent Flossie had knocked down half a dozen houses: but on the whole Kut enjoyed her. At least her fragments had produced the basic material for hundreds of cigarette cases – which was more than one could say for Johnny's shells and bombs.

Townshend found the daily bombardments irksome not because of the damage they did but because of the failure of his five-inch guns adequately to retaliate. 'I will never take these useless guns anywhere I may command in the future,' he raged to his diary. 'They are only fit for the scrap heap!'[16] But he kept his dissatisfaction to himself. His five-inch guns were doing their best, and the rest of his guns had functioned superbly – particularly his 4.7s on the barges: and a general does not bare his soul to his subordinates.

So when junior officers were assigned the duty of keeping him company on his roof, he talked about everything except the war. About actresses, and Gaiety Girls, and his friend George Grossmith, who was rehearsing a new play, *Tonight's the Night*, which would shortly open in the West End:[17] about plays he had seen and plays he hoped to see: about how they wouldn't see his bum for dust, once he got out of Kut.[18]

If they had joined him early, he would invite them to participate in his morning sport of sniping Turks as they squatted by the river and attended to the demands of nature.[19] 'Very unsporting', one complained, back in his dugout Mess. 'Shooting sitting Turks.'

Others failed to see how a general who insisted upon sparing the life of a German field marshal could so lightly destroy these squatting Turkish privates: but most of Kut approved Townshend's marksmanship. So long as they had to make do with empty ammunition boxes in one of their saps, Johnny Turk need expect no sympathy from them if he was mad enough to do what he had to do into the river. For one thing, they had to drink from the river.

The muddy, orange-coloured Tigris was many things to the men of Kut. She slaked their thirst, and was therefore blessed. She succoured their enemy, and was therefore cursed. She was their link with freedom, and was therefore friendly. She was a barrier against freedom, and was therefore hostile. She was their moat, and therefore protective. She was the spy's route to the enemy, and therefore threatening. She was their own escape-route, and therefore kindly. She flooded and drowned them, and was therefore malignant.

Men looked up the Tigris, and saw the enemy: looked down it and envisaged the thousands who battled only twenty miles away to free them. Occasionally, at night, a few Indians slid into the river and floated silently downstream on inflated goat skins, hoping to reach the Turkish lines: but usually they were shot as they passed the pickets stationed at intervals round the looping bank – and those who succeeded were dressed by the Turks in a special uniform of black so that they would be identifiable as renegades. The Tigris was the snake that writhed through the empty belly of Mesopotamia: and, like all snakes, no friend of man.

She made Kut irritable, as so many things nowadays did. Like the number of casualties wounded in the head and throat. Like the absence of tobacco and the inadequacy of lime or lemon leaves as a substitute. Like the privileged status of Townshend's favourites, the Norfolks, who lived in houses and rebuked the Dorsets and West Kents and Ox and Bucks for having dirty boots and unpolished buttons when they crept into town at night, hoping to buy a chapatti – or even a woman.[20] Kut's catalogue of things that irritated was inexhaustible. Lice. The especially heavy bombardments each time one Turkish battalion relieved another. The mysterious manner in which seditious pamphlets found their way by night into every Indian redoubt.

Only the Gurkhas remained good-humoured – but the Gurkha is incorrigibly good-humoured. Even when he was posted in no-man's-land at night, with orders to intercept the brave Turk who crawled across to drop pamphlets on the wire in front of the Indians' redoubts, he remained good-humoured: and, creeping up on the pamphleteer, cut off his head with a wide boyish grin. Then returned to his line to clean his kit and sew on his buttons. Very domesticated was cheerful Johnny Gurkha – except when he had a kukri in his hand.

Thus February grew older. Bombardment in the morning, sniping during the day, planes dropping bombs at dusk, bombardment in the evening: sappers working all night, every night, desperately building bunds of tamped mud against the day of the Tigris floods, due in March; ration fatigues; men toppling backwards off the fire-step, head or throat streaming blood; cooking horse-meat over shallow trenches of oil – everything, even the starlings, blackened by the smoke; the same shorts and tunic, but much dirtier, and very threadbare; watch straps suddenly loose round wrists grown suddenly thin; the hospital packed with victims of scurvy and fever; and boils appearing wherever the sand-fly had burrowed beneath the skin, boils that left a black scar the size of a penny. Baghdad sores. Even Baghdad had become a pejorative.

Townshend did what he could to cheer his men. Not that their morale was low: but their mood had become grim. He visited the hospital and the lines near the fort – but nowhere else – and offered cigarettes from his case and said that Aylmer would soon relieve them and that their siege would go down in history along with Ladysmith and Plevna. And he passed on to them a message from the King.

'I, together with all your fellow-countrymen, continue to follow with admiration the gallant fighting of the troops under your command against great odds,' the King Emperor had cabled. 'Every possible effort is being made to support your splendid resistance.'[21]

First the Viceroy and now the King: things must be bad.

Townshend replied that 'The knowledge that we have gained the praise of our beloved sovereign and our fellow-countrymen will be our sheet anchor in this defence.'[21] But then, just in case praise should not be sheet-anchor enough, dashed off another cable suggesting to Lake that he might adopt Napoleon's expedient of manning his line of communications with convalescents from the hospitals at Amarah and Basra. He had himself, he pointed out, done precisely that – thus releasing fit men for the fighting.[21]

Although it was February 17th, Lake had still refused to send Aylmer back into battle, so it was with a Russian victory that Townshend had to content himself, General Baratoff having cabled him that the Turkish fortress of Erzroum had fallen. Back at Amarah, months ago, he had sent Baratoff a message in clear (doubtless hoping that Nixon would intercept and learn from it) saying, 'You and I are alike. We both believe in economy of force.'[22] Now he cabled again, in complimentary French: but really he needed Baratoff at the gates of Baghdad, not of Erzroum. All that the loss of Erzroum did to the Turks outside Kut was to make them more determined than ever that its garrison should never escape. About 8,000 of them stood at Hanna; about 8,000 at Essinn; about 8,000 round Kut – and 6,000 more were in the pipeline.[23]

Two days later, Aylmer wired that he could afford to wait neither for the arrival of the 13th Division nor for the floods, so he would attack at once with the forces he had. 'It seems to me,' Townshend commented gloomily of this decision, 'I had better kill a lot more horses and save my barley, for it will be a long time before we are relieved.'[23]

Nor was he unduly pessimistic. Aylmer attacked at Hanna: and the Turks stood their ground. Three times more Aylmer bombarded the Turkish lines and sent in his bayonets. Each time the Turks stood fast –

and between times dug themselves in even deeper. As pointless as trying to catch birds by putting salt on their tails, Townshend grumbled.[23] Yet there was little more Aylmer could have done. Supplies from Basra were simply not enough. Not of troops, not of shells, not of food or medicines or anything else he needed. The only things Basra had sent him in any quantity were Japanese fly-traps: and battles are not won with fly-traps.[24]

All that day, as the battle flared and died, flared and died, Townshend's men stood to arms, waiting for Aylmer's force to appear over the sand dunes, waiting to board their maheilas, be towed across the Tigris by the cable of the flying bridge and then leap ashore, run twenty-five dangerous yards, and start firing like hell until the Tigris Corps joined hands with them: but all they saw of Aylmer's force was the distant smoke and flash of its guns.

And the Turks discouraged any idea of a break-out by launching a tremendous barrage, especially on Woolpress Village, and by sniping with increased ferocity. As Melliss inspected part of his line, one of his men let out a howl of fright and rage. 'The bastard,' he shouted, pointing at the Turkish lines. '*Look* what he's done to my rifle!'

Melliss looked, and saw that a sniper had put a shot down the barrel of the proffered rifle – which had done it no good at all.

'The bastard nearly killed me,' protested the owner of the ruined rifle, outraged by such liberties in time of war.

'Give it to him, my boy,' Melliss laughed, and moved on.[25]

All that day Kut stood to, in a state of 'complete readiness'; but at nightfall stood down again – reverting, as one wit put it, to the usual state of 'partial unreadiness'.[26] Yet another relief attack had failed.

CHAPTER SEVENTEEN

A YLMER wired that he would make his next attack in early March, deploying six brigades; but Townshend must co-operate – in whatever way he thought best. Had he cast his mind back twenty years to the last occasion on which he had marched to Townshend's relief, he would have realized that Townshend considered sitting tight the best way to co-operate: but after the fearful battles of January 8th, January 21st and February 22nd, Aylmer was doubtless too preoccupied with the present to hark back to the past.

In any event, Townshend wired that he would 'endeavour' to co-operate by crossing two brigades and two batteries of field guns by means of his flying bridge as soon as he saw Aylmer's turning attack come round the Dujeilah redoubt. The crossing, he warned, would take eight hours – which would make it of little use – and it would be anyway overwhelmed, but he would make it.

Townshend's officers were no less realistic than he, but rather more good-humoured, and determinedly more optimistic – even running a sweepstake at five rupees a ticket on the date of the arrival of the first relief ship full of food. 'The field' was a ticket marked MOSUL. If Kut were not relieved, Mosul, it was generally accepted, would be where they would see out the war, as prisoners of the Turks. To the amusement of all, Melliss drew Mosul.[1]

Refusing to be defeated by the monotony of their diet, one officers' Mess contrived to vary its menu with mule's tongue in aspic,[2] which it bravely declared delicious; another Mess celebrated the birthday of one of its members with roast starlings on toast; and the gunners' Mess at last debated whether or not to eat Mrs Milligan – who promptly decamped, leaving her masters both remorseful and dejected.[3] First the Viceroy, then the King, now Mrs Milligan: things must be black indeed.

Black everywhere, it seemed, as news reached them of the slaughter at Verdun. It was difficult, in Mesopotamia, to understand the war in

France. And difficult after those press jibes about the Mesopotamian picnic, not to be resentful of those on the Western Front. But this – Verdun – was frightful. Even in Kut, pitted with shell-holes, its houses round the one-time bazaar lying in ruins, everyone so thin, it was impossible not to be shocked by Verdun. Not even an optimistic telegram from General Baratoff's Headquarters in Persia could dispel their gloom. 'I am perfectly convinced', Baratoff had wired Townshend, 'that we shall be able soon to meet and shake hands in Mesopotamia':[4] and when he visited the trenches that day Townshend had told everyone all about it. 'The Russians are making great headway', he had said: but no one had really believed it.

After all, what did it mean? Always before he had said that *Aylmer* was making great headway – that he knew Aylmer – and that Aylmer would get them out of Kut like he'd got him out of Chitral. So where was Aylmer now? And where, for that matter, were the Russians?

'I dunno,' said one, and spoke for them all. 'I haven't seen 'em!'[5]

And the sappers reported that across one four-hundred-yard stretch of the front line they could no longer see a single wooden picket in what had once been a barbed-wire fence. All of them had been removed at night for firewood. The fence was repaired and an order was issued that anyone caught stealing such pickets in future would be executed.[6] Kut was becoming despondent and desperate.

March 1st was a disagreeable day. All twenty-one of the Turkish guns bombarded Kut, and Flatulent Flossie as well. Then three planes dropped a total of fifty bombs – some of them hundred-pounders – and hit the hospital, and blew up a lot of Arab houses, killing six, wounding four, burying sixteen and provoking a fearful wailing. Then more shells, one of which landed in the mosque, killing two more Arabs and blowing a lot of others clear out of the doorway.[7] Nine of Townshend's men were killed and twenty-eight wounded.[8] It was a bad way to start a month – the fourth month of their siege.

So was Townshend's decision to issue respirators – because of the rumour that the Turks were going to use gas.[8] His men were not pleased to be given respirators. 'Fancy this place having respirators,' they said. Fancy respirators being a bit of flannel you pissed on and wrapped round your mouth and nostrils. No food: but respirators you pissed on. Typical army.[9]

No gas attack, either, as it turned out. Typical rumour.

'You know the worst thing about this place?'

'Yes – no smokes.'[10]
'The worst thing is them Turkish corpses.'[11]
'The worst thing is these scrawny cats.'[12]
'Wonder what cat tastes like?'
Nothing to talk about. Except when you'd get out, food and fags and corpses.[13]

Down-river, Aylmer's force regrouped for its next attempt. Always the next attempt. Regiments so reduced they were being combined to make one: the remnants of the Dorsets and Norfolks and some other odds and sods amalgamated to become the Norsets.[14] This next push better succeed or there'd be no one left.[15]

For the Turks it was also a trying time. They had suffered as many casualties as their enemy, and had had so much difficulty replacing them that in some trenches they were even using dogs.

'Will any officer owning bitches on heat,' demanded an ever-resourceful Basra, 'please make them available for the purpose of luring over enemy watch dogs.'[16]

Bloody Basra. Short of guns, short of shells, short of ships – and all it could think of was bitches.

Townshend's sappers struggled desperately to prefabricate the flying bridge they would fling across the river from Kut town to a point on the opposite bank where the Turks were less formidably entrenched than usual. Their efforts were watched by some sullen Arab maheila-men, of whom three, on the night of March 4th, swam the river and told the Turks what they had seen. The following morning the Turks reinforced their trenches opposite the town.

On look-out duty that night a sentry peered into the darkness, down towards Hanna.

'Look,' he exclaimed. 'Look at all those stars.'
'That's gun-fire, you silly bugger.'
'Can't hear nothing.'
'It's still gun-fire.'[17]

The next night it was the same – except that the flashes seemed more distant.

And the next night again. Only this night Kut was less concerned with Aylmer's efforts than with an exciting enterprise of its own. The sappers had manufactured a large mine which, when it was floated down-river, would blow up one of Nureddin's bridges. And launched from Woolpress Village, it duly vanished from sight. But stuck on a nearby sandbank and, exploding violently, blew a hole in the bank of the Shatt al Hai.[18] Not much help to Aylmer – whose casualties since January totalled 8,700; and to whom Basra was quite unable to ship the 12,000 reinforcements and 26 guns waiting there to help him.

Helpless in Kut, cheered only by a Reuter's report of a Turkish mutiny in Smyrna and a riot in Constantinople, Townshend's mind had reverted to his obsession for promotion: he despatched a further telegram to Lake, urging him to 'expedite the gazetting of awards' to the officers of the 6th Division whose names he had submitted.[19] There was in Kut, he advised, a belief that those invested had suffered professionally in comparison with their comrades on the Western Front.[19]

It was a foolish complaint, since junior officers on the Western Front had an expectation of life so brief that the professional prospects of those in Kut seemed brilliant in comparison: but Townshend was not speaking of junior officers – Townshend was speaking of himself, as he proved when he continued that, in his own case, several major-generals junior to himself had been promoted to lieutenant-general over his head, even though they had neither his independent command nor his responsibilities.[19]

One can only guess at Lake's reaction to this second display within a month of blatant self-interest at a moment when he and Aylmer were frantically concerned with a battle whose sole object was the relief of Kut: but Townshend's motives for wiring as he did are entirely clear.

He lived for promotion; yet, so long as he remained in Kut, the swirl of battles must soon cast up some other lieutenant-general than he: already Gorringe had been made Aylmer's Chief of Staff. To the least Machiavellian mind in Mesopotamia it was obvious that Gorringe was being groomed for command of a new corps – and Townshend's was far from the least Machiavellian mind in Mesopotamia.

While Townshend fretted about promotion, Aylmer planned the battle he dare not lose if he was to retain command. Not surprisingly, he planned to the last second and the smallest detail every move of every unit and brigade.

As if he were building a bridge, he ordained that everything must be done in its proper sequence and at the stipulated moment. When rain began to fall, he postponed his attack. 'Luck seems against us all the time,' Townshend groaned at this decision:[19] but Aylmer was no longer relying on luck. Events in Mesopotamia had long since convinced him that luck was Nureddin's prerogative. He had to bluff the

Turks into sitting idle in their trenches while he marched his entire force leftwards and unobserved across three-quarters of their front until he could sweep round and through the redoubt at Dujeilah, between the Hai on his left and the Tigris on his right.

This done, he would charge over the sand dunes towards Kut, and Townshend's men, by means of their flying bridge, would cross from Kut to the bank below Woolpress; and between the two of them they would crush Nureddin's right flank.

For which purpose, Townshend had ordered a force of Norfolks, Dorsets, Oxfords, Punjabis and Pioneers, along with Melliss's 30th Brigade, to stand to in the palm groves near the town. Supported by the bulk of his guns, they would either attempt the river crossing *or* – and the alternative revealed his defeatist attitude – assist Delamain and Hoghton to repel any Turkish attack on his first line a mile and a half to the north.[19]

Though these were not the orders of a man dedicated to the concepts of a break-out and co-operation with his would-be rescuer, Townshend had no intention of laying himself open to any subsequent charges of passivity. The onus of failure, if it came, must lie on Aylmer: to ensure which he telegraphed Lake that only 8,000 Turks manned the entire thirteen miles of trenches between Essinn, Dujeilah and the Hai – which would be completely inadequate against the force Aylmer could muster.[19]

Having thus conjured up in the minds of Lake and posterity a picture of Aylmer romping virtually unopposed through lines manned only by one Turk every eight yards, he allowed his provisional force to stand to arms: but he clearly had no intention of ordering it to cross the river to co-operate with Aylmer until Aylmer had won the battle alone.

Not that those who stood-to knew this. On the contrary, alert and expectant, they intended fighting the battle of their lives. The strongest swimmers had already been selected as the first to cross in maheilas and on makeshift rafts.[20] Getting up the high, almost vertical bank would be their worst problem: then digging in under the furious fire that would inevitably assail them from the Turkish trenches facing the river and the town.[21] But Melliss's brigade, and Colonel Evans's provisional force, were ready to risk all of this.[22] Tomorrow, sometime, Aylmer's men would appear on the crest of those sandhills: and the men of Kut were determined to make them welcome. With bayonets fixed, 150 rounds of ammunition each and haversacks packed with a day's ration of horse-meat, they stood to and waited. Kut had never been so silent, nor so electric with excitement.

Even Townshend was excited. To the officer assigned to keep him company on his roof, he gleefully announced, 'Well, Burroughs, I've just sent a cable to George Grossmith. He's in *Tonight's the Night* at the Gaiety, you know. So I've said, 'Maybe Tonight's the Night, but Tomorrow's the Day.'[23] He seemed pleased with his play on words: and Burroughs was content to let him chatter on about his theatrical friends. Anything was better than the 'shop' the Regulars talked: and Townshend was amusing anyway.[23]

Aylmer's force, twenty thousand strong, with its guns and carts and inevitable impedimenta, set out from various bivouacs at nine that night. By 5.45 the following morning they must be ready to attack at their starting-point fourteen miles away, at the far end of the enemy line.

Fourteen miles across the Turkish front in slightly less than nine hours, when the accepted rate of progress for an army marching at night was one mile an hour: but nine hours was the most Aylmer could allow them if surprise were to be achieved against the redoubt at Dujeilah.

The force marched in silence, aware that it must be *exactly* in position at precisely the right time. Especially General Kemball's double column, whose task it was, having separated into two columns, to take and outflank the redoubt. So long as this column was in position on time, the redoubt would be lightly manned and vulnerable.

It would be lightly manned because the Turks had no reason to suspect so wide a sweep by so large a force against it; and because it lacked water, in consequence of which, most of the troops who guarded it by day withdrew four miles to the river every night. If Kemball's columns could get into position before daybreak, before the Turks returned from the river, Dujeilah must fall to them.

Kemball's columns therefore marched with fanatical care. Constant compass bearings were taken to keep it on course. The revolutions of a bicycle wheel were painstakingly counted, to measure the distance covered. A cross check was made with a parade ground pace-stick. And just before sunrise the column halted, only fifteen hundred yards from the redoubt.

So considerable a feat had not been achieved without distress. At each halt men had fallen asleep and only been aroused with the utmost difficulty; a supporting division had lost itself in the darkness and delayed the entire advance; but, just before sun up, Kemball's columns were more or less in position. Not as close as they should have been, but at least only fifteen hundred yards from the redoubt, as compared with four miles for the Turks who must return to man it.

Had Kemball attacked at once, Dujeilah would have fallen. But Kemball's orders were to attack Dujeilah only after it had been heavily bombarded – and his guns were nowhere near their appointed positions. Telephoning Aylmer's Headquarters, he asked what he should do. 'Stick to the programme,' came the reply.

So he stuck to the programme. And the sun stuck to its programme. And the Turks saw his two columns standing indecisive in the dawn light. And Khalil Pasha, their new commander, started rushing up reinforcements. Not just those troops bivouacking on the river bank, but, as the British bombardment began and continued, three thousand more from across the river as well. And when, at 10 a.m., Kemball's first column finally advanced, it ran into a murderous, massed and determined fire from a fully manned redoubt – and was slaughtered.

Even so, his second column, on his right, could have broken through the weaker lines flanking the redoubt, and attacked it from the rear: but Aylmer and his Chief of Staff, Gorringe, insisted that it also stick to its programme, so it remained where it was – only a battery of the Royal Horse Artillery venturing to the top of a mound about a mile across the Hai from Woolpress Village.

'Hurrah,' shouted Burroughs, 'we're going to be relieved.'

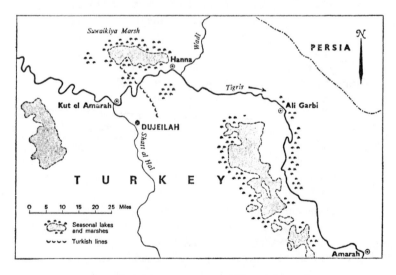

Turkish-held territory round Kut el Amarah

But the artillery advanced no further: Gorringe had said, 'Stick to the programme,' and one disobeyed Gorringe – whatever the outcome – at one's peril.

'But a fife and drum band could get through there,' an orderly wailed, and Burroughs had to agree; but no fife and drum band appeared; and the artillery disappeared. Well ... the battle was only young. They'd be back.[23]

From his roof-top in Kut, Townshend had watched and listened since before dawn – and been disconcerted to hear no gun-fire till 7.10. At 8.30 he was even more disconcerted to hear silence. Which meant that so far the guns had probably only been registering. Eight-thirty and broad daylight and a lull in the firing – it did not bode well.[24]

But then it started again, and continued till 10 a.m. A message came from Aylmer asking what he was doing by way of co-operation: but Townshend was doing what he had always intended doing – nothing positive. Slamming his glasses back into their case he had bluntly declared, 'I am not satisfied that they've taken Dujeilah redoubt. Let's have some tea!'[25] Kemball's fatal lack of initiative was not going to be made good by any diversionary action from Kut.

As Aylmer reported stubborn resistance, Townshend heard the crackle of heavy rifle-fire, which continued till 4 in the afternoon: but nowhere on that sand-dune crest did Kemball's column appear.

At 5, Aylmer reported that his attempts to break through had failed, but that he would try again.[26]

At 5.30, the sound of a fresh bombardment was heard.

At 5.45, a heliograph was seen urgently flickering.[27] Calling for Townshend's sortie? Probably, thought those who saw its winking light. But no one could read its message through the dust and haze, so Townshend ignored it.

Again Aylmer's exhausted men attacked: and again were beaten back, all along the line. And still, from every roof-top, men in Kut watched the flash of gun-fire; in the lines and the palm groves, stood to and listened; huddled close to the river, prepared to fling across two flying bridges and storm the opposite bank.

At 8.30, another bombardment. Flashes everywhere: each side blasting the other.

At 11, Aylmer wired, 'Enemy lost heavily today and it is doubtful whether they will be able to maintain their position. Will let you know tomorrow proposed plan'.[28] Then, bluffing desperately, 'which will include English Division which has now arrived.'[29]

Perfectly aware that the 13th Division was still uselessly marooned at Basra, Townshend realized that not only was Aylmer bluffing, but that the attack which, for want of supplies, had to succeed in one day had not done so. 'It looks', he muttered, 'like another failure.'[30]

And everyone in Kut was saying the same thing. 'If Charlie'd been out there, they'd have got through to us,' they told one another.[31] 'They should've flown him out right at the beginning. He'd have got us out months ago.'[32]

And almost certainly he would have done. Noted for the thoroughness of his reconnaissances, he would have reacted very differently at 7.10 that morning had Kemball asked *him* could he attack an almost empty redoubt without waiting for a preparatory bombardment. At Ctesiphon, when Delamain had found time running out if he was to achieve surprise, Townshend had agreed without hesitation to an immediate advance, even though his planned 'paralysis' of the opposite flank by Hoghton's column had not materialized. But Townshend was *not* out there by Dujeilah: for which he, as much as Nixon, whose ineptitude he had exploited, was to blame.

The following morning, Aylmer's promised message – written late at night – was dropped into Kut by plane, Aylmer being afraid that the Turks might monitor and decode a telegram. 'Today's operations', it read, 'terminated in a gallant but unsuccessful attempt to storm Dujeilah Redoubt. Unless the enemy evacuates the Essinn position tonight, we shall be obliged to withdraw to our previous position at Wadi. Casualties today have been very heavy.'

Townshend's reply was not sympathetic, a single glance from his roof-top having revealed to him the unpalatable fact that Khalil Pasha had not withdrawn from Essinn overnight. He rebuked Aylmer for having attacked Dujeilah with less than four, and preferably six, brigades; gave it as his opinion that Aylmer's aerial reconnaissances had provided false intelligence which had foolishly been believed; and advised that his force could now survive only until April 7th, and not, as he had previously suggested, till April 15th.

My troops are ready to live on short rations [he asserted] but they will become weak, and desertion among the Indians will increase. I hope that the next effort will be with such maximum force as will make an absolute certainty of success. This suspense is hard to bear; it breaks down the health and depresses. To all men and all people, uncertainty is intolerable. Twice now I have promised the men that relief was at hand. I ought to be relieved before April 7 ... [33]

It was peculiarly ironic that Townshend – who had kept Aylmer in a state of constant uncertainty for more than three months by giving him no less than six different deadlines before which he must be relieved – now rebuked Aylmer for leaving the 6th Division in a state of uncertainty. He ignored the fact that Aylmer had attacked when and with the force he did only at Lake's insistence, which was unsympathetic of him. But his complaint of poor reconnaissance and an inadequate maximum force was entirely justifiable: he had frequently warned against both.

Nevertheless, his message was ungenerous to a force that had just suffered 3,476 casualties on his behalf – and been obliged to suffer 7,000 casualties in previous battles prematurely precipitated by his own utterly unrealistic declarations as to how long his division could survive.

Already despairing, Townshend was further depressed to receive from Khalil Pasha a letter which proved that the Turks had no intention of withdrawing from any of their positions. Writing in French, Khalil was courteous but uncompromising.

Your Excellency:

The English forces which came to relieve you were compelled to retreat after giving battle at Felahiyeh and suffering 7,000 casualties. After this retreat, General Aylmer, who was a month and a half making his preparations, yesterday, when he thought he was strong enough, resumed the offensive, as you saw. But he was again compelled to retreat, with 4,000 casualties, and I am left with adequate forces.

For your part, you have heroically fulfilled your military duty. From henceforth, there is no likelihood that you will be relieved. According to your deserters, I believe that you are without food and that diseases are prevalent among your troops. You are free to continue your resistance at Kut, or to surrender to my forces, which are growing larger and larger.

Receive, General, the assurances of our highest consideration.

HALIL
Commanding Turkish Forces in Irak
Governor of Baghdad.[33]

Townshend promptly declined Khalil's invitation to surrender, saying that he believed there was every chance of relief, and asking if there was any truth in the Reuter's reports of Turkish mutinies and riots and the fall of Erzroum: but then, as if to make amends for his jibe, he thanked Khalil for his courtesy, and declared himself glad to find that the Turk was always a good soldier and gentleman.[33]

Khalil's letter may not have induced a surrender, but it had at least struck several most responsive chords in Townshend's unusually orientated mind. Khalil's assurances 'of our highest consideration' seem to have conjured up fresh visions of Junot besieged by the gallant British, and of the commandant of Belfort besieged by the gallant Prussians. Each had extracted from a gallant enemy the chivalrous concession that, upon surrendering his fortress, he and his command could pass unscathed through the lines investing him and return home: and Townshend found comfort in the precedents they afforded him.

So he wired Lake suggesting that Aylmer negotiate with Khalil for his own release upon similar terms. Such negotiations, conducted by a general known to be preparing yet another attack, must, Townshend considered, carry such weight that Khalil would be disposed to agree.[33]

In case Aylmer should still hope for some kind of break-out from Kut, however, and therefore be disinclined to negotiate, he warned, 'If I could get out with 300 men only, it would be great luck.'[33] With six weeks of the siege still to run, he had despaired of relief, and seemed to consider that his only hope was to be allowed by his enemy to leave Kut and Mesopotamia, cease his battles with the Turks, return to India, be posted to France and obtain promotion there. It was not defeat he feared, but the end of his career.

For his troops, March 10th was a day of almost querulous debate. Why had the guns stopped firing? What had happened? What was *going* to happen?[34] Why hadn't the order been given to break out when their own people had been so close?

'We'd have bloody well cleared 'em,' they insisted.[35]

'It's a funny blooming thing, isn't it? According to what Charlie says, we shouldn't bloody well still be here.'[36]

'Harry,' promised a Glaswegian radio operator to the colleague on duty with him, 'when we get out of this place, I'll take you to a pub in Sauchiehall Street and you'll sit in the one corner, and I'll sit in the other, each of us wi' a bottle, and we'll drink all night.'

'You sit with your bottle,' Harry retorted ungraciously, 'I don't drink.'[37]

'It's a bloody funny thing,' a supply officer at Woolpress Village commented as *Sumana* brought across that night's supply of mule carcases, 'but these animals apparently have no entrails! Where are their livers and hearts?'[38]

No one felt gracious on March 10th: and no one knew what had happened. But the Glaswegian had a gift for decoding messages as he tapped them out, and Harry suspected that he would not have issued so reckless an invitation had he not recently dispatched a wire of considerable grimness. Not that it was any use asking him: he never told you.

'What'd that last one from Charlie say?'

'Ah dinna ken.'[39]

But the Scot need not have been so secretive because, almost immediately, Townshend issued a communiqué – or, as his troops preferred to call it, a c'munick. Prefacing it with Aylmer's telegrams of defeat and failure, he said:

I know you will be deeply disappointed to hear this news. We have now stood a three months' siege in a manner which has called upon you the praise of our beloved King and our fellow countrymen in England, Ireland, Scotland and India, and all this too after your brilliant battles of Kut-el-Amara and Ctesiphon, and your retirement to Kut, all of which feats of arms are now famous.

Since 5th December you have passed three months of cruel uncertainty, and to all men and to all people uncertainty is intolerable.

As I say, on top of all this comes the second failure to relieve us. I ask you to give a little sympathy to me, who have commanded you in these battles referred to; and who, having come to the Division as a stranger, now love my command with a depth of feeling I have never known in my life before.

When I mention myself, I would couple the names of the Generals under me, whose names are distinguished in the Army as leaders of men.

I am speaking to you as I did before, straight from the heart and, as I say, I ask your sympathy for my feelings, having promised you relief on certain dates on the promise of those ordered to relieve us. Not their fault, no doubt – do not think that I blame them! They are giving their lives freely, and deserve our gratitude and admiration. I want you to help me again as before. I have asked General Aylmer for the next attempt, which must be made before the end of this month, to bring such numbers as will break down all resistance and leave no doubt of the issue. Large reinforcements are reaching him, including the 13th English Division of 17,000 men, the leading brigade of which must have reached Wadi by now, i.e., General Aylmer's Headquarters. In order then to hold out, I am killing a large number of horses, so as to reduce the quantity of grain eaten every day, and I have had to reduce your ration. It is necessary to do this in order to keep our flag flying. I am determined to hold out and I know you are with me in this heart and soul.[40]

The communiqué was not a success. 'Give a little sympathy to *him*?' a gunner sergeant muttered. 'Well – if General Melliss had said that, I'd have dropped dead from shock.'[41]

'Here we go again,' grumbled the West Kents,[42] who had come to equate c'municks with bad news and bullshit. And seasoned Regular officers were observed to have tears in their eyes: not because Kut seemed doomed, but because Townshend's order that a large number of horses be killed meant that the lives of their chargers were at last being threatened.

Woolpress Village's supply officer, on the other hand, was delighted that night to receive from *Sumana* not only his quota of carcases but ninety pounds of livers and hearts as well – delighted but infuriated: his suspicion that people in Kut were keeping the tit-bits for themselves had been confirmed.[43] But when it came to tit-bits, there was little Woolpress's garrison or Kut's rankers could do: they went to the favoured few.

'Sorry,' Delamain told his brigade as he toured their trenches. 'I've got to stop you four ounces of bread.'[44] No one complained; no one wanted to complain; but no one any longer felt certain that one day they would all be relieved.

'Roll on when they march in here,' they wrote in their diaries with their stubs of indelible pencil:[45] but somehow the words no longer looked real. And that night the voice of Johnny Turk sounded less amusing as he shouted to the Indians, 'Why you stay there and no eat? You come to us and eat plenty.'[46]

CHAPTER EIGHTEEN

FOR everyone the following few days were deeply depressing. An auction was held for the few possessions of an officer killed by a sniper. For his toothpaste, someone paid seven and sixpence; for a pound of biscuits, six shillings, for a penny bar of chocolate, half a crown, for a bar of soap, ten shillings, for a hundred cigarettes, ten pounds.[1] One man's carefully hoarded treasures – he dead and buried in the palm grove and his friends bidding for the right to dispossess him.

A few, though, still had cigars to smoke, or chickens that laid eggs worth five shillings each. One officer followed a brother-officer through miles of trenches, waiting to pounce on the last, discarded, bespittled butt of his cigar. Only to be out-pounced by a second officer, whom he would happily have killed.[1]

A colonel, realizing that his cigar was the object of a similar pursuit, turned pityingly and said, 'Sorry – I promised it to the adjutant.'[1] Life had become very primitive: yet no one any longer noticed it.

A thirsty private took off his boots, lowered one on the end of the tied-together laces into the Tigris, drew it up over his parapet and drank. 'Very tasty and all,'[2] he declared: and no one thought anything of it.

Another patiently cooked his few ounces of mule over the black-smoking oil-fire and then chewed it reflectively. 'Tastes rotten,' he pronounced: and no one even laughed.[3]

A corporal had a pair of shears for clipping the coats of mules: he cut men's hair with them – and it seemed perfectly reasonable.

For two days there had been heavy rain and already the flat desert around them glistened with water and their trenches were awash: it was as if the days of hope after January 21st had never existed.

'When are they going to get us out, sir?' Townshend's troops asked him when he visited the hospital.

'I don't know,' he admitted. 'I've made you so many promises ...

All I know is that if I had as many men and guns as *they've* got down-stream, I'd be in the bloody Caucasus by now.'[4]

'I can realize to the full,' Lake wired Townshend, 'the disappoint-ment which both you and your command must feel at our recent failure to relieve you. Rest assured, however, that we shall not abandon the effort and that for the next attempt the maximum force will be employed.'[5]

Townshend published the message as a communiqué, and everyone said, 'Here we go again.' He also ordered that horses and mules be killed at the rate of twenty-five a day, hoping thereby to survive with-out slaughtering a hundred of his finest chargers: and a hundred of his regular officers breathed again.

Then came March 12th: for Townshend the worst day of his life, because it brought a letter from Aylmer which said that he was being 'relieved of the command of Tigris Corps, in favour of Major General Gorringe'. With immense generosity, Aylmer added that he was grieved to have failed Townshend, but that his task had been harder than people realized.[5]

Not a hint of reproach for battles forced upon him too early by survival dates capriciously calculated. Just a generous apology and the final words, 'Goodbye and God bless you all, and may you be more fortunate than myself.'[5]

For Townshend the letter implied a personal calamity: which be-came real that same day when he learnt that Gorringe, now the com-mander of Aylmer's corps, had been promoted to lieutenant-general.

'But he's junior to me,' he protested to one of his staff officers. 'It's all wrong.'[6] And later, on his roof, in the company of a young subal-tern, he burst into tears and wept on his shrinking subordinate's shoulder.[7]

That night, as if to symbolize his despair, the Tigris rose six inches, and a million frogs, appearing from nowhere, croaked derisively.[8] The floods would soon be upon him: and through them Gorringe would never force his way.

On March 13th the siege was 100 days old and Kut's garrison began to wonder whether it might not break Ladysmith's record of 120 days. Some, perversely, even hoped that they would. Others, officers and therefore more realistic, began to wager that the relief would fail – for which one of them at least was reprimanded on the grounds that wagers like that were calculated to cause despondency and alarm among the troops.[9] He consoled himself with an entry in his diary that grass was beginning to grow on the dark wet earth around him, and that the distant Persian mountains looked very serene. One needed the serenity of distant mountains and the promise of green grass when one's seniors had become so fretful as to take umbrage at a perfectly harmless bet.

At least Woolpress Village was spared that: senior officers never came near it. Even General Hamilton, half of whose brigade was there, had only visited it once. And Townshend had avoided it entirely. Which suited Woolpress. Life was very pleasant, away from the brass. And morale was excellent, although there had been some resentment that Townshend had not thought fit to allow his Village troops at least to break out when Kemball was so close at Dujeilah. No river for them to cross – they were across it already. On the wrong side of the Hai, of course: but on the right side of the Tigris. Might have made all the difference.[10] But they'd not been allowed to try. Just as they were never allowed to try and shoot down the German planes that daily came in low above them to bomb Kut. Townshend was emphatic about that – though God alone knew why.[11]

And God alone knew why he sent out all those messages to actors and actresses in London. If he really did send them, that was. Might be no truth in it. Still ... if he did, surely there were more important things? Like messages from his troops?[11]

'Living not good on barley-coffee and bread,' Townshend wrote on one of the bits of paper Boggis had to carry down to the radio operators for transmission. Not that Boggis read it. But the operator did. No need to decode: it was in clear, addressed to that inimitable comic, 'Bunch' Keyes.[12] The operator tapped it out, and it was duly acknowledged from downstream.

Later that night, receiving messages from downstream, the same operator recognized the 'touch' of a close friend. Their official business done, he sent his friend a memo from Kut. 'Living not good on barley-coffee and bread,' he tapped cheerfully, in clear.

In the Mediterranean, an alert radio operator on a Royal Navy battleship picked up this distant signal, wrote it down and handed it to his superior. Some time later, the Fleet transmitted a message to Basra, who relayed it to Kut: whose operator was court-martialled and sentenced to seven years' imprisonment (to be served after the relief) for the almost treasonable crime of repeating verbatim to a service friend forty miles away the message Townshend had transmitted to a theatrical friend in London.[12] Doubtless he was thus savagely sentenced because messages like that might cause despondency and alarm among the troops of Tigris Corps!

Who could not have been rendered more despondent and alarmed than they were by anything less than a message advising that Germany had won the war. Every day the river rose perceptibly; the snows on the Caucasus were melting and soon the Tigris would flood; eventually the plain lands between them and Kut would become a lake. They'd never get through.[13] Least of all under Gorringe. Least of all against Turks elated by their recent triumphs on the harsh brown hills of Gallipoli.

Basra advised that Lake, though personally opposed to the idea of any negotiations with Khalil, had forwarded Townshend's proposal to the Commander-in-Chief in India and to the War Office in London. It was Lake's view that such negotiations would become pointless if Kut were to be relieved at the next attempt: and futile if the next attempt were to fail. In either event, Khalil would publish the fact that a British force had begged his mercy, and this would have an ill effect on Britain's prestige throughout the world.[14]

Townshend retorted only that successful negotiations would obviate any *need* for a further attempt to relieve Kut. Blind to the fact that he was besieged not by nineteenth-century Britons but by twentieth-century Turks, he apparently saw himself as a second Junot, and saw in Lake's regard for British prestige no validity at all.

Whilst Simla and London contemplated his curious proposal, the Tigris overflowed and both sides had once again to evacuate their first line of trenches. More convinced than ever, then, that he would not be relieved, Townshend awaited Simla's decision.

'Please tell Townshend,' Duff cabled Lake, 'not to make terms with Turks until he hears from me. Acknowledge.'[14]

Losing no time, Townshend acknowledged, 'Kindly inform Chief India that there was never the slightest intention of any negotiations with the Turks unless there was any doubt in the mind of the Army Commander about the possibility of relieving me; and not only that, but unless he and Government approved.'[14] A remarkable assertion, bearing in mind his insistence to Lake that immediate negotiations, if successful, would obviate the need for further attempts at relief. And 'unless there was any doubt in the mind of Army Commander about the possibility of relieving me' was a typical Townshend qualification.

It somehow deflected the opprobrium his suggestion had brought upon him back upon the very men who had originally disapproved it.

Like a nagging wife, Townshend had always to have the last word, and never allowed the point of the argument to inhibit him. 'The idea in my mind,' he elaborated, 'was to come away from Kut without any loss of prestige, if Kut has to fall, and to save Government humiliation.'[15] Yet one of his main arguments against attempting to capture Baghdad, four months previously, had been that to be obliged to come away from it, having once taken it, would mean Government humiliation and a loss of prestige too damaging even to contemplate.

'Very possibly the Turks would not give such terms, and then I would not take any others, but would stand till we were overpowered or no food left' – no mention now of fighting house by house and to the last bullet – 'when I should endeavour to cut my way out with those who volunteer to come with me.'[15] Thus blustering and shifting his ground, Townshend strove to undo the damage to his reputation implicit in Duff's cable to Lake: and, having started, was unable to stop.

'If Tigris rises before you can relieve me,' he telegraphed Gorringe, the new commander of Tigris Corps, 'which I doubt, I suppose you have considered the Sheik Saad to Kut road by right bank?'[15] When he had wanted to negotiate, he had been convinced that the floods would make relief impossible; now that he was forbidden to negotiate, he doubted the floods would come before he was relieved. Arguing with Townshend was like wrestling with an octopus: and to ensure that he won whatever argument it was he was now arguing, he also suggested that Gorringe remember Wolfe's tactics at Quebec[15] – which implied, since Quebec had been an amphibious operation, that he expected to be relieved *during* the floods.

Very sensibly Gorringe chose to discontinue a debate that had degenerated into a sort of berserk rondo and replied simply, 'We are all confident that next time we shall win through and so enable you to bring to a successful issue your gallant defence of Kut.'[16]

General Staff India, however, had tired of Basra's policy of deferring always to Townshend's omniscience and gallantry. 'It is essential,' they cabled Lake, 'both you and Duff know definitely to what date General Townshend can hold out. He has changed his estimation three times' – six, in fact: but Simla had been advised of only half of them – 'and the whole conduct for the relief is materially affected by the question of date'.[16]

Asked only for a date, Townshend instantly responded with recriminations and excuses. He had originally been given to understand, he protested, that he would be relieved by January 1st.[17] This was untrue (Nixon's best offer having been relief 'within two months'), but to Townshend it probably seemed the truth because he had told Basra, on December 3rd, that he could feed his British troops for only a month. Ipso facto, they must be relieved by January 1st. The fact that he had already fed them for three and a half months was beside the point. The point with Townshend was never facts: it was what he chose, at any given moment, to say – and he had said that he must be relieved within a month.

Not having been so relieved, he continued, he had been obliged to *buy* grain,[17] and, according to the amount bought, had made his second estimate. But sifting and cleaning had so reduced the amount available that he had had to make a third estimate. *Now* the date to which he could 'hang out' was definitely April 15th.[17]

For a week, wriggling like an outraged virus under the microscope of officialdom, he had defeated its every attempt at identifying the malady that afflicted Kut: now diagnosis was abandoned and the decision taken to risk yet another operation.

For Gorringe the planning of such an operation was no easier than it had been for Aylmer. To be sure of success, he needed 90,000 troops, fully supplied: available to him were 30,000 whose daily requirements could be only two-thirds fulfilled. Of these 30,000, one-third was made up by the 13th Division, whose sixty-per-cent losses at Gallipoli had been made good with raw recruits; and the remaining two-thirds were the 7th and 3rd Divisions, who had jointly suffered some 12,000 casualties in previous relief attempts – and had no reason to believe that they would fare better, or be more successful, in future attempts.

They knew too much to be confident. They knew Gorringe and his bull-headed tactics of frontal attacks. They knew that their artillery was inadequate to prepare such frontal attacks and their machine-guns too few to give them bite. They knew that the Turks had been heavily reinforced and now were dug in strongly not only at Hanna, but also at Fellahiyeh, three miles behind Hanna, then at Sannaiyat, three miles behind Fellahiyeh, and finally at Essinn a few miles behind Sannaiyat. Against four such positions their 30,000 and Gorringe's Boer War tactics were hardly likely to prevail.

The only general who could, in fact, have prevailed, they believed, was Townshend – who was locked up in Kut by the Turks. The only way to prevail under Gorringe was to reinforce with the thousands of troops down-river – who were locked up in Basra by lack of shipping. And the one slim chance they had with Gorringe, and without re-inforcements, was up-to-date intelligence from their aeroplanes – which were grounded by floods and gales. It was all singularly depressing.

But Kut refused to be depressed. When the mills' grinding-stones split in half, the sappers ingeniously shrank iron tyres around them and bound them together again.[18]

When one of the engines that ran one of the mills developed a crack in its cylinder-head, thus savagely reducing the day's usual out-put of 7,200 pounds of ground barley, the sappers made an oxy-acetylene lamp out of an old rifle barrel and welded it together again.[18]

As fast as flood waters threatened, the sappers, using hired Arab labour, erected more bunds of puddled mud, repaired breaches in parapets, and strengthened points that seemed threatened. It was at last, if only for the moment, comparatively safe to work above ground, because the Turks' sniping posts had also been flooded: but exhaustion made the work very slow.

A bomb was dropped in the middle of the bazaar hospital and Townshend sent a brusque letter of complaint, under a flag of truce, to Khalil.[18]

The gunner officers papered the walls of their dugout Mess with pictures from Japanese matchboxes, and kept a pet insect, a gerry-mundler, in a glass-topped box. Occasionally they put a scorpion in with the gerrymundler, and made wagers on their ensuing duel: but they quickly tired of this as a sport because the gerrymundler always bit off the scorpion's tail and ate its disarmed opponent at its leisure. It got very fat: until someone left the glass top off its box and it crawled out and fell on to the floor where someone else trod on it: then the gunner officers no longer had a pet. Nor a mascot, since Mrs Milligan had never returned. The more they thought about that, the surer they were that their servants had eaten her.[19]

Some Sikhs approached their medical officer. 'Sahib,' their spokes-man said, 'we need sāg.'

'Well, yes,' agreed the nonplussed medico, who knew perfectly well that their diet lacked green stuff, 'but what can we do about it?'

'There is sāg growing,' the Sikhs explained.

'Growing? Where?'

'The grass, Sahib. Everywhere, since the rains.'

The medical officer went to his colonel and asked could his men leave their trenches to collect grass. 'No,' said the colonel. 'They'd be sniped.'

'The Turks are a long way off now, sir; and if these men don't get something green soon, half the regiment will go down with scurvy.'

'No,' said the colonel.[20]

Clothing had become indescribably ragged and dirty.

'If only I could change my shirt,' someone snarled.

'Only thing *you* can change is your lice,' he was told.[21] Prophetically so, because that night the lice vanished, as mysteriously as they had arrived, and fleas took their place.

The Turkish bombardments grew daily more vicious and the German aviators daily more persistent. In spite of this, to the amazement of all concerned, a brigadier visited Woolpress Village just as the first plane of the day made its customary low approach – watched, as usual, by those whom Townshend had forbidden to fire on it.

But not by the brigadier, who dived into an Arab hut and stayed there until the raid was over. Emerging then, he seemed in no way ashamed: and, when a second plane appeared, dived shamelessly back into the hut and refused to leave it until assured that a third was nowhere in sight.

Later he was conducted round the Village's various breastworks, and shown the ingenuity with which every loop-hole had been blocked and camouflaged against snipers.

'Shall I uncover it, sir?' one of the men suggested, not without malice. 'So you can have a look at the Turkish trenches?'

'No, no,' the brigadier insisted – and left Woolpress as soon as it was dark, never to return again.[22]

He was not missed. His men had no further use for him and his officers would happily have shot him. An idiot brigadier they could have forgiven. Idiot brigadiers they were even used to. But a craven brigadier – he should be shot.[22]

Like that dog in no-man's-land. Someone had shot it. And eaten it. And died. Rumour had it that it had lived so long on putrid corpses its flesh had become contaminated. Probably true. Though not of all dogs. Another, belonging to a very senior officer, had been shot by the Forty Thieves, and one of the provosts had caught them cooking it.

'You know private fires are forbidden,' the military policeman rasped. If it was fence pickets they were burning he would have to report it, and then one or all of them would be shot.

'Can't eat it raw, can we?'

'Eat what?'

'Old Shitbag's dog.'

Abruptly the private fire became permissible: but could the military policeman – after what had happened to those who had eaten Fido from no-man's-land – allow them to eat another dog? It was too big a decision to be taken alone: so he carried the cooking pot to the nearest medical officer and asked his opinion.

'Dog, is it?' the medical officer mused. 'Whose dog?' The military policeman told him. 'Should be very nourishing,' declared the medical officer. 'Take it back and tell them I said so.'[23]

But *he* could afford to be charitable. That day, Gorringe's planes had dropped a load of saccharine tablets, and, since there was too little to issue it all round, it had been distributed only among the officers. Compared with dog, saccharine – sweet, lovely saccharine – was a gourmet's delight.[24]

The news from the Relief Force was that all was quiet down-river – which was more than could be said of Kut. In one day the Turks had fired thirteen hundred shells, killing and wounding sixteen, flattening a large number of houses, knocking bits off the mosque and wrecking one of the big 4.7 guns down on the barges. Townshend did not much care for Gorringe's inactivity, and appeared also to distrust his reports of enemy dispositions.

'I can hardly believe,' he telegraphed, 'that the Turkish Commander could be such a fool as to group one body at Hanna, one at [Fellahiyeh] and another at [Sannaiyat], all three groupings being much too distant for effective mutual support against a blow by your concentrated mass.'[25] Claiming to disbelieve Khalil's reported groupings was as good a way as any of bringing up the subject of a concentrated mass: and Townshend believed that Gorringe was going to fail just as resoundingly as Aylmer had unless he concentrated.[25]

Concentration of a mass in March 1916, however, was no simpler a procedure than it had been in June 1915. 'I doubt', Lake at last cabled his obtuse Commander-in-Chief in Simla, 'whether the paralysing effect which the inadequacy and late supply of river craft has had on operations up the Tigris is fully realized by the General Staff at home.'[26]

He doubted with good cause. In November 1915 Nixon had gone to some pains to delude Chamberlain on that very subject: and later still the Viceroy, in his cables to Whitehall, had suppressed Basra's specific reference to it. Admittedly a despairing British Government had assumed control of all decisions relating to the war in Mesopotamia in February, but India still executed those decisions, and it was still from and through India that Whitehall had to obtain its reports on the needs of the Tigris Corps. Which was like relying upon Ananias for the truth, or Jezebel for chastity.

Admittedly, also, Home Government had achieved a slight improvement in Mesopotamia's Medical Service: but its river transport remained as inadequate as ever. Gorringe, for example, needed 500 tons of supplies a day: assuming that none of the river craft had broken down, been disabled or got stuck on a sandbank, Basra's daily shipments upstream would amount to only 260 tons. And it was madness to assume that none of the river craft, on any particular day, would be broken down, disabled or grounded.[26]

More river steamers were on their way, of course. And docking arrangements were being improved. And reinforcements were coming out by the thousands. But Townshend had to be relieved within three weeks: and none of the extra ships, supplies or troops essential to that operation were going to reach Gorringe in time. It was all very well for Townshend to claim that Khalil's groupings were such that they would be vulnerable to the attack of a concentrated mass; the Turks had long since proved their ability to vanish overnight from a threatened position and to reappear next day in a strong one: and the Turks were going to have on their side floods which would so funnel and bog down any mass concentrated against them that it would be rendered more vulnerable than ever they would be in any of their four separate positions.

Nor was the news from Kut of the kind that gave any hope of a co-operative break-out. The daily toll of scurvy, beriberi and dysentery was rising; flood waters had become an even greater menace than the Turk, and the garrison spent its days pumping out trenches, and its night sleeping sodden in slime.

Even so – waterlogged, hungry, shelled, bombed, flea-ridden, thin, ailing and constantly sniped at – Townshend's troops remained disciplined and cheerful. It was March 22nd and, as the last of the day's thirteen hundred shells exploded in their midst, a gunner had half his face blown off. 'Give 'em hell, sir,' he said to the officer kneeling beside him; and died.[27] Those were days when officers would sooner be killed than fail to show themselves, and when a soldier's last words were predictably patriotic.

Again the Sikhs asked for permission to eat Kut's new, green grass, and their medical officer, worried by the smell of approaching death that clung to so many of them, sought out their commanding officer yet again, telling him of the smell, giving him the latest figures of cases of scurvy and beriberi. Convinced at last, the colonel nodded his assent.[28]

For some weeks thereafter Kut's monotonous diet was varied with what it chose to describe as spinach. Not that this change was due solely to the Sikhs. Everywhere, men had suddenly, simultaneously, developed an appetite for grass.[29] But care had to be taken. Some grasses were edible, others not. The Indians knew which were which, remembering the types their cattle had eaten back in their villages, and every night crawled out to pluck sackfuls of the right grasses. The British crawled out and plucked sackfuls of what they hoped were the right grasses. But whatever they plucked they cooked; into a greenish, blackish, gall-bitter mess, known to all as spinach. To General Hoghton, particularly, it was a welcome nutritional supplement. From the very beginning he had been as incapable of stomaching horse-meat as the most obdurate of his Indians: at last he could eat something more than bread.

Not, of course, that it made an enjoyable meal: no one any longer enjoyed anything he ate. Even Townshend had run out of delicacies by now. No more pig's cheek, no more plum pudding, no more Vichy or whisky-soda: just chlorinated water from the Tigris, barley-coffee, a pound of horse-flesh, eight ounces of bread, and spinach every day.

Never – outside of other sieges, other captivities – did men think more about food. Every meal they had ever eaten, they lovingly recalled. Every meal they hoped to eat, they planned minutely. Something sweet was what they craved most. Like *pêche Melba* or *zabaglione*, or *crêpes suzettes* with hot chocolate sauce poured over them, dreamed the officers. Like ice cream with custard and lashings of sugar, dreamed their men. They had forgotten their families, forgotten the smoothness of clean sheets, the bliss of hot water, the pleasure of silence, the luxury of light: all that they remembered, and craved, and discussed interminably, was food, the apotheosis of which was something, anything, sweet.

Lacking which, they had had to concentrate on essentials; in

February, a month ago, they had converted what had once been the Arabs' communal latrine into a garden, and planted in it vegetable seeds dropped by their loyal aircraft. Not enough vegetables would grow to feed their thirteen thousand, but at least, Townshend had decided, such as did grow would help those who languished in hospital – particularly the scurvy and beriberi cases, of whom there were almost a thousand.

Though generous and medically advisable, it had not been an easy decision for Townshend to take. Of course his wounded and sick needed extra greens; but so did his combat troops. And every day more of his combat troops reported sick with enteritis caused by eating the wrong kind of spinach. Who then mattered most? His sick and wounded: or the men who defended them? Ought his decision to be humane: or practical?[30] Humane, he had concluded: and had issued his order accordingly.

Yet obviously he had found no peace of mind because of it. His staff officers and subaltern companions on the roof of his Head-quarters saw clearly that he was concerned. And who, gazing out at the brown lake that spread for miles on all sides, only the Turkish positions protruding above them, could blame him?[31]

It was said that he mistrusted Gorringe:[32] and few blamed him for that either.[33] Gorringe had advised that the marshes round Hanna were spreading by the day, thus threatening the *Turks* in their trenches.[34] Didn't he realize that Tigris Corps would have to advance through the spreading marshes just as fast as the Turks withdrew? And if he did, did he really think it could be done?

As they looked down-river, those in Kut realized that the right bank was worse flooded than the left: but the only relief attempt so far to have come anywhere near success had been that wide sweep out to Dujeilah from the right bank. Townshend wanted Gorringe to try it again, but it seemed unlikely he would be able to. This meant he would have to attack by the other bank – through Hanna, through Sannaiyat, through Fellahiyeh, through the left Turkish flank at Essinn. The left flank with its two marshes, one in the middle, one at the end: bigger marshes now, though, than when Townshend had pushed between and around the farthest of them. There could be no pushing between now, and to push around, Gorringe's troops would have to march half way to Persia! No – one couldn't blame Townshend for looking concerned. Boggis even sought to comfort him.

Not with words (orderlies do not comfort generals with words) but with food. 'Have you got any kidneys?' he asked the butchers in the slaughter lines.

'*Horse* kidneys?'

'It'll make a change for Charlie!'

'But they're full of ammonia.'

'I'll try 'em all the same,' Boggis insisted: and, cooking the horse kidneys, offered them to Townshend – who was unable to eat them. Like everyone else, he now took his evening meal an hour later, to avoid the company of fleas at his dining-table, and was all the hungrier for the delay; but he simply could not eat the kidneys of horses.

'Sorry, Boggis.'

'I'm sorry, sir. Thought it'd make a change.'[35]

Kut's surviving horses and mules had to make the best of a change in their diet, which now consisted of chopped-up date-palm trunks, flavoured occasionally with the cooked, minced flesh of some of their fellow animals.

'Cannibals, we're making 'em,' those in the horse lines muttered, sickened by the sight of it. Although it was better, in a way, than watching them eat palm trunk on its own; they ate that like dogs, gnawing at it, holding it still with a hoof like a paw.[36]

'Poor buggers is starving.'

'*I'm* starving!'

'Least you aren't eating the hair off your mate's head.' To which, as each animal wrenched off and devoured the mane and tail of the other, there seemed to be no answer.[36]

'When I get home, sir,' an orderly promised his officer, 'I'm going to take your horse to every pub in town. Horses is noble animals and we've made 'em fly from tree to tree just looking for something to eat. When I get home, I'm going to give your horse as much to drink as she can swallow.'[36] In 1916, even the working classes felt sentimental about horses: and Kut felt almost as strongly about its cannibalized, semi-canine horses as it did about anything sweet.

About everything else, though, it was phlegmatic. A shell exploded in a sap, killing all who stood in it, and men near by congratulated themselves on having just left it.[37] A corporal on the firing-step had the top of his head blown off by a sniper's dum-dum, and the man beside him was shocked only by the mess of it.[38] A sentry standing sound asleep at the parapet was court-martialled, and his comrades were glad it was he, not they, who had been caught – because nowadays everyone fell asleep, standing, sitting or lying, after only the shortest spells of duty.[39] Feelings had become blunted, reactions slow. Unless someone was caught stealing meat from the ration carts on their long, stampeding trek through shell-fire and darkness from the town to the lines; then feelings ran high and the reaction was swift and vengeful. Two years' imprisonment, and not a day too much.[40]

Another week had passed, March was almost gone and the lethargy of chronic hunger had become apparent. Only a fortnight ago, each of those who made bricks had been turning out 250 a day: now they did well to make 100.[41] Only four days ago a regiment of Turkish cavalry had appeared nine thousand yards away. A good target. A target the gunners would once have obliterated: but four days ago they had hit it with their first round and then – as they slowly reloaded, as the Turks' horses stampeded – had allowed it to escape.[42]

Still ... at least, Kut had held out longer than Ladysmith. Plevna was the next to beat. A hundred and forty-three days to beat. Roll on the Relief Force.

Meantime, also, the daily routine. Servants washing their officers' shirts. Butchers slaughtering horses and mules. Fifteen hundred in hospital. Mills grinding. Bhistis bringing up water, thin legs thinner than ever. Shells screaming and blasting. Flood water seeping. German planes bombing. Fleas swarming. Rations arriving. Dixies simmering. Black smoke. Sentries bolt upright on the fire-step, trying not to fall asleep. Weather hotter. Stench of corpses. Talk food. Think sweets. Sleep in trenches and dugouts. Do nothing – except the daily routine.

The Turks were busy, though: putting up another bridge across the Hai. According to rumours, Charlie was going to send *Sumana* down one night to ram it.[42] So long as the Turks didn't sink her first, which they were doing their damndest to do, dragging a field gun to a new position each night and siting it in one hollow or another, about a mile away, where it couldn't be seen. Everyone watched out for the top of its wheels each morning, though, or for the top of its officer's head, as he lined it up. Just a few inches of wheel or a glimpse of a head. Tell the boys at the brick kilns and see if they could hit the gun. Meantime Johnny Turk has tied a lanyard to his firing handle, pissed off into another ditch and given it a yank. *Wham* at *Sumana*. *Bang bang bang* at Johnny. Marvellous that they can go on missing one another for so long. Been going on for weeks: but good old *Sumana*'s still there. And so, somewhere else, tomorrow, will be that bloody Turkish gun.[43]

'I suppose you have got your sixty-pounders by now?' Townshend

P.O. OF WATCH	
READ BY	
REPORTED BY	
PASSED BY	
LOGGED BY	M.T
SYSTEM	
DATE	2/4/16
TIME	9-15 AM

FROM **HQ. Kut.**

TO **H.Q. B.E.F**

To Sir Wilfred Peek of HQ Personal. Write Alice tell her the hole I am in here through the fault of others, When I think, tell her how all conduct of operations was put on to me & not one word of praise & no thanks for all I have done throughout this campaign. I have only one desire that to leave the Army as soon as peace comes. I am Ill and weak but a little better today Tell her I have some six or seven hundred pounds pay at ? Which I will instruct them to send her. If I have to go into captivity, It will kill me

Charles Townshend Apl 8

One of Townshend's last personal messages from Kut

Baghdad welcomes Kut's British prisoners of war
with organized demonstrations of hatred

Many months too late, a British force drives the
Turks back towards Baghdad and recaptures Kut

wired Gorringe and Lake. 'Is there anything more to come up? I feel certain you understand the great difference every day makes to us in this state of well nigh intolerable suspense ...' Even Basra must have realized that this was no cry of wolf. 'Today I am given the news that we have four days' less food than the figures [that my staff] gave me [indicated]. I suppose this is theft, although we have a guard of convalescents on the food magazine. I hope you will let me know, as soon as you have decided, which bank you will come by, and not let me be ignorant to the last minute ...'[44]

It was the cry of a man in despair: despairing any longer either of the goodwill of those outside or of the integrity of those within. Yet he should have known better than to leave the guarding of his food to convalescents.

'Jock ... went into a small room on the right and after a little while came out and passed us handfuls of sweet biscuits. He said that the man in charge sold the biscuits to officers at fourpence a pound. They were in a large barrel. When the artillery corporal on guard slept with his head on the step, they just stepped over him and helped themselves.'[45] Convalescents tire even more swiftly than those who are fit, and Kut's fit sentries fell sound asleep standing upright. No man who is starving stays hungry when all he need do is step over a sleeping head. And sweet biscuits to Townshend's troops would have been as honey to ants. It was not a guard of convalescents he needed, but a guard of fasting saints, closely watched by two archangels, who would watch one another, all of them to be watched by the Roman Catholic padré, while the Church of England padré sat on top of the biscuit barrel – bound hand and foot. Food would still have been stolen, by all of them, but not in such quantities that Townshend, on the last day of March, would have found himself short of four days' rations for thirteen thousand men.

CHAPTER NINETEEN

❧

O N MARCH 31st Gorringe wired Townshend:

> Preparations for your relief are well forward and you may be
> assured that I shall not be a day later than is absolutely neces-
> sary. According to Baghdad records ... the last flood was the
> maximum we are likely to have. Another of possibly equal height
> may be expected 10th to 15th next month. The floods threaten
> and are causing much trouble ... to the Turks ... their food
> supplies very short and casualties ... considerable.[1]

No mention of the bank by which he would advance; nothing new;
just a comforter for Townshend and his thousands of anxious, hungry
mouths. Nothing, it seemed, would ever go right again. Last night the
Turks had at last succeeded in damaging *Sumana*, shooting away her
stop valve; this morning the stench of Turkish corpses was so vile
that it had been decided to rake in their putrefied remnants and bury
them in the ditch in front of the fortress walls; this afternoon Aylmer's
planes had at last dropped a sackful of long-awaited mail – straight into
the middle of the Tigris; and now rain was deluging down and the
desert night flared with lightning.[2]

To compensate a little for the loss of mail, Townshend allowed
three hundred telegrams to be sent downstream for transmission to
England – all from officers – and just to stress that privates had no
rights, April Fool's day began with a second deluge and a hailstorm
so fierce that unprotected troops in the trenches felt battered and
alarmed.[2]

The following morning Townshend was handed a telegram from
Basra asking him what plans he had for ferrying his men across the
river should the need arise for a break-out in co-operation with
Gorringe's attack. How *could* he ferry maheila-loads of troops across
the Tigris without *Sumana* to tow them?[3] Especially when no one took

any notice of his plea for a new stop valve to be dropped to him from one of the aircraft. And what was the use of him planning to ferry troops across the Tigris when Gorringe refused to tell him whether he proposed attacking along the Dujeilah bank or the one opposite?[3] Irritably, he reminded Basra that he could no longer use *Sumana* and had no idea of the direction of Gorringe's attack.

> Nor do I think that Gorringe, with 29,000 men and 108 guns, which strength will easily give him a Maximum Force of 24,000 men and ample gunfire, will require assistance from me to win through a division and a half, or possibly two weak divisions, holding a front of fourteen miles, which extent should require three army corps to hold ... Had the Relief Force arrived in January, we could have co-operated with vigour: but now it is very difficult.[3]

Everything was very difficult. Even paying his troops was difficult. Today he was allowing those who wanted it to draw a few rupees, and then his Treasury would be empty. And even this – his men believed – had only been possible because the Crown and Anchor boys had come to an agreement with Treasury, whereby they had handed over all their winnings in return for promissory notes drawn on His Majesty's War Office and repayable after the relief – or the end of the war.[4]

Solemnly each man presented his pay book; solemnly the officer concerned wrote, 'April 2nd, 1916 ... 1 rupee ... Kut el Amarah,' and added his signature; solemnly each man took his few shillings' worth of dirty paper, saluted and departed. In four months they had been paid three times, on average £1 a head. And they had only drawn that to buy Arab tobacco at forty-eight rupees a pound.

Because the locals would no longer accept paper money, Townshend asked Basra to drop him enough gold to pay his force properly. They were clamouring for something to smoke, he said, and if they went into captivity – as was not unlikely – they should at least do so with some money in their pockets.[5]

Gorringe advised that he would attack on April 5th: but declined again to reveal along which bank. Townshend wished him luck. Gorringe replied that he would attack at dawn: and added – perhaps undertanding Townshend's anguish and disappointment – 'You are the rock on which I hope to split the Turkish forces'[5] ... a compliment too high-flown to have any basis in reality.

At 5.20 next morning the first flashes of gun-fire were seen by those who stood on the roofs of Kut. Gorringe's guns had been well placed and the Turkish wire in front of their first line was being chewed to pieces. Aware, however, that it was the bombardment of their first line itself that had alerted the Turk to Aylmer's intended infantry attack, and thereby destroyed any element of surprise, Gorringe did not now propose advancing his barrage. Instead, he would send his new division – the Gallipoli Division – straight in with the bayonet.

At 6 a.m. Kut noticed that the gun-flashes downstream had flickered and died. Downstream the troops of the 13th Division clambered out of trenches sapped to within 150 yards of the Turkish line and, bayonets forward, charged silently through the grey light. Charged all the way to the first enemy trench without a shot fired at them, leapt into it – and read a derisive sign, printed in French. 'Adieu,' it said, 'till the next battle.'[6]

Exultantly then they charged the second line: Johnny Turk could have his next battle. The 13th Division knew that everyone was watching it, waiting for it to prove itself after all its talk of Gallipoli: now let them see how a real division fought.[6] But the second line was also empty. As was the third. All of Hanna's lines, in fact, were empty. Johnny Turk had withdrawn to strengthen Fellahiyeh.

At 5.35 Townshend received the news that Gorringe had taken the enemy's first five lines, and passed it on to all those in his command, who were so overjoyed that a subaltern suggested some organized cheering. His colonel having agreed, the subaltern made his way from the command dugout to the trench and said, 'Pass the word, right and left, "When the adjutant blows a whistle every man is to cheer." I give you five minutes to prepare.'

To the left and right the order was passed. 'When the adjutant blows his whistle every man will cheer,' the Hampshires were told. 'Hala gir,' the Gurkhas were told. 'Hala gir,' as soon as the adjutant blows his whistle.

Five minutes later the subaltern returned, to supervise the cheering: and found all his Gurkhas smiling gleefully and dressed to kill, only awaiting the adjutant's whistle before they hurled themselves over their parapet to attack the Turks, a mile away across no-man's-land.

'But what are you doing?' he demanded.

'It is the order, sahib. When the whistle blows, we hamla gar.'

'Hala gir,' he corrected; and their smiles vanished.

They cheered loudly enough in the event: but they would much rather have attacked.[7]

From 10 a.m. onwards, like ants disturbed in their nest, Turks could be seen rushing this way and that on all sides of Kut. Full of optimism, gunners opened up on the enemy bridge over the Shatt al Hai, and on the ferry down the Tigris at Magasis, both eleven thousand yards away: but so ineffectually that they soon gave it up.

And down-river the 13th Division gave up its attack, having experienced at last some of Khalil's cunning. Advancing optimistically from Hanna to Fellahiyeh, across open ground, they had walked straight into his enfilading machine-gun-fire and been forced to dig in until nightfall.

The delay was fatal, because it gave the Turk time to prepare for their next attack – and darkness into which to vanish, once he had inflicted as much damage as possible. When eventually the 13th Division took possession of Fellahiyeh's abandoned lines, they were exhausted and had suffered 1,868 casualties.[8] Tomorrow, though, the 7th Division would take over for the attack on Sannaiyat: and after that the 13th Division would return to the fray, to force Essinn and relieve Kut.

Early next morning Kut heard the din of a violent bombardment, as violent as the one it had endured itself the day before: but received no word from Gorringe. Townshend wired him, asking for news, but was left to guess what might be happening at Sannaiyat. Anxiously he watched from his roof, peering into the sun, looking for gun-fire; but only a mirage appeared before him, through which nothing could be observed, or believed if it was observed. Unable to contain himself, Townshend wired Basra.

'Can you give me any news of Gorringe?' he begged. 'I have not heard from him since 8.30 yesterday morning ... No news is, I suppose, good news, but it makes my people uneasy. I do not want to bother Gorringe in the midst of work, but he should not keep me like this without news.'

Advised by his observers that the Turks were now sending troops across the Tigris by the Magasis ferry, he seized upon the excuse to contact Gorringe, telling him that enemy reinforcements were crossing to oppose him and that he was shelling them and that he would continue to do so, at a slow rate, all night 'if desired ... I have not heard from you now for thirty-four hours,'[9] he concluded reproachfully: but still Gorringe did not answer. His was a cruel silence, but Townshend was now his subordinate, and Gorringe was notoriously officious to subordinates.

To add to Townshend's distress, reports came in that the Tigris had risen thirty-eight and a half inches in the last twenty-four hours. Once again every man in Kut was fighting the flood waters: but it was the threat to Gorringe's troops, not to his own, that concerned him. With increasing anxiety he waited for any news at all from Sannaiyat.

Only to be told that atmospherics had so interfered with radio reception that it was no longer possible to receive a single dot or dash. Nothing ever went right. Not any more. Attempting to console him, Chaplain Spooner, upon whom one could always depend for an apt text, told him that the collect for the week of that fourth Sunday in Lent was most propitious. 'Grant, we beseech Thee, Almighty God,' Spooner recited, 'that we, who for our evil deeds do worthily deserve to be punished, by the comfort of Thy grace may mercifully be *relieved*.'[9] And for the first time that day Townshend smiled.[10]

But he would not have done had he known that the 7th Division, having advanced only three miles during the night, had been discovered at daylight half a mile from the Turkish lines at Sannaiyat, and had been halted entirely 150 yards farther on. Examining the battlefield from a safe distance through binoculars, one of Gorringe's staff officers had demanded, 'What's that line of khaki? Why haven't they dug themselves in?' 'Because they're dead,'[11] he was told. The 7th Division had suffered twelve hundred casualties and had never once been close to victory.

At last, at 10 p.m., Gorringe wired Townshend; but only to tell him that he did not require slow fire on the Magasis ferry for the moment – which was just as well since Townshend was perfectly aware that his guns were useless at a range of eleven thousand yards.

The rest of the night passed in uneasy silence – until 6.45 a.m. when the distant thunder of a fresh cannonade was heard. It lasted till 7.30. Later a message came from Gorringe advising that he was entrenched four hundred yards from the enemy positions at Sunnaiyat, but it gave no details, and Townshend spent the morning protesting thereat both to Gorringe and to Lake, neither of whom paid him much attention. Gorringe merely said he had pushed forward to a point from which he hoped to capture Sannaiyat, in spite of the hampering floods; Basra merely advised that he could award seventy assorted decorations to his troops, but none to his officers – and no promotions.[12] India had remained unmoved by his plea that he was being unfairly passed over.

He was not for the moment to become a lieutenant-general; and it seemed unlikely that he ever would.

'It is essential', Townshend wired Gorringe, 'you tell me more, for every military reason': and for once Lake supported him, advising Gorringe, 'Army Commander knows that you must realize how essential it is for you to keep Townshend fully informed of your progress.'

The difficulty was, of course, that there *was* no progress: there was simply a series of strong Turkish positions flanked by the Tigris on their right and by swamps on their left, so that no turning movement was possible, and a morass of mud and a moat of waist-deep barbed wire to impede what had therefore to be a series of frontal attacks, all of which had failed. Had it not been for Townshend's food situation, in fact, Gorringe would have abandoned the field: as it was, he had decided to resume his attack the following day.

Unfortunately the weather decided otherwise. A strong north-west wind blew the marsh waters knee-deep over much of the ground his troops would have to cross. The attack was postponed till April 9th: but 7th Division, in daylight, did edge closer to the Turks, to reduce the distance it must cover in its final charge.

That night 7th and 13th Divisions lay wet and frozen till 4.20 in the morning: then, rising stiff and numb, stumbled in three waves towards the Turkish lines. For several hundred yards they met no opposition, and the leading wave forgot its discomfort: but their advance had not gone undetected. When still four hundred yards from the Turks, one flare after another soared into the darkness – red, green and white – and bathed them in light.

Exposed and unprotected, they charged. But the second and third waves behind them faltered – lacking the exhilaration of the lead, still numb with cold, still befuddled with exhaustion, still with five or six hundred yards to go across mud vividly illuminated and spurting and spouting with bullets and shells.

Hearing the rumble and thump and stutter of battle, Townshend wired Basra for news of its progress: but Gorringe was too busy manoeuvring two divisions in an already doomed operation to advise even Basra of his progress.

In fact, having severely mauled the first wave, the Turks had withdrawn to their second line to fight off the expected onslaught of the second: but the second was already falling back – and the third following it.

At once the Turks sent out their bombers to blast the first wave as it gasped for breath in the forward enemy trench: and, after a bitter mêlée, drove the British out of their trench and back across the mud. For a loss of 1,807 casualties, no ground at all had been won.[13]

'We again failed to win through,' Gorringe wired Townshend, explaining that he was digging in and consolidating; that he was everywhere – even on the other side of the river, where the 3rd Division were keeping the enemy occupied – hampered by floods; and that all enemy positions were strongly held.[14]

It was the words 'digging in' that filled Townshend with despair.[14] He and all his officers had seen the Turks' flares during the night. First the red, that meant 'enemy advancing'; then the double red, that meant 'reinforcements wanted'; then the greens that meant 'ammunition required'.[15] Reading these signals, they had hoped for a limited break-through. 'Digging in' was what they least expected, what Townshend least wished to hear. When it came to digging in, no one in the world could match the Turk. By the time Gorringe had consolidated sufficiently to renew the attack, he knew that the Turks would have turned their trenches into a series of impregnable redoubts.

And digging in meant time lost, which his rations did not permit: not unless he cut them again. But dare he cut them? Already men were fainting after quite minor exertions. Already his brick-makers were down to a quota of ten bricks a day, compared with their original 250. On the other hand, either they ate less, fainted more and gave Gorringe a few days' grace, or they surrendered on April 15th. He cut the bread ration from eight ounces to five, and advised Basra he could hold out till April 21st.[16]

Perceptibly shaken, his men accepted the reduced ration with a wry 'Here we go again'. All that really worried them was that their bread now came in ten-ounce loaves to be shared between two men. How to cut it so that each man got exactly five ounces? The solution was beautiful in its simplicity. One man cut the loaf, the second took whichever portion seemed larger. Men thought long before they wielded their knives, and cut with the precision and concentration of neuro-surgeons as they split the loaves in two: men stared hard and took their time before they decided which portion would be theirs.[17]

That day was almost as bad for Gorringe's men in the desert. It was blisteringly hot; flood water lapped every step; and sandflies, mosquitoes and flies drove everyone – not least the horses – almost mad. The air, it seemed, seethed with flies. Breathe in – flies up your nostrils. Gasp – flies down your throat. Peer ahead – flies in your eyes. Every second another billion flies seemed to have hatched out in the hot, steaming mud. Every second another stinging sandfly bite. Every second another pin-prick mosquito bite – then the red, itching, maddening lump. Every day more work on the communication trenches, which now ran miles, it seemed, back from the front line. No one ever appeared above ground-level. It was like Flanders. It was as static and filthy as Kut, reinforcements constantly plodding their subterranean way up to the line from a tented camp downstream that had offered only half rations and a Salvation Army marquee to comfort them.[18] And out there, in front, across six hundred yards of squelching mud, the Turk, indifferent to it all, stolidly waiting, secure in his ever-deepening trenches, moated by river and marsh, quagmire and barbed wire.[19]

Gorringe and Lake discussed the position and agreed – since it would be futile to attack again on this side of the river – that the 3rd Division must try to break through on the other side. Not that it looked much better there: but, to relieve Townshend, it must be attempted.[19]

If the worst came to the worst, Townshend now wired Lake, he would take six or seven hundred of his fittest men and run the gauntlet in *Sumana*, whose stop valve had at last been replaced. He would leave the rest to surrender. Meantime, would it not be best if Gorringe were at once to begin negotiations with Khalil for a Junot-like exchange? Kut and its guns for Townshend and his troops? Would it not be best for Gorringe to negotiate now, while he, Townshend, still had food, could still endure? There was, he said, not the slightest chance of a break-out: on three sides the Tigris locked him in, and on the fourth lay a lake, beneath whose surface lurked Turkish trenches, death traps eleven feet deep, six feet wide, quite invisible, impossible to detect until his men plunged into them and, in their weakness and exhaustion, drowned.[20]

'It's a bloody muddle,' his wireless operators told one another as they tapped out his interminable messages. 'He's good at making speeches, of course: but it's still a bloody muddle.'[21]

As if to confirm their words, Townshend issued another communiqué, compounded as usual of fact, exhortation and attempted ingratiation.

The result of the attack of the Relief Force on the Turks entrenched in the Sannaiyat position is that the Relief Force has not yet won its way through, but is entrenched close up to the Turks

... General Gorringe wired me last night that he was consolidating his position as close to the enemy's trenches as he can get, with the intention of attacking again. He had had some difficulty with the flood, which he had remedied.

I have no other details. However, you will see that I must not run any risk over the date calculated to which our rations would last – namely 15th April. As you will understand well, digging means delay, though General Gorringe does not say so.

I am compelled therefore to appeal to you all to make a determined effort to eke out our scanty means so that I can hold out for certain till our comrades arrive, and I know I shall not appeal to you in vain.

I have then to reduce our rations to five ounces of meal for all ranks, British and Indian.

In this way I can hold out till 21st April, if it becomes necessary, and it is my duty to take all precautions in my power.

I am very sorry I can no longer favour the Indian soldiers in the matter of meal, but there is no possibility of doing so now. It must be remembered that there is plenty of horse-flesh, which they have been authorised by their religious leaders to eat, and I have to recall with sorrow that by not having taken advantage of this wise and just dispensation, they have weakened my power to resist by one month.

In my communiqué to you of 26th January I told you that our duty stood out plain and simple; it was to stand here and hold up the Turkish advance on the Tigris, working heart and soul together. I expressed the hope that we would make this a defence to be remembered in history as a glorious one, and I asked you in this connection to remember the defence of Plevna, which was longer than even that of Ladysmith.

Well! You have nobly carried out your mission; you have nobly answered the trust and appeal I made to you. The whole British Empire, let me tell you, is ringing now with our defence of Kut.

You will all be proud to say one day: 'I was one of the garrison at Kut!' As for Plevna and Ladysmith, we have outlasted them also. Whatever happens now we have all done our duty. As I said in my report of the defence of this place, which has now been telegraphed to Head Quarters – I said that it was not possible in despatches to mention everyone, but I could safely say that every individual in this force has done his duty to his King and Country. I was absolutely calm and confident, as I told you on 26th January, of the ultimate result; and I am confident now. I ask you all, comrades of all ranks, British and Indian, to help me now in this food question in the manner I have mentioned.[22]

In one way this latest effusion proved a success; in another a failure. It persuaded no less than 5,135 Indians to start eating the meat they had so stubbornly rejected for months: and it caused the first open discussion about Townshend's shortcomings as a commander.

'I told you, didn't I? Here we go again!'

'Not *another* bloody c'munick!'

'Only thing I'll be proud of is getting *out* of Kut.' So said his troops.

His officers were more explicit. Since 5,135 Indians had begun to eat meat the instant they were told it was that or almost nothing *and* an adverse report to India Government, quite clearly they should have been told (rather than asked) to eat it at the very beginning rather than the bitter end of the siege. Melliss, in fact, had long ago suggested that Townshend *order* them to eat it; but he had refused. And Delamain had several times pointed out that his successive communiqués, by invariably promising an early release – even though each new communiqué meant an old promise broken – had encouraged the sepoy to hold out on his full ration of grain rather than compromise his soul and his village status by eating horse. Delamain had suggested from the very beginning that Townshend should warn all his troops that the siege might well be a long one: but Townshend had always refused, saying that such a warning would be bad for morale[23] – with the result that not only had sepoys delayed eating horse and mule, but rankers of all descriptions had refrained from making themselves as relatively comfortable in dugouts as their officers had been.

Many officers also debated the wisdom of issuing frequent communiqués whose frank contents would instantly become known to the Arabs in Kut, not a few of whom were spying for the Turks. In each one he had mentioned the date before which the next relief attempt would be made: in each one, therefore, he had alerted the enemy to the period in which an attack was most likely to occur. Which may have been good for Kut's morale, but can hardly have helped the morale of those who sought to relieve it.

Others, whose knowledge of military history was not inconsiderable, pointed out that Townshend's constant references to Plevna were hardly encouraging to any but himself. Certainly Osman Pasha had deserved the honour and glory accorded him for his stand: but his garrison had been put to death! Had these erudite officers also known that their General was about to send Khalil a cordial message, bringing to his attention the fact that Kut had defied those investing it as long as Plevna had, they would have been even less happy. Though Khalil was to reply with equal cordiality, he certainly knew what had happened to Plevna's Turkish garrison. To remind him of it was hardly the way to ensure the safety of Kut's British garrison should it be obliged to surrender. Townshend was a very strange man.

Collating all Townshend's communiqués and messages from Kut, it can legitimately be deduced that after February 7th (when he had first asked Nixon to recommend his promotion to lieutenant-general) Townshend was always prepared to abandon his beloved command in the interests of either his own release or his own advancement. On March 5th he had again requested promotion. On April 9th, for the second time, he had suggested that he should attempt to escape from Kut and leave his division to its fate. Three times he had suggested negotiations to exchange Kut and its guns for the release of himself and his men, though he must have known that only he would be allowed to go. Twice he had sent ingratiating letters to the enemy commander in the field: and once he had insisted that no attempt be made on the life of an enemy field marshal.

But, for all its drama – a battle lost, surrender mooted, rations cut and incessant dispatches – April 10th was not yet over. In India, Lord Hardinge handed over his vice-regal powers to Lord Chelmsford: in Basra, General Lake decided to prolong Kut's expectation of life by dropping food from the air: at Sannaiyat, Gorringe decided that the 3rd Division should attack on April 12th: and at Bombay, an inspection of the Supply Base proved it to be as chaotic as the base at Basra.

At Basra, Lake was now having discussions with Admiral Weymiss. Why not, he suggested, strip down *Julnar*, armour her as strongly as possible, load her with several hundred tons of food, call for volunteers and ask them to run the gauntlet to Kut?[24] Because, Weymiss answered, the project was hopeless. It had been when Lake first suggested it: it still was. So hopeless that he was not inclined to ask either officers or ratings to volunteer for it.[24]

Lake persisted, however, pointing out that his six aeroplanes and three sea-planes were inadequate to drop a minimal requirement of five thousand pounds of food daily, and that without extra food Kut would probably starve before Gorringe could fight his way through to it. And finally Weymiss agreed that, if Gorringe's attack on April 12th failed, he would ask his men to attempt the impossible.[24]

At the same time, Townshend was talking long and earnestly with Delamain, and both were agreeing that relief seemed unlikely. 'Our people,' Townshend remarked grimly, 'are always a month late in their plans and a division short in their numbers: and the fundamental principles of Economy of Force and the Mass have often been either disregarded or violated.'[25] He had forgotten entirely that his own attack on Kut had taken a month longer to formulate and execute than Aylmer's; that it was he who had forced Aylmer to attack early and with inadequate forces; and that he, unlike both Aylmer and Gorringe, had never had to cope with the deadliest enemy of all – floods. He was a very self-centred man.

The day ended with a telegram from Basra suggesting that Townshend could prolong his resistance by evicting from Kut its six thousand non-combatant locals! What it had refused to permit at a feasible moment, it favoured now, when the encircling Turks made it unthinkable. To his credit, Townshend dismissed the suggestion, advising Basra that, however correct such an eviction might seem in theory, in practice it was abhorrent, because the Turks were determined that no one should leave Kut until it starved. Khalil had sent him a message promising that any Arabs attempting to escape would be shot; and the volleys of musketry that had greeted the nightly landings by Arab swimmers on the opposite bank had proved that Khalil meant what he said. 'Allah, Allah,' the idiot Arabs chanted with joy as soon as they reached the far bank – and promptly Khalil's troops mowed them down. If he were now to pack two hundred Arabs at a time on to maheilas, and send them drifting down the Tigris, the slaughter would be fearful and the horror of it would ring throughout Mesopotamia.[25]

As to the suggestion that *Julnar* should attempt to bring him supplies, he was equally forthright. The ship would be raked with fire from departure to arrival, he warned. His *Sumana* had survived only because she was walled with maheilas, which themselves had been buttressed with sandbags and mud:[25] and it was not likely that *Julnar* would make much headway against the raging Tigris if she had to carry with her a fortress of buttressed maheilas.

For a man in such desperate straits as he, it was a selfless answer.

Unless, of course, he had become so dedicated to the idea of a negotiated surrender that he was not interested in prolonging his investment – which is possible. As also it is possible that he was reluctant to sacrifice sailors on a suicidal mission to succour the Army. He had a handful of sailors in Kut, and they had fought magnificently, constantly manning his 4.7 guns on barges, contemptuous of the Turks' unceasing efforts to shell them into oblivion. Like everyone else, Townshend was grateful to them. He may well have wished to spare their friends downstream. He could be a warm-hearted man.

That night the rains started again, making Gorringe's attack next day seem most unlikely. And the Turks shot dozens of Arabs as they attempted to float on inflated goat skins to some point on the river bank whence they could vanish into the dark, drenched desert. And General Hoghton – big, genial, brave and unlucky to the last – died of a surfeit of spinach. Somehow, he had eaten the wrong kind of sāg. Shocked by his death, which was totally unexpected, Townshend ordered that the eating of grass must cease. For the rest of the siege, Kut's rations would be less adequate than ever.

CHAPTER TWENTY

M EN had only to look at one another now to know that they were
starving. Thighs were too lean, fingers too bony, teeth too big,
eyes too deep. 'If Kut falls because of starvation,' Townshend warned,
'its captors will have not a biscuit to spare for our men, and the drama
which will then be enacted is better not spoken of.'[1]

From Basra the officer commanding its handful of aircraft replied
that, so long as each plane flew three missions a day, five thousand
pounds of food could be dropped daily into Kut. For its garrison,
camp-followers and Arabs this would yield a daily ration of six ounces.
Begging only that such supplies as were dropped should be double
bagged, to resist impact, Townshend waited unconfidently for his
manna from heaven.

Not content simply to wait and see, his men looked for fresh sources
of nourishment. The Supply and Transport Mess, remembering the
tinned but rancid butter it had so contemptuously discarded in
January, retrieved and ate it. It tasted like engine oil.[2]

Some gunners, remembering the tins of jam they had buried in
December, whilst flinging up earth-works in front of their gun-pits,
greedily disinterred them.[3]

In every trench men examined the parapets they had so hurriedly
constructed at the beginning of the siege, looking for bullet-punctured
tins of rotten potato meal. And finding them, ate them. Did not share
their mouldy, reeking meal with the whole company, only between
those who had found it. Usually it killed a few, but the others ate on,
because everyone had 'starvation dysentery' and who was to say it was
not that that had killed them?[4]

An officer found a bag of rotting oats, once the food of horses.
He and his Mess having decided to make a porridge out of it, they sat
down to de-husk it: but after an hour had de-husked enough for only
one man: so they gave their sepoys half the bag on condition that they

de-husked the other half. Then they made and ate their porridge. It tasted like black glue.[5]

Bones in the meat ration were no longer discarded, but gnawed, dog-like, until they vanished. In the horse lines, maneless, tailless animals had eaten their halters, their tethering posts and their saddle cloths.[6] Officers' chargers had at last gone on to the menu. Everyone – literally everyone – envied and hated the butchers who slaughtered and the drivers who tended the animals waiting for slaughter, because *they* could eat livers and hearts. Not the hearts of officers' chargers, of course – they were the prerogative of whomever had ridden the hapless horse involved – but of all the others.

More eagerly than ever officers shot starlings in Kut and sparrows in Woolpress Village: until some idiot peppered a general's rump and bird-shooting was promptly banned.[7] Less fussily than ever men pursued and took captive anything that moved, and ate it. Hedgehogs fried in axle grease were pronounced delicious.[8] No cats survived, nor dogs – except Melliss's terriers and Townshend's Spot. All the time, suspiciously, men watched one another. Watched where they went, asked why they went there, followed them, suspecting a cache of moudy meal, or bleached bones, or something edible which previously no one had had the sense to eat.

Yet when Mrs Milligan clucked proudly back to her gunners' Mess – proudly, because she had a brood of chicks in tow – no one thought of cooking her. Instead, they marvelled at the way she had found herself a rooster, sat over her eggs, hatched them out and returned through shot and shell to her original home. She, meantime, ignoring their idiot delight, marched her brood out into the mud and taught them to eat bullets as if they were worms.[9]

Next morning the familiar roar of a downstream cannonade was heard, and Kut's hungry garrison paused in its scavenging long enough to wonder whether this attack could possibly be the real one: but it soon died, drowned by rain, so they buried Hoghton instead, but with considerable pomp, feeling that somehow the last rites of a general were very symbolic, though of what they were not sure. Of their indestructible capacity for doing things well? Of their impending doom? Of the immutability of a social order? They didn't know: but they were glad that they had done it well, and gave no thought to the fact that for a thousand others of less exalted rank they had done nothing at all – except begrudge them the wood for their crosses, because they had needed it for fuel. Death as such no longer moved them.

Not even the news that the Relief Force had suffered a further five thousand casualties between Hanna and Sannaiyat particularly moved them – apart from those who had brothers in the Tigris Corps, which a surprising number did. But the majority, devoid of fraternal anxiety, were too busy scavenging for food and hoping for relief to care what had happened to five thousand well-fed men who lived in that almost unimaginable world beyond the perimeter of shell-pocked Kut. Compassion, like one's stomach, shrinks with starvation: altruism, like one's bowels, degenerates with dysentery: dogma, like one's teeth, is loosened by a deficiency of vitamin B – as a result of which 9,239 hitherto dogma-bound Indians were now eating horse-meat.

The bread ration, on the other hand, had been cut to four ounces a day, to give Gorringe a few extra hours in which to achieve the impossible. He had to attack that night: the weather was vile: and none of his food-laden aeroplanes could even get off the ground, let alone fly. So they came later and dropped a few fishing nets instead. Surely, in some of those little creeks that straggled off the Tigris into Kut's peninsula, there must be fish for the netting? Apparently not. Then try dynamite! Dynamite was hurled into the river to explode with a roar and a spout of orange water: but the fish just came to the surface belly upwards and floated sadly down to Essinn, where the Turks ate them. For Kut, nothing went right. If only its Arabs didn't have to be fed. But its Arabs, vociferously importunate, did have to be fed. If only, lamented the officers, one could have a drink while one played bridge and read novels: but one couldn't. One hadn't been able to since the end of March. One had been too generous with one's alcohol in the early days of the siege.[10]

If only, lamented the rankers, there were some dates on the palms. But there weren't. And the fact that dozens of eighty-pound baskets of that delicious golden fruit had been used to build parapets in December no longer bore thinking about. Roll on the Blood Orange.

At 4.45 on the morning of April 15th Gorringe did his best: but his 3rd Division, knee-deep in water, could hardly roll anywhere. At least, though, it waded, sloshing through the darkness, following officers who peered at compasses, because they must all get to the right place at the right time before daylight, otherwise the Turk would see them coming – if he hadn't already seen them in the constant flare of lightning. Bayonets forward, boots full of water, they splashed on – but got lost, because lightning and steel bayonets had combined to drive their compasses berserk.

Nevertheless, they took some of the advance posts they were supposed to take, and everyone hoped that the weather would be better on the 17th. They would attack on the 17th, Lake cabled London: it was going to be a near-run thing, but he still hoped to relieve Kut.[11]

'We don't seem any nearer relief than we did a month ago,' a Kut R.F.C. corporal noted in his diary ... 'Everyone is looking worried and worn out ... Eight of the R.F.C. are excused duty. They can hardly put one leg in front of the other.'[12]

It was something they all noticed now: this sudden difficulty in walking. One kept lurching from side to side, from one trench wall to the other. Pity it had to rain last night and stop the relief. Weather's perfect today.[12]

So perfect that plane after plane flew high overhead – at five thousand feet, according to the R.F.C., who should have known – and dropped one double-sacked bundle after another, each one wrapped in what looked like a sheet. Just a white speck at first; then getting bigger, spiralling like a leaf, but unmistakably sacks of food, the Arabs gazing up in wonder and sighing, 'Aaah, Allah ... he's made it fall!'[13]

He made the first sack fall into the Tigris.

'Is the Relief Force quite sure it's on the right side?' Kut caustically telegraphed.[14]

Then a sea-plane made the last sack fall into the *Turkish* lines. 'Would His Majesty's Navy mind dropping *us* some food too?' Kut sarcastically demanded[15] – ignoring the fact that no less than 3,350 pounds of precious rations had already landed on target. Or perhaps only too aware that 3,350 pounds was 1,650 pounds short of their minimum requirements for that day alone. Every ounce counted now: and not even the miracle of man's first air drop could distract them from their awareness of ounces.

The food was taken to the magazines, where convalescents continued to guard it. 'I noticed one particular lot. It was very sweet stuff, like melted chocolate. When it was dark, I went to the sack where it had been stacked in the third row, untied it ... and we helped ourselves. In the morning we were told that there were about four pounds missing. We said it was just as it was dropped ... and our explanation was accepted.'[16] Stealing from thirteen thousand isn't really stealing – not when you're starving.

But stealing from one or two is unpardonable. Two sailors complained to the chocolate-eater that, while they had been away from their hospital charpoys, someone had stolen their ration of bread, 'which was one slice, as big as the palm of the hand. I felt very annoyed and could hardly believe it.'[16]

Gorringe advised Townshend that his men had rushed some pickets and taken forty-three prisoners.[17] Forty-three? Out of the entire 6th Turkish Army? What use was that?

The effects of an officer killed the day before were auctioned in the palm groves. His hundred cigarettes fetched twelve pounds; his binoculars six pounds ten shillings and his pouch of Arab tobacco three pounds ten shillings – as against the two shillings it was worth, presuming one was mad enough to smoke it.[18] Learning of the auction, those in the ranks were astounded that anyone, after four and a half months of siege, could possess either a hundred cigarettes and a pound of Arab tobacco, or sufficient rupees to buy them at an auction. But then both the deceased and the purchasers *were* officers: and that did make a difference.

'April 16, 1916,' another officer recorded. 'The day I ate the heart of my beloved Esmaralda.'[18] The day, also, that the 3rd Division steeled itself for its next attack on the Turk: that three Punjabis – would-be deserters from Kut – were sentenced to death: that seven bagfuls of rupees were dropped into Kut and evoked from Townshend the sharp rebuke, 'Food must come first.'[19]

A rumbling came from down-river and the night sky flickered. Another thunderstorm? No – too sustained: gun-fire. Gorringe's bombardment had started. Soon his infantry would be advancing.

But the infantry had already advanced, through their own bombardment: and caught the Turks crouching at the bottom of their trenches, waiting for it to stop, killing most of them and putting the rest to flight.[20] Townshend was pleased to learn of this initial success; and even more pleased to hear that the ground over which the 3rd Division must next advance was drying out well.[21]

Though the Turks counter-attacked with furious gallantry, they could not evict their enemy from the trenches they had captured: so they breached the banks of the Tigris and flooded the next battle-ground, and then counter-attacked again, overwhelming the Gurkhas, putting them to flight, disrupting an entire brigade and throwing into chaos all of 3rd Division's communications.[22]

For the moment, Townshend was not advised of this reverse, probably because his radio operators were fully occupied handling an entirely different dialogue. If relief was going to come too late, Basra telegraphed, Sir Beauchamp Duff had given permission for a volunteer force to attempt an escape on *Sumana* – but Townshend himself must stay behind, though the loss of his services would be regretted.[23] Even so, Duff qualified, such an attempt was only to be made as a last extremity, 'and that state of affairs has by no means been reached'.

'Quite so,' replied Townshend, who clearly thought it had: air supplies having provided only five thousand pounds of food in two days, so that he could now endure only till April 25th, his anxiety was understandable.[23]

His anxiety did not diminish that night when Basra wired that ten thousand Turks, led by German officers, were counter-attacking so determinedly down river that many of the trenches were blocked by piles of corpses:[23] and it increased sharply when he learnt next morning that they had continued their attacks all night, in some places as many as twelve times.[23] Gorringe had brought the 13th Division across the river to help, but the Turks had just come in again and again, killing and being killed in the mud, until, by daylight, fifteen hundred of them were lying dead in front of the trenches they had failed to storm and Khalil had decided that in future Gorringe could do the attacking.

This Gorringe had done, but to no great effect. He had suffered 4,500 casualties and the lines to which the Turks had withdrawn seemed impregnable behind their sea of water and mud, which grew deeper by the minute as the rain streamed down.

Perhaps, though, something had been gained by the last day's fighting. Khalil had brought many troops across from his Sannaiyat positions to reinforce his counter-attack: and to that extent Sannaiyat had been weakened and become vulnerable to a fresh attack by the 7th Division.

Gorringe decided to launch this attack on April 22nd. Admittedly he would only be able to muster 6,000 troops against a reported 8,700; but, if Townshend was to be relieved, he had no choice. No choice but to bluff Khalil into thinking the 3rd and 13th Divisions would soon renew the attack on their side of the river, keep the Turks guessing with bombardments on both sides of the river, pray that the ground would dry out in the next three and a half days on 7th Division's side of the river, and then rush Sannaiyat.[24]

For Kut, those three and a half days were less agreeable than ever. 'Got any livers or lights?' men begged at the slaughter lines.

'No.'

'Nothing at all?'

'Nothing.'[25] In desperation, two of them took a mule's head, carrying it by its ears, the blood still dripping from its severed neck.

'Must be *something* on it you can eat,' muttered one, ashamed of the thing he carried. His companion said nothing: but when they reached the communication trench they halted. Carrying a mule's head, could they outface those they must meet on their way to the first line? They could not. Crouching low, they began the long sprint across no-man's-land. *Ping*, went the sniper's bullets past them: *whirr* went the dum-dums. *Ping*, *whirr*. Then *thud* – into the mule's head. Bugger the blokes they'd meet! Diving into the communication trench they made their shambling way back to the front line, skinned the head, cooked it in a kerosene tin and ate it, bones and all, over the next two days.[25]

During which the three Punjabi deserters were shot, a 'bone roll' was established, so that each man would receive one bone a week to gnaw, a ration carrier was sentenced to four years' imprisonment for stealing meat, and duty on the fire-step was reduced to an hour at a time because men had begun to faint or fall asleep so easily. And officers who had just shot their chargers watched hospital patients crawling into the slaughter trench to cut out livers and lights. Days during which a Bombay gunner, on guard at the food magazines, and unable to differentiate between scrounging and theft, went almost mad resisting the temptation to steal from sacks of sweet molasses;[26] when Townshend was never seen; and when men became forgetful.

'What does thee mean,' an R.S.M. bellowed at a corporal, 'wandering about like that without revolver?'[27] Shells falling: bombs falling: rain falling. 'Hoard your ammunition as if it were gold.' Guns blazing from the brick kilns. Target C. Men dying every day: some said fifty a day. Dysentery, malaria, beriberi. But only British troops got beri-beri. Deserters. But only Indian troops deserted. And were shot in the river. Or against a wall. Von der Goltz died in Baghdad and Khalil took over his command. Gorringe bombarded both banks of the Tigris but reported his shells running low, wind blowing high, blowing the marsh waters back in front of Sannaiyat, which looked bad for Kut. Kitchener cabled Lake that British prestige was involved in the relief of Kut and Duff cabled Townshend, 'You can assure all ranks from me their relief will be executed shortly. They must not relax their gallant efforts during the next few days, and I am quite sure that you will continue to inspire them by your courageous example.'[28]

As usual Duff was talking nonsense: but Townshend published his cable as a communiqué and his men were still sufficiently loyal not to ask how his courageous example could inspire them when they no longer even saw him. It was April 21st, and the only good thing to happen that day was an air drop of flour.

But the next morning's drop fell half into the Shatt al Hai and half into the Tigris. Four hundred priceless pounds of whatever it was – to Mesopotamia's enormous fish. Everyone watched the white shrouded sacks spiralling downwards: everyone knew they were going too far either to the south or the east: some even wept and, as the guns downstream resumed their distant rumbling, Townshend wired Basra begging for news of Gorringe's advance, declaring himself as weak with ague as were his men with starvation and anxiety.[28]

Gorringe's news, had he been brutal enough to transmit it, would in no way have allayed Kut's weakness and anxiety. Across half his Sannaiyat front, water lay six inches deep: across the rest there was a flood.

In spite of it, he attacked – but only where the water was shallowest – and, advancing four hundred yards across a quagmire, sinking often to their armpits, their rifles clogged with mud, none of them with a clear idea of what it was they were supposed to do, except follow the man in front, or keep pace with the man alongside,[29] his advance brigade managed to storm the first Turkish trench, which was half full of water. According to their pattern, the Turks were no sooner driven out than they counter-attacked, and enfiladed a second British brigade as it attempted to reinforce the first. By early afternoon British and Indian dead outnumbered the living in that forward, flooded trench, and a gradual withdrawal from it began – except by the Highlanders, who refused to believe that the battle was lost.

But it was lost, and eventually even they fell back: whereupon a Turkish officer appeared with a white flag, under cover of which Turkish orderlies began to collect their wounded. Accepting this unofficial truce, the British then began to collect theirs, and for the rest of the afternoon both sides scoured the mud, examining bodies, abandoning the dead, carrying away the living.

Gorringe then told Lake that it was unrealistic to ask his force to attempt Kut's relief again before April 25th. In twenty days it had lost almost ten thousand men: and was still twelve miles from Kut. To attack again would involve further artillery preparation. There wasn't the time. There weren't the shells. His officers were too young and inexperienced and his surviving troops too raw. The floods, not the Turks, had beaten them.[30] The 2nd Black Watch had left only 48 of their original 842 men: the 6th Jahts only 50 out of 825: the 125th Rifles only 88 out of 848: the 1st Seaforth Highlanders only 102 out of 962. He could not ask them to attack again. Not before the 25th. And Lake, who had never before seen Gorringe anything but confident, believed him.[30] The Tigris Corps' strength by April 25th would be 23,450: since January, Tigris Corps had lost 23,000: to resume the battle before the 25th made no sense.

At 7.30 p.m. he telegraphed Townshend: 'Much regret that the attack at Sannaiyat position this morning was repulsed. Gorringe, however, will not relax efforts.' But in order to buy Gorringe the time he would need to mount those efforts, Lake now knew that he would be compelled to ask the Navy to run a twelve mile gauntlet to Kut. If *Julnar* could get through with several hundred tons of food, Kut could hold out another month – and Gorringe could attack again.[30]

Townshend's reply, dispatched next morning, Easter Sunday, was as realistic as it was rancorous. 'We must face the situation, namely that Gorringe with 30,000 men and 133 guns, has been repulsed again.' No mention of marshes, floods, rains, quagmires and gales, and only a grudging, 'I must suppose with heavy losses': but his bitterness is understandable. 'We are now at 23rd April,' he pointed out. 'My extreme limit of resistance is 29th; and Gorringe is not even at Sannaiyat. Therefore, short of a miracle, he cannot relieve me.' And therefore, he requested, would Lake immediately negotiate with Khalil for the free withdrawal of all those at Kut as he had suggested on March 9th?[31]

But this Lake was not yet prepared to do. *Julnar* had already been armoured with steel plating and manned by a volunteer crew, and by the 24th she would be fully laden with 270 tons of food. Kut must be given this last chance before Khalil was allowed to announce to the world that the British had implored his mercy.[32] At a well attended service in a makeshift chapel, Kut's gaunt troops prayed that *Julnar* might get through and that God's mercy might be with her and them.[33]

Julnar left her quayside berth at Amarah just after 7 on the night of April 24th, commanded by a naval lieutenant and piloted by Lieutenant-Commander Cowley, a one-time skipper of the Euphrates and Tigris Navigation Company whom the Turks, by virtue of his long residence in Mesopotamia and his invaluable work with Expeditionary Force D, regarded not only as a Turkish national but as a renegade as well. In spite of which Cowley had insisted upon taking part in a mission which everyone, from Admiral Weymiss downwards, considered doomed.

As secretly as was possible for a steamer upon which a large number of Arabs had worked for most of the past week, *Julnar* sailed upstream.[34] Probably not more than half the population of Amarah, the entire Headquarters Staff of the 6th Turkish Army and twenty thousand soldiers, camp-followers and locals in Kut knew her intentions: but Basra clung to the illusion that she sailed secretly.

Townshend clung not to illusion but to hope. After *Julnar*, he had only one other hope of avoiding capture and humiliation. Should *Julnar* fail, only the chivalry of Khalil and Enver Pasha could save him from unconditional surrender; and Enver Pasha was better known as an assassin than as a man of chivalry. Staring eastwards into the darkness, down the Tigris which ran like an extension of his own front line for ten crooked miles or so before it remembered that the Persian Gulf was its objective, and began to writhe southwards again – staring and straining his ears, he watched and listened for any hint of disaster.

Twenty-five miles of twisting, treacherous river, from whose banks came one assault of musketry after another, lay between *Julnar* and Kut; but through it all, for mile after mile, she drove her way, her steel plates ringing with shot, her sandbags filling with lead, her crew falling wounded, one after the other.

On Kut's river bank a company of Norfolks squatted, waiting to receive her; to protect and unload her. It was cool sitting there, and nothing happened for hour after hour; it was difficult to stay awake, and frightening to be so exposed, but it would be worth it – worth anything – if suddenly *Julnar* were to appear laden to the gunwales with food,[35] a white light at her masthead if she was undamaged and could berth, a red light if she was holed and had to go aground.[36]

Ten, and still no sign of her: neither a white light nor a red: the suspense unbearable. So unbearable that officers in the town even forgot that they had been issued with gold that day:[37] all they could think of was *Julnar*. Eleven, and still no sign of her.[38] But *Julnar* was still heading up-river.

'I hear rifle-fire,' Townshend exclaimed.[39] Impossible not to hear it. Then, silence.

When dawn came everyone peered downsteam. Even from the trenches men risked their lives to peer rightwards over the parapets, downstream.[40]

'There she is!' a Dorset shouted.

'Are you sure?'

'Can I have your glasses, please, sir?' An officer handed across his binoculars.

'Well?'

'She's high and dry at Magasis Ferry.'

'That's the end then,' said the officer, and took back his glasses.[41] With a hawser stretched diagonally across the river, the Turks had fouled *Julnar*'s screw, so that she had swung inshore, and boarded her. Her skipper and most of her crew had been killed; the rest, including Cowley, had been taken prisoner, and Cowley himself had been escorted into the desert and murdered.[42] Now only an outmoded tradition of magnanimity in victory stood between Townshend and the end of his career as a soldier, between his officers and the tedium of captivity, between his men and an ordeal which – to use his own words – would be 'better not spoken of'.

Advised of *Julnar*'s capture, Lake wired Townshend that he considered the time had now come to negotiate with Khalil. He had once more submitted to Government the proposal Townshend had made on March 9th, and even though it had then been flatly rejected, he now thought that, 'with your prestige, you are likely to get the best terms'. Admiral Weymiss, he said, agreed with this latter point of view – no one at Basra wanted any part of so humiliating a task – and he himself promised to supply to the surrendering force such food as Khalil, in deference to Townshend's prestige, would agree to. 'Please wire your views.'[43]

Townshend's views, which he wired promptly back to Basra, were that if *ordered* he would meet Khalil and suggest a six-day armistice during which terms could be agreed and food brought up[44] – though why he imagined that Khalil, whose victory over both Kut and the Tigris Corps had been complete, should so philanthropically indulge him he did not explain. Probably his mind was a century away with Junot. Certainly his was a different philosophy from Enver Pasha's. Equally certainly, his one-time insistence that he would fight house by house to the last bullet had been forgotten, his proposed break-out by six or seven hundred of his fittest men (since he had been forbidden to lead it) had been abandoned, and his Chitral complex had become plain at last for all to see.

That night Kitchener cabled Basra:

H.M. Government highly appreciate the gallant efforts made

to relieve Kut, and, having regard to all circumstances of case, feel that to call upon your troops immediately for a further effort would not be justified. Unless, therefore, you, Gorringe and the divisional commanders have reason to change the opinion already expressed regarding prospects of success, you are authorised, should the attempt to revictual Townshend fail, to open negotiations.[45]

At 3.30 a.m. on April 26th, Lake telegraphed Townshend accordingly. In the advance from Amarah to Ctesiphon, and the retreat from Ctesiphon to Kut, Townshend's force had suffered some 7,000 casualties. Kut's dead totalled 1,608, its wounded 1,836, its missing 48. Between January and the end of April, the Relief Force had suffered 23,000 casualties. In all, 33,000 casualties so that another 13,000 men could go into captivity and Force D end up where it had started. Whence it should never have advanced: Townshend himself had written, 'history always punishes such violations'.[46]

At 9 a.m. Townshend sent letters to Ali Neguib Pasha, Khalil's successor in the field, and to Khalil himself, advising that he was authorized to negotiate, requesting a ten-day armistice and seeking permission for two officers from Lake's command, Captains Herbert and Lawrence – the world was to hear rather more of the latter in years to come – to attend the negotiations. Khalil's answer arrived that night, suggesting that Townshend sail up-river to begin negotiations at once: but, when he attempted to comply, the Turks shelled *Sumana*, so he sailed the following morning instead. In an eerie silence, the men of 6th Division dragged themselves out of their trenches and, for the first time in 147 days, stood upright on the scarred peninsula of Kut to watch his departure. The siege was over.

CHAPTER TWENTY-ONE

୧୫୫୫

I T WAS a fine clear day; the flood had fallen and everywhere groups oı
men wandered aimlessly, content simply to savour fresh air, sunlight
and safety. Only the stink of corpses and clouds of inescapable, madden-
ingly persistent flies marred the perfection of a still desert morning. In
broad daylight, they stood on roof-tops, in the palm groves, on their
parapets and on the river bank. Some even swam. Some just watched the
Turks doing exactly what they were doing – stretching their legs,
sitting in the sun, bathing, gossiping. What, everyone asked (but not
fearfully; the euphoria of temporary safety had dispelled all fear) will
happen to us now?

To settle this not unimportant issue, Townshend sailed upstream
on *Sumana*, met Khalil's launch, transferred to it and started his 'negotiations'. No negotiations, Khalil insisted: just quit Kut and surrender.[1]
But that, Townshend protested, was tantamount to unconditional
surrender. Surely, after a siege that had outlasted Plevna and upon the
conduct of which Khalil had himself congratulated him, he deserved
better terms than that? Like permission to return on parole to India in
exchange for all Kut's guns and a million pounds in gold? At which
Khalil began to look interested, and allowed Townshend to return to
Kut on the understanding they would meet again tomorrow.[2]

Doubtless Khalil was as anxious to contact Enver Pasha before he
made a final decision as Townshend was to contact Lake – which he
did as soon as he stepped off *Sumana*. Lake replied promptly, authoriz-
ing him to offer the gold he had already offered, even though India
Government had not yet agreed to any such extravagance. Townshend
at once wrote a typical Townshend letter to Khalil, and a typical communiqué to his men.

He begged Khalil to reconsider his demand for an unconditional
surrender, repeating that his force deserved better, begging that Enver
Pasha be advised of his offer of gold, threatening otherwise, having
destroyed all his guns and material, to pay nothing at all, and warning

that at least a quarter of his force would die in captivity – so why should not Enver Pasha let them go home to India where, having promised never to fight the Turks again, they would live happily ever after?[2]

To his men, Townshend penned the last of his ingratiating, bombastic and self-pitying epistles and handed it to Boggis, who delivered it for transmission to the H.Q. signallers.

'It is hard to believe,' the H.Q. signallers tapped out to their various colleagues in their various Brigade headquarters – who duly took it all down and passed it on to orderlies, who carried the message to their respective major-generals, who promptly passed on its contents to every man in the lines, the gun-pits and the town – 'that the large forces comprising the Relief Force now could not fight their way to Kut: but there is the fact, staring us in the face.' To the bitter end Townshend intended blaming anyone but himself: on the contrary, as he went on to explain that Basra had told him that 'you with your prestige, are likely to get the best terms', he intended to praise himself and solicit sympathy. 'I have overcome my bodily illness and the anguish of mind which I am suffering ... Negotiations are still in progress: but I hope to be able to announce your departure for India on parole, since the Turkish commander ... has wired Constantinople to ask for this.'[2]

At once 2,800 Britons, 7,200 Indians and 3,200 camp-followers began to debate and argue: would Constantinople agree?[3]

'Of course they won't.'[4]

'Why not?'

'Do you believe it then?'

'Got to when you're as hungry as I am, haven't you?'[5]

'Only ones they'll let go home'll be the lads in hospital.'[6]

'Well ... that's something.'

But then the argument would flare again. 'Why shouldn't they let us go? Look at us! What use are we to anyone?'

'Been trying to kill them haven't we?'

'We'll give our parole.'

'Why *should* they let us go? They beat us.'

'Hunger beat us.'[7]

'We should have kicked out all the natives, right at the beginning.'[8]

'Well, we didn't, did we?'

But Enver Pasha rejected the offer of cash, guns and stores; and the Turkish press commented of it that the British, having failed to conquer with the sword, now sought to corrupt with gold.[9] The best that Enver Pasha would offer was that, for a million in gold and all of Kut's guns and stores, Townshend could go, alone.

Attempting to persuade Townshend to accept these terms, Khalil said that the guns would never be used against British troops, that their surrender would be the beginning of a long and mutually desired rapprochement between his country and Townshend's, and that Townshend's men, upon their surrender, would become Turkey's 'sincere and precious guests':[9] but Townshend, awake at last from his nineteenth-century dream, was not convinced.

'It is obvious,' he wired Lake, 'that I must go into captivity.' He had returned to Kut with his head held high,[10] but he felt as haggard and desperate[11] as Melliss, now ill in hospital, looked.[12] Then almost at once found another straw and, for a few hours, clung hopefully to that. If a million would buy *his* freedom, surely another million would buy the freedom of his men? Wiring Lake again, he suggested that Lawrence and Herbert offer Khalil *two* million pounds in gold.[13]

London co-operated, but Enver Pasha did not: 2,800 British soldiers and 7,200 Indians on display throughout his country were more valuable to the Turkish Government than two million pounds in gold. Turkey was so bankrupt that even a hundred million would not have helped, therefore Enver opted for prestige.

A whole day was consumed by these futile discussions: a whole day in which many who would have otherwise have planned and attempted an escape that night had their will sapped by the pipe-dream of re-patriation. And when, finally, that dream was dispelled, they could no longer attempt to escape because there was work to be done. Every-thing in Kut had to be destroyed – except one rifle per company as protection against the town's Arabs.

Thereupon gunners – who had been shocked to hear rumours that their treasured guns were to be handed over to the Turks[14] – promptly blew up their guns; troops broke their rifles; signallers shattered their sets, officers asked orderlies to bury their pistols; drivers hacked up harnesses and saddles; ammunition that had been 'hoarded like gold', rifles that had been soldiers' 'best friends', breech blocks that had slammed on thousands of shells, dial sights that had switched to dozens of targets, reels of cable that had carried a million dots and dashes, and bayonets that had jinked free of thousands of Turkish bodies were cast into the Tigris. The din was prodigious and the use of gun-cotton reckless. A breech block hurtled out of a howitzer and landed on Townshend's roof.[15] Fires blazed as they had not blazed for months, consuming rifle butts and trenching tools. The Treasury officer issued the last of his gold, mainly to officers. In every headquarters the duplicates of every message ever received were burnt – Townshend's c'municks amongst them. And code books. And records – the seven-year prison sentence on the radio operator who had dared repeat Townshend's message to London among them. And every other item that might have been of any use or comfort to the enemy, from binoculars to cameras. 'Now,' said Kut defiantly, 'come and get us. Because *we*'re all you'll get; and we're no use to anyone.'[16]

No use, but still hungry. Yesterday they had at last been given permission to eat the small blue tin of reserve rations they had carried in their tunic pockets for five months or more. Delicious bully, beautiful biscuits. Yesterday, rather than let her fall into the hands of the Turks, the gunner officers had eaten Mrs Milligan – who, not surprisingly, had been very tough indeed.[17] Now there was nothing. No mouldy potato meal, no cats or dogs, no air drop, no tiny loaf of bread.

Some days previously the troops had been promised that they would be given a golden sovereign each with which to march into captivity; but now they were told that *their* gold had fallen into the river. So tomorrow they must surrender penniless, their only possessions the ragged uniforms in which they stood, the dirty blankets on which they had slept. Nevertheless, they slept well that night: whatever else captivity might bring, at least – unlike fighting – it couldn't kill them. At least they would be fed; would get some mail; would be able at last to write home.

The morning of the 29th passed quietly, clear and warm, relaxed and strangely unanxious. No more decisions to make, orders to obey, battles to fight. Just captivity. And Johnny Turk was all right.

No more Regular officers playing at being soldiers, thought four of the junior warts who, having found themselves a tent, proposed isolating themselves inside it from bridge, captains, majors and colonels until such time as the war ended and they could return to some form of sensible, cultivated employment.

But they maligned the Regulars, whose awareness of their responsibility to their troops had not been diminished by defeat. Among the thousands of twenty-year-olds, there were a few older rankers who must somehow be spared the rigours of captivity.

'There's a job for you, Hayden,' a major announced. 'We're surrendering, and you know what that will mean, don't you? You'll be separated from your officers and we won't be able to protect you. So *you're* to be servant to General Melliss.' Not, would you like to be? or, will you be?; just an imperative, you *are* to be[18] – which was to save his life.

Several thousand men lay ill and wounded in hospital and for once hoped that they would *not* be discharged. The Turks had agreed that some of those not fit for immediate captivity could be exchanged for Turkish prisoners downstream.

Downstream, four divisions congregated at Amarah – whence, eight months ago, it had all begun. Eventually, they would retake Kut and advance to Baghdad – would take Baghdad and advance into Turkey. Eventually – after order had been brought to Basra: to the chaos of ships waiting at anchor five or six weeks in the middle of the green Shatt al Arab. After a railway line had been built to Nasariyeh, and a road up the Tigris. After river steamers had arrived in sufficient numbers to supply and maintain their offensive. After ambulances and hospitals had become available in respectable numbers. After sufficient reserves and artillery had arrived to support an attack. Eventually. But not now. Now Kut must surrender. One way or another, in battle or to captivity, forty-three thousand men had been lost for nothing.

Having ordered the last of his rifles to be destroyed, and the Union Jack to be lowered, Townshend wired Lake, 'I have hoisted the white flag over Kut ... I shall destroy our wireless set ... We are pleased to know that we have done our duty and recognize that our situation is one of the fortunes of war. We thank you and General Gorringe and all ranks of the Tigris Corps for the great efforts you have made to save us.'[19]

Then he issued the last of his many communiqués.

I have sent the following letter to the Turkish Commander in Chief:

'Your Excellency,

'Hunger forces me to lay down our arms, and I am ready to surrender to you my brave soldiers who have done their duty, as you have affirmed when you said, "Your gallant troops will be our most sincere and precious guests." Be generous then; they have done their duty. You have seen them in the Battle of Ctesiphon; you have seen them during the retirement; and you have seen them during the Siege of Kut for the last five months, in which time I have played the strategical role of blocking your counter-offensive and allowed time for our reinforcements to arrive in Iraq. You have seen how they have done their duty, and I am certain that the military history of this war will affirm this in a decisive manner. I send two of my officers, Captain Morland and Major Gilchrist, to arrange details.

'I am ready to put Kut into your hands at once and go into your camp as soon as you can arrange details, but I pray you to expedite the arrival of food.

'I propose that your Chief Medical Officer should visit my hospitals with my P.M.O. He will be able to see for himself the state of many of my troops – there are some without arms and legs, some with scurvy. I do not suppose you wish to take these into captivity, and in fact the better course would be to let the wounded and sick go to India.

'The Chief of the Imperial General Staff, London, wires me that the exchange of prisoners of war is permitted. An equal number of Turks in Egypt and India would be liberated in exhange for the same number of my combatants.

'Accept my highest regards.

GENERAL TOWNSHEND,
Major-General,
Commanding the 6th Division and the Forces at Kut.[20]

Commenting on this not entirely tactful epistle, he concluded his communiqué thus:

I would add to the above that there is strong ground for hoping that the Turks will eventually agree to all being exchanged. I have received notification from the Turkish Commander-in-Chief to say I can start from Constantinople. Having arrived there, I shall petition to be allowed to go to London on parole, and see the Secretary of State for War and get you exchanged at once. In this way I hope to be of great assistance to you all. I thank you from the bottom of my heart for your devotion and your discipline and bravery, and may we all meet in better times.[20]

For his command, the final paragraph of this communiqué was cruelly misleading. Perhaps Townshend included it to bolster his troops' morale; or perhaps to ensure that, as he abandoned them, he retained their goodwill; but, from the moment he left them until the war ended, he was to do almost nothing to improve the lot of his men in captivity, and nothing at all to procure their repatriation.

Khalil had asked him to tell his troops that they would be 'our most sincere and precious guests': so Townshend did so, even though, more than a fortnight previously, he had warned that the Turks would have not a biscuit to spare for them and that the drama which would then be enacted was better not spoken of.[21]

'General Townshend,' the Navy wired from Basra, 'We, the officers and men of the Royal Navy, who have been associated with the Tigris Corps and have, many of us, so often worked with you and your gallant troops, desire to express our heartfelt regret at our inability to join hands with you and your comrades in Kut.'[21] More accustomed to sending signals than the Army, and anyway more human, the Navy had said all that there was to say, and theirs was the last message to be received by Kut.

Which replied first, 'Goodbye',[22] and then, 'Piecemeal'[23] – the latter Townshend's prearranged signal that his radio sets were about to be destroyed. Piecemeal: the method of attack which, in his opinion, had doomed each of the plans to relieve him. Piecemeal: the antithesis of Maximum Force. Piecemeal: his last word. He had to have it.

Having tapped it out, his radio operators fired their rifles into their set until its inductor coils burst into flames: then, with the butts, destroyed the instrument completely and walked out into the sunlight to witness the arrival of their captors.

Led by a smartly uniformed colonel riding erect on a grey and glaring bleakly through pince-nez spectacles, marching to the rattle of drums, a long column of sturdy, grubby Turks in thick uniforms of yellowish grey, puttees of varying colours and boots of varying styles, plodded towards them, apparently as phlegmatic as Kut was apprehensive. As they drew closer they were seen to be carrying enormous packs with great-coats rolled and strapped on top of them. Their belts sagged with the weight of ammunition pouches and spherical grenades. Their bayonets were long, their enverris strange – half-cap, half-turban. But their officers sported gold braid and astrakhan collars and field-glasses and short swords and pistols.

As the column trudged towards the town, Arabs cheered and tried to kiss the colonel's boots; but he kicked them aside and asked his escorting British officer:

'How many guns are there?'

'Forty-three, sir.'

'Where are they?'

Mutely the officer pointed at the wrecked guns: and Colonel Nizam Bey was not pleased.[24]

The Turks, having hoisted the Ottoman crescent, took swift

possession of everything – stores, houses, billets, and Townshend's headquarters. In a matter of minutes Kut was transformed into something wholly alien to those who had held it for so long. Alien because those who had been its masters were now, clearly, of no significance at all. It was the Turks who mattered now. This grimy, uncouth rabble whose skins were so surprisingly pale; of whom so many, surprisingly, had blue eyes and ginger hair; a mongrel, pallid breed: but now the masters.

One by one most of Townshend's officers made their way through the town to his Headquarters, where now Colonel Nizam Bey was installed. To him they offered their swords; and he, bowing, accepted them and shook their hands. But some officers, not wishing to give Nizam Bey the pleasure of accepting their swords and shaking their hands, broke the blades and threw them into the Tigris.

For Townshend special arrangements were made. Khalil Pasha himself came to Kut, and it was to him he surrendered his sword. Courteously Khalil handed it back; a slight, straight-backed man patronizing the older, taller, fleshier Englishman. Townshend then asked a favour.[25] Would Khalil be so kind as to send Spot downstream, whence he could be repatriated to England? Gravely Khalil agreed. Captivity was for Englishmen, not for dogs.

Elsewhere there was less courtesy, as Turks who had marched a thousand miles without water bottles and in worn boots or Arab shoes sought to replace them with the bottles and footwear of those they had conquered. One was even rash enough to steal General Melliss's boots. Whereupon, roaring with rage, little old Blood and Thunder had leapt out of his hospital bed and pursued the thief until a Turkish officer intervened. The boots having been returned to their outraged owner, the officer struck the Turkish soldier repeatedly across the face: and the soldier stood to attention and saluted after each blow, his salute a curious gesture – a crumpled hand, like a monkey's paw, to his enverri.

As rumours of looting spread, Johnny Turk ceased to be the amiable enemy who had cheered the pyrotechnics of an illuminated rifle-grenade and waved aloft a whimsically bandaged shovel, and became instead a hard-eyed predator. And suddenly the prospect of captivity became alarming.

For the last time Townshend talked to some of his men.

'What'd he say?' asked those too far away to have heard his words.

' 'E said, I dunno where you're going, but it's every man for isself and God for the bloody lot of you.'[26]

Smiling, nodding, he moved on; a word here, a word there.

'What'd he say, bor?'

'I'm going to get you released on parole.'[27]

'What'd he say?'

'Goodbye men and God bless you.'[28]

Somehow they had all hoped for something more. It seemed strange that a man who had had such power over them could now volunteer nothing more positive than goodbye and God bless you.

The prospect of captivity became no less alarming when everyone was ordered to march nine miles upstream to Shamran. Nine miles! Who could march nine miles? Five months ago they had stopped at Kut because Townshend was convinced they could march not another inch: how could they now – weak, ill and exhausted – march nine miles? On the other hand, what else could they do? Because the Turks had made it clear that, until they reached Shamran, they would get no food. Collecting their few possessions, tying them in their blankets (their haversacks had long since rotted as camouflage over loop-holes or sandbags on parapets) filling their water bottles with Tigris water, they staggered up-river. And, when they arrived at Shamran, found no food. Enormous goat's-hair tents they found, black and big enough to hold a hundred men, enough of them to hold about half of those who had marched, but no food.[29]

Not everyone had marched. The officers and some of the men, the lucky ones, were taken to Shamran on a steamer: but when they arrived they were confronted by the same chaos. No food, no latrines, no organization, and bad-tempered Kurdistan guards.

For the officers it was not so bad. They had naturally brought with them small tents and camp-beds and folding canvas chairs and playing cards and spare clothes and servants to carry all of it: but for the troops, with just their blankets and their water bottles and occasionally their great-coats, it was a grim beginning to whatever lay ahead.

The four subalterns who had decided to withdraw from the barbarities of regimental life retired into their tent and talked of other things than discipline and wars: but were interrupted when a captain thrust his head inside and asked, 'Will you take me in?'

'No,' they said. 'Go away. We want to be on our own. And anyway, why have you come to us? We're only junior warts.'

'Oh dear,' he muttered. 'I'm so upset. Mushy Evans has been so rude to me. I can't understand it.'

'Mushy? What's he done to you?'

'Well, just when we were leaving Kut I said to him, "Is there *any-thing* I can do to help, sir?" And do you know what he said? He said, "Oh for God's sake, you stupid bugger, stop being so piss-begotten polite." '

Trying not to laugh, the four subalterns considered the dismay a newly promoted brigadier's rebuke, qualified as it had been by his favourite adjective, must have caused a captain notorious for his politeness and sense of protocol. 'Oh, all right,' they said, 'we'll take you in.'[30]

To General Melliss's tent came a stream of Turks, to peer in at the great victor of Shaiba. Melliss Pasha they called him: and sensibly he took them at their word. Thereafter he became His Excellency Melliss Pasha to every Turk of every rank, and wherever he went he was to attempt to improve the lot of his unfortunate men as General Townshend never did.[31]

It was only at dusk that some food arrived: a heap of Turkish army biscuits thrown to the ground off the back of a camel. The biscuits were disc-shaped, fibrous and tough as concrete. They looked like glazed, circular dog biscuits and tasted like reinforced dung. At their freshest, they contained too much straw and dirt to be palatable: flavoured with camel sweat, they were most disagreeable.

But to men already starving, better than nothing. Those with strong teeth began to gnaw and worry at their edges; others took off their boots and attempted to break them into manageable lumps; and the very patient soaked them for hours in water – and were astonished to see how much they swelled and expanded. One way or another, however, almost everyone ate his biscuit: then went to sleep, either in one of the big black tents, or sprawled on the desert under a high, black sky.

The following morning they began to die. Frothing at the mouth, their bowels and stomachs disintegrating into a greenish slime, dehydrated and moaning, they died one after the other. In a matter of hours they had changed from lean men into leathery skeletons, all eye-sockets and claw fingers and ribs and bared teeth. Enteritis, the doctors called it: but enteritis covers a multitude of sins. To some it looked like cholera. To others poisoning. To all of them, terrifying: because biscuits, six to a man, and no indication that more would follow, were almost all there was to eat.

'Soak them,' the doctors ordered. 'Soak them, then bake them, or they'll kill you.'[32] Easy to say: but not so easy to do when thousands of men scavenge for the camel thorn that will make the fires that will bake the biscuits that have been soaked in the fouled waters of the Tigris. So the weak and the lazy gave up the struggle, and ate their biscuits unbaked, even unsoaked, and died.

'Yok!' screamed the Kurdestan guards, when men tried to move those who lay dead in their own filth, black flies swarming round them, crawling in and out of their mouths and nostrils. 'Yok,' – and slashed with whips and rifle butts. So 'yok' meant no; and Johnny Turk was not at all the bloke he had seemed; and now, at last, those who were strong enough began to think about escaping.

'I'm going tonight, sir.'

'Going? Where?'

'Downstream, sir!' Floating in the darkness, a good swimmer might make it. Twenty miles or so. Eight miles an hour with the current. Two and a half hours to freedom.[33]

'Well, I have no authority to stop you, but if you do go, you know they'll shoot some of *us*?' Always the same argument. 'A soldier', the *Soldier's Small Book* insists, 'must be quick to devise a means of escape from capture.' Apparently sir had never read the *Small Book*.

'No, sir, I didn't know that':[33] and abandoned the idea of escaping.

'Let's make a break for it,' a Dorset suggested to his friends. 'There's only one sentry. We could easily do him.'

'No.'

'Why not?'

'Too weak.'[34]

Since biscuits so clearly meant death, many of the troops began to barter for other kinds of food. Boots, great-coats, blankets and tunics were all exchanged for a handful of dates or a tinful of rice or a few cigarettes. The officers in their tents seemed reluctant to impose any kind of discipline, and Shamran became a place of anarchy and pestilence.

Back in Kut the sick and wounded lay on their charpoys and watched Turks and Arabs steal anything that caught their eye. There was nothing they could do to prevent it. They were as helpless as the local townsfolk over whom the Turk had reasserted his authority by hanging everyone even remotely suspected of having helped or liked the British. Dozens of them, including the mammoth Fat Boy, were still swinging from their gibbets, hanged in the Turkish manner, which does not break the neck but merely, slowly, strangles. The medical officer said it was a practically painless death, because the blood to the brain was cut off almost at once, but it didn't look painless. And the death of such lesser citizens as had been garotted, rather than hanged, had certainly not been painless.

Eleven hundred patients were to be exchanged for eleven hundred specified Turkish prisoners of war. Of the thousands in the hospital, which eleven hundred would be chosen? How did you look sicker than you were to a Turkish doctor? How much, if anything, did Turkish doctors know? How, if you were lucky enough to be chosen for exchange, would you get to Basra? What would Basra do with you when you got there?[35]

But Basra had more pressing matters on its mind than the exchange of useless casualties for valuable prisoners of war. From Headquarters to Tigris Corps went an urgent signal inquiring as to the 'number of files killed in April in Japanese fly-traps'. By which one officer was so incensed that he scrawled the answer 'Balls' across the bottom of the message and sent it straight back to his signallers.

Another urgent message came from Basra. 'For files,' it said, 'read flies.'

'For balls,' replied the officer, 'read cock.'[36] After eighteen months of war, first things still came first.

The second day at Shamran the word spread that Townshend would soon be passing, going up-river on a launch to Baghdad. Hundreds of officers and men went down to the bank, ignoring the guards and their slashing whips and their screams of 'Yok, yok': and, when the little boat steamed past them, cheered the man who stood at the rail saluting them.

'I shall never forget that cheer. Tears filled my eyes as I stood to attention at the salute. Never shall I have such a command again. I loved the 6th Division with all my heart,'[37] wrote Townshend as – lavishly accompanied by an A.D.C., his principal staff officers, an Indian servant, a Portuguese cook and two British orderlies – he left his men at Shamran. For their present plight, he as much as anyone was to blame. For the ghastly deaths awaiting their majority, he more than anyone was responsible. Yet they cheered him then: and to this day not one of his troops can be found who does not praise him; and of his officers none can be found who blame him sufficiently to condemn him as the man who destroyed the division he claimed to love.

CHAPTER TWENTY-TWO*

WHILE Townshend steamed comfortably towards Baghdad – past Shadie, past Azizieh and Llaj and Ctesiphon – his troops continued to die of 'enteritis' at Shamran, and their captors started to separate them from their officers. The officers were to sail to Baghdad: they were to march.

Delamain tried desperately to persuade the Turks to allow some at least of the officers to march with the men, but the Turks were adamant. The only promise they would make was that no leg of the march would be longer than eight miles. Melliss might have won further concessions, but he was too ill: Townshend should have ordered some at least of his officers to remain with their men, but he had not thought of it.

And so began for the troops of the 6th Division that most soul-destroying of all the processes of captivity, the creation of a privileged class that will enjoy extra comfort, extra pay and extra rations with no attendant responsibility towards those for whom it is their duty to provide leadership and protection. No man who has not been a prisoner of war, and who has not, as a prisoner, been in the ranks, can begin to imagine the bitterness experienced by troops in captivity when they see their officers abandon them to enjoy a life of comparative wealth, comfort and safety.

'Well, they're not the bloody bosses now, you know,' some at least defended them. 'They got to do what they're told, just like us.'[1] Which was true. So Townshend should have ordered them to remain with their troops – to continue to show themselves – even if the Turks shot them for doing so. And Townshend should have had the authority of King's Regulations to reinforce his order. But he did not so order and his authority was not so reinforced. Nor is it for any commander of today's British Forces. Officers are still liable to be segregated from their men in future captivities;[2] and will accept the

* See the endpaper map.

segregation because it is a saint and a hero who does not, when the sole obligation to do so is a moral one; and whenever the captor is Asian, their abandoned men will continue to be destroyed, just as the 6th Division was destroyed in Asia Minor between 1916 and the end of 1918, just as the troops of Generals Percival and Gordon Bennett were destroyed in Malaya between 1942 and the middle of 1945.

For Mesopotamia's captives the abandonment began on May 4th, when the first party of officers sailed upstream. It continued until only one officer per regiment was left (and all of those would soon, without demur, depart – except for the C.O. of the Gurkhas, who refused to go, saying, 'They are my children. They will die without me.')[3] Otherwise, at Shamran, there was not a general, not a colonel, not a subaltern – not even a doctor. Led by N.C.O.s, tended by Indian apothecaries armed only with such drugs and instruments as each could carry, they were about to march more than a thousand miles and to perish in thousands of thirst, starvation, exhaustion, brutality and disease. Along the same route exactly, not more than a handful of officers would die, and they only of illness: because the officers had gold and silver, which their men did not, donkeys and carts, which their men did not, doctors and drugs, which their men did not, and the respect of their escorting guards, which their men did not.

No one regretted this more than the officers concerned, whose belief in the principle of 'no privilege without responsibility' was un-equivocal: they had proved it by their courage in battle and the horrifying casualties they had suffered. But, as the loyal and reasonable Private Sherlock had observed, 'They're not the bloody bosses now, you know.' Now the Turk was the boss. And the Turk had said to them, 'Go. Leave your men with us. They will be our honoured and treasured guests.' So, full of misgivings, they had gone, denied any means of helping their men other than to take with them, allegedly as orderlies, batmen and cooks, as many of their subordinates as the Turk would tolerate.

Yet had the Turk said, 'Officers, you will now tell us all you know of the strength and dispositions of General Gorringe's force down-stream,' they would have refused to a man. Because King's Regulations forbade them to do so. King's Regulations should equally have for-bidden them to shed their responsibilities to their troops. King's Regulations did not do so then, and did not do so in the Second World War: and Queen's Regulations do not do so today.

Advised at last of Kut's surrender, the British public became so resentful that – even as the first party of officers sailed away from Shamran – Kitchener had to speak soothing words from the House of Lords.

I am glad [said Lord Kitchener] that the noble and gallant lord has offered me this opportunity of paying a tribute to General Townshend and his troops, whose dogged determination and splendid courage have earned for them so honourable a record. It is well-known how, after a series of brilliantly-fought engagements, General Townshend decided to hold the strategically important position at Kut-el-Amara, and it will not be forgotten that his dispositions for the defences of that place were so excellent and so complete that the enemy, notwithstanding large numerical superiority, was wholly unable to penetrate his lines. Noble lords will not fail to realize how tense was the strain borne by those troops who, for more than twenty weeks, held to their posts under conditions of abnormal climatic difficulty, and on rations calculated for protraction to the furthest possible period, until, as it was proved, imminent starvation itself compelled the capitulation of this gallant garrison, which consisted of 2,970 British and some 6,000 Indian troops, including followers.

General Townshend and his troops, in their honourable captivity, will have the satisfaction of knowing that, in the opinion of their comrades, which I think I may say that this House and the country fully share, they did all that was humanly possible to resist to the last, and that their surrender reflects no discredit on themselves or on the record of the British and Indian Armies.

Every effort was, of course, made to relieve the beleaguered force, and I am not travelling beyond the actual facts in saying that to the adverse elements alone was due the denial of success; the constant rain and consequent floods not only impeding the advance, but compelling – in lieu of turning movements – direct attacks on an almost impossibly narrow front. No praise would seem extravagant for the troops under Sir Percy Lake and Sir George Gorringe, and that they did not reap the fruit of their courage and devotion is solely due to the circumstances which fought against them. The last message sent by General Townshend from Kut was addressed in these terms:

'We are pleased to know that we have done our duty, and

recognize that our situation is one of the fortunes of war. We thank you and General Gorringe and all ranks of the Tigris force for the great efforts you have made to save us.'

I think the House, no less than the country at large, will endorse these words, and I am sure that those who held and those who strained every nerve to relieve Kut have alike earned our admiration and our gratitude. I am glad to endorse what the noble lord has said in regard to the conduct of the Turkish Commander.[4]

Thereby placated, and distracted by other disasters closer to home, the British public forgot both General Townshend and his hapless troops. And even had that public been told that Townshend was at that moment three days' sailing away from his troops, and his officers in the process of leaving them, it would have had no idea how terribly these things mattered to those who lay in their black tents or under the blazing sun at Shamran, waiting for their march to start, and to those who lay in the hospital at Kut, waiting for a Turkish medical officer to decide which of them should be exchanged.

'Only Indians will be exchanged,' was the rumour:[5] and British troops too badly wounded or too enfeebled even to haul themselves on to a bed-pan bit their lips with despair, because those not exchanged must join their comrades at Shamran and march to Baghdad.

Next day the Turkish medical officer made his perfunctory inspection, pulling up eyelids, feeling triceps, prodding wounds, asking what the Senior British Medical officer meant when he said 'beriberi'. If a patient was Mohammedan, and not palpably fit, he was sick enough for exchange: if a patient was British, and not palpably helpless, he was fit enough to march through the length and breadth of Asia Minor.

That same day, at Shamran, the Turks issued rations for three days to each of those who must march: nine biscuits, three ounces of jam and a small handful of dates. Even the most optimistic of their prisoners realized that three biscuits a day, plus a gobbet of jam and a couple of dates, would hardly sustain them for eight miles across rough desert in temperatures close to 100°:[6] so, of those who had not already done so, many more began trading their tunics and great-coats, their watches and rings, anything and everything – except their water bottles, shorts and sun helmets – for an extra handful of dates or a slice of stale black bread.

Yet they clung to their pay books!

'It's my friend,'[7] one explained to a curious Kurdistan guard: and, opening it, inscribed on its fly leaf the legend:

Pte W. J. Sherlock,
2nd Dorset Regiment,
Prisoner of War,
Asia Minor,
Turkey.

Whatever happened to him now, and whoever found him, his name would become known, and his family be notified. Turning the page, he stared thoughtfully at its first entry – a stoppage of a penny a day, payable to his mother. Then he turned to the latest of its entries; payments received in Kut. Three over a period of five months: total – six rupees, or eight shillings.[7] He was young, blue-eyed, fair-complexioned. Almost all of them at Shamran were young. Twenty-six was old. But already several hundred had died, and their shrivelled corpses, looking like tattered, unopened umbrellas,[8] had been chucked into a near-by ravine. Carefully he pushed his pay book deep into his tunic pocket: whatever happened, he would not be parted from it.

And whatever happened to the officers steaming slowly upstream, they and their orderlies would not, they hoped, be parted. Not so much because a gentleman must have someone to wash his clothes and cook his meals, even in captivity, as because they suspected that all would not go well with those who marched. So General Melliss took his newly appointed orderly, Hayden, with him, even though Hayden had broken his leg carrying baggage on to the steamer.

There were a hundred British and eight Indian officers on board, each with his allotted two hundred pounds of baggage, so the British officers and their orderlies occupied the top deck, the Indian officers and their orderlies the lower deck. Looking down, they saw open barges attached to each flank of their steamer, and in them Turkish wounded, untended, fending for themselves, dying, uncomplaining. Across the river they saw Arabs jeering, boys gesturing obscenely and women uttering their shrill ululating cry of contempt. Three days to go, and then Baghdad.

At Shamran, the Turks were adamant in their refusal to allow the one officer assigned to each regiment to march with it to Baghdad. All officers must sail: all troops much march. Only one concession would Khalil make: those at Shamran could remove from stranded *Julnar* as much of her cargo of food as they could carry. And *Julnar* had naturally carried not only essential supplies but also all the orders that Townshend's officers had months ago dispatched to Bombay to tide them over a Christmas they had expected to spend in Baghdad. Champagne, brandy, whisky and port, plum puddings and chocolates, cigarettes and cigars – all had arrived at Basra, and all had been included in rations intended solely to enable Kut to survive until Gorringe could relieve it.[9]

For twenty-four hours, therefore, Shamran flowed with alcohol as men smoked ecstatically and gorged themselves on plum pudding[10] – which instantly bound up their biscuit-scoured bowels and cured their enteritis. Yet the chocolate, of which they had dreamed for so long, for which they had craved for so long, sickened them. After four months without sugar, they found it too sweet![11]

That night they slept deeply and comfortably; but the following morning a large party was ordered to assemble for the first leg of the march to wherever it was Enver Pasha had decided they should finally be imprisoned. Evil-tempered Kurds slashed at the ragged columns with their bull-penis whips and counted them again and again – and tried to buy or steal their boots and great-coats.[12] Harassed and irritable, their prisoners had to endure it all.

Lacking haversacks, they had bundled their few possessions in their blankets and now – bitterly regretting the balance of the food still lying in *Julnar* – waited to start. Eight miles. Noon already. The heat of the day. And suddenly screams of, 'Yellah, yellah,' and the cracking of whips, and the first column beginning to move.

Almost at once men began to straggle, and some to collapse. 'Yok, yok!' the Kurds bellowed, galloping up on their horses, forbidding anyone to help them; but tying an unconscious Naval rating on to the back of a camel. As it lurched along, he fell off, and was dragged, head downwards, across the desert, hour after hour.

'Yok,' the Kurds bellowed at those who had rushed to lift him back on to the camel. 'Yok' – and slashed with their whips.

At Umm al Tubul, where they had defeated a Turkish Army, they saw no trace of their last victory – except for a mule with its foot shot off. The mule had worn a circular track in the desert as it cropped alone for five months: and when they staggered past it, it ignored them. Just stood there on three legs, head down, resignedly cropping.[13]

After only a few hours, water bottles had been emptied. 'Yok!' bellowed the Kurds, galloping to cut off those who sought to refill them from the Tigris. 'How much farther?' the marchers groaned. 'Two hours,' said the Kurds.

Behind the stumbling columns lay a scattering of men too weak to go on, Arabs dragging off their sun helmets and blankets, their shirts and shorts, their boots and socks, stuffing sand down their throats, or slicing with their daggers, moving from quivering naked body to the next bundle of khaki. Soon the flies would come, picking at dead nostrils, exploring swollen tongues; then the hyenas and pariah dogs. Soon only bleached bones would remain.

'How much farther?'

'Two hours.'

Some of them began to discard everything they carried; everything except their water bottles.

Eight miles done, and still they marched. So much for the promises of General Khalil to his honoured and precious guests. Nine miles. And a halt. Thank Christ. Sleep. No – fill water bottle first. Stumbling to the river, they drank.

'Johnny!' Looking up, they saw smiling Gurkhas, offering back to them the coats and blankets they had miles and hours ago discarded. 'My men can fight,' their colonel had once asserted, 'but don't expect them to do long marches.' Because they were so small, their legs so short. Yet look at them now. That wide grin and the proffered coat or blanket. Which tomorrow might well be sold or stolen or discarded again. Unrolling their blankets (those who still had them) and laying them flat, unlacing their boots (those who still had them) and easing them off, a thousand men wrapped themselves up and fell asleep. Scores were dying. The Naval rating was already dead. But sleep was all that mattered. And, as they slept, their guards slipped among them, stealing dozens of pairs of boots.

At which moment, in Baghdad, Townshend, at a dinner given in his honour, was discussing strategy with his host, General Khalil.[14]

To Shamran now came hundreds of those to whom the Turkish medical officer had denied the right of repatriation: men helpless and incontinent with dysentery, shuddering with malaria and weak from wounds. At the same time, their more fortunate comrades marched in single file down to the river, took a last curiously nostalgic glance backwards at Kut and boarded a British hospital ship. From a near-by gibbet, six Arabs hung.

'Anything you want?' an orderly asked.

'A bath?'

'Down there.'

'What would you like to drink? Milk, coffee, or rum and milk?'

'Whose leg are you pulling?'[15]

But this was no leg-pull. This, at last, in Mesopotamia, was the Medical Service for which Chamberlain had been begging for almost a year: and the rum and milk was 'marvellous, like electricity going all through my body'.[15]

Fifty men died before they got to Basra: but, for the remainder, this was a voyage of bliss. And at Basra they found a new hospital – 'a lovely place, with proper beds and nurses too'.[15] Thence to Bombay; thence, back on their tracks, to Egypt, to the General Hospital in Alexandria.

'There were five of us from Kut ... and we had to go to the dining-tent for meals ... We would go round the tables eating all that was left ... When the doctors got to hear about this, we were confined to our wards.'[15]

At Alexandria they saw their first Charlie Chaplin film, and laughed as they had thought they would never laugh again; and heard the Arab newspaper boy crying, 'Very good news this morning. Lord Kitchener is dead'; and then home to England, to be photographed by the press. 'Survivors return from Kut.' Where's Kut?[15]

The officers' party had reached Baghdad and been marched in triumph through the city and its bazaar, Arab women spitting at them, German officers photographing them from balconies and they themselves so deliberately indifferent that voices from the crowd were heard asking time after time, in English and French, 'Well, who *are* the prisoners? Who *won* the war at Kut el Amarah?'[16]

The officers accepted it as their due. Studiously supercilious, some monocled, some with cigarettes in long holders, some visibly disappointed by women who resembled not at all the fabled beauties of legendary Baghdad, they dominated a procession designed to humiliate them. And, finding themselves installed in barracks where they were supposed to share a Mess with their Indian colleagues, and even eat after them, promptly advised their captors that this could not be: and had it changed.

Melliss and Delamain shared Townshend's lavish quarters in what had been the Italian Consulate: and Townshend at once consulted with Melliss, asking his advice. He had been 'invited' by the Turks, he said, to proceed to Constantinople. Should he go? What would others think of such 'preferential treatment'?[17]

It was a curious question. Curious because Townshend had justified his desertion of his troops by assuring them that he was *off to Constantinople* whence, on parole, he intended returning to London to arrange their mass repatriation. Curious also because he had wired Lake, just before his surrender, 'My duty seems clear, *to go into captivity with my force*,[18] though I know the hot weather will kill me, for the continuous strain I have suffered since August till now is more than I can bear ...'[19]

It was a curious question, because it proves that when he left Kut he had no idea where he was going, except that it was *not* into captivity with his troops; and that both his outrageous promise of repatriation for his troops and his selfless assertion that it was his duty to go into a captivity that would kill him had been lies. Townshend, in fact, survived his captivity not in hot weather that might have killed him but in great luxury – whilst his troops, for whom he never sought repatriation, though he constantly sought it for himself, died like flies in squalor and brutal deprivation.

Melliss's reply to Townshend's question has been reported only by Townshend himself. 'Clear out of this infernal country as soon as you can,' he quotes Melliss as saying.[20] Yet, a month later, Melliss had to be separated almost forcibly from his troops, on whose behalf he had raged constantly at every Turkish official unfortunate enough to cross his path; and Melliss was to make no effort at all to ensure that *he* was moved from infernal Asia Minor to somewhere else more comfortable. If, then, he advised as Townshend says he advised, it was more probably to get rid of his superior than to comfort him that he did so. 'Invited' to go to Constantinople and there to receive 'preferential treatment', the least Townshend could have done was to decline the invitation until all his troops had reached Baghdad and he had seen for himself how they were being treated and what he could do to improve their lot. Instead, he left at once.

CHAPTER TWENTY-THREE

THE first party of troops continued to stumble along leg after leg of their march up-river, and a second, larger party had begun to follow them. They trudged in a trance, intent only upon reaching those distant trees and streams that constantly lured them on, and just as constantly vanished before they could reach them. Not knowing which they hated more – their vicious guards or Mesopotamia's cruel mirages – they dragged one foot past the other, one foot past the other, one foot past the other, interminably. Maddened by incessant yoks, yellahs and yessuks, they had no thoughts but one foot past the other and rest and food and water. Terrified of the lurking Arab, they abandoned anything that burdened their progress and plodded mindless as thirst-crazed cattle towards the next mirage, the final waterhole.

Sometimes they marched by night, sometimes from dawn till midday, never eight miles, sometimes fifteen, always to some bend in the river where they would fall face down and guzzle blindly, indifferent to the Kurds' horses deliberately watered upstream of them, ignoring the splash of horses urinating into water they were drinking, unmindful of comrades no longer by their side, but back there, somewhere. Then gnawed at biscuits, voided outraged bowels, made a bivouac of tattered blanket against the searing sun, and slept.

Except those who had malaria. Huddled four or five or six under a single blanket, *they* would shiver monstrously, icy cold in the ferocious heat.

Except those who had sold, or discarded, or been robbed of their blankets. They would lie in the sun and feel the burn of it in their brains, the headache getting worse, making the desert spin faster. Lie there and know that when the yellahs started they would probably be unconscious and that then the Kurd would stove in their skull with his rifle butt. Better that, the Kurd explained, than leave them to the Arabs.

Arabs, Kurds, sun, blankets – none of them mattered. All that mattered was pain. The pain of a rifle butt against the skull, a knife through the throat, women's claws at one's crotch. To avoid that, they would even march again. Meantime oblivion: but such brief oblivion.

'Yellah, yellah!'

Those whips flaying the meat off your back. Those somehow obscene whips. Made each of a bull's penis split down the middle and then hung to dry, weighted down with a stone, twisting as it dried, drying into something only man could devise for a bull's penis. Strange that those who handled them most loving-cruelly were the officers with their caps of astrakhan and their carefully enunciated French.

'Yellah, yellah.'

Untie boots from round your neck – those who hadn't sold them, those who hadn't had them stolen as they slept. Force swollen, blistered filthy feet into leather dried tough as officers' whips.

The *Soldier's Small Book* '... Before marching, wash feet with soap ... rub inside of socks with yellow soap ... soak feet in salt or alum and water ... Nails should be cut straight across. Men are cautioned against getting boots too small for them.'

Filthy feet with long black nails thrust sockless, soapless, into creased boots shapelessly disintegrating. No alum. For some, no boots. Use puttees. Or strips of blanket. No blanket? Puttees worn away to holes and fraying thread? Go barefoot! Stand and feel instinctively with right hand at right hip for the familiar presence of one's rifle. No rifle? No! Rifles destroyed at Kut. Years ago.[1] Yellah, yellah.

For some, no yellah, yellah. Dead where they slept. Always the big ones. 'The generals like 'em thin and brown.'[2] Fall into column. Avoid the rear. At each halt the rear catches up only just in time to continue marching. Avoid the head. Too close to the Kurds. Try to get in the middle. Everyone trying to fall in in the middle: prepared to close ranks against the latecomer. Yellah, yellah. How much farther? Two hours. An Arab settlement. Milk and dates for sale, and meat and chapattis. No money. No rations, no money. How many dates for a pair of boots, you bastard son of Allah? Take 'em then.

In Baghdad their officers bought food with the gold and silver with which they had been paid in Kut, and were paid more gold by the Turks, and given more gold by Mr Brissel, the American consul.

Also they had their names taken, though for what purpose no one seemed sure. Even less sure were the Turkish soldiers who wrote down their names, which they were apt to confuse with their place of birth, surnames being a refinement not practised by the Ottoman.

'Votre nom?'

'Lieutenant Henry Curtis Gallup, Hants.'

'Henry Curse it Hants,' the clerk carefully inscribed.

'Captain Leonard Mathias, Bombay.'

'Leonard, son of Leonard, Bombay,' wrote the clerk;[3] and so on, until the list was finished, when it was sent to Constantinople, where doubtless it was lost.

With his entourage of two British officers, two British orderlies, an Indian servant, a Portuguese cook and a Turkish A.D.C., Townshend set off by train to Samarrah, whence by victoria, motor car and more trains he would make the long journey to Constantinople.

With their orderlies, camp-beds, stools, valises, gold and umbrellas – purchased locally and carried eccentrically, but with as much aplomb as they wore their monocles or brandished their long cigarette-holders – his officers followed him the next day. Unlike their General, however, they were not well-housed in Samarrah, being required to doss down in the station courtyard on the opposite side of the river from the old city with its magnificent gilded domes, and were not entirely pleased to see their commander sweep off, without a word to them, in a horse-drawn victoria. He had passed a pleasant morning shooting sand-grouse, and looked forward to more of this sport at his next stop, Tekrit.

'Funny way to go into captivity,' Boggis observed sourly to his fellow orderly: but Townshend, his gun across his knee, laughing in his victoria, seemed happy enough.[4]

The following morning, his officers set off to cover the same journey by donkey. In theory they had a donkey each: but in practice they needed half their donkeys to carry their baggage, which meant that for each two officers there was only one donkey to ride. And even that was theoretical, because each pair of officers shared three orderlies, which meant that five men must take it in turn to ride one donkey. Riding for an hour, walking for four hours, they made their way across the coarse-grained plain, stumping through rank grass and patches of brilliant poppies. They were, one of their intellectuals assured them, following the route of Xenophon's great retreat from Baghdad to the Bosporus more than two thousand years previously: but they were less concerned with Xenophon than with their tortured feet and their tortured forks. Straddling razor-spined donkeys was a pastime fit only for prepubic Arabs.

Not all of them, however, had left Samarrah for Tekrit that day. A few who were ill had been allowed to stay behind, one of whom was the subaltern who owed thirty rupees to a refreshment room babu in India. He had malaria and it is malaria's habit to rack its victims only on alternate days: so the following day he felt better, and asked for permission to visit the city to buy some quinine.

Permission granted, he crossed the river on a coracle, escorted by an Arab sergeant and an Arab soldier, and was led through the gates of Samarrah's massive walls to a hospital where the sergeant indicated a Turkish officer sitting on a bench, drinking coffee. Mellor approached him, saluted and was invited to sit and take coffee.

Having sipped his coffee, he asked for quinine. 'I'm sorry,' the Turk replied, 'we have no quinine. Your blockade has prevented it.'

Mellor asked for bandages, for chlorodyne, for iodine; but the answer was always the same, 'Your blockade has prevented it.'

'Well what *have* you got?' he demanded.

'I'll show you,' said the Turk. And led him through the hospital past two hundred patients for whom there were no drugs of any kind.

Outside again, the Turk said, 'It is a pity that Turkey and Britain are on opposite sides in this war. I hope soon our traditional friendship will be resumed.' And, each saluting the other, they parted, Mellor aware at last that the Turk – as distinct from the Kurd and the Arab – was not brutal, but simply the victim of a war on three fronts, an impenetrable blockade, a shortage of everything and a tradition of inefficiency as old as his coracles.[5]

For those officers left sick and wounded in Baghdad's hospital the situation was little better. Slightly better, perhaps, because they were regularly visited by French Dominican Sisters who were reckless in their generosity: and yet slightly worse because Enver Pasha was soon to arrive, and no Turk was prepared to seem sympathetic to them. Fortunately, they had enough money to eat fairly well and their quarters were not uncomfortable.[6]

Down-river, the two columns of troops continued their desert trek, the one a day behind the other, two desperate columns of head-down trudging men, each column about five miles long, its mounted guards tirelessly, goadingly circling. They had been given another six biscuits each, and some dates, and the promise of a good meal at Azizieh. But at Azizieh, they received nothing.

So they set off for El Kutunie, Zeur, Llaj and Ctesiphon, their stragglers now quartered in Arab huts as if the guards had tired of killing them. 'See you later,' the stragglers told their friends, shaking hands. 'Yes.' But they didn't believe it. Neither of them believed it.

The first column reached and passed the one-time battlefield of Ctesiphon. Now just desert, and the Arch lowering down at them.

The second column reached Ctesiphon, in it some of the West Kents who had joined Townshend's division at Azizieh as it retreated to Kut. For months they had heard of the marvels of the Arch: but, looking at it now, with the eyes of starving men, saw nothing marvellous. Just ancient bricks. 'Why didn't you blow the bloody thing up?' they demanded.[7]

And so along the Diyala, across it and into flag-bedecked Baghdad; a gaunt, shambling, scarecrow column winding its way through the bazaar, indifferent to the gobs of spittle and the clicking of German cameras, its only thought to lie down and sleep for ever. Thousands of lean-legged men, some heavy-booted, some barefooted, some gouty in swathes of torn blanket. Tattered shorts and blackened shirts. Or bare, blackened skin. Battered sun helmets. And hundreds fewer than when they had started.

Out of the bazaar at last – German sailors from *Goeben* spitting with the best of them – then across the river again to the railway station where there was a barbed-wire compound. No shade, no latrines. Halt, drink, unfold blanket, make bivouac in blazing sun, crawl under it and die.

The Norfolks' colonel, seeing them, rushed to help: but was driven back by the guards. Almost disinterestedly his exhausted men told him that it had been a bad march: that stragglers had been suffocated with handfuls of sand, or had their skulls stove in. So he demanded that in future he be allowed to march with them: but they drove him away.

At which moment General Townshend was again shooting sandgrouse, this time at Tekrit: but at three o'clock he and his party climbed into their carriages and set off across the desert, heading for Mosul, four days' ride away.

At four o'clock they passed a small party of emaciated Britons and, halting, discovered that they were the few survivors of *Julnar*'s selfless bid to run food through the Turkish lines to Kut. The sub-lieutenant who led them gave Townshend a vivid description of how it was to be marched through Asia Minor: and Townshend had only to look at them to know that all of it was true. But he found himself unable to help them. Did not suggest that he should march with them. Offered none of them a lift in his victoria. Just gave them money – and rode on.[3]

In Baghdad, Delamain and some of his medical officers tried to help those who lay in the barbed-wire compound; but there was little the Turks would let them do. Little either, at that moment of utter exhaustion, that their troops seemed prepared to do for themselves. Lacking latrines, they made no effort to dig them. Disorganized, they seemed too dispirited to reorganize. Aware how fatal it was to sell their boots and clothing, they continued to sell them – to locals who had bought from their guards a franchise to exploit the Ingleez. Sold them for food. Or cigarettes. A life for a fag.

It was the American Consul who saved them. As representative of their Protecting Power, he took his duties seriously, shaming the Turks into putting five hundred of the weakest and sickest of them into hospital and himself giving some of them money. Not, of course, as much money as he had given the officers (because they were not officers, and because their need was greater than the officers): but at least some money, for some of them at least.

America's record as the Protecting Power in Turkey from that time onwards is one of devotion and generosity, in spite of the fact that little of her protection was allowed for almost a year to shield those who would most need it. But for that the Turks were to blame. Determined to demonstrate their victory over the British to as many of their people as possible, and to use their prisoners as profitably as possible, they dispatched the survivors of the march from Shamran to the remotest parts of Turkey and there made them build the railway line which one day would link Baghdad to Constantinople.

At the moment that railway was merely a series of disjointed sections across illogical patches of desert. Wherever there were mountains, or structural difficulties to be overcome, there was no railway. Townshend's men were to pierce the mountains with tunnels and overcome the difficulties beyond. They would, of course, die, as thousands of Armenians had already died: but that was to be their role.

'Yellah, yellah.'

Collect and roll up blankets, strap on water bottles, stand and be counted, and recounted, and counted again: then to the station, to board the train to Samarrah, forty to a horse truck. And six hours later, at midday, reach Samarrah, astonished by its superb golden dome. Six biscuits issued to each of them, and four dates: and tomorrow the beginning of a two-day march to Tekrit. No donkeys, no victorias and – fortunately – no idea of what lay ahead of them in the next forty-eight hours; except that they must survive them on six biscuits, four dates and two bottlefuls of water.

And so they set off with their new guards in the heat of the day, and were exhausted by the first leg of their march, during which they had to ford an icy stream; and filled with hatred on the second leg, because their guards made them empty their water bottles[8] before driving them across a sun-glittering salt pan. Feet and boots crunching the glaring crust, tongues swollen, flogged on by mounted guards who themselves drank frequently, and filled with hate, they stumbled along.

'How much farther?'

'Two hours more.'

Meantime the train that had conveyed them the seventy miles to Samarrah was heading back to Baghdad; where, realizing that they could depend only upon themselves, many of those in the compound were beginning to acquire that capacity for improvisation and theft which, allied to an equal capacity for hatred, keeps men alive in times of deprivation. They made waterbags out of canvas stolen from tents. They sold more cautiously, and kept the money, aware that a mere four piastres – four hundredths of a lira – would buy a donkey-ride from one point to another. They convinced the Arabs that such mundane articles as safety-pins and cheap sun-glasses had great virtue, and obtained from them prices that were ludicrously high. And they began to listen to the language of their guards, and to learn it.

And then they too were herded into horse trucks, and carried to Samarrah; whence, leaving their seriously sick behind in a bug-infested barrack, they marched off again towards Tekrit, whilst their train returned for those who, having followed them from Shamran, had entered a Baghdad compound filthy with faeces, and made it even filthier.

All along the line, the story would be the same. March until exhausted; then halt at a filthy bivouac and make it even filthier. No organization. No officers to organize them. And they themselves too obsessed with mere survival to think of those who followed.

Beyond the horror of the salt pan lay other horrors: yet some who endured them were getting tougher, inured to the rhythm of trance-like marching and to a pattern that never varied. Given the rhythm, the trance was possible. Given the trance, the pattern impinged less. Almost blind to the pattern, only the acceptable was observed.

Distant fire gouting out of bare desert was acceptable. A French oil-well, their guards explained, which had blazed for years, because no one knew how to put it out.[9]

Guards whistling at their donkeys, to make them ease themselves each time they halted at a stream was acceptable. But donkeys easing themselves upstream of a point at which they themselves drank was unacceptable: so they reverted to their trance, and refused to be affected by it.

Turkish soldiers marching in the opposite direction – heading doubtless for Kut and the too-late battle that would recapture it for the British – were acceptable.

'Where are you going?'

'To the siege of Bombay.'[10]

To the siege of Bombay! That was most acceptable.

But twenty-mile marches were wholly unacceptable: so concentrate on the rhythm, count the steps, close the eyes, sleep a few paces, find the deadening trance – and survive.

Guards, half-Arab, half-Turkish, taking a fancy to the kids was not acceptable: so refuse to think how they were being used in the enemy's tent at night. No use thinking. No use resisting. Don't talk about it. Unless the kids are broken up: then tell them there was nothing they could do about it. ' 'Cos them Arabs is very angry with a whip. You don't do what they want, boy, they has their whack out of you and leaves you to die.'[11] So, whatever is happening in the guard's tent, tie your boots and everything else you own securely to you, wrap up in your blanket, and sleep. Tomorrow it will all start again.

Strangely, and happily, the Indians fared better than the British. Even their morale seemed better. From the moment they left Shamran, they looked after one another. Sikhs looked after Sikhs, Jahts after Jahts, Mahrattas after Mahrattas. All the Indians looked after their own, with the result that fewer of them died, or were throttled as they lay abandoned in the wake of their column. And they seemed able to digest the Turk's almost indestructible biscuit. And they were not, of course, the object of Enver Pasha's especial spleen, as the British were. They died, naturally: but not such a high proportion of them died as of the British.

A party of officers sat or lay in their courtyard at Samarrah, defiant under their umbrellas, unconcerned as they read their books of verse or talked or played bridge. A West Kent sergeant who could speak Arabic, and felt himself a person of some significance because of it, came strutting up.

'Just heard we stand to to march tomorrow, gentlemen.' Then, looking ferociously at the Failed D.S.O., 'Can you march?'

'Good God, no. Always been used to a car! Still, if one must, I suppose one can try.'

Next day they set off – the Failed D.S.O. with socks carefully soaped in the best *Small Book* manner, the West Kent sergeant full of zeal. For mile after mile they alternately rode and marched, scrupulously taking turns with their British and Indian orderlies to straddle the bony spine of the donkeys that carried no baggage. There was too little water and too many stones – which insinuated themselves into one's boots, where soaped socks provided astonishingly little protection: but on they went, five, ten, twelve miles, until the West Kent sergeant fell to his hands and knees.

'Well, sergeant,' greeted the Failed D.S.O., 'I thought you said you could march. I told you *I* couldn't: but I thought you said you could.' So much, he thought, for all that Aldershot nonsense:[12] and plodded on. Plodded on all that day and the next, until his party reached a river reeking of petrol and saw towering above it the rock-perched town of Tekrit. Climbing up to the town, they were housed in a building that reminded them of a barn, and were visited, some of them, by a group of curious German officers.

'How are you getting on?' the Germans asked.

'We're not getting on at all.'

'How are you being fed?'

'We're not being fed at all.' So the Germans gave them two bottles of whisky and two of brandy, and that, along with the meat and fruit and milk and yoghurt they bought made a quite enjoyable meal.[12] They were utterly weary, and not a little apprehensive, but they were coping.

'Treat the Turk like a sepoy,' was their motto.[13] The Turk knew that they were officers and *they* knew that officers were a class for whom the Turk had an abject respect: therefore, exploit his respect.

It could diminish the day's march by not one inch, because the Turk had to get them to the next halt or be thrashed by his own officers, but it *would* diminish the sensation of being captives. It could increase their rations by not one ounce, because the Turk had paid them in Baghdad solely to ensure that they could buy their own food thereafter, but it would mean that, whenever they wanted to halt and buy something, they would simply halt and buy it. It could shorten their captivity by not one day, but it would make captivity less passively intolerable.

Some of them, in fact, had even begun to feel sorry for their captors. Not, of course, for their officer captors, who were absolute shits, but for the ordinary Turkish soldier who fought so admirably, asked for so little, got even less and was guilty of no worse cruelties to his prisoners than those he daily and phlegmatically endured himself at the hands of his own superiors.

The officers' parties might have been exhausted, but they marched their four hours and rode their one hour with spirit and in good order. They were Xenophon's Greeks retreating, rather than slaves driven into the wilderness: and one day, just as Xenophon's troops had cried 'Thalassa, thalassa ... the sea, the sea,' because they had triumphed over the desert, so they would cry, 'It's over,' because their friends now concentrating at Amarah would have triumphed over the Turks. Theirs was an indeterminate sentence – perhaps a month, perhaps a year, even perhaps two years – but it was not a death sentence, and none of them doubted that he would see it out. Boredom would be their worst enemy, but that they would fight when they arrived wherever it was they were going: meantime, treat the Turk like a sepoy.

Meantime, said the Turks, treat British soldiers like slaves: and their slaves, to whom all thoughts of sea and peace had become as grotesquely unreal as the trees and streams they constantly saw, but knew to be illusions, marched in a trance of exhaustion, hunger and thirst, and looked no farther ahead than the moment when next they would be permitted to halt and drink and sleep.

CHAPTER TWENTY-FOUR

FROM Tekrit, Townshend had travelled by motor first to a small village boasting a bath for rheumatics and earth that oozed neglected oil. Here Boggis and his orderlies had made him a bivouac for the night, his Portuguese cook had prepared him a meal, his A.D.C. and two staff officers had been attentive, and his Turkish escorting officer properly respectful. The next day he had proceeded to Mosul, where he was accommodated in an officers' club. Across the Tigris lay the ruins of Nineveh, around the club was a pleasant garden, beyond the club lay a large barracks: it was all very comfortable and splendidly military.

After resting three days, he and his party, in three lorries, were driven to Nisibin, where again they rested, Townshend noting in his diary the presence there of a detachment of fit young Germans in new khaki uniforms and even newer steel helmets. Turkey, he concluded, had become an 'appanage of Germany'.[1]

From Nisibin they drove to Ras al Ain – where once, Townshend recollected, Belisarius had had a stronghold – and from Ras al Ain travelled by train to Aleppo, where a large reception committee of Turkish officers and gendarmerie met Townshend at the station, escorted him to Baron's Hotel and installed him in a suite that included both a sitting- and a dining-room.

From Baron's Hotel, bathed and in clean linen, he sallied out to see the sights and then called on the Turkish general in command and the resident American Consul. Everywhere he was accorded not just courtesy and respect but fawning admiration: but to no one, apparently, did he mention the plight of *Julnar*'s marching survivors, nor that of his troops, which, he can hardly have failed to realize, must have been as bad.

In all of Asia Minor, the only Britons as fortunate as he were the 345 sick officers and men exchanged from Baghdad for 345 Turkish prisoners of war from Basra: but even they, when they reached Basra, said nothing publicly about the plight of those they had left behind them. Not because new-found comfort and safety had made them indifferent to their recent comrades' suffering, but because Sir Beauchamp Duff, their mulish Commander-in-Chief, forbade it. In 1943, by making public the fearful conditions suffered by Japanese prisoners of war in Thailand, the British Government procured for them an almost immediate amelioration: in 1916, by saying nothing, and by muzzling those who wanted to speak, Townshend and Duff condemned ten thousand of their troops to months of agony and death.

In May 1916 Basra was preoccupied not with the fate of its captive troops but with aerial photographs that seemed to indicate that the Turks were damming up the Shatt al Hai, which would eventually dry up the lower Euphrates, below Nasariyeh, and leave all its river steamers stuck in the mud. What Basra wanted from those just returned from Baghdad was not atrocity stories but an accurate report of what they had seen as they had sailed round Kut, past Woolpress Village and the mouth of the Hai, of Turkish damming activities.

They had seen no such activities, the exchanged prisoners reported. What had been interpreted as Turks building bunds across the Hai was merely Arabs preparing gardens for melons and cucumbers on each of its banks! Vastly relieved, Basra proceeded to lose all interest in anything else the exchangees might have wanted to say – except to ensure that they did not say it.

Which was tragic for those not so fortunate as to be exchanged, because the march from Shamran to Baghdad, and from Samarrah to Tekrit, had been almost enjoyable compared with the marches that followed to Nisibin and Ras al Ain, and from Aleppo hundreds of miles across mountains and plainland into the farthest reaches of Turkey.

It was Enver Pasha who was to provide the next, and almost the last link between Townshend the fêted General and his unfortunate captive troops. At Baghdad, Enver Pasha had ordered the rankers to be paraded for his inspection.

As planes flew overhead dropping triumphal garlands, and a very tall German officer escorted him – who was very short – he had walked down the tracks of the railway line and inspected them.

'Where is your coat?' he had asked one of them through his interpreter.

'Your bloody blokes pinched it,' he was told and, on hearing this translated, had smiled and walked on.[2]

'Why are you not wearing your boots?' he had asked another.

'Because I've got an ingrowing toe-nail.'

'Then tie your boots to your foot and march,' he had retorted;[3] and had proceeded to the officers' hospital.

'Well,' he had said there to one of Mrs Milligan's recent owners, 'the Turkish Army has done what nobody has ever done before – captured a British division. What do you think of that?'

'May I reply as man to man?' the English officer had inquired.

'Of course.'

'Then, if the position of the two forces had been reversed, do you really think it would have taken the *British* Army five months to capture a Turkish division?'

'Take him out and shoot him,' Enver – always prone to shoot those who disagreed with him – had snapped to his A.D.C.

'But you gave him permission to speak as man to man,' the A.D.C. protested: and, glaring at them both, Enver had cancelled his execution order and stamped out.[20]

'Boy,' grinned the A.D.C., who had been educated in America, 'you sure gave him a bibful.' But, too powerful to be worried by bibfuls, Enver had moved on.

At Samarrah, to a group of derisive officers, he had repeated the familiar patter, 'You are our treasured and honoured guests': and at Mosul had met a batch of officers who, being officers, were in no desperate condition, though tattered and weary. One of them was a doctor who had been detached from a previous party to look after the sick.

'Are your men being well looked after?' Enver had asked.

'No, sir, they are not. They must be given proper hospital facilities. The barracks they are in are not good enough.'[4]

Nodding, Enver had ordered a hospital to be made available and had continued his journey to Bozanti, where he met Townshend, who had just arrived in a German lorry.

Received in the saloon of Enver's private train, Townshend at last sought better conditions for his men: but the Turkish Minister of War, who had seen even more of those conditions than Townshend, refused to commit himself, except to say that those who marched would be well looked after, which Townshend knew to be untrue. Enver had little difficulty in changing the subject, however, because he then referred to Townshend's skill as a general, than which nothing could have been more acceptable to the Englishman's ears.

'He spoke', Townshend reported, 'in very flattering terms of the defence of Kut, and of my ability in advancing nearly to Baghdad with what he called une poignée d'hommes. He said I should be the honoured guest of his nation, which appreciated the way I had done my duty to my country.'[5]

Flattery as fulsome as this could hardly have failed to distract Townshend from the tiresome matter of the safety of his men: and certainly he appears to have been distracted, because his subsequent requests for better treatment concerned only himself.

'I reminded him of his offer to me in a telegram to go home on parole if I did not destroy my guns. I told him it was impossible for me to purchase my liberty in that way, and so I had destroyed them, and now I hoped he would allow me to be exchanged and go to England.'[5]

But Townshend was no longer dealing with a Nixon whose poor brain he could addle with nimble words. Enver was not prepared to let him have things both ways as he had so often had them with Basra: was not prepared to let him preserve his honour by destroying his guns, which had been the price of his freedom, and to hope for his freedom at the same time. On the other hand, it would have been impolite, and most un-Turkish, to have said so thus bluntly.

> He said [Townshend noted] that perhaps it would be done: he would see. He said that I must not grieve at being a prisoner; it was the fortune of war ... He said he would see me on my arrival at Constantinople ... and, shaking hands cordially with me, ended the interview. A large staff of German and Austrian officers were with him, and, as I walked along the train, many of them saluted me, others snapshotting me with Kodaks ...[6]

General Melliss, well enough at last to proceed on his way, followed in the wake of his marching men. The white bones of those who had died shocked him: but the sight of men still living, but no longer human, outraged him. One, crawling across the desert on all fours, thought he was a dog. Others lay with their arms wrapped across their eyes, so that they could not see their comrades abandon them. Others lay huddled, the dead and the near dead, in Arab tents, the living doomed to die the day they could no longer crawl to the river for water.

Raging and bullying, refusing to accept denials, His Excellency Melliss Pasha attached those who still breathed to his party, even loading them on to his own cart, and ordered that they be given such drugs as were available. What money he had, he spent on those he collected: and at each town he would storm into the commandant's office and insist that they be put in hospital. He did it at Samarrah, he did it at Tekrit, and at Nisibin and Ras al Ain and Mosul and Islahiya: but still other parties dragged themselves up the line from Samarrah.

To Tekrit, where they were made to bivouac on the river bank below the town: from which the locals hurled stones down upon them; where there was no wood for fires to cook their issue of wheat and oil; where the only shade came from blankets; but where at least they could swim and, for the first time in three weeks, wash their clothes.

To Mosul, a three-day march, freezing at night, their ration one sheep to 250 men a day, the road flinty on feet almost all bare because those boots that had not been stolen had by now fallen to pieces. At Mosul they were packed into cells riddled with lice and devoid of latrine buckets. A sixteen-year-old bugler refused to give himself to a Turk who wanted him, and was bastinadoed. Mosul was the worst yet. Their water-point lay just below a hospital cess pit and when, trying to avoid the floating turds, they took too long filling their bottles, they were harried away with screams of 'Haidi git'. When they tried to buy food with what was left of their clothing, they were prevented with bellows of 'yessok'; and when they wanted to sleep, were driven on with shouts of 'yellah, yellah'.

To Nisibin, where the hospital was a charnel house, its dying men naked except for a loin-cloth, the flies crawling in and out of their mouths even before they died. The British medical officer did everything possible (even ingratiating himself with those Germans whose presence Townshend had noticed, and stealing from them anything that might help his men), but still they died. Wanted to die. 'Oh, pray God, sir,' groaned a skeletal, filthy travesty of a man, who a month ago had been a youth, 'pray God that I may die quickly.'[7] And as the padré to whom he spoke prayed for him, Russian prisoners, whose condition was even worse, sang their melancholic Slavic songs, and assured any who spoke to them that they had been glad to surrender, because even this was better than fighting a war in which they had had no interest at all.

'Yellah, yellah': and Nisibin receded into the distance as they climbed a mountain and looked back upon it. Looked back not because it had been anything less than frightful, but because it was their last glimpse of the Tigris – which had always been their source of water. Now they must rely on village wells, and most of the villages through which they would pass would be Armenian villages, long since deserted, and their wells would be choked with the corpses of those whom the Turks had slaughtered.

'That day's march was awful,' a diarist recorded.[8] Even compared with their trek across the salt pan, it was awful. And each succeeding day it got worse, a trail of skeletons and corpses – Armenians – warning them that the future offered them less hope than ever. And then came thunderstorms to make their progress slower, their nights icier.

In increasing numbers, men fell out and, lying on the ground, pressed their forearms across their eyes: and those beside whom they had marched failed even to notice that they were gone. Of all the horrors of a horror-packed trek that would last a thousand miles, no memory is more ghastly than that of men lying alone, knowing that they must die alone, covering their eyes to blot out the sight of their colleagues deserting them. For them the Arab with his dagger or his handful of sand, or the guard with his rifle butt, would have been a mercy: instead – solitude, despair, abandonment and long hours of thinking of... what? Impossible to say. They left no diaries. Would have been too weak to write anyway. But when they were found, dead, those outraged forearms had not moved. To the very last, they had refused to gaze again upon so alien a world.

Those who survived reached Ras al Ain: where, having struggled so far, one of them promptly threw himself down a well and drowned.[9] Then on again by train, briefly, to the mountains. Packed tight, robbed without mercy, and starving. Literally starving. They had marched through all of May and much of June and now, the railway having ended, would march again, across the Amanus mountains, through the rest of June as well. Village names meant nothing any longer: only the freezing mountain air, and marching, and dying on bare feet, any longer signified.

'Still with feet!' Corporal Candy's diary records. 'Rations for one day, a small quantity of rice in the morning, dinner at 4 p.m., two chapattis, tea, a small quantity of rice and ...' But Corporal Candy died before he could record what else he had had for dinner. He was one of fifty R.F.C. mechanics who had marched out of Kut – of whom seven, in 1918, would return to England.[10]

For the officers, the same trek; but at a pace they could to some extent control, with donkeys and carts they could occasionally ride, with food they could always buy, and with malicious delight at the sight of colonels ardently collecting camel dung for camp-fires towards the end of each day's march.[11]

And with spirit enough to rebuke the Turks for having rounded up the inhabitants of every Armenian town and either massacred them or driven them out to die of starvation and fever. Those who had been herded into churches and burnt to death had probably been the luckier ones. Luckier certainly than the children tossed into the air and spitted on bayonets. Luckier than those thrown alive down their own wells. Luckier than the women and girls sold into concubinage and slavery. Luckier than those pathetic bands of women, old men and children driven into the desert to die as they staggered towards 'agricultural settlements' that did not exist. Was it to achieve this that Gladstone had abandoned Britain's traditional policy of friendship with Turkey? To prevent it, he had claimed. Yet, lately, every stage of their march had proved how futile the change in policy had been. The bones, the putrid wells and the dead mother lying with her dead child, ghostly in pale moonlight, abandoned on stony ground,[12] had made them angry; so they rebuked the Turks.

'They were revolutionaries,' a Turkish officer explained. 'And besides, what are *you* doing in Ireland?'[13]

'What are *we* doing in Turkey?' they wondered: but continued to march with spirit along the way that had destroyed so many of their men. Humour helped: although the Turks' habit of planting his mount upstream of you as you drank, and then whistling at it till it eased itself, was hardly hilarious. But even that had yielded its moment of mirth, when a brigadier fell out of the column, dropped his shorts and squatted – to be affronted by the long, enticing whistle of a very non-Aldershot subaltern.

Again unlike their skeletal men, most of the officers had become merely lean and tough. Marching was no longer, to many of them, an effort. Some, perversely, were even enjoying it. And none were being abandoned. Nor were there any longer any prejudices against officers who were Indians. Subedar Majors Gitab Ghul and Dula Singh, for example, were admired by everyone in their party – especially Dula Singh, whose habit it had become to leave a few chapattis by the head of any sleeping officer who seemed to him to be weakening. He never said anything, and was never seen leaving his chapattis: but everyone knew it was Dula Singh.[14]

Through Mosul, Nisibin and Ras al Ain they made their wearisome but undejected march: and then by train to the mountains – to Islahiya, where the railway ended and they found a group of rankers lying naked in Arab tents, their dead lying outside until the sun went down, when those who were dying buried them.[15]

Ahead of all his men, Townshend travelled by train and arrived at Constantinople on June 3rd, to be met by the G.O.C. of the Turkish Army, his Staff, members of the War Office and a crowd of respectful locals. Introduced to everybody of importance at a reception in the waiting-room – while von der Goltz's coffin was removed from the train with no pomp or ceremony at all – he felt very flattered: and was even more flattered to be entertained later at Constantinople's best restaurant, then escorted by a detachment of cavalry through the city to the water-front, where a Naval pinnace awaited him. His baggage, Staff and servants aboard, he sailed ten miles down the Sea of Marmara to the fashionable island of Halki, where, high on a cliff, he took up residence in a comfortable villa.

That same day, in Mosul, a party of his troops was herded into the serai, 'where we remained on view to the population, who flocked around to see such strange and half starved people'.[16]

That same day, at Islahiya, as they began to march across the Amanus mountains – which he had found quite beautiful[17] – his troops were 'dying like sheep, shitting and falling back in it'.[18]

That same day, in the building the Turks called a hospital, those still too ill to march from Samarrah were being allowed by their captors to die in agony. There was no treatment for them and very little food, and those who fouled their beds were given an injection of brandy-coloured fluid after which they stopped fouling their beds because they were dead.[19]

By that same day, more than a third of the British troops to whom Townshend had vowed that he was leaving them only to procure their repatriation had died.

CHAPTER TWENTY-FIVE

Two days later, Townshend was taken back to Constantinople to see Enver Pasha, who told him not only that he was to consider himself a guest but also that the Sultan had ordered that he should receive the honours and salutes due to a corps commander.[1] At last someone had given him the promotion he had so long pursued: and if, ironically, it came from his enemies, Townshend seems to have been unaware of any irony.

But this was not the only inducement Enver offered to keep his guest quiet and happy. Townshend, he said, could go where he liked when he liked, so long as he would promise to warn the Minister of War if ever he was contemplating escape.

'Yes, I will do so,' Townshend promised.[1]

And would he like his wife and daughter to join him? Enver inquired. Yes, he would.[1] So Enver ordered a telegram to be dispatched to the British Foreign Office, advising that the Sultan had given permission for Townshend's wife and daughter to join him; and Townshend returned to Halki, to await their arrival, and walk in the woods, and study his books, and take daily swims, which he found 'delicious'.[1]

For his officers, still trudging north-eastwards, life was not quite so amiable; and for his men not amiable at all; but no purpose is served by tracing their entire itinerary. As it had started, so it continued, except that, after Islahiya, small groups were detached from the larger parties to work, under German engineers, as tunnellers through the mountains and navvies on the railway lines. The rest marched on – to Marmourie and Bagtshe: and General Melliss followed them, picking up their stragglers, raging at the Turks.

He arrived at Marmourie with thirty such stragglers and, when the Turks refused to help them because more than three hundred in one week had already died under their care, persuaded a German major to send them to a German hospital. To those working at Marmourie he gave his last five liras in gold before he left them: but the Turks, tired of his ceaseless interventions, then put him into a victoria and hustled him out of the way.

Almost all those stragglers whom Melliss failed to find died alone in the desert: yet there were exceptions. One such, having fainted on the march, woke up alone and began to stumble on again. Where, he had no idea: he just stumbled. Until an Arab with a revolver halted him and drove him to a railway camp manned mainly by Armenians.

There an Austrian woman gave him some bread, pointed and ordered him to go 'That way.' So that way he went, through two villages where everyone ignored him, because he was nothing to do with them, and on to a third, where he was rounded up with some criminals due for execution and, tied to them, flung into a shed.

'Why don't you petition the governor?' an Armenian fellow prisoner suggested: but he could not think how he could petition the governor when merely to visit the latrine he had to walk chained to another prisoner. Also he was bearded, naked except for a ragged pair of shorts, sun-blackened and very dirty. He did not consider himself the sort of person from whom a governor would welcome a petition. So he stayed in the shed, tied to a murderer.

Then a guard came and shouted for him, and took him outside to an Armenian woman dressed entirely in white. Surveying his bearded, blackened face, she said, 'You're not English.'

'I damned well am.'

'Yes,' she smiled, 'I believe you are,' and offered him bread and five liras. He accepted the bread, but refused the gold. 'They'd cut my throat for that in there,' he explained, pointing to his fellow prisoners. Then asked why she had come to him.

The brother of the Armenian who had suggested he petition the governor had told her he was there, she said. And Armenians were very pro-British. Thanking her, he allowed himself to be led back to confinement: where he languished another week. Then, as his companions were either executed or sent to various railway camps, he was taken by mounted escort to Bagtshe, where he rejoined the party from which he had fallen out.[2] He had had a typically Turkish experience. In the next two years, hundreds of his fellow rankers, and hundreds of officers, would find themselves in similar situations, where they would be casually imprisoned, bravely aided and fortuitously released.

At Bagtshe an N.C.O. was asked by the commandant, 'How many troops have you every one?' and was shocked to hear himself reply, 'A hundred and forty.' His party had left Kut over three hundred strong. Now it was 140: and among those 140, not one fit man. All were skeletal: 'many were fit to die with dysentery and various other complaints.'[3]

Various other complaints! Like beriberi, which made their legs elephantine and suety. Press a thumb into the leg and it left a dent for an hour. Like malaria, with its icy shivers and raging sweats every alternate day. Like Baghdad sores, which covered their legs and arms. Like cholera – except no one cared to call it cholera. Like starvation. Like typhus. Like sunstroke. Like digging tunnels and building a railway when suffering from all of them.

'Building a railway.' Today the words evoke visions only of prisoners dying under the Japanese in Thailand in 1943: but it was equally frightful in Turkey in 1916. Not because the Turks despised their prisoners as the Japanese did, but simply because they had no drugs to give them, and little food, and no organization. And because it was midsummer at first, and later mid-winter, and both were killers. And because those who started working on the railway in late June and early July 1916 were men sick and exhausted from a march that had lasted sixty days or more.

Few Turks, in fact, were brutal (and those who were were almost always officers), but they were all either lazy or indifferent, or both. The ordinary soldier was good-naturedly lazy; the ordinary officer was lazily inefficient; and had their prisoners been healthy, life would have been quite tolerable. But Turkish hospitals lacked everything a hospital should have had. There were only three remedies. Opium pills that deadened the pain and reduced the will to live; the brandy-coloured injection that killed; and the knife that cut without benefit of anaesthesia. And that, for men with beriberi, malaria, cholera, typhus, enteritis and sunstroke, meant death.

In these circumstances, then, the prisoners began to work, levelling the desert, boring through the mountains, filling skips, pushing them to near-by ravines, laying explosives, breaking rocks.

For those who levelled the desert, a quota of so many cubic metres a day. They rose at 2 in the morning and marched to work, each man carrying two sixteen-pound bricks. As soon as they arrived, their quota for the day was marked out. As soon as the 'posta' turned his back, they moved back the markers, to reduce their quota. Then work. And, at the end of it, march back to camp, carrying skinfuls of water; eat a small meal and retire to their tents, thirty to each bell tent; and sleep feet inwards to the centre pole, until 2 the following morning.

For those who broke rocks, a small hammer and large stones and the inevitable quota. The Indians being better at it than the British, as soon as the Indians turned their backs, the British stole some of *their* broken stones and so, again, reduced their quota.

For those who tunnelled, the endless pushing of skips to the nearest ravine: tip and return to the tunnel: load and push and tip at the ravine. Return to the tunnel. Push back to the ravine. The heat was wicked, the rations were negligible, the flies were myriad, the camps were filthy and no one bothered guarding them at night because there was nowhere they could go, except to death by thirst in the desert. They received no mail, they received no parcels and, at the end of their first month's work, they were paid five piastres. A box of matches cost three.

The officers also had reached the end of their march, and the lot of those who were installed at Kastamuni was typical. They found a number of empty Armenian houses awaiting them, and an empty Greek school, and plank beds with thick straw mattresses, a pillow, a sheet and a cotton quilt, and a basin and chair to each room. They found tables laid with clean napery and well-mannered young Greeks ready to wait on them as they ate meals provided by a contractor. They found a lazy commandant and middle-aged postas in ragged blue uniforms whose one desire was to avoid trouble. They found a diet of eggs, milk, butter, yoghurt, cheese, fruit, meat and bread. And they found that they had nothing to do.[4]

So, being British, they at once demanded that they be allowed to exercise, which their captors (who knew that they had just completed a 1,200 mile journey in 56 days, 640 miles of it on foot or on donkey) found very confusing.[5]

Then they examined their various contractors' invoices for food, service, accommodation, furniture, firewood and the like, and realized that they were being dunned six liras a month altogether when all that the most junior of them was paid by the Turks was seven. Which left very little for such necessary extras as alcohol, tobacco, jam and payments to orderlies: so they took their commandant in hand and had the system changed, and settled down to creating a civilized community, playing bridge, reading books, cashing cheques through their Armenian interpreter, attending lectures, learning languages, planning escapes and organizing games of rounders. At the end of their first month in Kastamuni, they were receiving letters and Fortnum and

Mason parcels from England, and were each of them paid at least seven liras – or seven *hundred* piastres.[6]

A second party of Indian Army officers had been sent to Yozgad, perhaps because they were Indian Army rather than British, or perhaps because they had annoyed the Turks when they reached Angora by singing:

> We won't, we won't, be buggered about,
> When we walk out
> We always shout,
> We won't, we won't be buggered about.[7]

The Turks had not cared for this song: but their officer prisoners soon made themselves at home in Yozgad.

Townshend also received his regular mail and parcels: but August and September, for him, were bad months. First came news that Mr Asquith, the Prime Minister, had refused to allow his wife and daughter to join him in Constantinople ('I am sorry to say', wrote Asquith to Alice Townshend, 'that the matter is not one in which I feel able to interfere')[8] and then came the worst blow of all.

'Boggis,' he snarled one morning, brandishing a letter from home, 'what do you think that bloody sixth marquis has done now?'

'I don't know, sir'.

'He's produced a son!' And raged at the injustice of it.[9] Since boyhood he had lived in the hope of succeeding to his grandfather's title. For eleven years the marriage of the one barrier between himself and that title had proved unfruitful and his hopes of becoming the seventh Marquis Townshend had soared even higher. But now there was a direct heir, and he would never become a peer. He would never even become a lieutenant-general; and, as a major-general, he would probably not even become a knight. More importunately than ever, then, he begged Enver Pasha to procure his repatriation: but the Sultan would not allow it and, embittered almost to the point of madness,[9] he had to continue his luxurious life in Constantinople.

Ironically it was mainly Townshend's troops who now were being repatriated. Determined to retrieve as many of their own prisoners of war as possible, the Turks were willing enough to exchange them for those who lay ill in Baghdad – who were both useless and an embarrassment, since they were dying in large numbers of diseases their captors were unable to cure.

The only trouble with these exchanges was that the Turk was so lamentably inefficient and reluctant to assume any responsibility. An exchange was easily ordered from Constantinople: but in Baghdad it involved weeks of havering, deciding who should go and when they should leave.

For the hundreds who lay ill, each hoping that he would be one of those chosen few, the delay was an added torment – as if they were not sufficiently tormented already. Dressed in loose white blouses, caftan-type over-shirts, and skull-caps, and shod in sandals, dragging themselves to squat over latrines long since filthy beyond all description, lacking food, care and money, they watched one after another of their comrades die, the good Sisters of Mercy praying by their bedsides. Assailed day and night by moans of, 'Water, water,' they watched their comrades go mad. Some so mad that they attacked their guards, who then ceased to be phlegmatic and took them outside and shot them.

'Water, water' – that incessant, whining, pleading moan was the worst torment of all. Melliss's batman, whose broken leg had almost knit, found that he could stand it no longer, so he crawled out of the long ward into the courtyard and drew from the well a bucketful of water. But he was discovered by guards who, alarmed at his temerity, beat him unconscious and had him carried back to his bed.

He awoke to see two Sisters praying by his bedside.

'If you think I'm going to bloody well die, you got another think coming,' he snarled, terrified lest he *was* dying. Smiling, the Sisters left him.

'You insulted them,' his companions at once rebuked him.

'I didn't know what I was saying,' he protested. But they were very angry with him, and he was ashamed of himself, and only the constant removal of those who *were* dying, the sight of them dead later in the courtyard, and the sound of the carts trundling them away, eventually made him forget his offence.[10]

In all the long days and nights they had spent in Baghdad their only moment of pleasure had been the explosion of a bargeful of ammunition salvaged from the Tigris outside Kut and anchored near their convent hospital. But that had not nearly compensated for the lack of all treatment except the occasional issue of a brown pellet of opium.

'I'm going to take mine, Alec,' Hayden's neighbour whispered.

'Don't,' begged Hayden: but he did; and next morning was dragged off his cot, dead. Bearded, dirty, bony and mad-eyed, they just lay on their cots, listened to the dirge of, 'Water, water', and hoped not to die.

'You may be exchanged,' a British officer advised one day: but warned that the Turks were demanding coal and gold as well as their own prisoners of war in exchange, so there would be delays. Always delays. The negotiations went on and on, and the sick at Baghdad almost forgot that some of them might be exchanged.

'Your people don't want you,' a Turkish officer told them day after day:[11] and it was only the tireless devotion of a handful of British medical officers who kept up their spirits and – by treating their wounds – kept them alive.

These medical officers the Turks tolerated because, true to their profession, they worked with equal devotion to heal the enemy's wounded. Only renegade Indians were turned aside.

'You don't belong to us, do you?' Captain Barker asked a Punjabi deserter. 'And you don't belong to the Turks. But you can go to them to get your wound dressed.'[11]

But still men died – or, if they had dysentery and were helpless, were killed off: and still the exchange terms were not agreed.

Then – with no warning – about a hundred men were ordered, 'Pack up!'

Having nothing to pack, they simply got up, gave their boots (if they still owned boots) to those who must stay behind, staggered to the river and boarded a paddle steamer.

'Too many,' objected a Turkish officer: and paraded them for yet another medical examination.

About fifty of them were sent back to the hospital, to die of disappointment: but the rest, dazed and incredulous, sailed down-river. Past Ctesiphon, past Azizieh, past Umm al Tubul, past Kut. Past Kut! At last they could believe they were going home.

Then stopped and were off-loaded at Sannaiyat, where there were only a few Turks, and no sign of any further plans to exchange them. Day succeeded day, then week succeeded week.

'If your people don't soon agree, you will all have to go back to Baghdad,' a Turkish officer warned. Ill-fed and weaker than ever, they waited helplessly: and two of them died.

'*Hey!*' – a terrifying shout – or was it excited? 'There's one of *our* boats!'

Ill or not, they managed to crawl to the river bank; and there, butting towards them, was a British steamer.

Things moved fast then. Aboard, care, food, drink, clean sheets, hot baths, sleep. It was like a dream. As was the hospital in Basra. New ... nurses ... cool ... unbelievable as they came back to life on their neat row of stretchers.

'Any Hampshires here?' a voice called.

'One down there' – pointing where Hayden lay.

'You a Hampshire?'

'Yes.'

'What's your name?'

'Same as yours, you bloody idiot!' – and two brothers were reunited.

'What've you been doing?' Hayden asked his brother, later, when they had become calmer.

'Taking this bloke Lawrence up and down the river.'

'What for?'

'I dunno: but dressed up he looks just like one of them bloody Arabs.'[12]

Hayden and his fellow ex-prisoners were fed only upon brandy and water for several days, then given some real food, and then shipped back to India. For them the war was over.

But now, from Baghdad, two more must be selected in place of those who had died at Sannaiyat, waiting for officialdom to make up its mind. Forty men were paraded; two would be chosen. Thirty-eight returned despairingly to their beds; two sailed down-river; one, an officer, the other a youth whose looks and build immediately attracted the Turkish captain of the steamer.

Beckoning the youngster to his cabin door, the captain offered money and indicated what it was he wanted. The offer was refused. Then the Turks called off the exchange: and again the captain called the youngster to his cabin, offering to arrange the exchange in return for favours granted. The favours were not granted, so the captain made a third approach, and was rebuffed for the third time.

Blindfold, both private and officer were then led off the boat, aware that they were about to be shot for no better reason than that the Turks had no idea what to do with them – except the captain, who hadn't been given the chance to do it.

They were placed in a cart, side by side, still blindfold, and trundled off. Then helped out of the cart and led by the hand, the hands on theirs strangely solicitous, to the river's edge again, and helped into a bellum.

'Are you there?' the officer asked anxiously.

'Yes, sir.'

They felt themselves punted downsteam; heard the voices of those who had helped them into the bellum receding; then growing louder again. What could it mean?

'Are you there?'

'Yes, sir.'

A jolt as the bellum grated ashore, and hands helping them out, helping them up on to camels, placing their hands carefully on the pommel of the saddle, slapping the camels, which lurched off. Uncomfortable ... and smelly ... and difficult not to fall off when you couldn't see ... and the camel lurching on, for hours.

Hands at their faces, removing the blindfolds. Blinking. Blind in the sunlight. And there, in front of them, an English sergeant and three English privates.

'Come on, mate,' said the sergeant, putting his arm round the seven-stone boy upon whom – whatever other designs he had had – the Turkish captain had taken pity enough to arrange a two-hour truce. 'We haven't got much time.'

Arms round his waist, they walked him and the officer a mile, or perhaps it was two miles, it seemed a long but effortless way, to a British camp – a city of tents beside the river. But he saw none of them.

His companion, the officer, took him into the officers' Mess – introduced him to the other officers. Everyone very kind. Very gentle.

'Like a drink?'

'Please.'

They gave him a whisky; and, as he drank it, he fell quietly to the floor. He woke up in a tent, was driven to a base camp, shells exploding near by, put on a boat, and carried back to India. He had no idea where he had been since he had left Baghdad: and he didn't care.[13]

CHAPTER TWENTY-SIX

LLOYD GEORGE having raged that the events leading up to the fall of Kut were 'a perfect example of what military administration is capable of if entirely freed from civilian interference', Britain, in July of 1916, had taken over the entire control of the war in Mesopotamia: but none of this had made the least difference to the victims of that military maladministration, who now were slaves in Turkey. Unfed, unkempt, unfit and uncared for, they continued to work on one section or another of the railway line until they were so ill that they had to go to one so-called Turkish hospital or another, where they died like flies.

No matter what they did, hundreds of them died. They learnt Turkish; they attempted to escape; they formed themselves into tight-knit groups – but still hundreds of them died. Others, though, grew mentally tough enough to refuse to die. Grew cunning enough to secure good jobs cooking for the German engineers. Grew un-chauvinistic enough to befriend Australians captured at Gallipoli, whose reckless contempt for authority seemed somehow, in the middle of Turkey, to yield dividends. Grew defiant enough to sabotage the line they were obliged to build. Drew strength from everything and from one another.

'What's that you're eating?'

'Locusts.'

'*What?*'

'It's in the Bible. Locusts and wild honey. Just peel 'em like a shrimp.'

'And?'

'Eat 'em raw.'[1] On five piastres a month – if the Turks remembered to pay it – there was little else they could eat. Thus the summer passed, and the winter began, and the railway grew longer, and they moved to other camps, and died in their hundreds of pneumonia and exposure as well as all the rest.

At Kastamuni the officers had quickly brought their captors to heel. 'One must train them like dogs,' they explained: and once their elderly, good-natured postas had ceased to be suspicious, it had been easy to train them. Mostly it was done by ignoring completely any posta who ordered them to do anything they were disinclined to do, or not to do anything they intended doing: but also they used their in-bred charm and good manners.

And when those failed, they used the Englishman's awful coldness, which made their commandant quite frantic. 'At the beginning of the war,' he raged, 'you stole two of our battleships, and now you have seized most of Egypt, and lately you have been cold to me and have not asked me to dinner or to have drinks with you. And therefore I will break up your house.'[2] So they asked him to dinner and drinks again and later extracted from him every concession conceivable.

They played Rugby and cricket; they boxed; they went on weekly picnics; they gave concerts; they formed a Higher Thoughts Club – which degenerated swiftly into a Tea Club; they received three liras a month from the American Embassy, as well as their minimum of seven from the Turks; and they had obtained from Constantinople an issue of clothing to replace their ruined uniforms.

About their new clothes they were not entirely happy, because striped suits cut very tight, and floppy hats lined with mauve silk made them look like a cross between Italian organ-grinders and sartorially minded gipsies; but the locals thought them very smart, so they made the best of it until parcels from home provided some-thing more suitable.

Such parcels came regularly, each one opened in the presence of the entire Turkish administration, everything in it handled and examined with a naivety they found almost touching. 'Allah, Allah', their nice old postas would mutter, handing from one to the next such Western marvels as razor blades and tinned food and electric-torch batteries. 'Allah, Allah.'[3]

With their parcels and their three liras from the Americans and their seven from the Turks, subalterns could manage well enough: and lieutenant-colonels and colonels, who were paid by the Turks ten and fifteen liras respectively, managed very well indeed. But there was no need for anyone to go short of money. Just write out a cheque on any old piece of paper and Anastas, the Armenian interpreter, would cash it at a very favourable rate of exchange with a Turkish leather merchant. Twenty-five liras to the pound was the official rate; Anastas got ninety; and changed about one thousand pounds' worth of cheques a month, repayable after the war. If the Turkish merchant had been caught, he would have been hanged, and if his debtors had been dishonest, he would have lost a fortune; but he so much preferred Englishmen's cheques to his own currency that he changed them every month – which made life for Kastamuni's gentlemen prisoners of war much more comfortable.

They could eat sufficiently, if not well, and they could drink themselves to death if they so desired – raki being an even swifter means of doing so than brandy – which worried their commandant sufficiently to evoke from him the order, 'As some officers drink more than is necessary they pour liquors throughout the windows down to the street upon the people and disturb the neighbours, making great shindy ...'[3]

Their habit of ignoring postas also worried the commandant. 'If any officers are not obeying the centeries,' he warned, 'the century will have the permission to strike with his steak and with his rifle.'[3] But the officers knew perfectly well that no Turkish posta would dare strike any officer, not even with his steak, and least of all with his rifle, so they continued to ignore their sentries' orders: and if they happened to dislike a particular posta, they ignored him in the presence of one of his own officers, who then struck *him*.[3]

Autumn came, and with it an issue of warmer clothing from the Americans, which made them look less like Italian organ-grinders crossed with gipsies than immigrants to God's own country queueing at a soup-kitchen: but they no longer minded. Their community was a lively one, and they were as happy as officers can be in captivity, playing bridge, talking, studying, producing magazines, playing practical jokes.

Woolley, they had heard, was an expert archaeologist, so they bought a cheap pot at the bazaar and painted it carefully to resemble something from an ancient tomb and, presenting it to him, asked him what it was.

'An impudent forgewy,' he instantly declared.[4] Life in Kastamuni was not dull, not even when winter came.

Nor was it dull in Yozgad, where the routine was the same, but enlivened by two officers who insisted that they received messages from the dead. Messages spelt out by the glass that moved under their fingers from one letter of the alphabet to another.

The Turks were fascinated by these messages – especially the commandant, to whom the two spiritualists had indicated the possibility of discovering where Yozgad's massacred Armenians had hidden their gold. The commandant was even persuaded that such messages were more easily received on water, and was even prepared to take them to the sea and get them a boat – on which they intended to make their escape. But then it all fell through: so Lieutenant Jones and his accomplice had to devise some other means of escape.[5] Meantime winter had arrived, so everyone in Yozgad went tobogganing instead.

To spare him the rigours of winds that swept down from the Russian Steppes and through the neck of the Bosporus, the Turks moved Townshend from exposed Halki to sheltered Prinkipo, a bigger island, where he was given a comfortable seaside villa, once the summer residence of the British Consul.

There he learnt that he had been awarded a Knighthood of the Companion of the Bath, but he seemed far from overjoyed. 'Not before time,' he grumbled to Boggis.[6] To become Major-General Sir Charles Townshend K.C.B., p.o.w., was little gratification to a man who had hoped, with good reason, to become Lieutenant-General Lord Townshend at the very least. Remembering his illustrious ancestor, he had probably hoped to become Field Marshal Lord Townshend: and, remembering his history, he still hoped to become a paroled rather than a captive knight. To this end he had asked the Spanish Ambassador to obtain Enver Pasha's permission for him to leave Constantinople and live in Spain; had fraternized with influential Turks in a most ill-advised manner; and had so plagued influential Englishmen with letters seeking their help that his loyal wife had felt compelled to implore him, 'Beware your enemies at home.'[7]

At a time when Melliss, from his camp at Broussa, was writing passionately to Enver Pasha on behalf of the 6th Division's ill-treated rankers, and Enver was denying that they were being ill treated, Townshend was concerned only with his own release from captivity. So much so that he wrote to Melliss trying to exonerate Enver Pasha from any responsibility for the fate of those who had marched from Shamran, and saying that everything that could be done for his troops was already being done.[7]

Fortunately, the American Ambassador, Mr Morgenthau, was a more compassionate and realistic man, who chose to believe Melliss rather than Townshend. Fortunately, his successor was equally compassionate and realistic. Fortunately, when America entered the war, the Dutch Ambassador proved to be as conscientious in his role of Protector as the Americans had. But it was a tragedy that Townshend had spent four months vainly attempting to procure his own repatriation instead of constantly harrying everyone in Constantinople to look after his dying troops. His apparent indifference to their fate, and his readiness to exonerate Enver Pasha, did not endear him to General Melliss in Broussa – who could also write letters back to England.

At home, at this time, those of his officers who had been repatriated were giving evidence in the House of Lords to a special commission set up by Lloyd George to investigate the Mesopotamian disaster. On his way to the War Office, one of them was halted by an angry old lady.

'Where have *you* been fighting?' she demanded, looking him up and down.

'In Mesopotamia,' he explained.

'Mesopotamia?' she exploded. 'Why not France or the Dardanelles?' And handed him a white feather.[8]

The winter months of 1916–17 killed many of those who worked on the railway: but at last the Americans had discovered where most of them worked and, by the beginning of 1917, warm clothing and some money had been sent to them. Again, not as much money as was sent to their officers, but still it did not occur to them that a system which assigns to non-working, comfortably housed officers at least four hundred liras during their captivity, and to hard worked, ill housed, starving troops a maximum of seventy-six might be a peculiarly unjust one. Unfortunately, the system had not changed by the end of World War II and will doubtless prevail at the beginning of World War VII. In the meantime, it does no harm to expose it.

Nor, at this stage, does it do any harm to reveal that no less than seven of the nine rankers' diaries read in the researching of this book faithfully listed every payment received, both from the Protecting Powers and from the Turks – who paid altogether about six liras for two-and-a-half-years' work. The six liras paid by the Turks seem to be regarded by those who still survive as money hard-earned: the seventy-six paid by America and Holland are still regarded as a gesture of tremendous generosity.

Equally, at this stage, it should be revealed that *nine* of the nine rankers' diaries read by the author contained carefully written and treasured copies of every one of Townshend's communiqués; that only four of the remaining rankers interviewed failed to produce similar copies made on loose sheets of paper; and that only two of those four rankers were prepared to describe Townshend as anything less than a superb and much loved general. And the majority may well have been right in their assessment of him: but, if they were, they knew a man very different from the one revealed by his own written words.

Certainly they were right about their officers, whose conduct in battle and siege they admired, and whose good fortune in captivity they did not begrudge. For what happened to them as a division, before they were captured, they blame only India: and for what happened to them during captivity, at the end of their march, they blame no one. Not Townshend, not their officers, not even the Turks – and, least of all, their postas.

For Turkish civilians they even felt sympathy. They seemed to have so little, apart from their wooden houses – which regularly burnt to the ground. Those who had marched to Angora had found half of it in ashes. And Changri had burnt while its prisoners were working there. 'It's the Russians!' one of them shouted as the flames leapt and houses tumbled. 'The Russians are shelling the town. We're going to be released.' So they spent all their money on a bottle of raki and got drunk: and next day wanted to die because it had not been the Russians at all, and because raki is a malevolent brew.[9]

In every town and village, fires were a regular occurrence: and the Government provided only the most primitive machines with which to fight them. The Government, in fact, provided nothing for any of its citizens except its officials, who were as indolent as they were greedy.

The commandant of the camp at Afion Karahissar, however, was not merely indolent and greedy, he was vicious, perverted and probably insane as well: and those of Townshend's troops unfortunate enough to find themselves in his hands had a worse time than most of their fellow rankers.

Under him, those found to be infested with lice were bastinadoed; those he found attractive were dragged to his quarters and raped; and, apart from a loaf of bread and half a pint of gruel daily, the ration was three small goats to four hundred men every three days.[10] Only the Germans offered any hope of protection against the brutalities of his regime, and even their goodwill was dubious.

'Are you Irish?' a German officer asked a dark-haired English private who weighed eight stone and looked pathetic enough to evoke sympathy from de Sade himself.

'Well,' said the Englishman slowly, wondering whether or not it would be to his advantage to become Irish, and deciding finally to compromise, 'me mother was!' And when the German seemed pleased by this, was sufficiently encouraged to tell him about Afion Kara-hissar's constant floggings.[11] The German at once rebuked the Turkish guards – but it made little difference to their behaviour. Their orders came from the commandant, and the commandant was mad. His brain, they explained, had been affected by the sun when he had served in the Yemen. Mad or not, however, they obeyed him.

At Yozgad, the second of the officers' camps, conditions were naturally vastly different. Yozgad, named after its hundred springs of clear pure water, lay 130 miles south of the Black Sea, was surrounded by bare, rugged hills and had gone to seed. Its streets were cobbled, its houses red-roofed and draughty, and its officer guests lived in two of the larger houses which previously had belonged to Armenians. They referred to their guards as 'the apes', but had quickly made friends with them, their passion for sport having convinced the Turks that they were eccentric but harmless.

'*Sit down* and play,' the postas would beg: but they preferred foot-ball, and long walks into the harsh high hills, and hunting and hockey. And, when winter came, they started tobogganing and even asked if they might ski, which so shocked their commandant that they had to wait till the following winter before he finally allowed them to do it.[12]

But some things they did without his permission. 'Now Darlenwch,' wrote Lieutenant Jones home to Wales, 'send tea and tobacco, Enos, underclothes, sugar, Antipon, tabloid ink, soap, Formamint, aspirin, cocoa, toffee, Oxo, razor, Yardley's dental extract, matches, alum, nuts, dates, Euthymol, novels, quinine, uniform. I remain Yozgad for present.'[12]

The Turks read his letter and allowed it to go to Britain. They knew all officers to be not only mad but fabulously rich as well, and it did not surprise them that their guests found life insupportable without every luxury from alum to tabloid ink, from Yardley's dental extract to Euthymol and novels. What they did not know, of course, was that darlenwch, far from being a term of English endearment, was Welsh for 'read'; and that the first letter of each word in the pre-posterous list that followed was all that Jones wanted read.

In fact his letter was swiftly deciphered, and his message – 'State unsatisfactory. Demand inquiry' – understood. As was proved by the answer: 'Darlenwch dear: Grape nuts, oil, Virol, Enos, razor, nuts, malt, elastic, novels, tea, envelopes, quinine, underclothes, ink, reels, india-rubber, needles, games'[12] ... Jones and his fellow officers were delighted to learn that the Government was inquiring: and it never occurred to the Turks to wonder what use their prisoners could possibly make of such unlikely gifts as oil, reels and india-rubber.

Jones sent more such cryptograms and received more. He advised that the troops were dying like flies and were pitifully hard up, and in return was given news of Zeppelin raids, Lloyd George's accession to the premiership, Romania's entry into the war and the fate of Russia's lumbering armies.[12] Happily, then, he and his colleagues settled down to make the best of their winter, tobogganing and rehearsing a Christmas pantomime. To help them survive, their allowance from the American Embassy was increased to seven liras a month, and later to fifteen.[12]

Thus the winter passed and March arrived and the Turks finally admitted that Kut had been recaptured – which inspired rumours that Baghdad had fallen too, and that America had at last declared war. These rumours the Turks countered with an announcement that the Russians had revolted against their Tsarist regime and that the British had been defeated in Syria. Instinctively, in the weeks that followed, their prisoners decided that the Russian Revolution was a fact, the fall of Baghdad and the British defeat in Syria wishful thinking on the part of themselves and the Turks respectively, and America's entry into the war a probability. In all, they were not dissatisfied.

Townshend, on the other hand, was dissatisfied in at least one respect: he found Constantinople in June so crowded with Germans and holiday trippers that he decided to avoid the city in future and spend his time swimming off the rocks in his garden, studying Napoleon's campaigns in his drawing-room, and sailing with his Turkish A.D.C. on a yacht lent to him by the Turkish Naval School.[13] He did not, however, take the trouble to sail across to Broussa to visit Melliss and Delamain and his other senior officers (and was never to do so for the whole of the war),[14] his mind now being concentrated upon Turkey's obvious bankruptcy and how he might exploit it.[15] After all, Baghdad had fallen, General Falkenhayn had arrived in Constantinople to take over command of all the troops in Asia Minor, and English planes had bombed battleships anchored in the Golden Hind – the Turks must realize that the war was going any way but theirs. Some day they would require an intermediary to seek, on their behalf, a separate peace: and what better intermediary would they find than Sir Charles Townshend, who had defended them against Melliss's charges of brutality to their prisoners of war?

CHAPTER TWENTY-SEVEN

AUGUST 1917 was a revitalizing month for some at least of Turkey's prisoners of war. From their house in Kastamuni four officers were led out of the town one night by Bombardier Prosser, one of their orderlies, whose nocturnal adventures over the past twelve months had made him familiar with every one of its alleys and by-ways. In his long overcoat, and with a fez on his ginger head, he had looked sufficiently Turkish to attract no attention as he prowled the town, and now he led his four officers surely and safely on the first mile of what was to be a very long journey indeed.

At the outskirts of the town, he left them; but bumped into a guard on his way back. Though he escaped, the guard raised a hue and cry and he had only just flung himself into his bed when the commandant came into the room he shared with the other orderlies of his house and placed a suspicious hand over the heart of each of the recumbent men. Prosser's heart apparently beat no faster than it should have done, and the commandant moved on – to discover that four of his treasured officer guests were missing.

Armed only with a forged document to the effect that all Turkish military and civil officers were to give them every assistance, because they were German surveyors, the four travelled north towards the Black Sea for night after night, and then marched boldly through village after village by day. No one seemed interested in them, nor in their forged document which, to the illiterate Turk, could well have said what they claimed it said. The villagers cared not at all who they were, so long as it was not tax-collectors; and the farmers cared not at all so long as they were not thieves.

So, weeks later, they reached the Black Sea – and were there captured by some Turkish soldiers who, unsportingly, made inquiries about their claim to be Germans and, finding it false, sent them off under escort, back towards Kastamuni.

En route, their party was ambushed by brigands. One of the

officers – Sweet, who had blown up Kut's bridge with Matthews – fled and vanished, but was recaptured, and died later of Spanish influenza: the rest were taken prisoner. Then the brigands explained that they, too, wanted to escape, so they returned to the Black Sea, stole a boat and sailed to Russia and freedom.

Meantime, the Turks, greatly annoyed by their departure from Kastamuni, decided to punish those they had left behind them, among whom a violent controversy erupted as to whether or not they should spare themselves such reprisals by promising to make no further escape attempts. Some had no chance of escaping themselves, because they were too old or unfit to walk hundreds of miles across Asia Minor either to the Black Sea or to the Mediterranean, but opposed the idea of a voluntary parole nevertheless; some had no chance and supported it, because they thought escapes brought unfair reprisals against those who remained; and some, though young and fit, were happy enough where they were and thought the whole idea of attempting to escape sheer lunacy. Kastamuni's days of carefully contrived freedom and gaiety were numbered.

For Townshend – comfortably ensconced on Prinkipo, and reading reports in his English newspaper on the findings of the Mesopotamia Commission set up by Lloyd George – August 1917 meant no escape but exoneration from all blame for the disasters of 1915–16. Hardinge, Duff, Nixon and Hathaway were blamed: but he not at all. Admittedly the Commission had expressed itself puzzled as to why he had told Nixon, just before the battle at Ctesiphon, that the promise of an extra division he knew to be unavailable had made all the difference to his appreciation; and admittedly the Commission had exonerated Aylmer of any blame for the failure to relieve him, on the grounds that he had been forced to attack prematurely;[1] but nothing explicit had been said against him, Townshend, and, not unnaturally, he was pleased by the Commission's findings.[2]

He was also pleased by a conversation he had with Enver Pasha, in the course of which, he claimed, the Turkish Minister for War told him, 'I wanted to send you directly home after Kut, but the truth is, General Townshend, the Germans would not hear of it, saying you were *un haut personnage* in England and your arrival would have a political effect.'[2]

If, in fact, Enver did make such a statement, it is surprising that Townshend believed it, because a year earlier – according to his own report – it had been the Sultan who had forbidden his repatriation. Now it was the Germans. But whichever it was, or even if it was neither of them, he was obviously taken with the idea of being so *haut* a *personnage* that his return to England would have an adverse political effect upon the Central Powers: and he returned from his interview with Enver in high enough spirits to indulge in a practical joke upon his Turkish equerry, whose room he sprinkled with a foul-smelling powder purchased, on his instructions, by Boggis.[3] For the rest of 1917 and the early winter months of 1918, he did little but cultivate influential Turks, lay plans for escapes that were never effected and write letters home to England.

From the middle of 1917 onwards hundreds of his troops' next-of-kin in England received a kindly but stilted letter from the War Office.

> Madam [or Sir]
> I am directed to transmit to you with regret the enclosed letter addressed to Pte —— which has been returned from Turkey with an endorsement to the effect that Pte —— is dead.
> No confirmation of this information has reached this office, but it is feared that, unless you have heard from him recently, it may possibly be correct. An enquiry is, however, being sent to Turkey with a view to learning whether the report is confirmed, and until the result of enquiry has been ascertained, the report will not be accepted for official purposes: but I am to point out that a considerable time will probably elapse before an answer can be expected.
> I am to express the sympathy of the Army Council with the relatives in their anxiety and suspense.
> I am, madam,
>   Your obedient servant,
>   F. WEATHERSTONE

In many cases, of course, the soldier to whom this letter referred had in fact died: but in hundreds of other cases he was still alive, the Turks having returned letters addressed to him simply because they had no idea where he was, or because their curious system of taking down names had made it impossible to identify anyone on their official rolls of prisoners of war. Officers, they could easily locate. They were either at Kastamuni or Yozgad or Geddos or Afion Karahissar or Broussa: but rankers were scattered all over Turkey; and which were

where, only the rankers – who had not yet been allowed to write home
– knew.

The Turks punished the officers at Kastamuni for having allowed three
of their number to escape by marching them further inland to Changri,
where they were housed in barracks as uncomfortable as they were
filthy.

From one officer, these conditions provoked a very English letter
to the Turkish Minister of War, Enver Pasha.

> Sir,
> I have the honour to report that, owing to the close confine-
> ment in which I have been kept, my health has now entirely
> broken down. I therefore request that, with a view to providing
> some slight possibility of recovery, I may be sent on a month's
> sick leave to England: and that, as far as the port of embarkation,
> I may be accompanied by Posta Ginger, as he alone, in all of
> Turkey, really understands my temperament. I have the honour
> to be, sir, your most obedient prisoner of war ...[4]

Such elegant whimsy was not, however, typical of the spirit of
Changri, many of whose inhabitants so resented their eviction from
comfortable Kastamuni that the controversy about one's duty, or even
one's right, to escape broke out afresh.

It came to a head when a notice was pinned to a board suggesting
that officers prepared to eschew further escape attempts, in the interests
of better living conditions, might care to sign it. What surprised most
of the officers was that the suggestion came not from the Turks but
from a British colonel: and what stunned them was that signatures
began to be appended to it in sufficient numbers for the colonel to feel
justified in coercing into conformity those who had not already signed
it.

These miscreants being required to line up outside the colonel's
office, and to appear before him one at a time, the interviews that
ensued were brief and repetitious.

'Hello, Miles. Do you intend to escape?'
'No, sir. Not at present.'
'That means you might go tomorrow?'
'I don't think so, sir.'
'Why do you want to escape?'
'Well, we're not here for our health, are we?'

'Matter of conscience, is it?'

'You could say so, sir.'

'Will it help if I give you an order *not* to escape?'

'Yes, sir. Until an opportunity to escape arises!'

'I see' – and looking down at his list, dismissing his subordinate, the colonel put a red X against the name Miles.[5]

Later, in one of the two non-conformist Messes, the subject having been debated calmly and without rancour, it was decided that everyone should for the moment accept the colonel's order because the hills round Changri were under three feet of snow, which made escape impossible anyway, and because a letter concealed inside a split post-card had already been sent to the War Office asking for planes to land on the football pitch as soon as the snows had cleared, and between certain specific dates. A coup had been planned to seize the camp – armoury, postas and all – and the instant the planes were sighted it would be put into effect. Then they would all fly away to a nicer place and that, regardless of any notices on any boards, would be that.

Accordingly they told the colonel that they would accept his order as long as the snows lasted, and the colonel was delighted. So delighted that he placed under close arrest the second Mess, which still refused to comply. The first Mess then revoked its acceptance, vowing, on the contrary, to escape at the first opportunity, so the colonel had to confess to the Turks that his officers had refused to obey his order. The Turks then asked each officer to give his parole, promising that those who did so would go to Keddos, which they said was comfortable, and that those who did not would stay at Changri, which they knew to be most uncomfortable.

In the event, both parolees and non-parolees profited, because those obliged by their principles to remain at Changri protested so vehemently about broken windows, cold and discomfort that eventually they also were moved – to the well-established and congenial community at Yozgad.

'Do you see that ravine there?' asked a nice old Turkish sergeant major escorting them on their march. 'Well, there I helped to massacre five thousand Armenians, Allah be praised.'[6] He was a kind man and very pro-British and Changri's officers understood him not at all. Nor did they enjoy the rest of their march through freezing weather to Afion Karahissar and finally to Yozgad.

Thereafter, however, they lived exactly the same kind of life as their friends at Keddos – except that twenty-five officers and Bombardier

Prosser made an immediate attempt at escape, and three officers feigned madness so successfully that they were eventually sent to Constantinople for observation and possible repatriation.

Of the twenty-five escapees, all but eight were soon recaptured; but those eight, despite freezing nights, hunger, blackmailing brigands, thirst and 450 miles of mountains, ravines and desert, staggered all the way to the Mediterranean seaboard. At their moments of worst pain they had doped themselves with opium pills – as a result of which the red rising sun appeared to all of them to be bright green[7] – and at their moments of worst danger they had bribed their way to continued freedom.

Arrived at the Mediterranean coast, they were exhausted by lack of food and distressed by the presence of a huge Turkish military camp. Nevertheless, they stole a motor-boat, paddled it well out to sea and started its engine. Almost immediately the engine stopped. They started it again. And it stopped again. And so it went on for hour after hour: until finally they landed on Cyprus – free men after more than two years of captivity.

Of those they left behind them no more were to escape from Yozgad. The mad ones still hoped for repatriation; others were to make unsuccessful attempts; but only they reached freedom.

But Yozgad and Keddos were hardly places of anguish and torment.

For officers the day began at 7.45, when the bubashi flung open their bedroom door shouting, 'Zabit gelior, zabit gelior, chabbuk.'

'All right, all right,' the four occupants would shout back at the Turkish corporal. 'All *right*! And how's your father?'[8]

Satisfied that his prisoners were awake, the bubashi would withdraw to the next room, shouting that his officer was coming to count them. Unhurriedly, those about to be counted would crawl out of bed and slip tunics over whatever they used as night-wear, in time to greet the Turkish officer with a polite, 'Bonjour, monsieur', and a salute, or a frozen stare, depending on how much or little they liked him.

Then they would wash and wait for the breakfast gong, which was an orderly bashing out 'Come to the cookhouse door, boys' with a spoon on a dixie, and rush down to the Mess (because the last to arrive got the worst cutlery), and eat bread and a porridge of wheat and barley with milk and salt, and eggs and buttered toast, and drink ersatz coffee.

After breakfast, they would take an hour's exercise, strutting up and down in front of the house, discussing when the war would end and all the latest rumours gleaned in the bazaar from Armenians and Greeks whose imaginations were both fertile and optimistic.

Having agreed that the war would end in two months' time, they would wait for the posta to shout, 'Tamam, haidi, chabbuk yellah,' when they had to go inside again: which was as well, because an hour of strutting and discussing when the war will end is plenty for anyone.

Most of them would read in bed all morning – plenty of books. Or have a game of patience, or bézique, or piquet, until lunch-time, which was 12.30.

Eat a thin stew, or a small omelette, or a cold-meat salad.

Read till coffee-time, at 3. Awful ersatz coffee – so write home once again and scream for tins of cocoa.

After coffee, they would read, because it was very hot – or write home and ask for material with which to make curtains. Or work at hobbies, which included carpentry, watch-mending, metal-work, cobbling, bird-watching, butterfly-collecting, geology, anthropology, archaeology, drama, music, painting, debating, lectures, writing and haircutting. No use talking. Conversation exhausted by 3.30. Exhausted by the heat as much as anything else. Everyone exhausted – except that powerful brute John Alcock, who was prepared to talk for ever and nonsensically about how he'd be the first man to fly the Atlantic. And was encouraged to do so by his Canadian friend, who had once cost a whole Mess its supper when the orderly asked him, 'What shall I do with this?' pointing at the left-overs they were going to eat that night, and he, who was occasionally careless with his aspirates, had said, ' 'eat it up': so the orderly ate it up.

Four-thirty was still too hot to talk.

But at 5 it got cooler: so they would go outside and sit in the shade till 5.30, when they washed for dinner in shorts and shirt-sleeves – dinner being stew and curry, or eggs, followed by stewed fruit, or a spotted dog made out of sodden bread and currants, which was a great luxury.

Then they would read, or play bridge, as long as the light lasted; be counted again by the Turkish officer; go to a lecture on anything from tea-planting to London eating-houses; and so to bed. A typical officer's day, between 1917 and 1918.[8]

Except for the days when there were games of hockey, or football; and the days when there were picnics; and, at Yozgad, in the winter of 1917, the days when everyone promised not to escape that afternoon provided they were allowed to go out to ski.

Except for the nights at Keddos when there was an orchestral concert, or a play, or a fancy-dress ball – at which one officer attended as a skeleton, to the fury of Dippy Dick, the bandy-legged commandant, whose motto was 'tranquillité' and to whom skeletons were 'absoluement défendu.'

Except for the night that Keddos burnt down in the middle of the play *Kill That Bug*, and all the officers rushed from the stage and audience to help the townsfolk rescue their bins of corn and their copper pots and their silkworm cocoons and their bedding and their sacks of flour, the women saying, 'You can always trust an Englishman,' while their husbands, as usual, did nothing. Of 2,300 houses, 2,000 became ashes that night, including some of the officers' houses – which caused great distress to one of *Kill That Bug*'s leading ladies, who was also the original junior wart, and the only Failed D.S.O.

'I don't know what the hell I'm going to do,' he confessed to a brother officer. 'I've got nothing to wear but what I stand up in – and that's only my panties and this very dirty dress.'

'But, my dear chap, you can't help it if your dress is dirty; you've been fighting fires all night!'

'*And* I've lost my glasses. I think I'll get Channer to ask Dippy Dick if I can go to Constantinople and get some new ones.'

'I think you should.'

So he went to Channer, who had learnt to speak Turkish fluently, and said, 'Why don't you tell Dippy Dick that the loveliest girl in the chorus has to go to Constantinople for some new glasses? I mean, he and his staff are very partial to me, always putting their arms round my waist, the dirty old men, so go on, tell him I'm the most gorgeous girl in the chorus and ask him can I go to Constantinople.'

No sooner said than, dressed in borrowed shirt and shorts, he was on a train to Constantinople. Only the train ran out of wood as usual and lurched to a halt quite close to the sea.

'I want to go for a swim,' he then announced to his posta, treating him like a sepoy.

'Yessok!' said the posta. 'You might swim to England.'

'Then I must make myself some tea,' he declared – and proceeded to light a fire and boil some water.

'What are you doing?' asked a girl who had appeared from nowhere to stand beside him. She wore the uniform of a German military nurse, but spoke perfect English, and was very lovely.

'I'm making tea.'

'But where on earth did you manage to find any tea?'

'Red Cross parcels.'

'May I join you?'

'Of course.'

'May I bring my friend?'

'Bring the whole bloody lot.'

So she and her German friend drank Red Cross tea with an English officer on the shores of Asia Minor, and she asked him where he came from.

'Haslemere.'

'But that's where *I* worked! I was governess to Sir Arthur Conan Doyle's children.'

'Then you'd know ...'

'Yes.'

'And ...?'

'Yes!' She knew everyone he knew.

But then the train started again, and he had to leave her to continue his journey to Constantinople, where he was put in a ward with three officers called Mouseley, Jones and Hill. The mad ones from Yozgad. Jones was anti-British mad, Hill was religious mad and Mouseley was just mad.

The hospital lay across the Bosporus from Constantinople, so they crossed to it with guards on a ferry to draw some money from the Dutch Ambassador.

'No escaping,' Mouseley warned. 'We've got an arrangement!' Which consisted of dropping their guards at a hotel run by a Greek friend of his, and then enjoying themselves alone in the city. Yozgad's loveliest chorus girl went to the Dutch Embassy to draw his money and then waited for Mouseley outside the gate.

Sentries with fixed bayonets stood on either side of the gate and he was standing between them, waiting for mad Mouseley, when a man in a seedy blue suit approached him. He had no desire to talk to anyone in a seedy blue suit, but the man said:

'Don't you know who I am?'

'No, sir.'

'Of course you do. I'm Sir Robert Paul and these idiots' – gesturing at the Turkish sentries – 'have been looking for me for two months.'

'But how did you get away, sir?'

'Got out with Yeates Brown. *He* was dressed as a woman. Bloody

316

fools, these Turks. Can't even say Sir Robert Paul. Call me Sir Rubber Ball.'

But at that moment Mouseley appeared, so Sir Rubber Ball wandered off in his seedy blue suit and the other two returned to hospital – whence, with a new pair of glasses, the Failed D.S.O. returned to the bosom of Dippy Dick whilst the Feigned Maniacs were repatriated to England.[9] It could only have happened in Turkey.

It was in December 1917 that various officers' camps at last received news which confirmed their worst fears for their troops. On the march to Kastamuni, they had been compelled to leave 41 of their orderlies at Angora: now only 18 of them were alive. From Shamran, 2,592 British troops had started marching: now only 600 were thought to be alive.[10] Profoundly shocked, the officers wondered how they might help, and were dismayed to realize that they could not help at all.

Not even at Afion Karahissar could they help, because the commandant kept them completely apart from their men. All they could do was complain constantly to the Red Cross, the Dutch Embassy and Enver Pasha about the commandant's dishonesty, brutality and perversion: but when finally he was court-martialled he was convicted only on the charge of thefts from his prisoners. As one of Enver's hired assassins in the ruthless days of the Young Turks, he knew too much to be severely punished. But at least, in 1918, he was removed from Afion Karahissar and his reign of bestiality and the bastinado ended.

Like their officers, many of the rankers also attempted escape; but their chances of success were nil. For one thing, they worked either in the desert or in the mountains, and therefore were even farther from the coast than their officers: for another, they were too conspicuous. Weighing eight stone if they were lucky, clad only in shorts and a hat, they could not pretend to be German surveyors: they were unmistakably prisoners of war. As they attempted to cross five hundred miles of desert without either food or money, and only the bottleful of water they had taken from their camp, Arab tribesmen invariably pounced on them. Then they would be returned to their camp and the commandant would shrug and say, 'I knew you would come back. I knew you could never get away.'[11] For the first attempt, there was no punishment; for the second, a flogging, or the bastinado; for subsequent attempts, imprisonment.

Two privates, marching by compass straight down the desert,

heading for the British Army they knew to be somewhere north of Baghdad, came so close to success that they actually heard the rumble of gun-fire. But they were captured nevertheless, and put in a cell with thirty-five others who were Turkish deserters, Arab murderers and Armenian innocents. Twelve weeks later, only three of them were still alive: but all thirty-four corpses had been left rotting in the cell with those who were too stubborn to die.[11]

Only one ranker is believed to have escaped. Trumpeter Inwood was a Eurasian who broke out of his camp with five others. Thirst, starvation and illness forced him to fall by the wayside while the other five pressed on – and were recaptured. Inwood somehow survived, joined a band of Arab tribesmen, organized them as a guerrilla force and, for the rest of the war, allegedly conducted a Lawrence-like campaign of terror and sabotage against his one-time captors.[11]

For the rest of the British force, however, captivity offered no such diversions. 'Angleez, Angleez,' the postas would call – and out they would go, to break stones, excavate tunnels, build hospitals and schools and make the railway. Split up into ever smaller groups, they were sent thirty here, thirty there, friend separated from friend, the frail fabric of their primitive society so constantly ripped to shreds that survival became a matter of luck and individual toughness.

Back to Bagtshe and Tekrit they were sent; and to Tarsus and Angora and Entillie; all over Turkey, in small parties that lacked identity and cohesion, to work on the railway and survive in isolation.

'Haide, Angleez, kok!' The Turkish choush would shout at them each morning. 'Hurry up, English, get up.' And they would stumble out of their bell tent, eat some of their previous night's rations – if they had saved any – parade, number in Turkish, be divided into parties and march off to work. And no one in the whole wide world seemed to know where they were – or to care.

Admittedly, representatives of some embassy or other had been sent to see them, and had taken their names and given them a couple of liras each, all of them squatting on a blanket out in the open during this solemn ceremony; but since then they had been dispersed again and again, so that the parcels sent to them from England very rarely reached them, and letters just as rarely.[12]

Though the Turkish official meant no harm, he equally meant no good. A British ranker was the equivalent of a Turkish ranker, upon whom the Turkish Government wasted neither consideration nor sympathy; and when the two found themselves together, the Turkish

318

ranker naturally helped himself to everything available – including parcels from England – before providing anything for his prisoners. Men went on dying throughout 1917 and 1918 not because of brutality, as they had in 1916, but simply because their captors had no better an organization to care for them than they had for their own villagers, farmers or military conscripts.

Even their infrequent gestures of solicitude were bungled. When lice arrived with the winter of 1917, the Turks helped get rid of them by boiling all their prisoners' clothing in huge copper cauldrons – their prisoners meantime standing naked and freezing – and then being ordered to dress in garments that were wringing wet.[12] And when typhus broke out, they sent their lice-infested prisoners to a Turkish bath, then shaved off all their body hair and ordered them to smear themselves with blue ointment that burnt so viciously that no one could work for days.[13]

At least, though, there had been something they could do about lice and typhus: for malaria they could do nothing. Which seemed to irritate them. Unable to cure it, they pretended it was a form of malingering and flogged those who collapsed shivering to the ground. As a result, it became their prisoners' practice to hide those who had malaria until they were fit enough to work again. It was a compassionate practice; but it made life on the railway no easier. Not when there were twenty-one tunnels to be bored through the mountains and hundreds of miles of line to be laid across one of the hottest deserts and some of the most malaria-ridden regions in the world. By looking after their own sick and sabotaging the Turk's rolling stock, they retained their pride: but pride alone could not keep them alive.

Nor could any of them be proud to eat even as little as they ate when daily, on some stretches of the line, they saw starving Armenian boys with testicles huge as footballs, starving girls with vast swollen bellies from which the navels were sickeningly extruded, starving children frenziedly banging their foreheads against the rocky ground until bloodily they fainted, mothers hopelessly tossing infants aside to die, new-born babies being brained with a stone by fathers too kind to let them utter their first cry.[14] The Turks had massacred half a million Armenians in 1915 and 1916: but the killings had by no means ended in 1918. British soldiers working on Turkey's railways may have been given little to eat, but Armenians were given nothing.

Nor could those who worked on the tunnels take much pleasure in the sabotage the Australians so constantly practised, because they

319

invariably looked so unconcerned that the Turks decided it must have been committed by the English – and punished them instead.[15]

It was therefore almost with relief that many of them found themselves packed into horse trucks and trundled off along the line to Konia. But this relief was short-lived. Too many died on the way – and their bodies were left inside the truck. Too many fell ill. At Konia the dead were buried and twenty-seven seriously ill men were put in hospital. An American doctor and an American nurse helped until America entered the war: but of the twenty-seven who entered Konia's hospital only two came out alive.[16]

'How old are you?' a German officer asked a ragged, child-like prisoner, who had surprisingly quieted his restless horse.

'Seventeen, sir.'

'You were captured when you were sixteen?'

'Yes, sir.'

'My God. Poor old England. Are they making sixteen-year-olds fight now?'

The boy's friends laughed. 'He don't fight, sir,' they mocked. 'He's a trumpeter.'[16] But the German's talk of England had disconcerted them. Here they were, in the middle of nowhere, weighing about seven stone apiece, clad only in a rough kilt made out of cement bags, PORTLAND CEMENT printed across and around their skinny thighs, and *he* talked of England. Why did no one from England send them food and clothing?[16]

By 1918 survival for the British ranker depended less upon food and clothing, however, than upon *not* going into hospital. The Dutch Embassy was as scrupulous as the Americans had been in sending money to those who worked for the Turks, and that money, little though it was, kept starvation at bay: but it could not buy drugs or anaesthetics in a country deprived of both by the blockade, and it could not buy medical skill in a country so conspicuously devoid of doctors.

'For Christ's sake, go *home* and die,' those already in hospital shouted at those from the railway so desperately ill or injured that they had decided to seek outside help. 'Go home! They'll kill you here.'[17] By home they meant camp – which happens when men are denied all contact with home for more than a year – but by 'kill you' they meant exactly what they said.

Operations were performed without anaesthetics, on the ground, by Greeks and Armenians, with kitchen knives. At Bagtshe hospital dozens of men were running round naked, bearded, weighing seventy or eighty pounds – raving mad. Too mad even to die. And the delirious were simply knocked unconscious and tied to their bunks.

At Angora a man with swollen testicles complained, 'Look what I've got here! I'm damned near finished.' Swollen testicles too often meant imminent death, and he was frightened: but there was nothing the British doctor to whom he complained could do. He was merely passing through Angora with some other Indian Medical Service officers; and anyway he had no drugs. So he took the matter up with the Turks – who at once dragged the private into hospital, pinned him down on a table and ordered a Greek doctor to lance his scrotum.

'Ow, you *bast*ards!' he screamed.

'Me no bastard,' protested the Greek. 'Chloroform London. Here no chloroform.'[18]

Into another railway hospital in 1917 had gone seventy-six men: a month later, ten came out. Their average age had been twenty-three and they had died possessed only of their pay books and, more often than not, their miniature Y.M.C.A. bibles. One of them died with his bible open at the fly leaf, upon which was inscribed Lord Roberts' personal message to all who cared to read it:

'I ask you to put your trust in God. He will watch over you, and strengthen you. You will find this little Book guidance when you are in health, comfort when you are in sickness and strength when you are in adversity.'[19]

If Roberts' message was true – and in 1917 it quite probably was – that little Book was the only comfort and strength to be found by British rankers in Turkish hospitals.

Or even in some Turkish camps. 'Entillie was a good camp. We were there three weeks and we only lost twelve. We worked at tunnelling and breaking stone for ballast.'[20]

For the ranker, then, no concerts or hobbies or picnics or ski-ing; no reading or debating or studying; not even many letters or parcels, of each of which most claim to have received only a half-dozen altogether in two and a half years. No leisure and no comfort; just work, and staying alive.

And occasional visits, later in 1918, either from Red Cross representatives or from English spies dressed as Arabs, both of whom took names, ranks and numbers and promised to advise their families that they were alive and well, the spies saying that this was the only way

Britain could establish the whereabouts of its lost prisoners of war. Asia Minor seemed to swarm with English spies dressed as Arabs: Englishmen who spoke Arabic seemed to have a passion for donning the burnous and swooping off into the desert to spy: and sometimes the men they visited wondered whether it was not a terrible waste of everyone's time.

But neither they nor anyone else realized how little time was left. Unbelievably, Germany and the Central Powers were within months of cracking: and when the break finally came, they were to be glad that someone had taken the trouble to discover where they were.

CHAPTER TWENTY-EIGHT

THEY still moved round, however; and the odd Turkish official was still capable of nastiness.

'Yozgad, May 14, 1918: Sergeant N. Neyland, Australian Infantry, threatened with having his eyes put out and being bayoneted because he was said to favour the English:'[1] and an officer, who had visited the post office at Tarsus, returned to his camp to report that he had seen there a mass of undelivered letters, some of them so old that they included a reply from the Corinthians to Saint Paul![2]

But cases like these had become rare. Even the rankers were now receiving food parcels: even Sergeant Neyland was repatriated, un-bayoneted, eyes and English sentiments intact: and even some of the railway-workers had been moved to quite congenial camps.

One such group was sent to San Stefano on the Sea of Marmara, to a camp run by Germans so sympathetic that they once agreed to an England-versus-Germany soccer match. Tactlessly, the British led 14–0 at half-time, so the commandant, von Bummel, stopped the game: but he bore no grudge because of it.

Then an Armenian priest suggested that the British should put on a concert, and the British were delighted, not having had any concerts for two years, and a large audience of Greeks and Armenians came to the school in which they were imprisoned to see them perform: but von Bummel ordered out all the Greeks and Armenians because his German troops wanted to see the show. So the concert party left too, and gave their performance on the jetty to the evicted audience: yet still von Bummel bore no grudge. He wore corsets, a gold bracelet, white kid gloves and a monocle, and was given to screaming, 'Put that man in a shit-house', but everyone liked him. And *he* seemed particularly to admire an English submariner called Bunce.

Bunce had been captured when the submarine A.E.2 failed to penetrate the Dardanelles and blow up the German and Turkish fleet at Constantinople; and he and von Bummel argued incessantly.

'Bunce!' von Bummel called one morning. 'What you for breakfast have?'

'Wasser,' replied Bunce, tersely.

'No Suppe?'

'Yok! Wasser.'

'Suppe!'

'Wasser.'

'Put him in the shit-house – keep him there all day,' von Bummel roared. And then, confident that this dire threat would have weakened his adversary's will, 'What you for breakfast have?'

'Wasser,' said Bunce, who had spent too long in tunnels to be alarmed by any shit-house.

'Suppe!' screamed von Bummel.

'Wasser.'

'Come with me,' von Bummel ordered then, changing his tactics: and, escorting his prisoner to the bazaar, bought bread and eggs and raisins and figs: and asked, '*Now*, Bunce, what you for breakfast have?'

'Wasser,' said Bunce, who was not to be bribed.

'You *still* say Wasser?'

'I still say Wasser.'

'You very good man,' von Bummel congratulated: and gave him the bread and the raisins and the eggs and the figs.[3]

In September 1918, Townshend was delighted to read in the newspapers sent to him from England that Marshal Foch's offensive had so shattered the Germans that 150,000 of them had been taken prisoner, 29,000 of them were roaming Berlin as deserters and two of their Bavarian divisions had mutinied.[4]

Later in the month the news was even better. There was a British air-raid on Constantinople and the Turks and the Bulgars had been whipped by the hitherto derided Anglo-French Army from Salonika.

But if September had been a good month, October was splendid. The Bulgars, it seemed, were suing for peace, the Turks were in a state of visible consternation and their War Cabinet had resigned. Now was the time, Townshend believed,[4] to achieve the glory that Kut had denied him.

While his officers and men, in their remote camps, were ravaged with Spanish 'flu, he laid the foundations of what he hoped would be a new career. While the officers of Yozgad grieved at the loss of 7 men out of 118, so unaccustomed were they to death in their community,[5] and his men accepted as a matter of course the death of scores, he advised the new Turkish Minister of Marine that he was willing to treat with the British Government on Turkey's behalf.

'I flattered myself that they would have confidence in my ability to conduct such a mission,' he subsequently wrote, 'and would have equal confidence in the genuineness of my endeavour to obtain honourable terms for their country.'[6] But first he required his personal liberty!

All of this he put in a letter, which was delivered to the new cabinet by his Turkish equerry, and on October 17th he travelled by launch from Prinkipo to the Sublime Porte and there delivered to Field Marshal Izzet Pasha the terms he was willing to negotiate.

They were that Turkey should open up the Dardanelles and the Bosporus; that Mesopotamia, Syria and the Caucasus, whilst still acknowledging the Sultan as their ruler, should become autonomous states; and that all British and Indian prisoners of war should at once be released. In return for which, Allied troops would evacuate Mesopotamia and Syria; Turkish territory in Europe would remain Turkish; and Great Britain would provide bankrupt Turkey with financial aid.

'Then you are willing to help us?' Izzet asked.

'With all my heart,' replied Townshend.

Izzet told Townshend he was at liberty to go and meet the British: Townshend told Izzet there was not a moment to be lost. Izzet compared Townshend's defence of Kut with Osman Pasha's defence of Plevna, and Townshend – not thinking to compare the fate of Osman's troops with that of his own – shook Izzet's hand most warmly[6] and returned to Prinkipo.

He reflected that he had cause to be proud! He had persuaded the Turks to open up the Dardanelles. He had achieved by diplomacy what he had been ordered to achieve by force of arms at Ctesiphon. All twenty thousand of the German troops at Constantinople would have to surrender. And because he alone had induced the Turks to sue for peace, Austria must capitulate.[6]

He gave no credit to the enormous British Armies that had, since Kut, assembled and fought bitterly for two years to drive the Turks and Germans out of Mesopotamia and Egypt and Syria; he gave no credit to the millions who had died in France as they destroyed Germany's will to fight on; he gave no credit to the Royal Navy which had deprived Turkey of all supplies by sea: he gave no credit to the

Russians who had threatened from Persia; and he gave no credit to the Salonika Army that had crushed Bulgaria ... Turkey was about to sue for peace because he had suggested it. She was about to open the Dardanelles in response to his diplomacy – just as she would have opened them to his 6th Division had fate been kinder at Ctesiphon.[6]

Presumably this last lunacy was sparked off by a recollection of Sir Percy Cox's remark, made to him during his conference with Nixon in August 1915, that the capture of Baghdad would have the same impact upon Islamic opinion as the capture of Constantinople: but sadly he now apparently believed that the capture of Baghdad would have led immediately to the capture of Constantinople itself.

And so this new Metternich set sail, on a Turkish tug, for British-held Mitylene. The moon was high, the sea was flat and the Turkish officer in command was terrified of mine-fields. Not so Townshend. Mad, he may have been: but he was as fearless as ever.

'But, Excellency,' protested the Turk, 'if we touch a mine and you are injured, I shall be tried by court martial.'

'If we touch a mine,' retorted Townshend, 'neither you nor I will know a thing about it!'[6]

On October 20th, at 3 in the morning, they arrived in Mitylene harbour – apparently undetected, because they had to whistle to attract attention.

'Who are you?' shouted a Royal Navy officer from a motor-boat.

'General Townshend,' Townshend shouted back.

'Good God,' the officer exclaimed, shining a torch on his face, 'I am glad to see you, sir.'[6] And at last Townshend had achieved his liberation. Typically, however, he had embarked on his momentous voyage of peace without first ensuring that his unfortunate officers and men were likewise liberated.

A week later, a conference between British, French and Turkish officials was held on board the battleship *Agamemnon*. Its purpose was to negotiate an armistice: and Townshend the Peacemaker was not invited to attend it.

On October 30th, the Armistice was signed, and every day thereafter, for several weeks, one group or another of Townshend's men discovered that they were free.

'We're marching out of here at 8.30 tomorrow morning,' a colonel advised the commandant of a camp in Constantinople.

'But, Colonel, you are in my charge.'

'You think so? Try and stop us and you'll be strung up.'

At Afion Karahissar, and Yozgad, and Keddos, officers found themselves free to wander where they liked, and to fraternize with whom they wished: but such sudden freedom seemed strange, and they mostly stayed where they were.

One of the three officers who had escaped from Kastamuni, now Lieutenant-Colonel Keeling, set off with three armoured cars to liberate rankers in camp after camp, and to arrange their transport by rail to Smyrna, whence ships would remove them for ever from hated Asia Minor.

Other camps found out for themselves that they were free. By the second week of November everyone knew that the war was over. But for 1,755 of the original 2,592 British rankers captured at Kut, and for 3,063 of the 10,486 sepoys and camp-followers captured, it made no difference: they were either dead or missing, and would never go home.

CHAPTER TWENTY-NINE

ᕙᕗ

F OR those who have been its prisoners, a war ends strangely, and
usually anti-climactically. The defeated captor is scarcely in the
mood to celebrate, and to celebrate in his presence is hardly tactful,
since he is usually armed, and morose as well.

Each returning prisoner of war has, therefore, his own peculiar
story to tell of how he became free, and was repatriated: yet basically
all the stories are the same, so one will suffice for the 837 British
rankers who returned to England from Asia Minor.

Private Wadham was a Dorset – one of the thirty from an entire
battalion who had survived their battles and their captivity – and he
had worked as a tunneller until a party of officers passed through his
camp, of whom one had bought a goose and, with consummate lack of
tact, asked him, who was starving, to cook it for him. Obediently
little Wadham had started to cook the goose, but had fainted clean
away at the mere smell of it. He had come to lying on top of the
officers' baggage, which was trundling away from his camp on a four-
wheeled araba.

'You're coming with us,' the officers had explained, making hand-
some amends for their earlier thoughtlessness: so he had reached
Kastamuni, and become an orderly, and had remained an orderly until
Russia capitulated, when he was sent with a small party to clean up the
barracks the Russian prisoners of war had hitherto inhabited.

He had been in no hurry to finish the job and had established an
amicable working relationship with his commandant, who preferred
sitting on a bench in the sun, smoking, his feet in comfortable slippers,
to the tedium of supervising prisoners: and being anxious to spend
some of the Red Cross liras he had just received, he asked his lazy
commandant to assign him a posta to escort him to and from the bazaar.

'Posta yok,' the commandant indifferently replied. 'Bombom bitti!'

Wadham then went back to his fellow prisoners and told them that
the commandant had said there were no more postas because the war

was over: so they all went for a walk, and one of them even celebrated this rather dull end to their war by knocking out the first Turkish soldier unfortunate enough to pass his way.

Next morning that same soldier appeared in their camp. 'Now we're for it,' they told one another: and to be sure the Turk walked straight up to his assailant and seized him by the arm. But then smiled broadly and said: 'Gel, emsherri ... come, brother' – and took them all for a drink.

Some days later, when no one had come to take them home to England, the Turks suggested that they should make their own way to Angora and there catch a train to Smyrna: so they walked to Afion Karahissar, where the line started. But found it trainless. Unperturbed, and English to the last, Wadham produced some tea he had found in a pile of undelivered Red Cross parcels, made a fire and began to boil water on the station platform.

'Brewing up then?' a voice demanded. He looked up to see an Austrian soldier.

'Yes.'

'Don't you know me?'

'No.'

'Yes, you do.'

'Bloody well don't.'

'Name Butcher mean anything to you?'

'Yes. He fell out and died on the march.'

'I *fell out* all right, mate; but some Austrians on their way to Palestine picked me up. Been with them ever since.'

'Dressed like that?'

'Been cooking for them.'

A train arrived and they managed to board it and travel to Angora: but at Angora all the trains to Smyrna were full. So they camped on the station until Wadham saw a familiar figure, whom he approached and saluted. 'Good morning Sherif Bey, sir,' he greeted the one-time commandant of his officers' camp. 'How are we going to get to Smyrna?'

Having bought each of them a glass of mastik, Sherif Bey ordered some Greeks off the next train, installed them in it and waved them goodbye: and for the next few days they clanked westwards across Turkey, feeding their engine the wooden buildings of each station through which they passed until at last, through groves of trees hanging heavy with purple figs, they entered Smyrna.

There they accommodated themselves in the one-time American mission and each day Wadham went down to the station to wait for other trains bearing more self-liberated stragglers.

'Machina geldi?' he would ask the station master each morning – is there a train coming?

'Yok. Charbon yok, machina yok.'

Until finally he realized that he and his party were the last of Turkey's prisoners of war, and a small steamer carried them off to Alexandria, where their curious suits and battered hats caused a deal of comment among the thousands of properly uniformed Britons stationed there.

They were sent to a camp full of Scots and, after a few days, it was with nothing short of relief that Wadham, taking a walk through Alexandria, heard his name called in accents that were English. Glancing across the road, he recognized a friend from India.

'You're in a funny state,' his friend remarked.

'We've been through some funny times,' retorted Wadham.

Later that day a group of Australians announced that he was to go drinking with them, and led him boldly down a street marked OUT OF BOUNDS TO ALL H.M. TROOPS.

An English officer with a picket of troops halted them: 'You can't come down here,' he snapped.

'You talking to me, mate?' the leading Australian inquired.

'I am.'

'Well, don't! Tell you what, why don't you just take your bloody picket and bloody well piss off.'

The next day was Christmas Day – for which the ex-prisoners' breakfast was porridge, and their lunch a small slice of beef garnished with an even smaller cabbage leaf.

'Any complaints?' the duty officer inquired.

'Yes. Call this Christmas dinner?' Wadham demanded.

'You're not on our ration strength, you know,' the officer rebuked.

'So you're living on charity!'

Rejecting such charity, the ex-prisoners of war left the Mess tent and went to the canteen instead, there to dine on cheese and onions, for which they paid themselves.

That night a steamer took them to Taranto in Italy, where no one was expecting them, so there was again no food.

'Who are you?' asked a very fat major; so they told him. 'Been having a thin time, eh? Well ... wait here.'

330

Half an hour later he returned and escorted them to a Mess where enormous West Indians served them an enormous meal.

'Thank you, sir,' they said, when they had eaten.

'Don't thank me; thank my boys. They paid for it.'

'Thank you,' they said to the big, black, smiling men: and took their places in horse trucks on the train for France, with no money in their pockets, and very little food.

In France they changed into a proper carriage, but still had no money, and now no food either, so an old woman selling fruit took pity on them and emptied her basketful of apples into their compartment, and they lived on apples till they arrived at Calais. Where they were locked up in a compound surrounded by barbed wire.

'How do I get out of here?' Wadham asked a fellow inmate.

'I'll show you the hole in the wire.'

'How'd you find it?'

'I'm the Provost R.S.M.'

But Calais had no attractions for a man who had spent two and a half years in Turkey, and Wadham was not sad to leave it when at last a steamer arrived to take him and his companions home.

At Dover an R.S.M. offered them the choice of a bath, a drink or a session with him telling him which Turkish – or for that matter British – officers had treated them brutally. 'Ah,' they said, then, 'it's a long time ago' – and opted for baths and drinks.

The girls who worked in the canteen allowed them to pay for nothing and they spent an agreeable time waiting for their train to London. Then an officer handed each of them a voucher to Waterloo; and off they set again. And at Waterloo stepped out on to a dirty, vaulted concourse, free to find their own way home.

For Wadham this was easy enough, because he lived at Bournemouth, and the Bournemouth train departed from Waterloo: so three hours later he was talking to his family.

Next morning his sister asked, 'What would you like for breakfast?'

'Nothing, thanks. Think I'll go for a walk.' That day he ate only at dinner-time. And the next, and the next, and the next.

'Something wrong with my cooking?' his sister demanded.

'No. Dinner's all I can eat,' he explained: but she didn't believe him. She didn't understand. No one understood. No one ever would.[1]

Having thus conspicuously failed to arrange for the comfortable repatriation of his troops, Townshend raced home ahead of them, via

Rome and Paris, rather than Taranto and Calais, and refrained from welcoming any of them; just as Whitehall refrained from welcoming him. Whitehall, in fact, had decided that Townshend no longer existed, any last chance he had had of restoring himself to its favour after his desertion of his troops having been dispelled by an interview he had just granted the Paris correspondent of *The Times*, in which he had boasted that the Turks had treated him as 'an honoured guest'.[2]

Rebuked in a letter from the Army Council for so tactless an admission, when more than sixty per cent of his troops had died as guests of the Turk, Townshend's reply was that he felt aggrieved at receiving such a communication, 'more especially in view of the trials I have undergone at having become a prisoner of war and for seeing all my juniors go over my head, thus ruining my career in the Army'.[2]

Only Townshend could have described life in a luxury villa on a fashionable island, yachting and swimming, whipping insolent locals, discomfiting harmless equerries, dining with wealthy Turks and being attended by a large retinue as 'trials undergone at having become a prisoner of war': and only Townshend could so blatantly have confessed to the lust for promotion, and the malice he bore to those who might be or had been promoted over his head, which had led him first to tempt Nixon with the suggestion of a raid on Baghdad and later to coerce Aylmer into a series of relief attempts so unnecessarily premature that they had all failed.

Yet still – as the War Office icily ignored him – he could not see how monstrously his own words read. So he bombarded everyone, from Lord Curzon to Winston Churchill, with requests for military appointments; but was rejected by them all. When so eminent a man as Haig had described him as a semi-lunatic,[2] and the King Emperor himself had grumbled that he should have remained with his troops at Kut, to share their fate,[2] there could be, and was, no hope for him.

So he became a Member of Parliament.

However, lacking whatever quality it is that enables an M.P. either to endear himself to the Commons or to succeed as a politician, he soon sought diplomatic employment instead. Turkey, he felt, was his métier, and the settlement of peace terms with Turkey something about which no one was wiser than he. Lloyd George and the Cabinet might not think so – indeed Lloyd George and the Cabinet emphatically thought not – but, he wrote to Austen Chamberlain, the Lord Privy Seal, 'Kemal has invited me to Angora and says they will give me a reception never equalled to any Englishman before.'[2]

The Lord Privy Seal did not reply, and the Cabinet refused to accept him as a representative of the Foreign Office in Turkey; but he went there nevertheless. And convinced himself that he had dominated Mustafa Kemal when he met him; and refused to admit that the Turks might be using him; and enjoyed their flattery; and made no reference at all to the treatment of his troops in their hands ... and continued to be snubbed by His Majesty's Government.

Poor Townshend. His wife and daughter loved him. His friends loved him. His dog, Spot – repatriated, as promised, by Khalil – loved him. Society accepted him, and knew him simply as 'Kut'. A fashionable artist painted his portrait, and actors and actresses still enjoyed his company. But, denied his family title, and denied his field-marshal's baton, he *had* to have something else. Like the adulation of the Turks, as he decided their fate on behalf of the British Government. Denied this also, he died in France on May 16th, 1924.

Just before he had surrendered at Kut, he cabled a friend, Sir Wilfrid Peek:

> Write Alice tell her the hole I am in here through the fault of others. When I think, tell her how all conduct of operations was put on to me and not one word of praise and no thanks for all I have done throughout this campaign. I have only one desire that to leave the Army as soon as peace comes. I am ill and weak but a little better today. Tell her I have some six or seven hundred pounds pay ... which I will instruct them to send her. If I have to go into captivity, it will kill me.[3]

But it was the peace that killed him: and at his memorial service in Paris, neither the British Government nor the War Office was represented: and neither Melliss nor Delamain attended his burial service at Raynham in Norfolk.

To have been members of the garrison of Kut, and to have survived the captivity which followed its fall, became a source of justifiable pride to Townshend's officers and men. They had fought and won some remarkable battles; they had beaten their enemy at Ctesiphon and only withdrawn from the field when he had returned in greater numbers than ever; and they had themselves been defeated, after the longest siege in history, only by hunger.

Remarkably, none of them bore a grudge against the Turks. On the contrary, those who still survive go out of their way to explain that the

Turk could not help what happened on the railway, and that those who murdered on the march were not Turks, but Kurds and Arabs.

Dozens of officers returned to Turkey, as much to visit Turks as to revisit the scenes of their battles and captivity. Channer even became a friend of Khalil's and arranged his admission to a London hospital when he was dying of cancer.

And dozens of officers called on the War Office, to insist that the cheques they had signed in captivity be honoured – which, without exception, they were.

For rankers, however, repatriation meant something more prosaic, because they belonged to a class that had to work. So they joined the Post Office, or the Railways, or the Police: or simply signed on for another term as Regular soldiers.

'Well,' the medical officers said of most of them, 'his heart's all right, and that's the main thing.'[4] And back they went to India. It was the only life, really, that many of them knew. That, and Kut, and captivity.

For what had been done to them by generals, they received no recognition – except a letter from King George V.

The Queen joins me, [the King wrote] in welcoming you on your release from the miseries and hardships which you have endured with so much patience and courage.

During these many months of trial, the early rescue of our gallant Officers and Men from the cruelties of their captivity has been uppermost in our thoughts.

We are thankful that this longed for day has arrived and that, back in the Old Country, you will be able once more to enjoy the happiness of a home and to see good days among those who anxiously look for your return.

GEORGE R.I.

It was a page-long letter, reproduced in the King's own handwriting, and it said exactly what needed to be said. Doubtless the King had other things to do, but he, unlike Townshend – who so loved his command: to whom the writing of letters was so compulsive – had found the time to write it.

Not that Townshend's troops resented their General's lack of attention. They had his c'municks: that was enough. He had done all he could for them, they were sure. What had happened had been no fault of his. But ...

334

'I shall succeed,' he had promised Lady Nixon, 'or never return.'

'I shall fight house by house till my ammunition and food are exhausted ...' he had promised Lake.

'I must go into captivity with my troops', he had vowed, 'even though the heat will kill me ...'

And had done none of them. On the other hand, as his mentor Napoleon himself once sadly observed: 'Du sublime au ridicule il n'y a qu'un pas.'[5]

NOTES TO THE CHAPTERS

(Details of the books not cited in full below are given in the
Bibliography)

CHAPTER ONE

1 A. J. Barker, *The Neglected War*.
2 Maj. F. Castaldini.
3 *Mesopotamia Commission 1917*: Separate report by Commander Wedgewood, D.S.O., M.P.
4 Lytton Strachey, *Eminent Victorians* (London, 1918).
5 *Mesopotamia Commission 1917*.
6 B. F. Lake (letter).

7 Mr D. R. Holzmeyer (diary).
8 Col. W. S. Spackman, *Never Come Back No More* (private papers).
9 Barker, op. cit.
10 Mr D. R. Holzmeyer (diary).
11 Mr R. Hague.
12 Mr D. R. Holzmeyer (diary).
13 Mr H. Eato.

CHAPTER TWO

1 *Mesopotamia Commission 1917*: Separate report by Commander Wedgewood, D.S.O., M.P.
2 *Mesopotamia Commission 1917*.
3 Maj.-Gen. Sir Charles Townshend, *My Campaign in Mesopotamia*.
4 *Mesopotamia Commission 1917*.
5 Mr H. Eato.
6 Mr D. R. Holzmeyer (diary).
7 Mr W. D. Swan.
8 Col. R. O. Chamier.
9 Capt. G. H. G. Burroughs.
10 Maj.-Gen. G. O. de R. Channer.
11 Lt.-Col. G. R. Rae.

12 Townshend, op. cit.
13 A. J. Barker, *Townshend of Kut*.
14 Townshend, op. cit.
15 Barker, op. cit.
16 Direct quotations from officers and gentlemen who do not wish to be identified.
17 Barker, op. cit.
18 Townshend, op. cit.
19 Barker, op. cit.
20 Townshend, op. cit.
21 Barker, op. cit.
22 Townshend, op. cit.

CHAPTER THREE

1 Maj.-Gen. Sir Charles Townshend, *My Campaign in Mesopotamia*.
2 Mr J. Boggis.
3 *Mesopotamia Commission 1917*: Separate report by Commander Wedgewood, D.S.O., M.P.
4 Mr J. Boggis.
5 *Mesopotamia Commission 1917*: Separate report by Commander Wedgewood, D.S.O., M.P.
6 A. J. Barker, *Townshend of Kut*.
7 Townshend, op. cit.

8 Mr A. Hayden.
9 *The History of the 43rd and 52nd Light Infantry in World War I*, vol. 1.
10 Barker, op. cit.
11 Townshend, op. cit.
12 A. J. Barker, *The Neglected War*.
13 *The History of the 43rd and 52nd Light Infantry in World War I*, vol. 1.
14 Mr R. Hague (papers).
15 Townshend, op. cit.
16 Barker, op. cit.
17 Townshend, op. cit.

CHAPTER FOUR

1 Maj.-Gen. Sir Charles Townshend, *My Campaign in Mesopotamia*.
2 Mr J. Boggis.
3 Mr E. J. Mant.
4 H. V. Wheeler, *Wartime Wanderings of the 4th Hampshire Regiment* (private papers).
5 Mr A. Hayden.
6 Townshend, op. cit.
7 Lt.-Col. E. W. C. Sandes, D.S.O., O.B.E.
8 *The History of the 43rd and 52nd Light Infantry in World War I*, vol. I.
9 *Mesopotamia Commission 1917*.

CHAPTER FIVE

1 *Mesopotamia Commission 1917*.
2 Lt.-Col. J. W. Gallaway.
3 Mr G. Sporle.
4 Mr W. J. Sherlock.
5 Arthur G. Kingsmill, *The Silver Badge*.
6 Capt. F. W. Page-Roberts (letters).
7 Maj.-Gen. G. O. de R. Channer.
8 Mr E. J. Mant.
9 Lt.-Col. G. R. Rae.
10 Maj.-Gen. G. O. de R. Channer.
11 Capt. F. W. Page-Roberts (letters).
12 Kingsmill, op. cit.
13 Capt. F. W. Page-Roberts (letters).
14 Mr D. R. Holzmeyer (diary).
15 Kingsmill, op. cit.
16 Mr H. J. Porter.
17 *Mesopotamia Commission 1917*: Separate report by Commander Wedgewood, D.S.O., M.P.
18 Sir John Mellor.
19 Mr W. J. Sherlock.
20 Mr H. V. Plumb (papers).
21 Capt. G. H. G. Burroughs (papers).
22 Edward Mousely, *Secrets of a Kuttite*.
23 Sir John Mellor.
24 Lord Elton, *Among Others*.
25 Mr W. D. Swan.
26 *Mesopotamia Commission 1917*.
27 Maj.-Gen. Sir Charles Townshend, *My Campaign in Mesopotamia*.
28 Mr H. S. Soden.
29 Brig. K. B. S. Crawford (diaries).
30 Maj. W. H. Miles.
31 Mr W. J. Sherlock.
32 Elton, op. cit.
33 Col. G. W. R. Bishop.
34 Townshend, op. cit.
35 Author's italics.
36 Townshend, op. cit.
37 Mr W. J. Sherlock.
38 Mr H. Eato.
39 Townshend, op. cit.
40 Col. W. S. Spackman, *Never Come Back No More* (private papers).
41 Townshend, op. cit.
42 Mr D. R. Holzmeyer (diary).
43 Mr W. S. Finch.
44 Mr W. D. Swan.
45 Townshend, op. cit.
46 *Mesopotamia Commission 1917*.
47 Sir John Mellor.

CHAPTER SIX

1 Maj.-Gen. Sir Charles Townshend, *My Campaign in Mesopotamia*.
2 *Mesopotamia Commission 1917*.
3 Townshend, op. cit.
4 *Mesopotamia Commission 1917*.
5 Townshend, op. cit.
6 Sir John Mellor.
7 Capt. F. W. Page-Roberts (letters).
8 Capt. G. H. G. Burroughs (papers).
9 *Mesopotamia Commission 1917*.

CHAPTER SEVEN

1 Maj.-Gen. Sir Charles Townshend, *My Campaign in Mesopotamia*.
2 Lt.-Col. C. A. Raynor.
3 Townshend, op. cit.
4 *Official History, World War I*, vol. II.
5 *The History of the 43rd and 52nd Light Infantry in World War I*, vol. I.
6 *Mesopotamia Commission 1917*.
7 Lt.-Col. E. W. C. Sandes, D.S.O., O.B.E.
8 Sir John Mellor.

9 Mr A. Vanstone.
10 E. W. C. Sandes, *In Kut and Captivity.*
11 Mr J. Boggis.
12 Townshend, op. cit.
13 Col. W. S. Spackman, *Never Come Back No More* (private papers).
14 Maj. W. H. Miles.
15 Townshend, op. cit.
16 Mr J. Boggis.
17 Lord Elton, *Among Others.*
18 Mr H. Eato.
19 Maj. F. Castaldini.
20 Townshend, op. cit.
21 Maj. F. Castaldini.
22 Lt.-Col. C. A. Raynor.
23 Mr J. Boggis.
24 Lt.-Col. C. A. Raynor.
25 Mr J. Boggis.
26 Lt.-Col. C. A. Raynor.
27 Spackman, op. cit.
28 Mr H. Eato.
29 Mr D. R. Holzmeyer (diary).
30 Maj. W. H. Miles.
31 Maj.-Gen. G. O. de R. Channer.
32 Mr H. V. Plumb.
33 Capt. G. H. G. Burroughs (papers).
34 Mr A. Ariss.
35 Lt.-Col. H. G. Thomson, D.S.O.
36 Mr W. D. Swan.
37 Townshend, op. cit.
38 Mr J. Boggis.
39 Mr J. Wadham.
40 Townshend, op. cit.
41 *Official History, World War I*, vol. II.
42 Lt.-Col. H. G. Thomson, D.S.O.

CHAPTER EIGHT

1 *Mesopotamia Commission 1917.*
2 Maj.-Gen. Sir Charles Townshend, *My Campaign in Mesopotamia.*
3 Lt.-Col. J. McConville.
4 Mr W. S. Finch.
5 Maj. W. H. Miles.
6 Sir John Mellor.
7 Mr W. J. Sherlock.
8 Mr J. Wadham.
9 Mr W. J. Sherlock.
10 Arthur G. Kingsmill, *The Silver Badge.*
11 Mr H. V. Wheeler.
12 Lt.-Col. J. McConville.
13 Col. G. W. R. Bishop.
14 Mr J. Boggis.
15 Col. G. W. R. Bishop.
16 Mr E. J. Mant.
17 Capt. H. S. D. MacNeal.
18 Lt.-Col. J. McConville.
19 Col. G. W. R. Bishop.
20 Capt. H. S. D. MacNeal.
21 Mr J. Wadham.
22 Mr J. Boggis.
23 Mr G. H. Cheeseman.
24 Col. G. W. R. Bishop.
25 Townshend, op. cit.
26 Lt.-Col. E. W. C. Sandes, D.S.O., O.B.E.
27 Mr E. H. Firman.
28 Townshend, op. cit.
29 Maj. W. H. Miles.

CHAPTER NINE

1 Maj. T. R. Wells.
2 Mr H. V. Plumb.
3 Mr W. J. Sherlock.
4 Lt.-Col. J. McConville.
5 Maj.-Gen. Sir Charles Townshend, *My Campaign in Mesopotamia.*

CHAPTER TEN

1 Brig. L. W. H. Mathias, D.S.O. (diary).
2 Charles H. Barber, *Besieged in Kut – and After.*
3 Capt. H. S. D. MacNeal.
4 Mr E. J. Mant.
5 Mr J. E. Sporle.
6 Mr H. Eato.
7 Lt.-Col. J. McConville.
8 Maj.-Gen. Sir Charles Townshend, *My Campaign in Mesopotamia.*
9 Mr G. H. Allen.
10 Brig. L. W. H. Mathias, D.S.O. (diary).
11 Townshend, op. cit.
12 *Official History, World War I*, vol II.
13 Townshend, op. cit.
14 *Official History, World War I*, vol. II.

15 Townshend, op. cit.
16 *Official History, World War I*, vol. II.
17 Townshend, op. cit.
18 The Rt. Hon. D. Lloyd George.
19 *Official History, World War I*, vol II.
20 Lt.-Col. E. W. C. Sandes, D.S.O., O.B.E.
21 Mr H. S. Soden.
22 Lt.-Col. E. W. C. Sandes, D.S.O., O.B.E.
23 Maj. T. R. Wells.
24 Townshend, op. cit.
25 *Official History, World War I*, vol. II.
26 Townshend, op. cit.
27 Mr H. V. Plumb.
28 Capt. H. S. D. MacNeal.

29 Lt.-Col. E. W. C. Sandes, D.S.O., O.B.E.
30 Mr H. S. Soden.
31 Mr J Boggis.
32 Lt.-Col. E. W. C. Sandes, D.S.O., O.B.E.
33 Mr A. Ariss.
34 Mr G. H. Cheeseman.
35 Sir John Mellor.
36 Mr A. E. Roach.
37 Mr G. H. Blower.
38 Mr H. V. Plumb.
39 Mr W. J. Sherlock.
40 Mr A. Vanstone.
41 Maj. T. R. Wells.
42 *Mesopotamia Commission 1917.*

CHAPTER ELEVEN

1 Maj.-Gen. Sir Charles Townshend, *My Campaign in Mesopotamia.*
2 Arthur G. Kingsmill, *The Silver Badge.*
3 Brig. L. W. H. Mathias, D.S.O. (diary).
4 Col. W. S. Spackman.
5 Lt.-Col. E. W. C. Sandes, D.S.O., O.B.E.
6 Lord Elton, *Among Others.*
7 Lt.-Col. E. W. C. Sandes, D.S.O., O.B.E.
8 Townshend, op. cit.
9 *Official History, World War I*, vol. II.
10 *Mesopotamia Commission 1917.*
11 Townshend, op. cit.
12 Charles H. Barber, *Besieged in Kut — and After.*

13 Sir John Mellor.
14 Townshend, op. cit.
15 Mr H. V. Plumb.
16 Maj. T. R. Wells.
17 Cpl. Candy (diary).
18 Brig. L. W. H. Mathias, D.S.O. (diary).
19 Maj. T. R. Wells.
20 Mr E. H. Firman.
21 A. J. Barker, *Townshend of Kut.*
22 Townshend, op. cit.
23 Barker, op. cit.
24 Brig. K. B. S. Crawford.
25 Lt.-Col. E. W. C. Sandes, D.S.O., O.B.E.
26 Townshend, op. cit.

CHAPTER TWELVE

1 Charles H. Barber, *Besieged in Kut — and After.*
2 Arthur G. Kingsmill, *The Silver Badge.*
3 Mr W. D. Swan.
4 Mr H. S. Soden.
5 Mr W. D. Swan.
6 Mr A. Ariss.
7 Lt.-Col. C. A. Raynor.
8 Brig. L. W. H. Mathias, D.S.O. (diary).
9 Mr H. J. Porter.
10 Lord Elton, *Among Others.*
11 E. W. C. Sandes, *In Kut and Captivity.*

12 Col. G. R. Rae (personal papers).
13 Maj.-Gen. Sir Charles Townshend, *My Campaign in Mesopotamia.*
14 *Official History, World War I*, vol. II.
15 Townshend, op. cit.
16 Col. G. W. R. Bishop.
17 Townshend, op. cit.
18 *Official History, World War I*, vol. II.
19 Brig. L. W. H. Mathias, D.S.O. (diary).
20 Maj. T. R. Wells.
21 Brig. L. W. H. Mathias, D.S.O. (diary).

CHAPTER THIRTEEN

1 Cpl. Candy (diary).
2 Maj.-Gen. Sir Charles Townshend, *My Campaign in Mesopotamia.*
3 Cpl. Candy (diary).

4 *Official History, World War I*, vol. II.
5 Cpl. Candy (diary).
6 Townshend, op. cit.
7 Brig. L. W. H. Mathias, D.S.O. (diary).

8 Townshend, op. cit.
9 Brig. L. W. H. Mathias, D.S.O. (diary).
10 Mr H. Eato.
11 Brig. L. W. H. Mathias. D.S.O. (diary).
12 Townshend, op. cit.
13 *Official History, World War I*, vol. II.
14 Capt. F. W. Page-Roberts (letters).
15 *Official History, World War I*, vol. II.
16 Mr J. Boggis.
17 Townshend, op. cit.
18 *Official History, World War I*, vol. II.
19 Townshend, op. cit.

20 *Official History, World War I*, vol. II.
21 Townshend, op. cit.
22 Lt.-Col. E. W. C. Sandes, D.S.O., O.B.E.
23 Brig. L. W. H. Mathias, D.S.O. (diary).
24 Mr J. Boggis.
25 Mr J. E. Sporle.
26 Mr G. Sporle.
27 Mr G. H. Allen.
28 Maj.-Gen. H. H. Rich.
29 Maj. T. R. Wells.
30 Townshend, op. cit.

CHAPTER FOURTEEN

1 Maj.-Gen. Sir Charles Townshend, *My Campaign in Mesopotamia*.
2 Mr J. Boggis.
3 *Official History, World War I*, vol. II.
4 Townshend, op. cit.
5 Capt. H. S. D. MacNeal.
6 Maj.-Gen. G. O. de R. Channer.
7 Capt. H. S. D. MacNeal.
8 Townshend, op. cit.
9 Khalil Pasha in a post-war interview with Maj.-Gen. Channer.
10 *Official History, World War I*, vol. II.
11 Townshend, op. cit.
12 *Official History, World War I*, vol. II.
13 Townshend, op. cit.
14 *Mesopotamia Commission 1917*.
15 *Official History, World War I*, vol. II.
16 Capt. F. W. Page-Roberts (letters).

17 *Official History, World War I*, vol. II.
18 Edward Mousely, *Secrets of a Kuttite*.
19 Capt. F. W. Page-Roberts (letters).
20 Brig. L. W. H. Mathias, D.S.O. (diary).
21 Mr D. R. Holzmeyer (diary).
22 Col. W. S. Spackman.
23 Lt.-Col. E. W. C. Sandes, D.S.O., O.B.E.
24 Khalil Pasha in a post-war interview with Maj.-Gen. Channer.
25 Mr E. J. Mant.
26 Mr R. Hague (papers).
27 Brig. L. W. H. Mathias, D.S.O. (diary).
28 *Official History, World War I*, vol. II.
29 Townshend, op. cit.
30 *Official History, World War I*, vol. II.
31 Townshend, op. cit.
32 *Official History, World War I*, vol. II.
33 Townshend, op. cit.

CHAPTER FIFTEEN

1 Mr J. Boggis.
2 Mr E. J. Mant.
3 Maj.-Gen. H. H. Rich.
4 Maj. T. R. Wells.
5 Mr E. J. Mant.
6 Mr G. H. Cheeseman.
7 Maj.-Gen. H. H. Rich.
8 Mr G. H. Allen.
9 Mr E. J. Mant.
10 Mr T. A. Lloyd (letters).
11 Mr G. Roff.
12 Brig. L. W. H. Mathias, D.S.O. (diary).
13 Sir Joseph Napier (diary).
14 A. J. Barker, *The Neglected War*.
15 Maj.-Gen. H. H. Rich.
16 Capt. H. S. D. MacNeal.

17 Maj.-Gen. Sir Charles Townshend, *My Campaign in Mesopotamia*.
18 Maj.-Gen. H. H. Rich.
19 Maj. T. R. Wells.
20 Maj.-Gen. H. H. Rich.
21 Sir John Mellor.
22 Maj. G. L. Heawood (letters).
23 Capt. H. S. D. MacNeal.
24 Mr D. R. Holzmeyer (diary).
25 Cpl. Candy (diary).
26 Mr H. J. Porter.
27 Mr W. J. Sherlock.
28 Townshend, op. cit.
29 Mr A. Hayden.
30 Mr H. S. Soden.
31 H. V. Wheeler, *A Short History of the Siege of Kut el Amara* (private papers).

32 *Mesopotamia Commission 1917*: Separate report by Commander Wedgewood, D.S.O., M.P.

33 Lt.-Col. E. W. C. Sandes, D.S.O., O.B.E.
34 Townshend, op. cit.
35 Mr H. Eato.

CHAPTER SIXTEEN

1 *Official History, World War I*, vol. II.
2 E. W. C. Sandes, *In Kut and Captivity*.
3 Lt.-Col. E. W. C. Sandes, D.S.O., O.B.E.
4 Maj.-Gen. Sir Charles Townshend, *My Campaign in Mesopotamia*.
5 *Official History, World War I*, vol. II.
6 Townshend, op. cit.
7 *Official History, World War I*, vol. II.
8 Townshend, op. cit.
9 Col. R. O. Chamier.
10 Townshend, op. cit.
11 Cpl. Candy (diary).
12 Maj. T. R. Wells.
13 Capt. G. H. G. Burroughs (papers).
14 Townshend, op. cit.
15 Mr G. H. Blower.
16 Townshend, op. cit.
17 Capt. G. H. G. Burroughs.
18 Brig. K. B. S. Crawford.
19 Capt. G. H. G. Burroughs (papers).
20 Mr D. R. Holzmeyer (diary).
21 Townshend, op. cit.
22 Mr H. S. Soden.
23 Townshend, op. cit.
24 Sandes, op. cit.
25 Mr A. Hayden.
26 Brig. L. W. H. Mathias, D.S.O. (diary).

CHAPTER SEVENTEEN

1 E. W. C. Sandes, *In Kut and Captivity*.
2 Brig. L. W. H. Mathias, D.S.O. (diary).
3 Mr W. J. Sherlock.
4 Maj.-Gen. Sir Charles Townshend, *My Campaign in Mesopotamia*.
5 Mr W. J. Sherlock.
6 Brig. L. W. H. Mathias, D.S.O. (diary).
7 Cpl. Candy (diary).
8 Lt.-Col. L. Bell Syer (diary).
9 Mr G. Roff.
10 Mr W. J. Sherlock.
11 Mr A. Vanstone.
12 Mr G. H. Allen.
13 Mr W. J. Sherlock.
14 Sir Joseph Napier (diary).
15 Mr R. H. Yorke (letters).
16 Sir Joseph Napier (diary).
17 Mr R. Hague (papers).
18 Sandes, op. cit.
19 Townshend, op. cit.
20 Mr G. H. Cheeseman.
21 Mr G. Sporle.
22 Mr H. Eato.
23 Capt. G. H. G. Burroughs (papers).
24 Townshend, op. cit.
25 Brig. L. W. H. Mathias, D.S.O. (diary).
26 *Official History, World War I*, vol. II.
27 Brig. L. W. H. Mathias, D.S.O. (diary).
28 *Official History, World War I*, vol. II.
29 Townshend, op. cit.
30 Mr J. Boggis.
31 Mr R. H. Murray.
32 Mr R. Hague.
33 Townshend, op. cit.
34 Cpl. Candy (diary).
35 Mr R. H. Murray.
36 Mr W. J. Sherlock.
37 Mr H. S. Soden.
38 Col. R. O. Chamier.
39 Mr H. S. Soden.
40 Townshend, op. cit.
41 Capt. H. S. D. MacNeal.
42 Mr E. J. Mant.
43 Col. R. O. Chamier.
44 Capt. G. H. G. Burroughs.
45 Cpl. Candy (diary).
46 Mr R. Hague.

CHAPTER EIGHTEEN

1 Capt. H. S. D. MacNeal.
2 Mr W. J. Sherlock.
3 Col. G. W. R. Bishop.
4 Mr A. Vanstone.
5 Maj.-Gen. Sir Charles Townshend, *My Campaign in Mesopotamia*.
6 Mr J. Boggis.
7 Maj. J. H. Harris.

8 Brig. L. W. H. Mathias, D.S.O. (diary).
9 Charles H. Barber, *Besieged in Kut – and After.*
10 Col. R. O. Chamier.
11 Maj.-Gen. H. H. Rich.
12 Mr H. S. Soden.
13 Mr R. C. Plumley.
14 *Official History, World War I,* vol. II.
15 Townshend, op. cit.
16 *Official History, World War I,* vol. II.
17 Townshend, op. cit.
18 Brig. L. W. H. Mathias, D.S.O. (diary).
19 Capt. H. S. D. MacNeal.
20 Col. W. S. Spackman, *Never Come Back No More* (private papers).
21 Mr W. J. Sherlock.
22 Maj.-Gen. H. H. Rich.
23 Mr A. Hayden.
24 Brig. L. W. H. Mathias, D.S.O. (diary).
25 Townshend, op. cit.

26 *Mesopotamia Commission 1917.*
27 Capt. H. S. D. MacNeal.
28 Capt. G. H. G. Burroughs (papers).
29 Mr H. Eato.
30 Townshend, op. cit.
31 Sir John Mellor.
32 Maj.-Gen. G. O. de R. Channer.
33 Maj.-Gen. H. H. Rich.
34 Townshend, op. cit.
35 Mr J. Boggis.
36 Mr H. J. Porter.
37 Mr H. Eato.
38 Mr D. R. Holzmeyer (diary).
39 Mr H. V. Plumb.
40 Mr R. H. Murray.
41 E. W. C. Sandes, *In Kut and Captivity.*
42 Townshend, op. cit.
43 Sandes, op. cit.
44 Townshend, op. cit.
45 Arthur G. Kingsmill, *The Silver Badge.*

CHAPTER NINETEEN

1 *Official History, World War I,* vol. II.
2 Cpl. Candy (diary).
3 Maj.-Gen. Sir Charles Townshend, *My Campaign in Mesopotamia.*
4 Mr H. Eato.
5 Townshend, op. cit.
6 Sir Joseph Napier (diary).
7 Maj.-Gen. G. O. de R. Channer.
8 *Official History, World War I,* vol. II.
9 Townshend, op. cit.
10 Mr J. Boggis.
11 A. J. Barker, *The Neglected War.*
12 Townshend, op. cit.

13 *Official History, World War I,* vol. II.
14 Townshend, op. cit.
15 Brig. L. W. H. Mathias, D.S.O. (diary).
16 Townshend, op. cit.
17 Maj.-Gen. H. H. Rich.
18 Mr R. H. Yorke (letters).
19 *Official History, World War I,* vol. II.
20 Townshend, op. cit.
21 Mr H. S. Soden.
22 Townshend, op. cit.
23 Col. W. S. Spackman.
24 *Official History, World War I,* vol. II.
25 Townshend, op. cit.

CHAPTER TWENTY

1 Maj.-Gen. Sir Charles Townshend, *My Campaign in Mesopotamia.*
2 Col. W. S. Spackman.
3 Mr T. A. Lloyd.
4 Mr W. S. Finch.
5 Brig. L. W. H. Mathias, D.S.O. (diary).
6 Mr T. A. Lloyd.
7 Maj. T. R. Wells.
8 Mr A. E. Roach.
9 Capt. H. S. D. MacNeal.
10 Brig. L. W. H. Mathias, D.S.O. (diary).
11 *Official History, World War I,* vol. II.
12 Cpl. Candy (diary).
13 Charles H. Barber, *Besieged in Kut – and After.*

14 Brig. L. W. H. Mathias, D.S.O. (diary).
15 Barber, op. cit.
16 Arthur G. Kingsmill, *The Silver Badge.*
17 Townshend, op. cit.
18 Capt. H. S. D. MacNeal.
19 Townshend, op. cit.
20 *Official History, World War I,* vol. II.
21 Townshend, op. cit.
22 *Official History, World War I,* vol. II.
23 Townshend, op. cit.
24 *Official History, World War I,* vol. II.
25 Mr E. J. Mant.
26 Mr A. Ariss.
27 Mr G. H. Cheeseman.
28 Townshend, op. cit.

29 Mr R. H. Yorke (letters).
30 *Official History, World War I*, vol. II.
31 Townshend, op. cit.
32 *Official History, World War I*, vol. II.
33 Townshend, op. cit.
34 *Official History, World War I*, vol. II.
35 Mr H. Eato.
36 Brig. L. W. H. Mathias, D.S.O. (diary).
37 Barber, op. cit.

38 Lt.-Col. J. McConville.
39 Mr J. Boggis.
40 Mr E. C. Burwood.
41 Mr J. Wadham.
42 Col. W. S. Spackman.
43 *Official History, World War I*, vol. II.
44 Townshend, op. cit.
45 *Official History, World War I*, vol. II.
46 Townshend, op. cit.

CHAPTER TWENTY-ONE

1 *Official History, World War I*, vol. II.
2 Maj.-Gen. Sir Charles Townshend, *My Campaign in Mesopotamia*.
3 Cpl. Candy (diary).
4 Mr H. Eato.
5 Mr W. J. Sherlock.
6 Mr H. J. Porter.
7 Mr H. V. Wheeler.
8 Mr G. H. Allen.
9 E. H. Keeling, *Adventures in Turkey and Russia*.
10 Charles H. Barber, *Besieged in Kut – and After*.
11 Mr J. Boggis.
12 Barber, op. cit.
13 Townshend, op. cit.
14 Brig. L. W. H. Mathias, D.S.O. (diary).
15 Lt.-Col. H. G. Thomson, D.S.O.
16 Mr W. J. Sherlock.
17 Capt. H. S. D. MacNeal.
18 Mr A. Hayden.

19 Townshend, op. cit.
20 H. V. Wheeler, *A Short History of the Siege of Kut el Amara*.
21 Townshend, op. cit.
22 *Official History, World War I*, vol. II.
23 Mr H. S. Soden.
24 E. W. C. Sandes, *In Kut and Captivity*.
25 Townshend, op. cit.
26 Mr W. J. Sherlock.
27 Mr H. Eato.
28 Mr D. R. Holzmeyer (diary).
29 Mr G. H. Blower.
30 Capt. G. H. G. Burroughs.
31 Col. R. O. Chamier.
32 Col. W. S. Spackman.
33 Mr G. H. Cheeseman.
34 Mr A. Vanstone.
35 Arthur G. Kingsmill, *The Silver Badge*.
36 Sir Joseph Napier (diary).
37 Townshend, op. cit.

CHAPTER TWENTY-TWO

1 Mr W. J. Sherlock.
2 Army Legal Service (Ministry of Defence).
3 Mr J. Wadham.
4 *The Times*, May 5th, 1916.
5 Arthur G. Kingsmill, *The Silver Badge*.
6 Cpl. Candy (diary).
7 Mr W. J. Sherlock.
8 Mr J. Wadham.
9 Maj. W. H. Miles.
10 F. A. Harvey, *The Sufferings of the Kut Garrison*.

11 Maj. W. H. Miles.
12 Harvey, op. cit.
13 Mr A. Vanstone.
14 Maj.-Gen. Sir Charles Townshend, *My Campaign in Mesopotamia*.
15 Kingsmill, op. cit.
16 Lord Elton, *Among Others*.
17 Townshend, op. cit.
18 Author's italics.
19 A. J. Barker, *Townshend of Kut*.
20 Townshend, op. cit.

CHAPTER TWENTY-THREE

1 Mr J. Wadham.
2 Mr J. Boggis.

3 Maj.-Gen. Sir Charles Townshend, *My Campaign in Mesopotamia*.

4 Mr J. Boggis.
5 Sir John Mellor.
6 Capt. H. S. D. MacNeal.
7 Mr J. E. Sporle.
8 Mr R. Hague.

9 Mr G. H. Allen.
10 Mr G. H. Blower.
11 Mr W. J. Sherlock.
12 Capt. G. H. G. Burroughs.
13 Col. R. O. Chamier.

CHAPTER TWENTY-FOUR

1 Maj.-Gen. Sir Charles Townshend, *My Campaign in Mesopotamia*.
2 Mr R. Hague.
3 Mr G. H. Blower.
4 Col. W. S. Spackman.
5 Townshend, op. cit.
6 A. J. Barker, *Townshend of Kut*.
7 F. A. Harvey, *The Sufferings of the Kut Garrison*.
8 Cpl. Candy (diary).
9 Harvey, op. cit.
10 Maj. T. R. Wells.

11 Col. G. W. R. Bishop.
12 Lord Elton, *Among Others*.
13 Charles H. Barber, *Besieged in Kut – and After*.
14 Lt.-Col. C. A. Raynor.
15 Barber, op. cit.
16 Lord Elton.
17 Townshend, op. cit.
18 Mr W. J. Sherlock.
19 Mr H. V. Plumb.
20 Capt. H. S. D. MacNeal.

CHAPTER TWENTY-FIVE

1 Maj.-Gen. Sir Charles Townshend, *My Campaign in Mesopotamia*.
2 Mr H. S. Soden.
3 *The Times*, May 5th, 1916.
4 C. L. Woolley, ed., *From Kastamuni to Keddos*.
5 Lord Elton.
6 Woolley, op. cit.

7 Col. G. W. R. Bishop.
8 A. J. Barker, *Townshend of Kut*.
9 Mr J. Boggis.
10 Mr A. Hayden.
11 Mr A. Vanstone.
12 Mr A. Hayden.
13 Mr H. V. Plumb.

CHAPTER TWENTY-SIX

1 Mr W. J. Sherlock.
2 Maj.-Gen. G. O. de R. Channer.
3 C. L. Woolley, ed., *From Kastamuni to Keddos*.
4 Maj.-Gen. H. H. Rich.
5 Capt. G. H. G. Burroughs.
6 Mr J. Boggis.
7 A. J. Barker, *Townshend of Kut*.
8 Capt. H. S. D. MacNeal.

9 Mr W. D. Swan.
10 Mr G. H. Blower.
11 Mr G. E. Palmer.
12 E. W. C. Sandes, *In Kut and Captivity*.
13 Maj.-Gen. Sir Charles Townshend, *My Campaign in Mesopotamia*.
14 Barker, op. cit.
15 Townshend, op. cit.

CHAPTER TWENTY-SEVEN

1 *Mesopotamia Commission 1917*.
2 Maj.-Gen. Sir Charles Townshend, *My Campaign in Mesopotamia*.
3 Mr J. Boggis.
4 E. W. C. Sandes, *In Kut and Captivity*.
5 Maj. W. H. Miles.
6 C. L. Woolley, ed., *From Kastamuni to Keddos*.
7 Johnston and Yeardley, *Four Hundred and Fifty Miles to Freedom*.

8 Sir Joseph Napier (diary).
9 Capt. G. H. G. Burroughs.
10 Woolley, op. cit.
11 Mr A. E. Roach.
12 Mr R. Hague.
13 Mr A. Ariss.
14 Mr G. H. Cheeseman.
15 Mr J. Wadham.
16 Maj. F. Castaldini.
17 Mr G. H. Cheeseman.

18 Mr R. Hague (papers).
19 Mr T. A. Lloyd (letters).

20 Lt.-Col. C. A. Raynor.

CHAPTER TWENTY-EIGHT

1 Cpl. F. Castaldini (diary).
2 E. W. C. Sandes, *In Kut and Captivity.*
3 Mr H. S. Soden.

4 Maj.-Gen. Sir Charles Townshend, *My Campaign in Mesopotamia.*
5 Capt. G. H. G. Burroughs (papers).
6 Townshend, op. cit.

CHAPTER TWENTY-NINE

1 Johnston and Yeardley, *Four Hundred and Fifty Miles to Freedom.*
2 A. J. Barker, *Townshend of Kut.*
3 Signals from Kut, Imperial War Museum.

4 Mr H. Eato.
5 To the Polish Ambassador at the retreat from Moscow.

APPENDIX

THE GARRISON OF KUT

THE ROYAL NAVY
H.M.S. SUMANA

H.Q. 6th INDIAN DIVISION

DIVISIONAL CORPS
AND ARMY TROOPS:

1 Squadron 7th Hariana Lancers.
1 Squadron 23rd Cavalry.
34th Div. Signal Company R.E.
30th Brigade Signal Company R.E.
Wireless Signal Squadron.
17th and 22nd Companies R.E.
Bridging Train 3rd Sappers and Miners R.E.
Sirmoor Sapper Company, R.E.
Searchlight Section Company, R.E.
48th Pioneers.

ROYAL ARTILLERY

'S' Battery, R.H.A. (one section).

10TH BRIGADE R.F.A.

(63rd, 76th and 82nd Batteries)
1/5th Hants Howitzer Battery, T.A.

R.G.A.

86th Heavy Battery.
104th Heavy Battery (1 section).
Volunteer Artillery Battery (Rangoon) (15 Pdr.).
6th Divisional Ammunition Column.

MACHINE GUN BATTERY.
16TH INFANTRY BRIGADE:

2nd Battalion Dorset Regiment.

66th Punjabis.
104th Wellesleys Rifles.
117th Mahrattas.

17TH INFANTRY BRIGADE

1st Battn. Oxford and Buckinghamshire Light Infantry.
22nd Punjabis.
103rd Mahratta Light Infantry.
119th Rajputana Infantry.

18TH INFANTRY BRIGADE

2nd Battn. Norfolk Regiment.
7th Rajputs.
110th Mahratta Light Infantry.
120th Rajputana Infantry.

30TH INFANTRY BRIGADE

Half Battn. 2nd Royal West Kent Regiment.
1 Company 1/4th Hampshire Regiment.
24th Punjabis.
67th Punjabis.
76th Punjabis.
2/7th Gurkha Rifles.

ADMINISTRATIVE SERVICES

Supply and Transport Corps.
Supply Units.

Transport Units (Animal) Detachments, 13th, 21st, 26th and 30th Mule Corps.
Jaipur Transport Company.
Mechanical Transport Corps.

MEDICAL UNITS:

3 Field Ambulances.
3 Field Hospitals.

1 Section Veterinary Field Hospital.

MISCELLANEOUS:

3 Chaplains, Army Chaplains Dept.
Military Governor.
Survey Party, Field Post Office.

ROYAL FLYING CORPS:

Detachment.

BIBLIOGRAPHY

GENERAL

Barber, C. H., *Besieged in Kut – and After* (Blackwood, 1917).
Barker, A. J., *The Neglected War* (Cassell, 1967).
—— *Townshend of Kut* (Cassell, 1967).
Candler, Edmund, *The Long Road to Baghdad*, 2 volumes (Cassell, 1919).
Elton, Lord, *Among Others* (Collins, 1938).
Harvey, F. A., *The Sufferings of Kut Garrison* (private papers).
Johnston and Yeardley, *Four Hundred and Fifty Miles to Freedom* (Blackwood, 1922).
Jones, E. H., *The Road to En-Dor* (John Lane, 1919).
Keeling, E. H., *Adventures in Turkey and Russia* (Murray, 1924).
Kingsmill, A. G., *The Silver Badge* (Stockwell, 1966).
Long, P. W., *Other Ranks of Kut* (Williams and Norgate, 1938).
Mouseley, E. O., *Secrets of a Kuttite* (John Lane, 1922).
Neave, Dorina, *Remembering Kut* (Arthur Barker, 1937).
Sandes, E. W. C., *In Kut and Captivity* (Murray, 1919).
Thesiger, Wilfred, *Arabian Sands* (Longmans Green, 1959).
—— *The Marsh Arabs* (Longmans Green, 1964).
Townshend, Major-General Sir Charles, *My Campaign in Mesopotamia* (Butterworth, 1920).
Woolley, C. L., ed., *From Kastamuni to Keddos* (Blackwells, 1921).

OFFICIAL SOURCES

History of the 43rd and 52nd Light Infantry in World War I, vol. I (H.M.S.O.).
Mesopotamia Commission 1917 (H.M.S.O.).
Mesopotamia Commission 1917, Separate Report (H.M.S.O.).
Official History, World War I, vol. II (H.M.S.O.).

INDEX

349